Social History
of Western Civilization
Volume II

Social History of Western Civilization

Volume II

Readings from the Seventeenth Century to the Present

RICHARD M. GOLDEN

Clemson University

St. Martin's Press　　　　　　　　　　**New York**

Library of Congress Catalog Card Number: 87–060525

For information, write St. Martin's Press, Inc.
175 Fifth Avenue, New York, NY 10010

Project Management: Publication Services

ISBN: 0-312-00431-1

Acknowledgments

"Misbeliefs about Our Ancestors. The Absence of Child Marriage and Extended Family Households from the English Past." Peter Laslett, excerpted from *The World We Have Lost*, 3rd edition. Copyright ©1984 Peter Laslett. Reprinted with the permission of Charles Scribner's Sons.

"Misbeliefs about Our Ancestors. The Absence of Child Marriage and Extended Family Households from the English Past." Peter Laslett, *The World We Have Lost*, 3rd edition. Reprinted with the permission of Methuen and Company, Ltd.

"The Constraint of Bodies." Reprinted by permission of Louisiana State University Press from *Popular Culture and Elite Culture in France, 1400–1750*, by Robert Muchembled. Translated by Lydia Cochrane. English translation copyright ©1985 by Louisiana State University Press. Originally published in France as *Culture Populaire et Culture des Élites dans la France Moderne (XV–XVIII siècles)*, ©Flammarion, 1978.

"Guilds." Excerpted from Mack Walker: *German Home Towns: Community, State, and General Estate, 1648–1871*. Copyright ©1971 by Cornell University. Used by permission of the publisher, Cornell University Press.

"The Peasants." Jerome Blum, *The End of the Old Order in Rural Europe*. Copyright ©1978 by Princeton University Press. Excerpt, pp. 29–49, reprinted with permission of Princeton University Press.

"Entertainment in the Parisian Fairs in the Eighteenth Century." Robert M. Isherwood, "Entertainment in the Parisian Fairs," *The Journal of Modern History*, vol. 53, March 1981, pp. 24–48. Reprinted with the permission of The University of Chicago Press.

"Finding Solace in Eighteenth-Century Newgate," W.J. Sheehan. J.S. Cockburn, ed., *Crime in England, 1550–1800*. Copyright ©1977 by J.S. Cockburn. Excerpt, pp. 229–245, reprinted with permission of Princeton University Press.

"The Devils of Toulon: Demonic Possession and Religious Politics in Eighteenth-Century Provence," B. Robert Kreiser. Richard M. Golden, ed., *Church, State and Society Under the Bourbon Kings of France* (Lawrence, Kansas: Coronado Press, 1982), pp. 173–200. Copyright ©Richard M. Golden. Reprinted with permission.

"Death's Arbitrary Empire." John McManners, *Death and the Enlightenment*, 1981, pp. 5–23. Edited selection reprinted by permission of Oxford University Press.

"The Sans-Culottes." Albert Soboul, *The Sans-Culottes*, trans. Remy Inglis Hall. Published by Princeton University Press. Excerpts reprinted with permission of Princeton University Press.

"Factory Discipline in the Industrial Revolution." Sidney Pollard, "Factory Discipline in the Industrial Revolution," *Economic History Review* (16), December 1963, pp. 254–271. Reprinted with permission.

"Urban Man." Pages 410–421 from *A History of the World* by Hugh Thomas. Copyright ©1979 by Hugh Thomas. Reprinted by permission of Harper & Row, Publishers, Inc.

Acknowledgments and copyrights continue at the back of the book, on page 326, which constitutes an extension of the copyright page.

Contents

Topical Table of Contents

Preface

Social History of Western Civilization is a two-volume reader for freshmen in Western Civilization courses. The twenty-five essays in each volume focus on social history because I believe that the most original and significant work of the past two decades has been in this area and because Western Civilization textbooks tend to slight social history in favor of the more traditional political, intellectual, and cultural history, though this bias is slowly changing. In the dozen years that I have taught Western Civilization, I have used many books, texts, and readers designed specifically for introductory courses. I decided to compile this reader because I perceived that other readers generally failed to retain student interest. My students found many of the essays in these other books boring, often because the selections assumed a degree of background knowledge that a typical student does not possess. To make this reader better suited to students, I have attempted to include essays that are not only important but readable as well. This has not been an easy task, for many significant history articles, which have been written solely for specialists, are, unfortunately, dull or simply too difficult for college undergraduates. I have gone through hundreds of articles searching for the few that are challenging, fascinating, important, and readable. Also, with readability in mind, I have translated foreign words and identified individuals and terms that students might not recognize. (All footnotes are my own unless otherwise indicated.) I, for one, cannot understand why anthologies intended for college students do not routinely translate foreign expressions, phrases, and book titles and, moreover, seem to take for granted that students will be familiar with Tertullian, Gustavus Adolphus, or Pearl Buck, to mention some examples.

A Western Civilization reader cannot be all things for all instructors and students, but I have consciously tried to make these two volumes useful for as many Western Civilization courses as possible, despite the widely varying ways in which such courses are taught. The readings in these volumes cover many geographical areas and a broad range of topics in social history. Some historians argue that Western civilization began with the Greeks, but I have included in Volume One a section on the Ancient Near East for the courses that begin there. Both volumes contain material on the seventeenth century; indeed, Volume Two includes in its first selections some material that precedes the seventeenth century. This chronological overlap is intentional because Western Civilization courses break differently according to the policies of instructors and institutions.

To show how the vast majority of articles in *Social History of Western Civilization* may be used in most Western Civilization courses, there is a correlation chart at the beginning of each volume that relates each essay to a relevant chapter in the major Western Civilization textbooks currently on the market. Though the textbooks do not always offer discrete discussions on all the subjects covered in the essays, many of the subjects are touched upon. As for the others, students will at least be able to place the articles in a historical context by reading the standard history of the period in the relevant textbook chapter and, more important, will gain fresh insight into that historical period. I have also provided introductions to the major periods in history for each volume as well as an introduction to each selection where I have asked pertinent questions in order to direct the students into the essays and encourage them to think about the problems and issues they raise. These introductions do not contain summaries and so may not be substituted for the reading of the selections.

The preparation of this reader was more time-consuming than I had originally thought possible. There always seemed to be somewhere a more attractive article on every topic. Thus many people suggested essays to me, critiqued what I wrote, and helped in other ways as well. I thank Jay Crawford, Fara Driver, Phillip Garland, Leonard Greenspoon, Tully Hunter, Charles Lippy, Victor Matthews, Mike Sutton, and Carol Thomas. Especially generous in their time and comments were Robert Bireley, Elizabeth D. Carney, Suzanne A. Desan, Hilda Golden, Alan Grubb, Thomas Kuehn, Donald McKale, John A. Mears, Thomas F. X. Noble, and D.G. Paz. The staff of St. Martin's Press—Michael Weber, Vivian McLaughlin, Beverly Hinton, Kristen Heimstra, and Andrea Guidoboni—have been gracious, efficient, professional, and supportive.

Correlation Chart For Western Civilization Texts and Volume II of Social History of Western Civilization

The seven readings (columns) are:

1. Peter Laslett, Misbeliefs about Our Ancestors. The Absence of Child Marriage and Extended Family Households from the English Past
2. Robert Muchembled, The Constraint of Bodies
3. Mack Walker, Guilds
4. Jerome Blum, The Peasants
5. Robert M. Isherwood, Entertainment in the Parisian Fairs in the Eighteenth Century
6. WJ. Sheehan, Finding Solace in Eighteenth-Century Newgate
7. B. Robert Kreiser, The Devils of Toulon: Demonic Possession and Religious Politics in Eighteenth-Century Provence

Text	Laslett	Muchembled	Walker (Guilds)	Blum (Peasants)	Isherwood	Sheehan	Kreiser
Willis, *Western Civilization: A Brief Introduction* (1987)	10	10	12	12	11	12	11
Willis, *Western Civilization*, 4/e (1985)	15	15		16		19	16
Wallbank et al., *Civilization Past and Present*, 6e (1987)	20	19	20	20	20	20	21
Strayer & Gatzke, *The Mainstream of Civilization*, 4/e (1984)	18, 19	18	19	22	21	21	18
Perry, et al., *Western Civilization: Ideas, Politics & Society* (1985)	16	16	18	16	18	18	17
Palmer & Colton, *A History of the Modern World*, 6/e (1984)							Prologue
McNeill, *History of Western Civilization*, 6/e (1986)	III, C-1	III, C-1	III, C-2	III, C-2	III, C-2	III, C-2	III, C-2
McKay, Hill, Buckler, *A History of Western Society*, 3/e (1987)	20	20	19	17, 19	18	20	18
Langer et al., *Western Civilization*, 2/e (1975)		1		5		7	5
Kagan, Ozment, Turner, *The Western Heritage*, 3/e (1987)	15	15	15	15	15	15	17
Harrison, Sullivan, Sherman, *A Short History of Western Civilization*, 6/e (1985)	36	36	36	36	38	38	38
Greer, *A Brief History of the Western World*, 5/e (1987)		10		10		10	10
Goff et al., *A Survey of Western Civilization* (1987)	17	17	22	24		24	24
Chambers et al., *The Western Experience*, 4/e (1987)	17, 20	16	20	20	19	19	16, 19
Burns et al., *Western Civilizations*, 10/e (1984)	17	17	17	17	17	17	16
Brinton et al., *A History of Civilization*, 6/e (1984)	15	15	16	17, 18	17	17	15

	John McManners, Death's Arbitrary Empire	Albert Soboul, The Sans-Culottes	Sidney Pollard, Factory Discipline in the Industrial Revolution	Hugh Thomas, Urban Man	D.G. Paz, Popular Anti-Catholicism in England, 1850–1851	Eugen Weber, Is God French?	Edward Shorter, Men, Women, and Sex	William L. Langer, Infanticide: A Historical Survey
Willis, *Western Civilization: A Brief Introduction* (1987)	12	13	14	17	16	16		17
Willis, *Western Civilization*, 4/e (1985)	16	16, 17	19	21	20			20
Wallbank et al., *Civilization Past and Present*, 6e (1987)	20	22	23	23		25	23	23
Strayer & Gatzke, *The Mainstream of Civilization*, 4/e (1984)	21	23	25	25	25	28	28	28
Perry, et al., *Western Civilization: Ideas, Politics & Society* (1985)	18	19	21	21,26	26	24	26	26
Palmer & Colton, *A History of the Modern World*, 6/e (1984)		Pro-logue	52	72	56	76	71	71
McNeill, *History of Western Civilization*, 6/e (1986)	III, C-2	III, C-3	III, C-3	III, C-3	III, C-3	III, C-3	III, C-3	III, C-3
McKay, Hill, Buckler, *A History of Western Society*, 3/e (1987)	19,20	21	22	24	24	24	24	20,24
Langer et al., *Western Civilization*, 2/e (1975)	5	8	11	16	14	14	16	16
Kagan, Ozment, Turner, *The Western Heritage*, 3/e (1987)	15	18	21	23	24	24	23	23
Harrison, Sullivan, Sherman, *A Short History of Western Civilization*, 6/e (1985)	36	40	44	44,50	46,51	51	50	50
Greer, *A Brief History of the Western World*, 5/e (1987)	10	11	12	12	12	12	15	
Goff et al., *A Survey of Western Civilization* (1987)	24	27	29	29	32	33	35	35
Chambers et al., *The Western Experience*, 4/e (1987)	19,20	21	22,23	23	24	24	23	25
Burns et al., *Western Civilizations*, 10/e (1984)	17	20	21,22	22	22	26	22	22
Brinton et al., *A History of Civilization*, 6/e (1984)	17	18	20	20	20	20	20	20

Book																
Theresa M. McBride, *A Woman's World: Department Stores and the Evolution of Women's Employment, 1870–1920*	20,21	22	25	34	12	50	23	16	24	III, C-3	73	26	28	23	21	17
Colin Veitch, *'Play Up! Play Up! and Win the War!' Football, the Nation and the First World War, 1914–15*	23	28	26	38	13	53	25	20	27	III, C-4	86	30	30	31	22	18
Alistair Horne, *The Price of Glory: Verdun 1916*	23	28	26	38	13	53	25	20	27	III, C-4	86	30	30	31	22	18
Alex de Jonge, *Inflation in Weimar Germany*	24	29	27	42	13	55	26	24	28	III, C-4	98	32	31	32	24	19
Michael Laffan, *Violence and Terror in Twentieth-Century Ireland: IRB and IRA*	23,25, 27	28,32	27,30	34,42		56	26,29	18,24	25,28	III, C-4	102,113	26,35	28,31	27,36		19
Henry Friedlander, *The Nazi Camps*	26	30	29	43	14	57	28	27	29	III, C-4	107	34	33	35	24	19
Peter H. Juviler, *The Soviet Family in Post-Stalin Perspective*	27	32	30	40	15	60	30	26,30	29,31	III, C-4	110,114	36	34	37	26	21
Philippe Ariès, *Forbidden Death*	28	32	30	40	15	60	30	22	28,31	III, C-4	114	33	Epilogue	39	26	20
Georges Friedmann, *Leisure and Technological Civilization*	28	33	30	39,41	15	60	30	26	31	III, C-4	114		Epilogue	32	26	20
Juliet du Boulay, *Past and Present in a Greek Mountain Village*	27	31	30	44	15	58	29	28		III, C-4	110	35	34	36	26	21

Introduction

This is a volume of selections in the social history of Western civilization from the seventeenth century to the present. Social history encompasses the study of groups of people, avoiding prominent individuals such as kings, prime ministers, intellectual giants, and military leaders. Over the last two decades, social historians have examined a host of topics, many of which are included here: the family, women, sex, disease, death, social groups (such as the peasantry and nobility), entertainment, work, leisure, popular religion and politics, criminality, sports, the experience of soldiers in war, economic conditions, and collective mentality (the attitudes, beliefs, and assumptions held by a population). Social history, then, sheds light both on previously neglected areas of human experience and on forgotten and nameless people. Indeed, some recent historians, perhaps a bit too optimistically, have offered as a goal the writing of "total history," including all aspects of people's lives.

Unlike political, military, diplomatic, or biographical history, for example, social history rarely includes specific dates. The problem of periodization, always a thorny one, is especially difficult when covering topics that can often be understood only as long-term developments rather than as ephemeral events. Social historians tend to be interested in trends that unfold over a long duration rather than in daily episodes and yearly happenings. Thus, infanticide, though surely declining in frequency in the late nineteenth century, cannot be understood without looking back to antiquity and to the Middle Ages. Another example is human sexuality. Any discussion of sexual practices of the Victorian Age must be set against the durable sexual relations that, in significant ways, changed little in the course of millennia. In social history, then, what has not changed is often more important than what has changed. The political historian can conveniently end a chapter or a period of history in, say 1648, with the Peace of Westphalia, or in 1789, at the outbreak of the French Revolution. Even then, the periods of history are arbitrarily chosen, but the decision of where to divide, cut off, or end a subject is much easier for the political or diplomatic historian.

As a way out of the difficulty, social historians have come to favor a simple division between pre-modern (or traditional or pre-industrial) society and the modern (or industrial) world. This split has several advantages. One can present a cogent argument affirming that the Industrial Revolution constituted a watershed, affecting lifestyles and human relationships throughout society. The Industrial Revolution raised new

problems and new questions involving workers' movements, nationalism, mass democracy, and women's emancipation, to name a few topics.
In the industrial era, developments have occurred more rapidly than
in pre-industrial society, where dietary habits, family relationships, and
work patterns, for instance, inclined to change much more slowly over
time. Second, the terms "traditional" and "pre-modern," on the one
hand, and "modern," on the other hand, are loose enough to permit historians to use the words while disagreeing about their meanings. What,
exactly, does it mean to be "modern"? What is the process of modernization? Were people in the nineteenth century modern?

I am sympathetic to the division between pre-modern and modern,
but, for the sake of convenience, I have grouped the selections in this
volume into three parts. Part I, "The Old Régime," concerns traditional
Europe. The essays focus on the seventeenth and eighteenth centuries—
the final two of pre-modern Europe—but several necessarily go back to
the sixteenth century or even farther. Part II, "The Nineteenth Century,"
begins with the Industrial Revolution. But, because the Industrial Revolution actually began in England in the late eighteenth century, a few
of the articles start there. Some of the selections discuss much earlier
material as they trace developments that reached fruition or ended in
the nineteenth century. Part III, "Contemporary Europe (World War I–
Present)" treats the Great War as a great divide. Here again, some essays
go back in time to discuss the prior century and traditional Europe. In
sum, historians impose periods on history that are always debatable and
sometimes capricious but certainly essential in providing some order to
the study of the past.

In any case, social history well researched and well written should
convey excitement, for it brings vividly to us the daily lives, habits, and
beliefs of our ancestors. In some ways, their patterns of behavior and
thought will seem similar to ours, but in other ways our predecessors'
actions and values appear quite different, if not barbaric or alien. Those
living conditions and attitudes that have survived to the present are not
by definition superior to those of the distant or recent past. Social history
does not teach progress. Rather than drawing facile lessons from the daily
lives of those who came before us, we might, as historians, attempt to
immerse ourselves in their culture and understand why they lived and
acted as they did.

Social History
of Western Civilization
Volume II

THE OLD RÉGIME

Politically, the Old Régime was the Age of Absolutism, the era before the French Revolution; intellectually, it encompassed the Scientific Revolution and the Enlightenment; artistically, the Baroque and Rococo styles set the tone. Socially, the seventeenth and eighteenth centuries saw the nobility preeminent over a rural order marked by the growth of towns. Most people were poor physical specimens who worked hard, suffered from vitamin deficiency and malnutrition, and lived short lives. Although it is often hard to read the minds of people who left little documentation to record their feelings, one can suppose that happiness and enjoyment seemed out of the reach of the majority of Europe's population, save for that happiness that accompanies survival or the brief interlude of an exceptional occasion, such as a religious feast, a wedding, or some small victory extracted from a harsh and severe world.

Although there were, to be sure, some outside the Christian fold—Jews, Moslems, and a sprinkling of atheists—nearly all Europeans in the Old Régime were Christians. After the Protestant Reformation had exploded a relatively united Christendom in the sixteenth century, most states maintained an established church and discriminated legally against Christians who belonged to other denominations. Christians venerated order and authority, though some found it in a church, some in the pope, and some in the Bible. The body politic likewise signified harmony and obedience, monarchy being the model, for that government mirrored God's supremacy over the cosmos. Few were the religious and political visionaries who dared affirm the possibility or desirability of an alternative to monarchical rule.

Deference and order permeated the social structure. Kings governed subjects, lords dominated peasants, men ruled women, and parents regulated their children's lives. Rank in the Old Régime was everything, and it certainly had its privileges. If men of commerce and industry rose in stature—in Great Britain and the United Provinces, for example—this in no way implied an assault on the belief that hierarchy provided the ideal basis for society. Throughout most of Europe, the aristocracy stood at the pinnacle of the social pyramid, and, in many

1

places as far apart as France and Russia, the nobles experienced a resurgence of power and prestige. The aristocratic ethos offered a model of behavior, a set of values that others could only wish to emulate. Again, only a small number of individuals, primarily some intellectuals or those on the fringes of society, dreamed of a democratic revolution that would sweep the aristocracy and their privileges into the dustbin of history.

The Old Régime therefore possessed a certain unity in the midst of great diversity, a unity grounded in the respect, even veneration, of religious, political, and social order. Though changing, the Old Régime welcomed a stability that accompanied faith in respected institutions. The preferred form of change was individual change, a modest improvement in one's personal fortunes or those of one's family. Such alterations of stature, however, did little to dispel the terrible and brutal conditions of daily existence that faced the vast majority of Europe's population before the deluge of the Industrial and French Revolutions, which together helped create a new régime.

Misbeliefs about Our Ancestors. The Absence of Child Marriage and Extended Family Households from the English Past

PETER LASLETT

This selection is from Peter Laslett's book, The World We Have Lost: England before the Industrial Age, *already a classic in the burgeoning discipline of social history. Here Laslett dispels several misbeliefs about marriage and family life in sixteenth- and seventeenth-century England. He contends that people did not marry at an early age in any social rank. In fact, they married quite late, especially considering their short life expectancy (as compared to that of the twentieth-century English). Why did the early modern English postpone marriage until well past the twentieth birthday? Were the reasons social, physical, or perhaps both? What constituted a marriage? What type of courtship was involved?*

Laslett also points out that the family unit was small, not large, and nuclear, not extended. Grandparents were seldom found in the parent-children family. Was old age not venerated? Were grandparents callously disregarded and discarded? How did wealth affect household size?

Because people married late and life expectancy was short, the death of a spouse tore the family asunder, much as divorce does in the modern world. What fate awaited widows and widowers? A woman had to possess economic assets in order to be considered an attractive catch. Would women in early modern England want to remarry? Do you think family life and human relationships were so different in pre-industrial England that they truly formed a "world we have lost"?

Laslett begins this selection with a reference to Romeo *and* Juliet, *claiming that Shakespeare's play misleads us about social conditions in England. What sources does Laslett use to analyze Shakespeare? Is literature of any value in reconstructing the lives of people in the past?*

Peter Laslett, *The World We Have Lost Further Explored. England before the Industrial Age,* 3d ed. New York: Charles Scribner's Sons, 1984, 81–87, 89–97, 99–104.

My child is yet a stranger in the world,
She hath not seen the change of fourteen years.
Let two more summers wither in their pride
Ere we may think her ripe to be a bride.

Capulet says this in the second scene of *Romeo and Juliet*. But whatever he said and whatever he felt, his child Juliet did take Romeo to husband at about her fourteenth birthday. Juliet's mother left her in no doubt of what she thought.

Well, think on marriage now. Younger than you
Here in Verona, ladies of esteem,
Are made already mothers. By my count
I was your mother much upon these years
That you are now a maid.

So she had married at twelve, or early thirteen, and all those other ladies of Verona also. Miranda was married in her fifteenth year in the *Tempest*. It all seems clear and consistent enough. The women in Shakespeare's plays, and so presumably the Englishwomen of Shakespeare's day, might marry in their early teens, or even before, and very often did.

Yet this is not true. Every record so far examined, and the number is now considerable, clearly demonstrates that marriage was rare at these early ages in Elizabethan and Jacobean England. Marriage and childbearing in the late teens were not as common as they are now and at twelve marriage as we understand it was virtually unknown. Girls could be *espoused* then, or even before, but that was a different matter.

Some of the evidence for these blank statements will have to be presented here and we shall have to be clear as to what constituted marriage. Espousals, so common in Shakespearean drama, were not marriages as we think of marriage, but counted as such if the undertaking was made before witnesses in the present tense. They became marriage itself when made in the future tense, if, but only if, sexual intercourse took place. . . .

People could marry by license as well as by banns in England then, just as they still can in the Church of England today. They had to apply for the license to the bishop of the diocese they lived in, and very often they were required to give their ages. The reason was that no one under twenty-one could be married by the church without parental permission: it was a grave sin to do so at an older age without good reason. We have examined 1007 such licenses containing the ages of the applicants, issued by the diocese of Canterbury between 1619 and 1660 to people marrying for the first time. Our results are set out in Table 1. The mean age of brides, as will be seen, was over ten years later than Juliet's, about 23 1/2. Bridegrooms were a good three years older, though some of the age gaps recorded were wider. When individual ages are looked at, however, we

Table 1: *Mean age at first marriage*

	Mean age of bridegrooms	Mean age of brides	Difference
All applicants for licenses, Diocese of Canterbury, 1619–60 (1007 bridegrooms, 1007 brides)	26.65	23.58	3.07
Gentry only amongst Canterbury applicants (118 bridegrooms, 118 brides)	26.18	21.75	4.43
Marriages of nobles, from about 1600 to about 1625 (325 brides, 313 bridegrooms)	24.28	19.39	4.89
Marriages of nobles, from about 1625 to about 1650 (510 brides, 403 bridegrooms)	25.99	20.67	5.32

do find very occasional marriages in the early teens. One girl gave her age as thirteen, none as fourteen, four as fifteen, twelve as sixteen, but all the rest of the brides in the sample, 990 of them, were seventeen or over, and more than four out of five had reached the age of twenty. Only ten of the men were younger than this. The commonest age for women was twenty-two, for men twenty-four; the median—the age below which as many got married as above it—was some 22.75 for women, 25.5 for men.

Put in the familiar form we use in conversation, the average age of this sample of Elizabethan and Jacobean brides was about 23 1/2 and the average age of bridegrooms was about 26 1/2. Our results have been amply confirmed from other sources and from many parts of England and other areas of west and north-west Europe. . . . Surely these facts by themselves ought to be sufficient to dispel the belief that our ancestors married much younger than we do.

But the literary references are so straightforward, and Shakespeare at least so influential that we must go further: there seems to be some desire in our day to believe in this particular mistake. Did the gentry[1] marry early?—after all Romeo and Juliet were not ordinary people.

Table 1 gives an answer to this more difficult question, showing that gentle brides were younger than the others in the middle years of the seventeenth century in the Canterbury diocese, that is eastern Kent. Bridegrooms were of much the same age as the rest of the population. When the first marriage of peers from all over the realm are added, this contrast is made a little sharper, but it cannot be said to be very impressive, and further research has not always confirmed the figures.

[1]The English social group below the peerage and above the yeomen.

Later in the century gentry seem to have been a little older at first marriage than craftsmen, and the age at marriage of peers went up. No class of the English population as far as we can see ever seems to have married at anything like the ages suggested by Shakespeare's plays.

The mean age at marriage, all marriages, in our day is twenty-eight or twenty-nine for men and twenty-five or twenty-six for women. When everything now known is added to the evidence presented here the conclusion is inescapable. It is not true to say that in England in earlier times, in the world we have lost as we have called it, people, either ordinary or privileged, married much younger than we marry now. In fact they were markedly older in relation to the number of years for which they lived. Whereas a woman marrying at twenty-five in Elizabethan England would on average live for some thirty-two or thirty-three years, and her husband at say twenty-eight for three or four years less than that, an Englishwoman of twenty-five in our day has fifty years or more in front of her.

Juliet's mother's statement is a little extraordinary in quite another way, since it is doubtful whether she or her daughter were capable of sexual relations, and above all of procreation, at age thirteen. It has been established that the age of sexual maturity in women has fallen in western Europe in the last century or so, and in all other industrialized areas of the world. In Manchester in 1835 working-class girls could expect their first period at an average of 15.6 years, but middle-class girls at 14.3, a difference to be noted. In 1890 the level seems to have been about the same for the middle class, but the working class showed an average of 15.0 in 1910. Ages could be higher than these in the 1800s: 16.8 in Copenhagen and in Munich in 1820 for poorer people, 15.0 in Norway for the middle class. The fall after 1900 can best be observed in the USA, where the general age was 14.1 in that year, but 12.9 in 1951 and 12.8 today, the current Japanese figure. In southern England it is now about 13.1, but in northern England 13.4 for the middle class, 13.6 for working girls.

This is an intriguing but difficult subject, for it should be evident that age at menarche varies from class to class and area to area as well as from time to time. No single average age at sexual maturity, meaning full physical development and capacity to bear children, can have existed in England in Elizabeth's day, or in pre-industrial Europe generally. But there are fairly persuasive grounds for supposing that the average or mean age cannot have been much lower than sixteen anywhere in Shakespeare's day, or earlier. If both these persons, Juliet and her mother, had been able to behave as the play requires, then both must have been a long way from the average, the average experience of the audience. They would have had to have reached childbearing age well before the young English aristocrat who, as far as we know, produced a baby at the earliest point in the life course, that is Elizabeth Manners, wife of the second

Earl of Exeter. She was brought to bed in 1589 at about fourteen years five months. Even in the 1980s a girl would be hard put to it to deliver a baby much before the age of fourteen, if she matured at the lowest of the average ages set out above.

But such deliveries do occur, since there is always variation about any mean. The extent of this variation has been determined for the present day, and, within limits, for earlier times. There is a fairly remote chance, perhaps one out of every hundred or more, that Juliet would have been capable of accepting Romeo's advances, considering that she was a very exceptional young lady, in her diet and general living standards, even if she could not possibly have borne a child by then. But the chances against *both* Juliet *and* her mother having been able to behave in the way we are asked to suppose have to be reckoned in the thousands. The more the point is laboured, the less credible the view that there was anything realistic whatever in the literary intentions of the play in these respects. . . .

. . . One quite exceptional case in the fifteenth century is of a noble-woman being 'married' at a time when she could not have been capable of sexual intercourse. Margaret, Lady Rowecliffe, first had a husband in 1463 at the age of four, but had lost him by the age of twelve, when she was given another one. The bridegroom's father then undertook that 'they should not ligg togeder til she came to the age XVI years', which is the plainest indication I have seen of the time at which an Englishwoman of late medieval times could be expected to be sexually mature. Such early 'marriages' should properly be called espousals *de futuro*, . . . promises to marry in the future. . . . Life was uncertain amongst commoners as well as amongst aristocrats. The marriage partner to be taken by an heir apparent was always a matter of the first importance where there was an estate and name to be safeguarded.

In 1593, Robert Furse, of Moreshead in Devonshire, for example, a substantial yeoman on his way up in the world and engaged like every other yeoman of ability in building up his family, matched his son at the age of nine years and three months to Susan Alford, an orphan and the ward of a kinsman: the actual marriage was to take place when Robert's son reached the age of fifteen. . . . This was obviously a fairly usual arrangement; the postponement of the actual union must have been usual too. . . .

. . . But everything we can get to know about differences between the privileged people and the rest in pre-industrial times is of significance. It is pretty clear from the body of evidence which has been expertly analysed by auxologists, that is students of growth, evidence which ranges over height, weight, breaking of the voice in males, the swelling out of the breasts in girls, and so on, why it is that these things vary from social group to social group and time to time. It is the better health and maintenance, as well as the better feeding, of the middle classes and of those in the more prosperous areas at the present time which are the operative reasons why they mature earlier, put on weight and height more quickly than the working classes. This must mean that everyone, even the most privileged, matured later in pre-industrial times than we all do now. But it also means that differences between classes in these respects may have been greater.

Now if this was indeed true of all privileged people in the world we have lost, of all members of the ruling stratum as we have called it, in relation to the rest, and of the gentry as a society in relation to those below them in the social scale, then it implies a very remarkable contrast between the two sections of the population. The privileged were no doubt taller, heavier and better developed than the rest just as they were in Victorian times. In the Elizabethan age, and in pre-industrial times generally, gentlemen may have had beards and broken voices earlier than the rest of the population, and ladies may have become full women more quickly. . . .

As widely held as the assumption about child marriage, and certainly more deeply rooted in belief and in opinion, about the self as well as about society, is the supposition that our ancestors lived in large familial units. Family groups, it seems to be almost universally agreed, ordinarily consisted in the pre-industrial past of grandparents, children, married as well as unmarried, grandchildren and often relatives, all sleeping in the same house, eating together and working together. This was so, it is supposed, because wedded sons and perhaps daughters too, but especially eldest sons, were permitted or even expected to live with their parents. A widowed mother would accordingly stay in the household after her son had taken over, or join him or another of her children in their establishments. If her children were all unmarried and her parents were still alive, she might go to live with them, taking her offspring with her. An unmarried uncle, aunt or cousin might do the same. Married brothers might share households too, perhaps after the death of their father, but under other circumstances, and for working purposes. Given conditions like these, households would have had to be bigger than our households are, and more complicated in their inner relationships as well: extended families is the phrase which is nearly always used.

Now all these statements have been demonstrated to be false, false for traditional England that is to say, as false and as misleading as the statements about age at marriage. It is not true that most of our ancestors lived in extended families. It is not true that industrialization brought the simple nuclear family with it. In England there was actually an increase in the tiny proportion of more complicated households in the period of economic transformation. It is not true that the elderly and the widowed ordinarily had their married children living with them, or that uncles, aunts, nephews and nieces were often to be found as resident relatives. It is not even true that the casualties of earlier, harder times, the victims of age, sickness, bereavement or want, could usually rely on their kin for continuing maintenance even though they did not live with them. Although the average family group was half as large again as it is today, four and three-quarters persons instead of a little over three, the reason for this has almost nothing to do with the extended family. The difference has to be attributed to demography, and to the presence of servants.

. . . [T]he huge household run by the Hales at Goodnestone in 1676 with twenty-two persons in it, and the even greater one at Chilvers Coton kept by the Newdigates in 1684 with thirty-seven, contained many more children than we are used to. But it was the servants, fourteen in one and twenty-eight in the other, which made them really large. Since servants, life-cycle servants as we have called them, were transferred children, their presence ensured that the important households should be bigger and the unimportant households smaller. This did not increase the *average* number of persons making up the domestic unit in the traditional world, of course; a simple transfer of persons between them could not have done so. The larger size of the average household then than now must be due to other causes, of which our much reduced fertility is one. The more modest, servant-supplying families of pre-industrial society had fewer births and usually fewer survivors of infancy and childhood than the more substantial, servant-keeping families. This intensified the contrast. But the grand domestic establishments of traditional English society were rarities, numerically. . . . They bulk much too large in the view we take of it. . . .

The wish to believe in the large, extended, kin-enfolding, multi-generational, welfare- and support-providing household in the world we have lost seems to be exceedingly difficult to expose to critical evaluation. There are a number of reasons for this. One may be the conviction that those whom we regard as the casualties of our industrial world, of whom the vast numbers of our elderly people are conspicuous examples, have been exiled by history, exiled from the family to which of right they belong. It is of great importance that we should efface this impression; the proper understanding of ourselves in time is what we are charged with as historical sociologists.

But it is also our duty to be just to our English predecessors, in their terms as well as in our own. If they had an individualistic familial system very like the one which we live under, if they showed forth the principle of neo-localism, as the anthropologists call it—setting up your own household at marriage that is to say, and living in it for the rest of your life—as conspicuously as we do ourselves, they did not lack familial solidarity outside the compass of the nuclear family.

The claim that few families were multi-generational, the figure being about one family in twenty, does not mean that there were no multi-generational families at all. Nor does it mean that elderly widows, or even widowers, never lived with their married children, for it was quite common for this to happen. The neo-local rule against living with your parents after marriage does not imply that your parent should not finally come to live with you. Since the widowed elderly were a small proportion of the population, their not infrequent presence in the household did not give rise to as much multi-generationality as might be expected. The neo-local rule itself was sometimes broken, since children did stay at home after marriage occasionally, for a few months or even a year or so until they could move into their own place. Orphans were found familial niches, though these were by no means always with their kinfolk, and the finding, as far as we can see, was not infrequently done by the parish, or other non-familial authority.

The wider kin, as distinct from the immediate, could be of considerable importance on particular occasions in the life of an individual all the same. They frequently appear when it was a question of getting a job, or making a trading connection, raising some capital or migrating for any of these or for other reasons. They come forward at critical junctures in the life course: at the births of children, when illnesses became disabling, at marriages, at deaths, even if they were so seldom sources of permanent support, psychological or financial. But it must be noticed that neighbours and friends are found in those positions too, and in some respects, such as standing surety for debts, were more important than kinsfolk, in the fourteenth century as much as in the eighteenth. It is not without interest that in the language of the time 'friends' covered both kinsfolk and other intimates. Nevertheless, some of the negatives which we have laid down about familial interaction seem to have been absolute. Two brothers living together after marriage and collaborating in the work on the same farm have never made an appearance in the English record. And the famous stem family household, where the heir, the eldest or perhaps the youngest son, stays at home, marries and has children whilst the rest either leave or go unmarried, is conspicuous by its absence too.

Neither the stem family nor the simple or nuclear family is as straightforward as might seem. For the familial group is a process, rather than a state, changing and developing from the time of its formation to the time of its dissolution in a cyclical manner. Its membership at one point in the family cycle cannot be taken as necessarily representing its membership at other points. A stem-family tendency may therefore exist in a society when only a few of its constituent households show forth the stem-family form. There were far too few housholds in traditional England with this constitution to allow such a thing to be taken as a usual practice, but English family households could change enormously in their membership during the family cycle, a cycle which occurred only once of course in every individual case in the simple family system. Under other systems an individual household could persist while the family within it underwent several cycles.

If the parents, or one parent, of a man or his wife heading a simple family household paid a visit to them, the kin composition of the family household of the younger couple would become complex for that time, and bigger too. Similarly if a brother or sister should dwell with them, or a more distant relative. Most alterations in the family itself changed its size rather than its kinship composition, however, and here the birth, and perhaps the early death, of children, and their leaving home when they were mature, were conspicuous events, and sometimes the death, or remarriage, of one of the spouses. But it was in the membership of the household, rather than in that of the family part of it, that the changeover was most marked, if servants were usually employed. For servants came and went at the end of every servant year, which was in the early or late autumn in most parts of the country, and the numbers which a family employed changed too. A family household could be a very different thing from decade to decade, year to year or even month to month, although it never became complex in its kinship composition.

These circumstances have led to confusion as well as to misunderstanding and disagreement when scholars have tried to compare family systems from region to region and time to time. But we now know enough to state with some confidence that the familial arrangements of northern and western Europe as a whole were like those we have described for traditional England, if not quite to the same extent and not so uniformly over time and from place to place.

We can also show that late marriage and a high proportion of life-cycle servants fitted in to a familial system which distinguished England and the west from much of the rest of the world, even from southern and eastern Europe, and to some extent from central Europe too. . . .

. . . [H]ouseholds could be small; indeed . . . [a family] size [of] three was commonest and nearly two-fifths of the population lived in [households] of three, four or five. But over half were members of groups consisting of six or more. . . .

There is evidence that by the 1850s and 1860s these things had started to change, but in a way very different from what traditional opinion might lead us to expect. It begins to look as if the poor and very poor, especially those long resident in one village and accepted as established members of the community, were more likely to have relatives living with them than anyone else. The hierarchy which puts the élite at the top, with most kin in the households, was being reversed. A possible explanation of this might be that it was pressure on space which compelled these poor people to double up with their relatives. This would scarcely account for the facts. The unsettled, footloose members of the mid-Victorian village examined had fewest relatives alive, and as for the gentlemen and aristocrats, almost universally supposed to be most likely to live in complex family households, they could and did afford houses of any size they pleased.

It seems clear, moreover, that the relative cost of housing in pre-industrial times was less, perhaps considerably less, than it is now. The humblest dwelling of all, a cottage for the labouring poor, could, it seems, be put up new for less than two years of the annual wage of a labourer, and the justices of the peace seem always to be authorizing or ordering such undertakings as if they were a casual matter. . . .

Where lists of the houses in a village have survived, however, some seem always to have been vacant, especially in the later seventeenth century. . . . Not that homelessness was unknown in those years or at any time in that era of endemic poverty and wretchedness. One Simon Gibbs, writes the clerk to the Justices of Warwickshire in January 1667, 'is destitute of an habitation for his wife and five small children, having long lain out of doors'. A cottage was ordered to be erected on the common of his village. . . .

The neo-local rules which have governed the shape of the English family for so long can be written out as follows. Under ordinary circumstances no two married couples could make an appearance in the same co-resident familial group. Even the remnant of a nuclear family, a widowed parent with a child, tended to count as a married couple for this purpose, and servants in the household had also to conform. When a son or daughter took a spouse, therefore, he or she had to leave, even if there was an expectation of taking over the family farm, and a new household has to be established. If this was not possible, then no marriage could take place. Once the wedding was over, the child lost the right of living in the parental family as or when it was convenient, a right which we can observe servants taking advantage of from time to time, returning to live for a while with their own parents when they were 'between places'. The mother and father of a married child were held to the neo-local rule as well. They had no *right* of residence in the family established by a child, even after widowhood, although it is clear that they were often brought in to that household in their final years of dependency. Indeed when it was advantageous for both parties, and for reasons of loyalty and affection, these principles could always be manipulated. . . .

The creation of a new familial unit was brought about by the enterprise of the young couple, of both of them. But it usually also required the co-operation of each set of parents, or of those of them who were still alive and accessible. The bride's dowry came from her own family, but to this was added her savings, which were often the wages and the 'vails', that is the tips, which she had hoarded when in service, as well as her experience, her skill and her strength. These were not always and entirely a matter of housewifery, learnt from her mother or in the households where she had served. . . . [A] few young women had served apprenticeships, and others would even have managed little undertakings of their own, as midwives, perhaps, or as teachers. But spinning or weaving were by far the most important sources of such earnings. If a woman were lacking in these possessions or accomplishments, then she could not get married, though sexual attractiveness would always count, at all times and on all social levels. . . .

Neither sons nor daughters had to wait upon family inheritance before marriage could take place, except sometimes where land was at issue. For it was not always, or even in most instances, access to land which had to be acquired. Children decidedly did not marry in order of their age, nor is it easy to discern in the records before the nineteenth century any tendency for one or other of them, especially a daughter, to wait behind to look after ageing, widowed or infirm parents. There were other aspects of marriage strategy, for the parents of the parties as well as for the parties themselves. Marriage was a family affair, or rather a two-family affair, affecting the policy of the immediate and sometimes the more distant relatives of both partners.

There was the consolidation or extension of a family's land, which might be secured by the match, amongst those who controlled land. A dowry could consist in broad acres, or the expectation of them, as well as in an assembly of household goods in a chest. There were political alliances to be forged or extended, and these could be in the politics of the vestry and the village pump as well as of the county or the diocese. Parental arrangement of the matches of children was much more likely when the issues were of this kind, much less so with the most numerous of the brides and bridegrooms, where property was small and power unlikely to count for very much. In such cases, especially when a bride or bridegroom was an orphan and distant from home, parental consent could be of little consequence. Nevertheless it was always secured when possible. When, as was so frequently the case, one or both of the parties had been married before, parental consent was not in question, for the spouse was at his 'own dispose' as they put it. For each and every would-be married couple, however, the decision to set up a family for the first time could only be made when there was an opening, an opening in the social fabric so to speak.

For marriage, and particularly first marriage, we must repeat, was an act of profound importance to the social structure. It meant the creation of a new economic unit as well as of a lifelong association of two persons previously separate and caught up in existing families. It gave to the man full membership of the community and to the woman something to run; she became mistress of a household. . . . A cell was added to society, in the town as well as in the country. It is understandable, therefore, that marriage could not come about unless a slot fell vacant and the aspiring couple was able to fill it up. It might be a cottage with its patch of ground and rights annexed to it on the common land, which became available to a manservant and a womanservant, and enabled them to set up as 'cottagers or labouring people'. It might be a bakery, or a joinery, a tailor's, butcher's, wheelwright's, blacksmith's or weaver's shop, each with its 'practice' attached, the body of customers that is to say in the habit of buying what was there turned out. Only for the truly fortunate would it be an assemblage of fields to own, or fields to rent, and this, often but not always, meant inheritance.

For all these slots there was a waiting period. Hence all young people had to wait to marry, and some could not marry at all. Once it is recognized that our English ancestors had the same rule as we have, two married couples not to be together in one family, then size and structure of household, age at marriage and proportions marrying can all be seen to be tied together and to be tied in their turn to the economics of the time as well as to the situation as to births and deaths. How long the waiting period had to be was affected by the numbers of the younger generation in relation to the numbers of the older generation, so that the fertility history of those in possession was at issue as well as their disposition to die. By and large there were bound to be niches for all but a few provided that the population was not increasing so fast that the new generation was greatly in excess of the old, and provided that economic activity increased proportionately. The time taken in actually locating the slots which were vacant, or about to become so, has also to be added to the queuing interval to marriage which society imposed on our ancestors.

No wonder then that they were interested in births, marriages and deaths. No wonder every mother of daughters became notorious for her curiosity about potential husbands. Since all these ineluctable circumstances as to succession applied with peculiar force to the literate and genteel, where finding an heiress meant heightened wealth and consequence, and failure to find a slot might mean social descent, it is comprehensible that so large a part of their lives and their literature was given up to the marriage market. To understand the demography of the world we have lost, always in relation to its productive activities, is therefore to begin to see how its social structure actually worked over time and at any one time, for rich and poor, élite and proletariat alike. . . . [L]et us look at our ancestors as they were when actually engaged in marriage as a *rite de passage*,[2] in Yorkshire in the 1630s.

We have learnt to be wary of high literature as a photographic portrayal, and of what nobles and gentry can be shown to have done as a guide to what everybody did. The actors in the following passage must have been genteel too, or at least of yeoman stock; certainly landed. . . .

Concerning our Fashions of our Country Weddings

Usually the young man's father, or he himself, writes to the father of the maid to know if he shall be welcome to the house, if he shall have further-

---

[2]Rite of passage.

ance if he come in such a way or how he liketh of the notion. Then if he [presumably the woman's father] pretend any excuse, only thanking him for his good will, then it is as good as a denial. If the motion be thought well of, and embraced, then the young man goeth perhaps twice to see how the maid standeth affected. Then if he see that he be tractable, and that her inclination is towards him, then the third time that he visiteth, he perhaps giveth her a ten-shilling piece of gold, or a ring of that price; or perhaps a twenty-shilling piece, or a ring of that price, then 10s. the next time, or the next after that, a pair of gloves of 6s. 8d. a pair; and after that, each other time, some conceited toy or novelty of less value. They visit usually every three weeks or a month, and are usually half a year, or very near, from the first going to the conclusion.

So soon as the young folks are agreed and contracted, then the father of the maid carrieth her over to the young man's house to see how they like of all, and there doth the young man's father meet them to treat of a dower, and likewise of a jointure or feoffment [this was what was settled on her] for the woman. And then do they also appoint and set down the day of the marriage, which may perhaps be about a fortnight or three weeks after, and in that time do they get made the wedding clothes, and make provision against the wedding dinner, which is usually at the maid's father's. Their use is [it is usual] to buy gloves to give to each of their friends a pair on that day; the man should be at the cost for them, but sometimes the man gives the gloves to the men and the woman to the women, or else he to her friends and she to his. They give them that morning when they are almost ready to go to church to be married.

Then so soon as the bride is tired [attired] and that they are ready to go forth, the bridegroom comes, and takes her by the hand, and saith: 'Mistress, I hope you are willing', or else kisseth her before them, and then followeth her father out of the doors. Then one of the bridegroom his men ushereth the bride, and goes foremost, and the rest of the young men usher each of them a maid to church. The bridegroom and the brides brothers or friends tend at dinner: he perhaps fetcheth her home to his house a month after, and the young man comes to fetch away his bride some of his best friends, and young men his neighbours, come along with him, and others perhaps meet them in the way, and then there is the same jollity at his house. For they perhaps have love ? wine [*sic*—as in original] ready to give to the company when they light [alight], then a dinner, supper and breakfast next day.

There are clear signs here of the betrothal which, as we have already seen, was then separate from the later marriage. It is also quite plain that although the parents of the couple were principal actors in the business, everything depended on the consent and the willingness of the young people themselves. What may be most surprising is that the married pair did not go away together after the feast in the home of the bride, but weeks later. . . .

The marriage customs of Stuart Yorkshire may have differed widely from those elsewhere in England and Wales. . . . Ralph Meers . . . had been a servant in the house of the Wawens who were 'lords of the soil' at Clayworth, and he became a labourer in the village. He could surely not have afforded the rings, the sovereigns or half-sovereigns to give to Anne Fenton, his bride who had been his fellow servant. There can have been no family portion to speak of for Anne, though she may well have saved her wages, all of them, at 30s. or £2 a year against that wonderful day, and no question of a horse for them to alight from at the cottage door.

Anne was already pregnant at the time as we know, and both of them had been in trouble with the parson on that account. Nevertheless, and this is a highly significant fact for the disciplinary system . . . , Ralph Meers became churchwarden within a year or two, and himself took responsibility for reporting on the sexual lives of the parishioners. There are plenty of other signs that the romantic respectability which has now attached itself to marriage and the married state in traditional England may be to some degree misplaced. Many of the brides and bridegrooms had been married before: something like a quarter of them were widowed persons in the seventeenth century, though their numbers were to fall within a generation or two. A far higher proportion had lost their fathers than their mothers, perhaps a third or even as much as a half, depending once more on the prevalent mortality. You could not with confidence expect to see your grandchildren in the world we have lost, not in England anyway. . . .

The Constraint of Bodies

ROBERT MUCHEMBLED

How often do we hear calls for increased discipline in society and greater parental authority in the home! Robert Muchembled returns us to the society of sixteenth- and seventeenth-century France, where church, government, and fathers imposed strict discipline and "moral" behavior on flocks, subjects, and family members, creating in the process what may seem like a utopia to today's opponents of women's equality and sexual diversity. Muchembled uses as evidence archival sources from regions in northern France; thus his thesis that a dynamic popular culture throughout France came to be suppressed is speculative, though provocative.

Why were authorities in early modern France so intent on constraining people's bodies? The late Middle Ages had not been so concerned about nudity, illegitimacy, sexual relations before marriage, prostitution, adultery, and masturbation. Why did French society grow to be less tolerant of such behavior? Muchembled links the new disquietude about so-called sexual deviancy to a developing sense of good manners. The élite taught the masses not only that they were no longer free in their sexual lives but also that other natural bodily functions—such as spitting and blowing their noses—had to be controlled. What evidence does Muchembled offer to document "the prison of the body"?

The education of children was the obvious place to begin the inculcation of these new moral values. From infancy one learned to relinquish control of one's own body. What methods were employed to teach children obedience? The father proved a willing and eager support in the effort by church and state to eliminate autonomy in the population. In turn, religion and government buttressed the father's authority. How? In what ways did the father control the lives of family members? Thus did a revived, stronger Christianity, political absolutism, and the father—king in his castle as never before—unite to bring a new type of order to society. It was not sentiment or love that bound people together but ideas of hierarchy and authority.

It would be false to claim that the popular masses were not subjugated in the fifteenth and sixteenth centuries. In the first place, they were slaves to the elements, to sickness, and to omnipresent death. They were subjected to men: to the king, to the seigneurs,[1] and to the ecclesiastical authorities, all of whom extracted taxes and demanded services and unfailing obedience when need arose. But the common people were

---

[1]Lords.

Robert Muchembled, *Popular Culture and Elite Culture in France, 1400–1750*. (Baton Rouge: Louisiana State University Press, 1985), 187–201.

relatively free to make use of their bodies as they saw fit and were not required constantly to rein in their sexual or emotional impulses. Roman Catholicism, furthermore, demanded of them that they perform the gestures of religion, but it lacked the means to penetrate profoundly into their souls, which remained for the most part dominated by magic and by "superstition." All in all, the masses were neither totally alienated nor very tightly supervised. As long as order and the established values were not questioned, they enjoyed a relative autonomy, particularly in cultural matters. . . .

This situation changed radically with the establishment of a truly absolute royal power. The epoch of Louis XIII[2] and Louis XIV[3] was for the masses a century of duress. Not only because taxes increased enormously, because war, famines, and epidemics raged . . . , but also because of a tightened ideological domination. The monarchy, supported by a minority of the privileged and by the Church, undertook the task of regimenting the masses, working people and idlers alike. The strictly institutional history of this grandiose effort is well known. It is symbolized by the creation of *intendants*,[4] the eyes of the king in the provinces, and by a political activity that it would be difficult to summarize in even an entire volume. The hidden face of this phenomenon, however, has to my knowledge not yet been the object of any systematic study. I mean by that the fabrication of consent or even the fabrication of simple submission. The multiplication of royal agents or the progress of centralization cannot alone explain why more than 90 percent of the population accepted, practically without revolt after 1675, a yoke more severe and an exploitation more systematic than in the past. In truth, the real base of the new political domination was the social conformity of each individual, and this was accomplished by a joint subjection of body and soul. The absolutist State discovered and used, with the aid of the Church and of the social elites, a "political technology of the body," and it learned to make use of the soul, "the prison of the body," as "the effect and instrument of a political anatomy." The end result was a diffusion throughout society of a model of vertical political relations that was organized around the notion of total obedience to the king, himself the image and servant of God on earth. . . .

. . . [T]he constraint of the body did indeed proceed from a strategy of power, designed to obtain the most perfect obedience possible on the part of the subjects, but it in no way constituted a coherent and systematic plan. Bodies would be constrained because the logic of absolutism and of centralization demanded it and led in that direction; there was no need to reflect on the impact or the validity of this fact. Bodies

[2]King of France, 1610–1643.
[3]King of France, 1643–1715.
[4]The chief royal agents in the provinces.

would be constrained in several ways: by sexual repression, by training in bodily control on all occasions, by judiciary mutilation and by torture, all of which marked the social limits beyond which each individual could no longer make use of his own body as he saw fit.

"It has been demonstrated time and again that the attitudes and the way of life of the fifteenth and the sixteenth centuries were pro-sexual." . . . Indeed, . . . both peasants and city-dwellers showed little hesitation or sense of guilt about the exercise of lower body functions. Sexual repression started around 1500, and it continues into our own times, with a particularly strong surge between 1550 and 1700.

A widespread change in behavior was behind this repression. New rules of proper conduct developed. As early as the end of the Middle Ages there were "Babees' Books" that circulated in western Europe and offered a new civility to the children of the governing classes. Mores evolved. The bedroom came into being, first as a separated area and then, in the eighteenth century, as a room set apart from the other rooms in the house. The bed, which had welcomed adults and children pell-mell in the sixteenth century, . . . gradually lost occupants, in the upper classes of society at least. The habit of sleeping nude disappeared, and in the sixteenth century underwear came into use, at first as a way to prevent indecent contact. Nudity even became taboo, whereas people frequently washed and dressed in public in the sixteenth century and even under Louis XIV. Entire families no longer went nude or partially nude to the *étuves* (steam baths). Modesty increased. Sexual brutality . . . gave way to more restrained sexual behavior. The sexual vocabulary that had been so very rich at the time of Rabelais[5] shrank and was transformed. Cruder, more symbolic words came to be used to speak of parts of the human body that had become taboo. Barbarous instruments were invented to prevent children from masturbating, and so forth.

In a general way, everything connected with excretion or with sexuality came to make up a sphere of individual intimacy. People learned to blow their noses, to spit, to sleep, and in general to comport themselves with civility. They learned to control their bodies and avoid impropriety. The lower body became a world apart, to the point that it seemed not to exist for the Précieuses[6] of the seventeenth century, or even for the cultivated man of the time. On the other hand, it is certain that the popular masses reflected this change only slowly and partially, and this accentuated the gap between their mores and those of the dominant circles. The elites found all the more reason to scorn the common people: weren't humble folk dirty, smelly, ugly, vulgar, coarse, and oafish, according to the canons of the new urbanity? Even though the villages and the popular districts of cities and towns did not take to the mores of the elites,

[5]François Rabelais, French writer, 1494–1553.

[6]Women in Parisian salons.

the discrediting of sexuality that was one of the principal aspects of these new mores was imposed on the masses.

Demographic data show this at a glance, and even literary sources before 1550–1600 give us a preliminary impression of a fair amount of sexual permissiveness in the popular world. One of the few works of historical demography concerning the sixteenth century insists on the fact that illegitimacy, in the Nantes region, oscillated between 3.9 percent and 0.3 percent of all births in urban parishes, and between 4.6 percent and 0.1 percent in rural communities. Furthermore, 50 percent of the parents of illegitimate children whose family situation is known lived in concubinage, and 8.5 percent had had children adulterously. We cannot speak of generalized license in this connection, but neither can we interpret these data in terms of evident sexual inhibition. In contrast, the seventeenth century quite certainly shows efficient repression in this domain. At a time when mass means of contraception were nonexistent, the rural illegitimacy rates now hardly ever rise beyond 1 percent. They are even 0.5 percent in the Beauvais region between 1600 and 1730. Illegitimate births, more numerous in the larger cities than in the village, show a tendency to decrease everywhere in the seventeenth century, and sometimes up to the middle of the eighteenth century, before they rise quite sharply after 1760–1770. Prenuptial conceptions also rose everywhere beginning with the middle of the eighteenth century, and sometimes even beginning in the 1650s.

These data are obviously difficult to interpret. Globally, they indicate, according to current interpretation, that sexual repression was at work in France between 1600 and 1750, whereas the preceding and the following periods saw a greater liberty in this domain. Some scholars consider that the Church had succeeded, between 1600 and 1750, in imposing almost total chastity outside of marriage (and marriage came late at the time and was even more delayed during the Ancien Régime).[7] Girls were seldom wed before they reached the age of 25, and boys married at around 27 and even 30 years of age. Taking into account the brevity of average life expectancy, a great many unmarried men and women must have died without ever having known the delights of the flesh. This seems aberrant to other historians, who prefer to raise questions concerning possible forms of sexual expression that escape demographers' counts, notably the practice of masturbation. Let us say, without attempting to settle the question, that popular sexual behavior seems to have been dominated between 1600 and 1750 by a respect for the norms imposed by the Church. Even if individual appetites were less restrained than it might be thought, it is certain that it was no longer possible to dispose of one's own body as freely as during the preceding centuries. At least, anyone who failed to be circumspect and to avoid overly free expression

---

[7]The Old Régime, the period before the French Revolution of 1789.

of desires ran the risk of being dragged before the tribunals, since a great many types of crimes against morality were on the books at the time.

The *officialités*—that is, the ecclesiastical tribunals—repressed sexual deviance among flock and shepherds alike. In the seventeenth century, the archdiocesan *officialité* of Cambrai judged 142 moral offenses involving rural priests, and 664 sexual offenses among the laity, in the majority rural. Carnal relations between unmarried young people make up 38 percent of the lay crimes; adulteries, sometimes involving incest as well, 32 percent; and simple incest 11 percent. Moral offenses among the clergy, which were few between 1600 and 1630, rise sharply from 1630 to 1650, return to their previous level between 1650 and 1670, then reach new heights between 1670 and 1700. Trials of the laity, numerous from 1644 to 1664, disappear almost entirely from 1664 to 1674, then increase during the last quarter of the century. Furthermore, when we look beyond the rise and fall of punished offenses, we can see that the court showed a quite clear absence of rigor at all times, toward priests and laity alike. Women, however, generally received harsher sentences than men.

These data show, on the one hand, that sexual repression intensified in the Cambrésis, particularly toward the middle and the last quarter of the seventeenth century, and, on the other, that the sexual conduct of villagers and of many priests remained fairly free. Indeed, the high number of trials and the relative indulgence of the judges indicate that the Church was far from having won the day in this region. There is no doubt, however, that in the long run the behavior of the masses and of their pastors was indeed modified. In the eighteenth century, the same *officialité* in Cambrai judged 46 cases of defloration, 105 cases of adultery—26 of them incestuous—and 20 acts of incest committed by laity. Even if there are lacunae in the documentation, we are far from the two hundred and more cases of adultery and the 73 cases of incest of the seventeenth century. However, 90 percent of the sexual crimes in the eighteenth century concern peasants, which leads us to think that sexual repression was less widespread in the countryside than in the cities. As for priests, they surely became more and more virtuous. The *officialité* of Troyes, for example, judged only two priests for fornication between 1685 and 1722, and two parish priests were reproached only with having taken too young a servant.

That the church undertook the surveillance of morality and that it met with success is hardly surprising. But it was not alone in the effort to establish a "moral order" by infusing sexuality with a sense of guilt and by repressing sexual deviance: lay courts did their share. Hadn't the king set the example by publishing in 1556 "one of the most terroristic edicts in previous French legislation," punishing with death any woman found guilty of "having murdered her child"? In reality, all the king did was to make this particular case conform to the evolution of repressive practice in the sexual domain.

This evolution is clear in the city of Arras. During the Middle Ages, moral offenses do not seem to have attracted the judges' attention to any great extent. In Antwerp, to pick a point of comparison, they represented less than 1 percent of all crimes from 1358 to 1387. In Arras between 1528 and 1549, on the other hand, the *échevins*[8] brought forty-two persons to trial, including ten women and two adolescents: twelve for procuration, three for rape, seven (married men) for the frequentation of prostitutes, ten for violence against women or girls, one for incest, two for child abandonment, and so forth. On the whole, these crimes represent nearly 8 percent of all people brought to trial for the period. More important, the accused were women in 24 percent of the cases involving moral offenses, whereas females in general averaged only 15 percent of all criminals.

Sexual repression increased even further in later periods in Arras and in Artois. . . . [A]dultery did not usually involve the death penalty, but honorable reparation and amends, if the guilty parties were of *condition honneste* (well-to-do) and flogging and banishment if they were *personnes viles et abjectes* (lowborn, abject persons). Compliant husbands were exposed in public with distaffs or banished, after having made honorable amends, and their wives were exposed and flogged.

Incest in the direct line (between father and daughter) bore the death penalty, but not incest committed *en ligne transversale*[9]—initiated by a brother, for example. As to incest in the broader definition, it merited no more than banishment, after flogging and honorable amends. Unless there were aggravating circumstances: Gilles, known as Joly Filiot, was hanged in Béthune 19 March 1584 for carnal knowledge of two sisters, one of them thirteen years of age. These girls were first cousins of his wife. He had induced them to drink . . . contraceptive potions, and they had lived for some time with him and his wife.

In cases of *stupre*—seduction of a virgin—the guilty party might be forced to dower the victim or marry her. This crime was not often pursued in Artois, our author tells us. Bestiality led to death by fire. Thus Oghuet from Sainte Marguerite perished in Béthune, in spite of his *grande simplicité* (mental retardation) and his youth. His mare was executed on the same spot. The author notes than in France the trial records were burned with the condemned person to erase all trace of the crime. Masturbation was not considered with as much severity . . . in Artois.

Abnormal forms of intercourse were judged with "indulgence" when the wife had submitted to them against her will: the *échevins* of Bapaume simply burned a *chapeau d'estouppes* (literally, a burlap hat) on the head of a wife guilty of such sodomy. Simple fornication outside of marriage involving widows or girls was not prosecuted, but couples living in

[8]City fathers, aldermen.

[9]In the transversal line, that is, horizontally, between siblings or even cousins, uncles, and aunts.

concubinage . . . were sent packing by the courts if the pastor or the neighbors requested it.

Prostitutes were tolerated only in the public *bordeaux*.[10] Otherwise, they were obliged to leave the city . . . in the particular case of the city of Arras. . . .

These remarks on judiciary practice in Artois are corroborated by an anonymous jurist in a collection of sentences copied down around 1630 and concerning the preceding hundred years or so. We find here twenty-two examples of condemnations for adultery in Arras between 1562 and 1613. . . . [I]ncest, on the other hand, was often punished . . . with less than death, even incest in the direct line. For example, on 9 May 1573 a married man who had gotten his daughter-in-law pregnant was flogged and banished from Artois for ten years. The Parlement of Dôle, to give a comparison, on 7 March 1600 sentenced a villager guilty of incest with his widowed sister-in-law to perpetual banishment after he was flogged and branded with a hot iron. . . .

. . . [T]he anonymous jurist offers some supplementary information. He describes thirteen sentences of married men who had frequented prostitutes between 1533 and 1578 who were obliged to make honorable reparation, to pay a fine, and to spend three days and three nights in prison on bread and water or who were banished for a maximum of five years. He notes ten examples of polygamy between 1555 and 1593. Pierre le Clercq, a brewer, was decapitated on 15 January 1557 for having married three women, one of them from Arras; another man was sent to the galleys for life; and still others were humiliated, whipped, flogged, banished, and so forth. Finally, infanticide is represented by seven sentences given between 1530 and 1634, three of which, in 1530, concerned a father and his two daughters. All of the accused were executed, with the exception of one girl proclaimed innocent and one widow flogged and banished for ten years.

Quite obviously, lay judiciary practice closely followed the religious moral code of the Counter Reformation. The anonymous jurist we have cited . . . notes in connection with this last instance that . . . celibacy is not a favorable estate if it is not pursued with a simple vow of chastity. His manuscript is embellished with formulas such as: . . . carnal love is very dangerous . . . it lowers [man] to the level of beasts, dulls all wisdom, resolution, prudence. Or: . . . carnal pleasure is not proper to the nature of man.

All the courts became avid defenders of Christian morality. The supervision of morals was one of the principal functions of the *échevins* of Arras at the end of the seventeenth century. Out of 232 sentences that they passed between 1694 and 1717, 102 concern moral offenses and 92 of these—nearly 40 percent—concern *libertinage*, that is, prostitution

---

[10]Brothels.

in all forms, 3 concern rapes, 4 concubinage, 2 the abandonment of children, and 1 polygamy. . . . [T]hese figures indicate an extremely high degree of sexual repression, and, in particular, an active struggle against urban prostitution. Out of 130 dossiers on moral offenses in Arras for the period 1674–1701 studied . . . 93 concern questions of prostitution and 11 concern procuration. The sentences were often severe: there were 104 banishments, 60 percent of which were for life, with one or several additional punishments, such as honorable amends, exposure with the carcan,[11] flogging, branding with a hot iron. There are few bourgeois among the condemned. On the other hand, 60 percent of the accused were not citizens, but vagrants or, in many cases, sixteen to twenty-two-year-old *libertines* of modest origins, camp followers to the soldiers garrisoned in the city.

During the eighteenth century sexual repression became less severe. In Bordeaux from 1768 to 1777, moral offenses that came before the *jurats*—the local equivalent of the northern *échevins*—were no more than incidental. Kidnapping seductions make up the greater part of them, while prostitution was tolerated unless there were complaints from the neighbors. In Paris during the second half of the eighteenth century, moral offenses represented only 1.6 percent of the cases presented before the criminal court of the Châtelet. Only bigamy and particularly rape were pursued. Prostitution and adultery now "fell under the jurisdiction of gossip alone."

Sexual repression, which for the most part was concentrated in the period from 1550–1600 to 1700–1750, is thus attested by literary, demographic, and judiciary sources. It was more than a systematic struggle on the part of the Church alone: the authorities and the members of the governing classes joined to promote a new type of civilization in a new type of state. In this sense, the surveillance of everyone's sexuality, through the establishment of laws and taboos, was aimed at subjecting people's bodies, and in particular the bodies of the popular masses, in order to obtain the highest possible level of obedience. Rules of proper conduct and modesty and obligatory continence outside of marriage, which came late in life, were social norms imposed on all. So was the obligation to enjoy the pleasures of the flesh only with moderation, within the authorized limits, and within the confines of marriage. Ecclesiastical and lay justice alike defined the boundaries of the permissible, the possible, and the forbidden to everyone's conscience. By different channels, each individual learned that his body did not completely belong to him. In twentieth-century terms, he was persuaded that sexuality was a social function and not an erotic or individual function. But there was more: he was also taught to control his entire body in order to put it to the service of society.

---

[11]An iron collar and chain.

Both Protestant and Jesuit pedagogues had understood, as early as the sixteenth century, that the best way to form good Christians was to concentrate on the education of children. More generally, along the same lines, childhood became in the Ancien Régime the principal area for the efforts of a "political technology of the body"—childhood, but also adolescence, and even the married state if the married man remained dependent on his father. Up to twenty-five or thirty years of age, sometimes even longer, people now learned to control their bodies.

From birth, and this was true long before the age we are considering, the infant willy-nilly learned to control his body. Since he was tightly swaddled until he was old enough to walk, the search for autonomy that psychologists consider so important for babies was totally impossible. . . .

More recently, David Hunt, studying the childhood of Louis XIII, has stated that French children of the seventeenth century labored under a serious complex, due to the frustration of their search for physical autonomy during early childhood. The dauphin Louis was weaned at twenty-five months (whereas the prescriptive literature usually recommended weaning at eighteen to twenty-four months). His guardians showed little attention to his personal cleanliness and they purged him frequently, depriving him of control over his own bowels. After a stage of total liberty and of sexual games permitted or provoked by his nurses, at the age of three he began to be "broken" by regular whippings. Hunt's description speaks of this as an inhibition of desires for autonomy accompanied by training in total obedience to a highly authoritarian father. The image of the "good" Henry IV[12] loses some of its shine. Was this princely education somewhat atypical? Perhaps, but a strong hand was used in all of French society of the time to inculcate respect for parents or superiors in children. Childhood, Hunt adds, was considered by adults as "a kind of infirmity," as a danger, as long as the little being had not learned to conform to the desires of adults—that is, until six or seven years of age.

After that age and up to the age of fourteen or fifteen came the second stage of childhood, which was the period of training for a trade or an office. Children of all social levels generally left their families to live under the rod and suffer the corporal punishments of a master previously unknown to them. In the eighteenth century, however, only the nolbles and the artisans continued to place their offspring to apprentice for later functions. The *collège*,[13] for its part, took in a social elite: there were fewer than fifty thousand students in these schools in all of France in 1789. This "great confinement" of children in schools usually involved frequent corporal punishment. Finally, an extremely long adolescence permitted the sons and daughters of the popular masses to earn enough,

---

[12]King of France (1589–1610) and father of Louis XIII.

[13]Equivalent to a high school.

slowly, to enable them to become established independently and to marry.

All in all, the child and the adolescent alike underwent a paternal tutelage that became heavier and heavier during the seventeenth and eighteenth centuries. Daughters of the well-to-do were often promised to the convent against their will or forced into marriage to prevent them from dipping too much into the capital that would come to their brothers. Noble and particularly bourgeois boys were confined, disciplined, and supervised in the *collèges*. They were taught to conduct themselves as *honnêtes hommes*.[14] They were cut off from death and from sexuality, in short, from the adult world. They too were married as their family—their father in particular—wished, for paternal authority was backed by legislation that permitted, by means of a *lettre de cachet*,[15] the imprisonment of a rebellious child. At the end of the seventeenth and in the eighteenth century measures were to be taken against arbitrary parental powers in this connection but with no modification of their essence, which was to avoid possible misalliance by preventing an adolescent from marrying as he wished.

Paternal power was just as strong among the popular masses, particularly in parts of France under Roman law. In Languedoc around 1690–1730, the father could exercise total justice over his children. Thus one peasant attached his twelve-year-old son to a stake for an entire day for having run away and committed a theft. Quarrels and murders were not infrequent in the bosom of the family, since the father would favor the eldest to the detriment of the younger children and a strict and heavy-handed respect for hierarchies of age, work skills, and sex ruled over domestic relations. . . .

The family, then, was founded in the power of the father. It was a power reinforced, on all levels of society, by the will of religious and political authorities. The absolute authority of the father, who stood at the peak of the familial hierarchy, guaranteed and reflected the immutable order of the world willed by God. Every father was also a small-scale king—that is, one of the millions of docile and unwitting agents for establishing centralizing absolutism. In Alsace under Louis XIV, family members learned the gestures of submission to the king in their daily contact with their father. Every gesture was connected to authoritarian and hierarchical concepts: "The master of the house [sat] at the head of the table, his wife at his right, his sons to his left, his daughters beside his wife, then the servants." At mealtime, the father drank his wine first, then passed the glass to the eldest of the males present, before other males could drink, in order of age and prestige. Restif de la Bretonne,[16]

[14]Upright men.

[15]A sealed letter addressed to a private person that usually ordered imprisonment or banishment.

[16]French novelist and chronicler of society, 1734–1806.

in the eighteenth century, describes his own father, a wealthy Burgundian peasant, as a domestic tyrant who whipped his son for flirting with some young lady without paternal permission and who ruled over the women, children, and servants. A true "priest" in a cult of authority, Restif's father demanded submission from all his household, as did all fathers and family heads of his epoch. The chastity of Burgundian girls was thus "built on the rigor of fathers."

The child's body, from birth to marriage, was trained in the gestures of submission and passive obedience to his parents, his father in particular. Obviously, the father did not have life and death power over his offspring, but with that exception, he wielded truly absolute power over his sons and even more so over his daughters as he also did over his domestic servants or his apprentices. By this fact he worked to ensure his children's social conformity in a physical sense. We have seen that he decided their future, their marriage, even their sexuality. He was quick to use corporal punishment or force to impose his will on them. He remained enthroned in the place of honor when his married son lived with him. Moreover, through daily rites of interaction he gradually infused obedience into all of his offspring. . . .

My hypothesis is that this interaction ritual evolved during the Ancien Régime in the direction of a permanent training in the values of authority and hierarchy within the family. The relations between parents and children at that time seem to bow before a ceremonial that accentuated discipline and diminished intimacy (except among the bourgeoisie, where a change in the opposite direction pertained). Thus it was with the strictly hierarchical relationships around the Alsacian peasant's table or with the peasant in Burgundy or Languedoc. A complex network of ritual gestures defined according to sex, age, skills, and local conditions set the place of each person in relation to the master of the house. The literate, who mirrored a society of hierarchy and privilege, were instrumental in this evolution. In a more insidious fashion, the law courts defined gestures of submission to parents, for grave disobedience on the part of children was judged as a crime in the sixteenth and seventeenth centuries, as several examples from Arras will demonstrate.

In 1561, a son accused of having killed a cow that belonged to his mother and of having committed . . . several offenses, indignities, and threats against her, [and] chased her from her house with violence because she had lived too long was sentenced to make honorable reparation, to go to prison, then on the next Sunday to repeat his public penance after high mass in the parish church. One woman who had beaten and insulted her mother-in-law was sentenced in 1572 to make honorable amends . . . carrying an unlighted candle, after which she was banished from Artois for three years. In 1594, a son who had differed with his father concerning money and who had called him . . . lackey, beggar, and thief paid a fine of twelve *florins* and was ordered to behave . . . with all humility and reverence toward his said father or face banishment. It was not infrequent to see these honorable amends carried on in public: a drunken shoemaker who had beaten his father and blasphemed paid his penalty by wearing a placard on his breast proclaiming: . . . denied God and beat his father, after which he spent a month in prison.

Justice thus came to the aid of an offended father or mother, dramatizing the deference due parents by the sanctions imposed on the guilty children. The spectators undoubtedly saw in this the solemn reaffirmation of interaction ritual. They also could read in it the lesson that maternity, and even more paternity, was sacred, and this notion lay at the foundation of all life in society. Judges condemned with utmost rigor incestuous fathers, who throw the normal order of things into question. Overly indulgent fathers were recalled to reason as well, such as one man in Arras in 1593 who was forced to watch the flogging of his daughter, condemned for her . . . lascivious, depraved life, since he should have avoided this state of affairs by supervising her better. Cuckolded husbands were banished for the same reasons. As for the crime of adultery, it was considered . . . a heinous and horrible thing because it destroys all human society, corrupts families, perverts republics.

Justice defined parental functions clearly. Men and women guilty of negligence in the death of a child were condemned, in Arras, to expiatory pilgrimages or honorable reparations. In addition they were ordered to . . . pay better attention to their children. . . .

In these various sentences the law presents us with an ideal model of the father, who supervises his wife and his children carefully, who avoids sexual deviation himself and forbids such to them, and who has a nearly unlimited authority over his family. The law guaranteed this authority, probably more firmly from the eighteenth century on than before. The model of the ideal good son or good daughter . . . was one of obedience, submission, and filial respect. . . .

Once again, the period from 1550 or 1600 to 1750 differs greatly from the preceding and the subsequent periods. Just as sexuality was repressed, so bodies were subjected to a total obedience to the will of the paterfamilias.[17] Finally, from birth to their late marriage, boys and girls both were constantly taught to leave decisions concerning their destiny to their families, to remain in their places, and to show deference and obedience to their parents. Everyone thus underwent a training for social conformity and respect for authorities and hierarchies.

It might be said that this enhancement of parental authority existed before the triumph of absolutism. This is quite possible. In any event, there was certainly an element of novelty in the fact that adolescence and increasingly delayed marriage led children to remain under the tutelage of their families until they were almost thirty years old, in an age in

---

[17]Father of the family.

which life expectancy was low. Furthermore, pedagogical and moralizing manuals insisted on the image of the virtuous and terrible father, reflection of a vengeful God or of an all-powerful king who dominated the world. Let us thus admit the idea that the father figure grew in stature but reserve the right to look closely at regional and local variation and to correct this image, as the central Pyrenees or Breton-speaking Brittany granted greater importance to the woman and mother than other regions of France.

The father was, from this point of view, an agent essential to the centralization and the ongoing stability of society to the extent that millions of agents had a clear and unswerving perception of the political system. . . .

Guilds

MACK WALKER

The guild, an economic and social association of practitioners of a specific craft or trade, was a prominent and characteristic feature of medieval and early modern urban life. Guilds regulated the quality and output of goods and limited competition in order to maintain prices and so guarantee guild members a secure living. Additionally, guilds offered a social life and took care of their members and of their widows and children. Traditionally, historians have argued that guilds decayed in the early modern period, weakened by capitalism and state centralization, until the Industrial Revolution finally swept them away. Recently, however, historians have reexamined guilds and have come to believe that they continued to exercise significant social and economic functions even as late as the eighteenth-century. Mack Walker examines the guilds in the eighteenth-century German home towns (those towns, with a population no greater than ten to fifteen thousand, that were relatively independent of outside authority and that, unlike larger cities, did not have a patrician class). He finds the guilds to have been active, powerful, and cohesive.

The selection opens with an account of a tinsmith's attempt to force his guild to approve his marriage, which the guild considered indecent. Why was the guild steadfast in its refusal to recognize the marriage? The guild, after all, fought the marriage for many years and ostracized the offending tinsmith, probably for as long as he lived. Why did guilds pay so much attention to the personal lives of their members, going even so far as to investigate the legitimacy of grandparents? What was guild morality? How did guild moralism define and defend the community?

To become a master in a guild, one had first to become an apprentice and then a journeyman. Exactly how did a man successfully pass through those stages? Why did so many fail to attain the coveted status of master? Why were guilds so suspicious of those from outside the town? Masters had both obligations and privileges: their widows and children likewise had certain rights. Here the economic and social functions of the guild came together, as the guild performed roles later taken over by modern governments. Why did the guilds become so much more important in the eighteenth century than they had been earlier?

The tinsmith Flegel, citizen of Hildesheim, was in love, and he wished to marry. That he should marry was in itself seemly, for the proper pursuit of his trade required a solid domestic establishment supporting and surrounding the workshop: a wife to help out and meet customers, and to provide relatives; a decent home for apprentices and a

Mack Walker, *German Home Towns; Community, State, and General Estate, 1648–1871* (Ithaca, NY: Cornell University Press, 1971), 73–91, 102–107.

gentling influence on journeymen; an assurance of Flegel's own diligence and reliability as a valuable member of the community. The trouble was that Flegel had set his heart, not wisely but too well, on the daughter of a fellow citizen named Helmsen; and when he went to register his intention to marry with the tinsmith's guild he was barred from doing so on grounds of indecency. The prospective bride's father—not she herself—had been born out of wedlock and then subsequently legitimized. . . . Helmsen's legitimacy was recognized by the territorial law of the Bishopric of Hildesheim, in which the community was located, but that did not make him legitimate in the eyes of the Hildesheim guildsmen. Indeed the citizen status of the sometime bastard Helmsen suggests that outside influence had forced him on the community, ensuring the unending rancor of the real Hildesheimer. The guild constitution, to which Flegel had subscribed, provided that wife as well as master must show proof of four irreproachable grandparents; and inasmuch as a master's children were automatically eligible for guild acceptance and support, Flegel's determination to marry the Helmsen girl demanded of the tinsmiths that they sponsor the grandchildren of a bastard before the community.

Flegel had become engaged in 1742. Eleven years before, in 1731, an imperial edict had appeared which provided, among other things, that legitimacy established by "the authorities" should be recognized as valid by the guilds. Accordingly Flegel appealed to the Hildesheim Town Council against the guild decision, citing the imperial decree. But who were the authorities in Hildesheim? The important guilds of the town were directly and constitutionally involved in town government, ostensibly as representative of the citizenry: the *Ämter*[1] of the butchers, the bakers, the shoemakers, the tanners, and the *Gilden*[2] of the tailors, the smiths, the wool weavers, the retailers, and the furriers. Moreover the first four, the *Ämter*, had a special relation with the bishop which they used as leverage against the Council when they felt need of it. The Council therefore . . . turned the case over to its committee for artisans' affairs; and there nothing was decided. After a year, Flegel took the extraordinary step of marrying Fräulein Helmsen anyway, in a ceremony held somewhere outside Hildesheim. When the guildsmen heard of it they were enraged: never before, they said, had a Hildesheim master artisan thus defied his guild's jurisdiction in marital matters. For Flegel to get away with it would violate one of the most important sanctions the guild had for controlling the composition and the behavior of its membership. And it would make the Hildesheim tinsmiths look bad,

[1]Councils.
[2]Guilds.

and with them all the other Hildesheimer. The guild excluded Flegel from its meetings and functions, and it goes without saying that it imposed economic and social boycott against him, master tinsmith though he was.

For three years, Flegel appeared repeatedly before the Town Council asking that the imperial decree be enforced in his favor; repeatedly he was turned away. In 1745 he appealed to the episcopal government, declaring that the guilds in their defiance of the law sought only after their own "gloire."[3] Also, inasmuch as they were represented in the town government and thus in the highest town court, they were acting in their own case against him. Here he was entering on dangerous ground, for if the guild-influenced town government indeed constituted "the authorities" with the right to establish legitimacy, then his case was lost. But locally it was lost anyway, and his appeal to the bishop invited the episcopal government to assert that they, not the Town Council, were "the authorities" in Hildesheim. The bishopric demanded that the Council issue formal judgment; but the Council, caught between state on one side and guilds on the other, found a temporary way out in a request for an opinion from the faculty of law at the University of Halle: Was the requirement of four legitimate grandparents legal? Was Helmsen legitimate (as book law said) or not (as the Hildesheimer said)? The Halle professors decided for Flegel and against the guilds, and the Council announced that decision. The smiths thereupon countered with the argument that the Halle faculty was not learned in Hildesheim local law and circumstance: community law breaks book law. Flegel was not reinstated nor his wife recognized. In 1747, five years after his marriage, he asked the Council to enforce the Halle decision; the Council issued the order, but nothing else happened. The Council then urged all concerned to try "good will" as a means to solution, and still nothing happened; but finally the bishopric ordered enforcement within two weeks. The Council summoned a meeting of the guild to admit Flegel, fearing military intervention by the bishop, but the hall remained empty; not a single master tinsmith appeared. Finally the Council ordered the guild to readmit Flegel and acknowledge the validity of his marriage lest episcopal soldiers and bureaucrats put an end to the privileges and autonomies of Hildesheim. The guild officers all resigned, and then there was nobody for the law to talk to.

Probably that is enough about the tinsmith Flegel. Eventually he was formally readmitted and his marriage registered, but that did not settle the case; after dragging on for several more years it disappeared into the episcopal courts. It is safe to say that Flegel never found a peaceable life in Hildesheim, for he had defied the procedures upon which community peace was founded. . . . Defense of their honor against incursions like

[3]Glory.

Flegel's was nothing new to the citizen-guildsmen of Hildesheim: they had defended it before against a master shoemaker who wanted to marry a piper's daughter, against a tailor who turned out to have a wet nurse for a mother, and against a smith who tried to register a miller's daughter as his wife. The social prudery and political stubbornness of the Hildesheim guilds were part of the character of every hometown community, and a role of guild organization was to lock those characteristics institutionally into the community as a whole. "For their functions," wrote Wolfram Fischer [*Handwerksrecht und Handwerkswirtschaft um 1800*, (Berlin, 1955), 15], "extended far beyond the economic, and their legal status placed them as integrating constituents of the political and social order of the old Empire. Only when we start with the social location of the guild and bring all its functions into consideration do we see the true role of the economic in the guild system." That "social location" was the home town; only there—not in the city and surely not the countryside—could the guilds assume so broad a role and still remain basically economic institutions. Only in the context of the home town is it comprehensible how the time of the notorious "decay" of the early modern German trades guilds should have been the period probably of their greatest power to impress their values and goals upon the society of which they were components.

To begin to describe them it is useful to separate out the several ways in which the hometown guilds entered into community life: economic regulation, political organization and representation, and guardianship of social or domestic standards. . . . As occupational groupings within the community—of butchers, shoemakers, carpenters, and the rest—guilds supervised the recruitment, training, and allocation of individual citizens into the community's economy, and their economic character placed its stamp upon hometown morality and the nature of citizenship itself. As primary political organizers of the citizenry . . . , they bore political and civic factors into economic practice and moral standards. And finally as moral and social watchdogs they saw to the quality of the citizenry—the *Ehre*, the honor, of the hometown workman and Bürger.[4]

Still in the exercise of all these linked functions they worked as economic media; their special influence on the community and its membership rested ultimately on that role. . . .

The hometown guild artisan ordinarily sold his own products, on the same premises where he produced them; or he performed skilled services within the specifically defined limits of the community. The customs and statutes that governed his training and regulated his activities were quite similar from one place to another. . . . Craft guild rules which assumed a local but diversified economy set him apart from the merchant guildsmen

[4]Citizen, townsman.

of the cities (although some small towns had retailers'. . . . guilds entitled to sell certain imported goods locally), and set him apart also from
the state-licensed or unorganized rural artisan. The rules were usually
set down in written articles, statutes or charters prepared by each guild
and confirmed or tolerated by some authority, much as the statutes of
the towns themselves. . . . [U]sually confirmation came at the instance of
the guild from the local magistracy or a local court. The guild's formal
authority rested on that confirmed or acknowledged statute, which out-
lined its training program, the regulations governing the exercise of the
trade, its powers to elect and to limit membership, the specific economic
activity over which guild members held local monopoly . . . , and the
geographical area . . . within which the monopoly prevailed. . . . [R]ules
to implement training programs were used to serve the economic and
familial interests of the guildsmen, by holding down membership and
excluding outsiders; conversely the economic interests of the trade were
subject to pressure upon the guildsmen as members of the community to
see to the useful education and social incorporation of the citizenry. . . .

Guild statutes often set forth rules of guild life in remarkable
detail, although of course much guild activity took place informally and
unrecorded . . . and in conjunction with the cousins and brothers on the
town councils and in the other trades. . . . In the countryside, in profes-
sionally governed or mercantile cities like Hamburg and Nürnberg, and
in the Prussian centralized country, incorporated craft guilds either did
not exist or their structure was used as the channel for government regulation of the economy. But craft guilds within the hometown communities could not be reached by that kind of legislation or control because
the civic community of uncles and brothers lay between, and because
the guilds themselves were part of the communal system of authority.

A guild's affairs were administered by a collegial body of from two to
four Overmasters . . . chosen by a process incorporating both the will of
the membership and the choice of the civic authorities. . . . The Overmasters decided internal conflicts, spelled out rules, levied fines and imposed
minor punishments, administered guild finances and properties, saw to
the inspection of masterworks prepared by candidates for mastership
(though this might be done by a specially appointed inspector), and generally represented the interests of the trade, within the community and
to the outside if need be. A guild court composed or dominated by these
officials could expel any member who did not accept its decisions, and
thus foreclose his practice of the trade; and frequently such a court punished members for civil or criminal misdeeds like theft or adultery, on
the grounds (if anybody asked) that the transgression had brought the
trade into disrepute, so that the trade must punish the offender to clear
its name. . . .

The Overmasters were custodians of the Guild Chest, . . . repository
of its official documents and secrets, ceremonially opened on the occasion

of meetings of the membership. Plenary meetings . . . were supposed to be held regularly—quarterly as a rule—but extraordinary meetings might be called to consider special problems, like a serious infraction of the rules by one of the members or some action by the authorities or by another trade that threatened the interests of the guild. . . .

The several aspects of guild life converged on the master's estate, as citizen, head of household, and independent craftsman. The process of selection and induction began with apprenticeship. Active masters were expected to undertake the training of the sons of fellow townsmen as apprentices; apprentices were required to be Christians of honorable estate and parentage. After a trial period of a few weeks in a master's shop, petition was made to the Overmasters for formal registration of the apprentice with the guild; if his birth was properly certified and his other credentials met conditions set by the guild, he was admitted upon payment of a registration fee . . . to the guild and a training fee . . . to the master. . . . The apprentice was bound to serve the master loyally for a stated period, some three or four years, during which time the master for his part was obliged to give the apprentice real training and practice in the trade—not just use him as an errand boy—and a decent place in his domestic establishment. Now: often the sons of masters within the guild were forgiven the fees, or paid reduced fees, or were excused from apprenticeship altogether, or signed in and out on the same day without the regular period of training. The grounds were . . . that a boy already knew what went on in his father's trade as well as an ordinary apprentice from another trade was expected to learn it; but it amounted to group favoritism and encouraged inbreeding within the trades. . . .

When the apprenticeship was done the young man paid another round of fees, usually underwent some convivial hazing, and thus was promoted to journeyman. The journeyman was presumed to have learned the basic skills of his trade, but he was not yet ready to carry it on independently. First he was to go on a round of travels, working at a wage for other masters in other places, and getting the behavior of late adolescence out of his system, away from home but still free of the responsibilities and encumbrances of a domestic establishment of his own. His training and good reputation were certified by the guild in which he had served his apprenticeship, so that the guild, its reputation at stake, was careful with the certification; similarly the journeyman relied on the good name of his home guild (or absence of a bad name) for his acceptance abroad. . . .

When a journeyman arrived at a new town he went to the journeymen's hostel sponsored by his trade there, and applied to the host . . . for work. The host directed him to a local master looking for help if there was one; if no work could be found within a stipulated short period, probably no more than a day and a night, the journeyman was sent on his way with the help of a small grant from the guild treasury. . . . If he stayed in town without work he was treated as a vagrant, for that is what he was; strange unemployed journeymen meant beggars and thieves to the home town.

There at the hostel he ordinarily lived, while he was locally employed; and his papers were deposited in the guild chest controlled by the Overmasters. Only a master or a master's widow in his learned trade could legitimately employ him: if he valued his prospects as master and Bürger he would not enter the service of a noble, nor of the state, nor work at a factory, nor go as a soldier or a servant. After a given minimum term of employment in one place the journeyman might leave to resume his wandering, or be dismissed by his employer, when proper notice was given and the piece he was working on was finished. . . . His papers were endorsed by the local guild to show that he had worked there, and how he had behaved. . . .

. . . [T]wo or more years of attested wandering was a customary condition for application for mastership. Far and away the best place for a journeyman to apply for mastership—barring a palatable widow or orphan—was in his home town, so there he usually returned when his wanderyears were done. His application was filed with the Overmasters of the guild to which he sought entry, and after their evaluation it was laid before the assembled masters and usually before the civil authorities as well. He had to provide certification of apprentice training that the local masters would accept, proof of his travels to proper places and of proper behavior when he was there, and of course above all he had again to prove legitimate ancestry. All of these conditions were more easily met by a local boy, unless there was something wrong with him, than by an outsider.

The examination of all these qualifications offered plenty of opportunities to exclude the candidate if the masters so chose, and if they could exclude him without offending colleagues, relatives, neighbors, and customers. Yet another hurdle was the masterwork, an exhibition of the candidate's skill prepared in the place where he applied. . . . It was easy to assign a difficult piece of work or an expensive one, and then if need be still to reject it in the name of the guild's high standards: where, young man, did you learn to make things *that* way? If the trade was overfilled . . . then the candidate might be rejected on that ground, or told to wait; and there was no guarantee that he might not later be bypassed for a more recent candidate who found greater favor. Another economic condition was that the candidate must prove he had the resources to establish his shop and assume the burdens of citizen and family head, some combination of tools and cash, perhaps; and often he was obliged to commit himself to the community by building or buying a house. Guilds commonly denied mastership to any bachelor, a practice that not only enjoined domestic commitment but helped the marital prospects of guild widow and orphan, not to mention unplaced daughters of the community as a whole: thus marriage ordinarily coincided with admission to mastership. . . .

The stranger upon whom these conditions were imposed was a stranger no more by the time he had fulfilled them all: proof of family background and domestic intent, locally produced masterwork, material resources in the town and a place in its economy, and time to learn about the community and for the community to learn about him. Familiarity and community acceptance was the real purpose of it all. That is why waiving the rules for local boys of respectable family made perfect sense to the hometownsmen, though to anyone from outside the home town, to anyone who thought of guilds purely as economic instruments, the communal working of the system smelled—and still does—of corruption, decadence, and economic malfunction.

The new master now shared in the local guild monopoly and agreed to abide by its rules. The guild monopoly made good economic sense within the community insofar as it maintained an appropriate balance and relation in and among the trades without exposing any citizen to ruinous competition, and assured that only skilled and responsible practitioners would pursue each of them. It was, to be sure, a system of mutual defense by guildsmen-citizens. But any guild that showed itself so restrictive as seriously to undersupply the local economy . . . , or to exclude citizens' sons without economic justification, incurred community pressure to erase entries into the trade, and it invited breaches of its monopoly which the community and its authorities would consider justified. If a trade grew very rich, it would attract sons of influential families who could not easily be excluded by numerical limitations. The hometown guild monopolies were enforcements of the rules whereby the community kept its soundness and autonomy, directed first of all against outsiders but also against any citizen who failed to go along with the rules.

Outside trespassers were mainly non-masters who produced or sold articles within the area where the guild claimed monopoly. . . . A glover who made a wallet might have his windows knocked out by the bagmakers, and then a carpenter be hazed by the glaziers for repairing them. The boundaries between respective trade monopolies made for endless controversy when they were not clearly understood in local custom and abided by. Within the trade, a master was punished by his guild or suspended if he stole customers from his colleagues, sold from door to door instead of working and waiting in his shop, cut prices or departed from standard materials and method, hired too many journeymen, or otherwise introduced disturbing elements of competition and conflict within the trade. The aforesaid tailor even if he was licensed might be using an improper stitch or improper cloth in his attic; or worse yet, he might try to sell clothes ready-made for pay by somebody outside the town. . . .

Only a master might take on apprentices and journeymen, and even he only so many, and only so often, as the guild allowed: the rules differing among trades and places but usually on the order of one apprentice at a time and no more than two journeymen. Masters' widows had important status and rights within the guild (recall the insistence on respectable backgrounds for wives), and the guild had a responsibility for their welfare. A widow could continue the operation of her husband's shop; if she had no journeyman she could demand one from one of the masters; if she married a journeyman of the same trade he was made master promptly, cheaply, and free of limitations on membership because she was already one of the admitted number. She did not attend meetings or vote, for there was no place for women there, nor could she take on an apprentice; but she was freed of most guild obligations and fees. A master's blood son usually enjoyed, along with the special dispensations of fees and training, a presumptive right by birth to enter his father's guild. A master's daughter possessed in a latent way much the same rights, transferring them with marriage to a journeyman of the same trade as her father and working in his shop, so that the journeyman became in effect a son; if she was orphaned those guild rights were her main inheritance. The social and familial appurtenances of mastership were very important, where there was no life insurance and no state social security system; but they pertained only within the familiar home community; nobody recognized them anywhere else. . . .

The structure and working sphere of the guilds show the place of economic institutions in hometown life. There is no doubt that the guild system was unsuited to economic growth and social mobility. . . . But that was the obverse of the guild's vital function in communal society and politics. Their close oversight of membership and their social and moral restrictiveness, their preservation of economic security for citizen-members: the very practices that made them such valuable and effective components of the community are what historians and others have meant by the decay or the decline of the early modern German guild. What appears as decadence by general economic standards was really the absorption, into these economic structures, of the important social and political functions they had in the stable communities of postmedieval and preindustrial Germany. . . . [T]he guild assumed the character described in this chapter sometime around the seventeenth century. . . . The guilds of the economically livelier medieval towns apparently did not behave that way. . . . There the guild seems to have functioned as a system of economic regulation and training, and indeed as a frame for political action, but without the character of social exclusiveness, communal integration, and the enforcement of morals that it has in this story. It may be that the isolation and stability (stagnancy) of the later hometown economies is what made the difference, compared with the flourishing medieval towns. . . . If so, that would be to say that the guild system, like any other economic system, worked more freely and more flexibly at times of economic vigor and expansion than at times of weakness and contraction. Yet it may remain a distinctive characteristic of the communal guild system that it responded to the pressure of bad times or of change by shrinking into conservative exclusiveness, rather than by the adaptation or renovation that might be expected of freely individualistic or of state-controlled economic systems. That characteristic came to matter a great deal.

In histories of the early modern German trade guild an inconsistency crops up that is very like the one that appears in the histories of the towns themselves. "Decadence," though agreed upon, takes two contrary forms. On the one hand guild decline appears as degeneration at the hands of the absolutist state which, by converting guilds into its own economic instruments or undercutting their powers, robbed them of their truer older functions; on the other hand guild decline is shown in stubborn, selfish behavior *contrary* to the interests of the whole population and the state, defying the common welfare and the public economy the state sought to further. . . . [T]he period of guild decline was precisely that at which guilds were best able to defy state or public policy broadly conceived. . . .

[T]he hometown guild was formed and stabilized in the quieter times that followed the wars of religion and empire; it was post-Westphalia[5]. . . .

The extremes and the eccentricities of guild moralism remain puzzling. . . . One explanation is that the notion of honorable status, of *Ehrbarkeit*, with which they were intensely concerned, was so broad and vague a slogan that it provided no reasonable or functional limits. . . . Its imprecise character led the guildsmen into absurdities of prurience and persecution when they tried to judge and act upon it. There was no check on their eagerness to show their own morality by the severity with which they judged others.

The main preoccupation with legitimacy of birth, which extended by easy stages into questions of sexual behavior and social background, had a reasonable foundation in the domestic character of community and economy: the importance of knowing who somebody was, and the soundness of his family circumstances. The guild encompassed the citizen-master's life, not just his occupation. His family was part of his occupation and his guild; his widow and his orphans were cared for by it and his sons were specially privileged within it. . . . *Ehrbarkeit* meant domestic, civic, and economic orderliness and these were undermined by the promiscuity and irresponsibility implied by illegitimate birth. Legitimate childbirth resulted from sober and responsible intention to have a child, whose conception bore the community's sanction; illegitimacy implied the contrary. . . .

It might be argued that moral sanctions were directed less against

---

[5]The Peace of Westphalia in 1648 ended the Thirty Years' War.

loose sexual behavior as such than at its social consequences: the foisting upon the community of persons with uncertain origins and uncertain qualifications for membership. The hometownsman's pride was closely involved in the guild's quest for purity. More mobile elements of German society were held by hometownsmen to be sexually and maritally promiscuous, so that sexual and marital purity were a caste mark that guildsmen-citizens employed to set themselves apart. It was important to be different from lower elements especially, from the rooting peasantry with its servile origins and style. Then there were the merchants and peddlers, traveling salesmen of their day, trying like cuckoos to pass off their bastards into the artisanry; and loose-living aristocrats had to be watched for that too. . . .

No doubt the guilds used ostensibly moral grounds to exclude persons held undesirable for reasons not strictly moral—not directly concerned with sex or marriage, that is, but exclusion for economic or civic reasons. . . . Put moralism for the sake of exclusion together with sexual purity as the hometownsman's mark of caste, and guild moralism becomes a specific instrument for excluding unwanted social elements from the community, and as such its use was stretched to the borders of credibility. It helped screen out unwanted outsiders, regardless of social estate, because it was so much harder for them than for natives to prove honorable family background. In other moral questions too, not only did the outsider have little evidence to offer for himself, his very arrival at the gates made him suspect of having become *persona non grata* elsewhere, and chances are he had. Why hadn't he applied in his own home town, where people knew him? . . .

The taint of illegitimacy lasted for generations; the same was true of other dishonorable estates. The list of dishonorable occupations . . . is almost without limit because each guild and each place had to show itself more discriminating than the rest, and no one could dissent from any instance without jeopardizing his own honor. Hangmen first of all: the usual taboo of the executioner, but hometown hangmen got a lot of other disgraceful work as well: clearing carrion, burying rotten fish. . . . Skinners worked with dead bodies too. . . . The line between what skinners did with carcasses and what butchers and tanners did with meat and hides was elaborately guarded, but not well enough to keep the tanners free of taint. Barbers and surgeons worked with wounds, a disgusting and servile business. So did bathers, and doubtless besides there were promiscuous goings-on at the baths. The lofts of mills were morally suspect too, and millers swindling middlemen and speculators to boot. Shepherds were contemptible everywhere. What kind of a man would be a shepherd? They skinned dead sheep . . . , and the same stories about a shepherd's relations with his sheep seem to have been told that I heard in New England as a boy. The weaving of linen was another primitive occupation, and like shepherding had suspect rural overtones and connections. Musicians and players moved from place to place, like itinerant peddlers and beggars. And officials of the state: their sons were adjudged dishonorable by the guildsmen. . . . It was a mark of dishonor to have worked as a peasant, or for a noble, or in a factory. . . .

Guild morality equated the outsider with dishonor; those two factors of repulsion multiplied together to produce guild moralism's intensity and its righteousness. It is important to note here that guilds, economic institutions, bore this spirit in the hometown community. The fervid moral preoccupation of the guilds, like their social and economic restrictiveness, seems mainly to have developed in the seventeenth and eighteenth centuries. There had been dishonorable occupations for long before that . . . , but little sign that moral fervor had been an important part of guild life. It was a part of the multiplication of their role beyond the custody of economic standards and training. That role was multiplied by the maintenance of social continuity and stability, and that by the guardianship of civic standards, and finally all united into morality in the sense of personal justification, of the kind traditionally in the hands of religious institutions—*moral* morality, the morality of conscience. The curious stock expression, "The guilds must be as pure, as if they had been gathered together by doves," seems to have originated in the seventeenth century. It may be that in the background of the early modern German craft guild's moral guardianship was the weakening and dispersal of religious institutions after the wars of religion: institutions perhaps with more experience and discrimination in moral questions than the home town. Civic authority had taken up moral custody first: not only state laws but seventeenth-century town statutes were full of religious and moral exhortations. But these had nearly disappeared by the mid-eighteenth century. And when the guild assumed the moral role, it adapted moral questions, unsurprisingly, to its economic structure and interests and to its place in the civic community. The guild, first habitat of the hometown Bürger, blended economic and civic and personal standards together into the moral quality of honor, in such a way that a man's personal morals—and his ancestors'—determined his economic competence and his civic rights; at the same time economic competence was prerequisite for civic and moral acceptance; and at the same time responsible civic membership was requisite for economic rights and personal justification. Such a combination might be called bourgeois morality, but like the political standards mentioned before it was the morality of the hometownsman, not the mobile and sophisticated high bourgeois. Hometownsmen did not have the multiple standards and compartmentalized lives that so many modern moral and social critics deplore: one set of standards for church on Sunday, another for relations with friends, another for business relations. They were whole men, integrated personalities, caught like so many flies in a three-dimensional web of community.

The totality of the web made the moralism with which the home-townsman defended his economic interests, and the righteousness he brought to his politics; it provided the aura of depravity and evil he attributed to rivals and strangers. The guilds in their connective func-tions—between citizen and community, and among compartments of life we incline to treat separately—were vital institutions of communal defense and also main determiners of what it was that would be defen-ded, and against whom. . . . The hometown community rested on the guild economy, and fell only when the guild economy was overwhelmed.

The Peasants

JEROME BLUM

In the eighteenth century, approximately 90 percent of Europe's population were peasants, though some areas, such as northern Italy and the Rhineland, were relatively urbanized. The peasantry was not a homogeneous social group, as Jerome Blum takes care to demonstrate. What different types of peasants were there? Which areas of Europe had the greatest concentration of free peasants?

Although serfdom existed throughout Europe, there were pronounced differences between the condition of serfs in Eastern Europe and those in Western Europe. How, for example, did the lives of serfs in France differ from those in Russia? What, exactly, did serfdom entail? What obligations did a serf owe to his lord? How did a peasant become a serf? Serfdom was not slavery, but the cruel treatment and oppression accorded many serfs and their families distinguished them little from slaves. In Old Régime Europe, the many worked and suffered so that the few could live well, and all over Europe the few, the élite, looked upon the peasants as contemptible inferiors put on earth to serve their lords. What cultural and intellectual assumptions lay behind these attitudes?

Blum depicts the peasants as an unenviable lot, leading wretched and difficult lives. It is no wonder that peasants drowned their misery in heavy drinking.

With the ownership of land went power and authority over the peasants who lived on the land. There were a multitude of variations in the nature of that authority and in the nature of the peasants' subservience to their seigniors[1] in the compass of the seigniors' supervision and control, and in the obligations that the peasants had to pay their lords. The peasants themselves were known by many different names, and so, too, were the obligations they owed the seigniors. But, whatever the differences, the status of the peasant everywhere in the servile lands was associated with unfreedom and constraint. In the hierarchial ladder of the traditional order he stood on the bottom rung. He was "the stepchild of the age, the broad, patient back who bore the weight of the entire social pyramid. . . the clumsy lout who was deprived and mocked by court, noble and city."

[1]Lords.

Jerome Blum, *The End of the Old Order in Rural Europe* (Princeton, NJ: Princeton University Press, 1978), 29–39, 41–49.

In all of the servile lands there were peasants who enjoyed full or partial freedom from seigniorial authority. Many of these people traced their free status to forebearers who had settled as colonists in newly opened regions, drawn there by the promise of freedom for themselves and their dependants. Others owed their liberty to emancipation freely given by the seigniors or purchased by the peasants. In the Swiss cantons of Uri, Schwyz, Unterwalden, Appenzell, Glarus, the Toggenberg district of St. Gall, and the uplands of Bern, the peasants had never paid servile obligations, or had freed themselves of these payments long ago. In France an undetermined but not extensive amount of peasant land, located especially in the center and south, had managed to evade the seigniorial net, despite seigniorial and governmental efforts to enforce the rule of *nulle terre sans seigneur*.[2] In western Germany there were settlements of free peasants called imperial villages. Created centuries before, these villages, like the imperial cities, recognized only the Holy Roman Emperor as their lord. By the eighteenth century, however, most of the imperial villages had fallen under the control of local rulers and had lost their special status. Other free peasants lived along the French-German border. In medieval times, lords had freed these people to keep them from leaving to become colonists elsewhere, or because as borderers they had special military value. All together, the free peasantry made up a small fraction of the rural population of western Germany, and despite their free status most of them had to pay dues and fees to seigniors who had established authority over them.

Eastern Germany, and especially East Prussia, had a much larger free peasant population than did the west. In 1798 in East Prussia 12,790 (21 per cent) out of 61,301 peasant holdings belonged to free peasants. . . .

. . . Those freemen who rented land from private seigniors sometimes had to pay dues in kind and labor in addition to a money rent. They often lived in their own villiages or on isolated farmsteads. Increasingly, however, manorial land encircled their holdings, they became fellow-villagers of the seigniorial peasants, and by the eighteenth century some of the *Kölmer*[3] had lost much of their freedom to the lords in whose villages they now lived. . . .

In Denmark, too, free peasants often found themselves at the mercy of seigniors. Their number, never large, fell sharply after the establishment of royal absolutism in 1660. By the end of the seventeenth century they made up less than 1 per cent of the peasant population in most of the kingdom. . . .

Most of the Austrian Monarchy had only a sprinkling of free peasants. In the Slav provinces of Bohemia, Moravia, and Silesia they comprised scarcely 1 per cent of the rural population. . . . Liberty came

[2]"No land without its lord."
[3]Freemen in East Prussia.

typically through individual acts of emancipation, usually in return for a money payment by the peasant. Other so-called free peasants actually were runaway serfs. . . .

Hungary had about 250,000 free peasants in the 1820's out of a rural population of about nine million. Some of these freemen were prosperous farmers, others had no land at all and earned meager livings as hired workers of noblemen and of landed peasants. . . .

In eighteenth- and nineteenth-century Russia serfs won freedom by voluntary emancipation by their seigniors, or by purchasing their freedom, or by military service. A handful of wealthy peasants, who had gained their riches through trade and industry and who paid heavy prices for their emancipation, became members of the bourgeoisie. The others, once freed, were enrolled in the category of state peasants and so remained in an unfree status, albeit one not as constraining nor as degrading as that of the serf. In the second half of the eighteenth century the government offered special privileges to foreigners to persuade them to colonize unpeopled regions of European Russia. The colonists, most of them Germans, whose descendants numbered nearly half a million by the 1850's, had much more freedom than did state peasants but still had certain external restraints placed upon them. . . .

Among all the servile lands, Poland and the Danubian Principalities had the largest proportions of free peasants in their populations. In Poland at the end of the eighteenth century between 20 and 30 per cent of about one million holdings were held by freemen. Many of these people came from neighboring lands, especially runaways from Pomerania and Silesia. They were welcomed by Polish landowners, who asked no questions and demanded only a small quitrent[4] of the newcomers. Others were residents of towns that in the sixteenth and seventeenth centuries had received city privileges. This allowed the townsmen to hold land on free tenures. . . . Still other freemen were runaway serfs who enjoyed freedom in their new places of residence so long as their owners did not reclaim them. Not all free peasants, however, remained in that status. Many of them voluntarily became serfs of a lord. Some did this in return for the seignior's assumption of the debts of the peasant, some to find peace and security or seigniorial protection from criminal prosecution, but by far the largest number became serfs because they married a serf and thereby acquired the status of their spouse.

An estimated 107,000 or about one-fifth of the more than 500,000 peasant families in the Danubian Principalities were free. Most of these people lived in the hill country, where they owned their land and where they had rights to the use of forests and pastures. The Principalities also had peasant colonists who cleared and settled seigniorial land in return for special privileges stipulated in written agreements. . . . They

---

[4]A rent paid in lieu of labor services.

agreed to do only three to six days of labor a year for the seignior and most of them had the right to commute this small obligation into a cash payment. They received the right to the perpetual use of the land they cleared. The state levied a reduced tax on their land and allowed them to pay it directly to the state treasury, and thereby escape the extortions inflicted on other peasants by the agents of the treasury. In a land where official extortion and corruption was a way of life that was a valuable concession.

The peasants of western Europe, save for a relatively small number, had long ago thrown off the bonds that held them in serfdom. Nonetheless, they still owed servile obligations to seigniors, and they were still subject, to a greater or lesser extent depending upon the locality, to the jurisdiction and punitive authority of seigniors. Some historians have made much of the fact that the dependence or servility of these peasants was not attached to their persons (as it was to the person of a serf). Rather, they argue that the dependence adhered to the land. It became part of the price the peasant paid for the use of his holding to the seignior who had the superior ownership of the land. Since nearly all of the land in these societies belonged to seigniors—whether prince, nobleman, institution, or burgher—nearly all of the peasants owed servile obligations. It seems to me to be a matter of little practical consequence, except perhaps to nationalistic historians, whether the servility and dependence adhered to the person or to the land. If, however, the argument must be pursued, there is much that shows that servility often did adhere to the person. Thus, peasants who were landless and who earned their livings as hired farm laborers or as artisans were under seigniorial jurisdiction and had to pay servile obligations, albeit in smaller amounts than peasants with land. In many parts of central and western Europe, peasants owed services and obedience to other seigniors in addition to the seignior who had the superior ownership of the land on which the peasant lived. Indeed, in some places the payments owed to the superior landowner counted among the lesser obligations of the peasant. The other seigniors could include a lord who had jurisdiction over the peasant, another to whom he had to pay a share of his produce, and a so-called *Vogtherr*, or patron. It was quite common to have one or more of these seigniorial roles divided among several people who had acquired their partial ownership through purchase, inheritance, gift, or exchange. Usually, one individual filled several of these roles, or joint owners consolidated their claims through exchange or purchase, so that probably few peasants had a different person in each of these seignioral roles. Two or three seemed the usual pattern, though in southwestern Germany it was not uncommon for a peasant to have four separate seigniors. . . .

The fact was that peasants in the western lands were dependent upon seigniors and stood in a servile relationship to them. Surely it made no difference to the individual peasant whether that dependence was acquired by birth into the peasantry, or by virtue of occupation of a certain piece of land. The dependence was still there. Even peasants who were recognized as fully free and who were alodial[5] proprietors of their holdings had to pay obligations to seigniors that were not demanded of property owners who belonged to other orders. . . . The peasants themselves recognized their unfreedom and servility. The *cahiers*[6] of grievances they sent to Paris on the eve of the Revolution were filled with complaints and anger at the servile obligations and the seigniorial privileges that oppressed and confined them. The judgment . . . that "the principle of the absolute freedom of the human person was not generally recognized" before the emancipations of the peasantry was true not only of his homeland, but of all the servile societies of western Europe.

The relatively small number of serfs in western Europe were called *mainmortables* in French-speaking lands and *Leibeigene* or *Eigenhörige* in German-speaking ones. Their serfdom was vestigal, a remnant of the serfdom once so common in western Europe, and with little resemblance to the far harsher serfdom that prevailed in eastern Europe. Peasants acquired the stain of serfdom in several ways. One, of course, was through inheritance—in Germany through the mother's side only. Residence in certain towns and villages automatically converted people into serfs of the local seignior, who in some instances was the town itself as a corporate entity. . . . People became serfs, too, after they had occupied for a specified period, such as a year and a day, a holding that carried with it the status of serf. This kind of serfdom, found in parts of Swabia, Hannover, northwest Lorraine, parts of Luxembourg, and in Franche-Comté, was called *Realleibeigenschaft* or *mainmorte réelle*, because the serfdom adhered to the land.

Some regions held a high concentration of serfs, others had smaller numbers or none at all. In France about 400,000 of the estimated one million *mainmortables* in that country lived in Franche-Comté, where in 1784 a contemporary estimated that they made up half of the population. . . . In Savoy the majority of the peasants were *mainmortables*. Among the German states, Baden and Hannover had relatively large concentrations. . . . Lesser densities occured in other states of western Germany; central Germany had almost no serfs. Several of the Swiss cantons had *mainmortables* among their population. . . .

Serfs could legally be bought, sold, exchanged, or given away by their owner. Nearly always such transactions involved the alienation by the serfowner of his seigniory, and with it his rights over the serfs who lived there. The only effect this sale had on the serfs was that now they had a new lord to whom they owed their obligations. There were instances, however, in which serfowners sold or exchanged their serfs

[5]Free lands (without a lord).
[6]Lists.

without land, as if they were chattels. The serf then had to move to the seigniory of his new owner. Such sales remained legal in a number of German principalities up to the end of the servile order, though in practice they seem rarely to have taken place.

The western European serf could own land in his own name, or hold land on hereditary tenure from a lord of whom he was not the serf. Like other peasants, he could have several seigniors to whom he owed obligations. Like other hereditary tenants, he could buy, sell, exchange, mortgage, or bequeath his land at will. However, none of these conditions applied to land he held from the seignior whose serf he was. He had to have his master's consent to alienate or mortgage the holding, or face confiscation and eviction. When lords gave their serfs permission to alienate, they demanded a fee. In Franche-Comté the charge was one-twelfth of the sale price, but sometimes seigniors demanded as much as one-half. The serf could not bequeath his holding and his personal property to whomever he pleased. Again he had to have his master's consent. In France and in Savoy he could leave his property only to those children who lived with him. Failing such heirs, all of his property escheated to the seignior. Some serfowners in France and Savoy even claimed as their own the property of those of their serfs who lived away from the lord's seigniory and who died leaving heirs. A royal decree of 8 August 1779 . . . ordered the end in France of this practice. . . .

In southwest Germany the lord once had claimed all of the property of a deceased serf on the ground that all which the serf possessed belonged to the lord, who out of grace had permitted the peasant to own and use the property during his lifetime. Traces of this persisted into the eighteenth century, when the seignior claimed all of the property at the death of a childless serf. In general, however, the lord took only a set percentage of the serf's property, or his best animal, or his best garment, or a small cash payment, and allowed the serf to bequeath the rest of his property as he wished. In northwest Germany the lord customarily took half of the movables of the decedent and his second best animal. . . .

In principle the serf could not leave the seigniory of his owner, but it had been a long time since lords had been able to enforce that rule. Now the serf could leave if he received permission from the lord and met certain conditions. In Franche-Comté and in Lorraine if the serf left without authorization the lord could take the income from the departed peasant's hereditary holding. If he did not return within a specified period—ten years in Franche-Comté—the holding escheated to the seignior. In many places the peasant who wanted to leave had to pay an exit fee to his lord. . . . By paying the exit fee the peasant freed himself from serfdom. If he left without paying the fee, he remained a serf and his lord had a claim on his property when he died. If the departing peasant who left without paying was a woman, she not only remained a serf, but in the Germanic lands her children were legally serfs of her lord, no matter where they were born or where they lived.

Serfs did not have to leave the seigniory in order to gain their freedom. They could purchase it if their owner was willing, and remain in their homes. The price was set by agreement between lord and serf, although in some places it was a fixed amount. On occasion an entire village bought its liberty at what must sometimes have been a great financial sacrifice. The people of Pusey in Franche-Comté paid their lord 50,000 livres and ceded a meadow to him in return for their emancipation from serfdom and from the obligations they owed him. In Bavaria, and after 1701 in Lorraine, serfs who entered the priesthood or who married a noble or who were ennobled (these two latter events must have been most unusual) were automatically freed.

Nearly everywhere seigniors required their serfs, male and female alike, to make a small annual payment, usually presented in person, as an acknowledgment of their serfdom. Sometimes, too, the serfs had to do homage and take an oath of loyalty to the lord, either periodically or when the serf became the occupant of a holding. . . .

The degree of freedom enjoyed by the serfs of western Europe, especially when compared with that of the serfs of eastern Europe, has persuaded some historians to maintain that their serfdom was "nothing more than a special kind of taxation" and a device to increase seigniorial revenues. It is said that their obligations were no more onerous, and sometimes less onerous, than those of other peasants, and that their status was neither degrading nor socially incapacitating, so that serfs rose to high rank in church and state and remained serfs. If, indeed, the obligations and status of serfdom made so little difference, it becomes difficult to understand why serfs bothered to redeem themselves from it, at sometimes excessively heavy prices. It is worth noting, too, that as a rule serfs who rose to high office were allowed to redeem themselves. . . . The fact that legally serfs could be bought, sold, exchanged, or given away certainly distinguished—and degraded—their status as compared with other peasants of western Europe. And it seems clear that serfs themselves considered their position as both demeaning and intolerable. They ran away to escape it and they entered lawsuits against their lords. . . .

In general the status of the peasantry worsened as one moved eastward across the continent and it reached its nadir in the lands that lay on the other side of the Elbe River. Most of the peasants there were held in a serfdom that was far more onerous and far more degrading than the vestigal serfdom of western Europe. In the last part of the eighteenth century the term *Leibeigenschaft*, slavery, came into use in German-speaking lands as the name for serfdom, instead of the more accurate *Erbuntertänigkeit*, hereditary subjection. It was employed especially by reformers in the hope that the use of the odious word "slavery" would lend force to their arguments for change. Actually, serfdom in eastern Europe was not slavery (though sometimes it seemed scarcely different from it), if only because the serf was recognized as a legal individual, within certain limitations could initiate and participate in court actions, and possessed certain individual, albeit severely restricted, rights.

There were, of course, differences among the eastern lands in the extent to which the peasants were "servile subjects of the manor". . . . In Russia, Livonia, Poland, Schleswig-Holstein, Denmark, and in much of eastern Germany, especially in Mecklenburg, Swedish Pomerania, and Upper Lusatia in Electoral Saxony, the law placed few limits upon the authority of the seignior. Often the only effective restraint on the lord was his knowledge that his demands might reach the point at which his serfs would run away to escape them. The peasants in the Austrian Monarchy and in Electoral Saxony (except for Upper Lusatia) and other lands of east-central Germany were considerably less dependent upon the will and whim of their seigniors. Reforms of the second half of the eighteenth century had given the peasants of the Hapsburg realm many rights they had not before possessed. They still bore "the marks of the yokes and chains of their earlier slavery," for they remained the hereditary servile subjects of their lords. But now the central government had established norms that curbed the powers the lord once had over his peasants. For example, he could not now demand more labor services than the laws specified, nor could he prevent his peasants from leaving, providing they complied with the complex provisions set out in the legislation, nor could he evict them from their holdings without proper cause. . . .

Serfdom in the Danubian Principalities differed from the serfdom of the other eastern lands, notably in that the seignior had neither civil nor criminal jurisdiction over his peasants. In practice, however, the serf there had no real protection against excessive demands and harsh treatment by his seignior. . . .

The alienation of serfs without land, often involving the break-up of families, reveals the depth of the degradation to which serfs had been reduced in many of the eastern lands. They were sold, mortgaged, exchanged, and gambled away. This concept of the serf as a chattel, a thing that could be made over to another person, apparently was a phenomenon largely of the seventeenth and especially of the eighteenth century. The practice assumed especially large proportions in Russia. The law code of 1649 had forbidden the sale of serfs, but serfowners quickly and freely disregarded the ban. The central government did nothing to stop them. Instead, it gave its tacit recognition by such legislation as a ban on the use of the hammer by auctioneers at public sales of serfs, or in 1833, and again in 1841, outlawing the separation of parents and their unwed children by sale or gift. In 1761 the Livonian diet gave legal sanction to the sale of serfs without land, though it forbade their sale for export and the separation of a married couple. A contemporary in the 1770's reported that serfs and their children were exchanged for horses and dogs. When famine struck in the winter of 1788–1789, seigniors in one district of Livonia, in order to save on the support they had to provide their serfs, were reported to have sold orphan girls of six to twelve for a pittance and even given them away. In Mecklenburg, where peasants probably suffered worse treatment than anywhere else in Germany, there was an active and open trade in serfs from the mid-seventeenth century on, though it did not receive official sanction from the government until 1757. . . .

. . . In 1759 the government ordered an end to the active commerce in serfs in Prussian Silesia. The ban seems not to have been entirely effective, since sales continued there until as late as 1795. By a decree of 8 November 1773 Frederick II[7] expressly forbade the sale of serfs without land in East Prussia. In contrast, in Swedish Pomerania as late as the 1780's legislation specifically permitted the sale of serfs without land and mortgaging and exchanging them. A writer in 1784 compared the traffic there in serfs with the African slave trade. In Schleswig-Holstein the law forbade the sale of serfs without land, but serfowners paid no heed to the prohibition. Reports told of a lord who exchanged a serf for two dogs and of serfowners who used their serfs as stakes in gambling at cards.

In Poland the law was silent on the right of lords to sell their serfs without land, and eighteenth-century jurists decided that they did have the right. . . . Some of the transactions broke up families. Some were made on the condition, insisted upon by the church, that the serfs had to remain Catholics. If they did not, the seller had the right to demand back his serfs. Most of the sales were to nearby lords, but sometimes the serfs were sold to more distant masters and even to buyers from Germany.

In Hungary and Transylvania, too, the laws said nothing about the sale of serfs without land. Lords there bought, sold, mortgaged, exchanged, and gave away serfs from the sixteenth to the late eighteenth centuries. The last known sale of a serf without land in Hungary occurred in 1773 and in Transylvania in the 1780's. . . .

In Russia there were servile peasants other than the serfs of private proprietors. By far the most numerous of these people were the state peasants. Early in the eighteenth century Peter[8] had created the state peasantry as a separate legal and social category, as part of his program to simplify administrative procedures such as the collection of taxes and other obligations. He formed the core of the new category from peasants who had never been enserfed, the *odnodvortsy*, descendants of minor servitors who had been settled on the frontiers, migrants to Siberia, and the non-Slavic peoples of the Volga basin and beyond. Later rulers added other groups, notably the peasants of the church after the secularization

---

[7]Frederick the Great, King of Prussia, 1740–1786.
[8]Peter the Great, Tsar of Russia, 1689–1725.

of the church's lands in 1764, and the peasants who lived on the manors owned by the tsar and his close kinsmen. By 1858, on the eve of the emancipation, state peasants actually outnumbered the serfs; a contemporary estimate put the population of state peasants at 27.4 millions and that of the serfs at 22.8 millions.

The state peasants lived on land that belonged to the government. . . . The peasants were subject to the will of the government, which put them under the supervision of bureaucrats. They had far more autonomy over their lives and activities and far more personal freedom than serfs had. Their obligations to the state were considerably less than the obligations that serfs had to pay their owners, and the compulsory labor service that bore so heavily upon the serfs did not figure among their obligations. However, theirs was an insecure status, for the tsar could give them and their land to private persons, whose serfs they then became. That happened to many thousands of state peasants. The government also assigned them to full or part-time employment in state-owned and privately owned industrial enterprises, especially in mining and metallurgy.

After the state peasants, the appanage peasants were the most numerous category of non-seigniorial peasants in Russia. They lived on the estates owned by the imperial court. . . . By 1860 there were over 800,000 male appanage peasants. . . . Like the state peasants, the appanage peasants paid only a money fee and did not have other obligations in kind or labor. . . .

The gypsy slaves of the Danubian Principalities were the last true thralls in Christian Europe. In the mid-nineteenth century there were about 200,000 of them, or between 5 and 6 per cent of the estimated population of the Principalities. They were the property of monasteries and private persons who used them principally as domestics, though monasteries sometimes assigned them to work in the fields. Others, in return for payments to their owners, were allowed to go off and earn their livings as nomads, or as sedentary artisans in towns and villages. Being slaves, they had no legal personality and so possessed no civil rights. . . . They were bought and sold like beasts of the field, and because they were poor workers they usually did not command good prices. And, like a beast, they could never acquire freedom or a legal personality because it was not possible to enfranchise them any more than it was possible to enfranchise a beast. If their owner did release them, another person could claim ownership, just as he could of an ownerless animal or object.

There was also a smaller group of gypsies who theoretically belonged to the sovereign (initially all the gypsies had belonged to the ruler who had alienated them to monasteries and private persons). These gypsies, numbering around 37,000 in 1837, had nearly complete personal freedom, paid only a small fee to the ruler, lived the traditional tribal nomadic life of the gypsy, and earned their living in traditional gypsy fashion as artisans, bear trainers, musicians, beggars, and thieves. . . .

The subservience of the peasant and his dependence upon his lord were mirrored in the attitudes and opinions of the seigniors of east and west alike. They believed that the natural order of things had divided humankind into masters and servants, those who commanded and those who obeyed. They believed themselves to be naturally superior beings and looked upon those who they believed were destined to serve them as their natural inferiors. At best their attitude toward the peasantry was the condescension of paternalism. More often it was disdain and contempt. Contemporary expressions of opinion repeatedly stressed the ignorance, irresponsibility, laziness, and general worthlessness of the peasantry, and in the eastern lands the free use of the whip was recommended as the only way to get things done. The peasant was considered some lesser and sub-human form of life; "a hybrid between animal and human" was the way a Bavarian official put it in 1737. An eyewitness of a rural rising in Provence in 1752 described the peasant as "an evil animal, cunning, a ferocious half-civilized beast; he has neither heart nor honesty. . . . " The Moldavian Basil Balsch reported that the peasants of his land were "strangers to any discipline, order, economy or cleanliness . . . ; a thoroughly lazy, mendacious . . . people who are accustomed to do the little work that they do only under invectives or blows." A counselor of the duke of Mecklenburg in an official statement in 1750 described the peasant there as a "head of cattle" and declared that he must be treated accordingly. . . .

A few were more understanding. Stanislaus Leszczyński (d. 1766), twice elected king of Poland and twice deposed, wrote that in that country "the nobleman condemns his peasant to death without any legal ground and even more frequently without legal proceedings and without any ceremony. We look upon the peasant as a creature of an entirely different sort, and deny him even the air which we breathe with him, and make hardly any distinction between him and the animals who plow our fields. Often we value them even lower than the animals, and only too often sell them to cruel masters who compel them to pay for their new servitude by excessive toil. I shudder when I mention the law which imposes a fine of only 15 francs on the noble who murders a peasant.". . .

The conviction of their own superiority harbored by the seigniors was often compounded by ethnic and religious differences between lord and peasant. In many parts of central and eastern Europe the masters belonged to a conquering people who had established their domination over the native population. German seigniors ruled over Slavic peasants in Bohemia, Galicia, East Prussia and Silesia, and over Letts and Estonians in the Baltic lands; Polish lords were the masters of Ukrainian, Lithuanian, and White Russian peasants; Great Russians owned manors peopled by Ukrainians and Lithuanians and Poles; Magyars lorded it over

Slovaks and Romanians and Slovenes—to list only some of the macro-ethnic differences. Few peoples of the rest of the world can match Europeans in their awareness of and, generally, contempt for or at least disdain for other ethnic and religious groups. . . . The dominant group, though greatly outnumbered, successfully maintained its cultural identity precisely because it considered the peasants over whom it ruled as lesser breeds of mankind, even pariahs. . . .

Schooling for most peasants was, at best, pitifully inadequate and usually entirely absent, even where laws declared elementary education compulsory. . . . [B]y far the greatest part of Europe's peasantry lived out their lives in darkest ignorance.

The peasants themselves, oppressed, contemned, and kept in ignorance by their social betters, accepted the stamp of inferiority pressed upon them. "I am only a serf" the peasant would reply when asked to identify himself. They seemed without pride or self-respect, dirty, lazy, crafty, and always suspicious of their masters and of the world that lay outside their village. Even friendly observers were put off by the way they looked and by their behavior. One commentator complained in the 1760's that "one would have more pity for them if their wild and brutish appearance did not seem to justify their hard lot.". . .

A few thoughtful people recognized that the responsibility for the misery and ignorance of peasant existence lay not in the nature of the peasant himself, but in the nature of the social and economic order in which he lived. J.C. Schubart (1734–1789) . . . a distinguished German agriculturist . . . explained that "the more industrious the poor peasant the more miserable; for almost everyone wants to refresh himself from his sweat and fatten himself from his blood; he is thereby beaten down, discouraged, and in the end becomes slothful because he realizes that he is more tormented and more ill-treated than a beast of burden.". . .

In their hopelessness, their desperation, and perhaps their self-hate, peasants everywhere, men and women and often children, drank heavily and even passionately. In many lands their addiction was encouraged by their seigniors, who had the monopoly on the manufacture and sale of spirits, who owned or leased out the village inn, and for whom these activities provided an important source of income. Some Polish seigniors even paid their hired labor in scrip redeemable only at the village tavern for drinks. Contemporaries frequently commented on the endless drinking and on its destructive effects. An account in an official publication in Silesia in 1790 that told of the crushing poverty and misery of the Polish peasants of Upper Silesia, reported that "Brandy or the mere thought of it transports these people from laziness, sluggishness and slackness to lightheartedness, happiness and exuberance. . . . They consume it with a frenzy. . . . The consequences of their intemperance are to be expected, the destruction of their health, disorder, neglect, need, confusion, discord, and sometimes murder." . . .

In light of their subservience and of their lowly condition, it could be expected that the peasantry would be politically powerless. Unlike the other orders of the traditional society, most peasants did not have institutionalized instruments, specifically representation in assemblies and estates, by which they could express their interests and voice their demands. Peasants were represented as an order in the diets of some of the lesser German principalities . . . and in the Austrian provinces of Tyrol and Vorarlberg, where the peasants were free. . . . In the rural cantons of Switzerland, the free peasantry dominated the cantonal assemblies; in other cantons, urban oligarchs ruled over townspeople and country people alike. In some parts of France, peasants had sometimes been allowed to participate in the choice of delegates to the Estates General, the national assembly, which had last met in 1614. When the Estates General were summoned on the eve of the Revolution, representatives of the third estate were chosen by the system of indirect elections in which all heads of peasant families were allowed to participate.

Peasants did have scope for political activity and for some degree of self-government at the village level. Nearly everywhere seigniors had allowed their peasants much autonomy in the management of their village communities. In the eighteenth and nineteenth centuries, however, communal autonomy declined significantly as seigniors, for their own private reasons, intervened increasingly in the internal operations of the peasant community. . . .

Entertainment in the Parisian Fairs in the Eighteenth Century

ROBERT M. ISHERWOOD

Eighteenth-century Paris was the home of fashionable salons where the social élite could mingle with the continent's leading intellectuals, who shined with their mordant wit and moralizing critiques of the tradition, authority, and privilege that characterized the Old Régime. But Paris also offered a different world of entertainment that is not so well-known. At the fairs, available to everyone, Parisians found extraordinarily rich forms of entertainment. The variety of spectacles was fantastic. What were the major types of entertainment found at the fairs? Were there any entertainments new to the eighteenth century? Who went to see the shows? That is, what was the social composition of the audiences? What attracted people to the fairs?

Robert Isherwood believes the entertainment had very serious functions and argues that street shows created a culture transcending boundaries between upper and lower social groups. What does he mean by the term "marketplace culture"? What characterized the humor at the shows? How did the entertainment reflect the aspirations, the collective mentality, of the crowds that flocked to the fairs?

While the French philosophes *popularized the achievements of the seventeenth-century Scientific Revolution, particularly the Copernican theory and Newtonian physics, the spectators at Parisian fairs saw little difference between science and magic. What sorts of shows convinced the people that science and magic were virtually indistinguishable?*

Much of the entertainment Isherwood describes can, of course, still be seen today at a circus or a county fair. The way the eighteenth-century Parisian population thought is not uncommon in the modern world. Does Isherwood's fascinating account of the social history of fairs suggest the extent to which the Enlightenment affected ordinary Parisians on the eve of the French Revolution?

Robert M. Isherwood, "Entertainment in the Parisian Fairs in the Eighteenth Century," *Journal of Modern History* 53 (March 1981): 24–48.

The fairs of Saint-Germain, Saint-Laurent, and Saint-Ovide were the principal centers of popular entertainment in Paris throughout most of the eighteenth century. Saint-Germain and Saint-Laurent were begun in the Middle Ages by monks to accommodate pilgrims congregating on certain days of the year to honor relics. The monks rented stalls to merchants to sell food and wares and eventually permitted entertainers to perform.

The Saint-Laurent fair was situated after 1662 on five acres of land above the church of Saint-Laurent between the faubourgs[1] of Saint-Denys and Saint-Martin, where the Gare de l'Est is today. In 1663 the priests of the mission of Saint-Lazare, whose proprietary rights over the fair had been upheld several times since the fourteenth century, built eight tent-covered markets for the merchants. Over a hundred boutiques were set up along the intersecting alleys. The merchants sold pots of rich soil and sandstone, crockery, and crystal. At the eastern edge of the fair, cabarets, restaurants, and *spectacles*[2] were installed in a spacious yard surrounded by gardens. . . . The fair opened in late July and closed on the feast day of Saint Michel in September, though it was usually prolonged.

The more fashionable Saint-Germain fair ran from February 3 until Palm Sunday. It comprised two huge markets 130 steps long and 100 wide, covered by a magnificent timbered roof built in the sixteenth century at the instigation of the abbé of Saint-German. . . . Beneath it a series of nine unpaved streets, lined with boutiques, crisscrossed the fair. Established on the site of the old hôtel[3] of the kings of Navarre, the whole terrain was sunken, forming what one observer called "a mere hole in the middle of the faubourg. . . . " The ground, much lower than it is today, was in some places six to eight feet deeper than the surrounding land. Visitors complained about the narrow passageways that had to be crossed to gain access to the fair. The danger of being hit by carriages . . . did not deter thousands of people from attending the fair every day.

A sumptuous array of food products was sold at Saint-Germain including pastry, spiced breads, jams, waffles, fruit, candy, wine, liqueur, tisane,[4] beer, and *eau de vie*.[5] The merchants who had stalls in the fair, some from Paris but many from Amiens, Rheims, Beauvais, and other communities, included wigmakers, engravers, linen sellers, cask makers, coopers, druggists, cabinetmakers, and locksmiths. The seventeenth-century writer Charles Sorel declared that the fair "was a place

[1]Suburbs.
[2]Shows.
[3]Mansion.
[4]Herb-tea.
[5]Brandy.

of joy and even debauchery where one must certainly sell merchandise which would serve intemperance and vanity." He added that "peasants and other people of low stock take as much pleasure in the grotesque paintings made to distemper, as people of taste get in seeing the most beautiful tableux."

Although ordinances were issued repeatedly against it, gambling also provided merchants with a source of revenue. A few at Saint-Germain earned several hundred livres a day by running dice games, lotteries, spinning wheels, cards, and skittles in their boutiques. . . . Since the boutiques with gambling were usually packed with people, they were favorite haunts of pickpockets who were adept at cutting off the backs of men's coats or women's dresses. In 1778 the Secrétaire d'Etat[6] for Paris cracked down hard on games of chance, which some believe contributed to the decline of the fairs at the end of the century.

The last of the great Parisian fairs was that of Saint-Ovide, which did not become a major entertainment center until the second half of the eighteenth century. The genesis of the fair occurred in 1662, when the Pope's Corsican guard insulted the Duc de Créqui, the ambassador to the Vatican. In reparation Pope Alexander VII gave the duke the remains of Saint Ovide discovered in the catacombs, which Créqui in turn gave to the Capuchins,[7] whose quarters bordered the Place Louis-le-Grand (Place Vendôme), where the fair was established. The saint's annual fete thus attracted crowds which drew merchants and entertainers to the fair. Coming into vogue in the 1760s when the fair ran from August 14 until September 15, Saint-Ovide sprouted boutiques of jewelers, dressmakers, bakers, grocers, hardware dealers, handkerchief merchants, and turners. The hottest selling item in 1762 was wax figures of Jesuits who were expelled that year from France. In 1766 there were 23 different entertainments listed at the fair including marionette and optical shows, a billiard parlor, a sea monster, [and] a Passion play . . . .

Typically, the fairs were clogged with soldiers, beggars, guardsmen, prostitutes, clerks, lackeys, students, shopkeepers, porters, and petits-maîtres.[8] Everyone mingled in a jangling din of shouts, insults, and banter amid a cacophony of whistles, tambourines, flutes, and street cries. "It was a continual ebb and flow of people who pushed each other from one side to the other," wrote Charles Sorel. "It seemed that that day had been chosen by all the people of low rank in Paris to come there. . . . One heard those who suffered from the discomfort screaming from every direction, and in vain pregnant women imagined that they would be more spared than others; one could not have lightened their

---

[6]Secretary of State.

[7]An order of monks that broke away from the Franciscans in the sixteenth century.

[8]Fops.

burden if one had wished to." For Joachim Nemeitz, who wrote an instructional guide for visitors to Paris, everyone at Saint-Germain moved "helter-skelter, masters with valets and lackeys, thieves with honest people. The most refined courtesans, the prettiest girls, the subtlest pickpockets are as if intertwined together. The whole fair teems with people from the beginning to the end."

These crowds generated their own marketplace culture . . . built on humorous mockery of the ranks, restraints, and privileges of the official world. In the fairs there was little distinction between spectator and performer, between the actual life of people in the streets and the representation of life and mentality in the *spectacles*. The fair was itself a show in which everyone participated in derisive laughter at the behavior of civil society and one in which the entertainments incorporated the songs and cries of the people, their gestures and postures, their language, and their aspirations and fears. Audiences and entertainers profaned and satirized the accepted standards of etiquette and decency, helping to create a familiarity in the fairs among people often separated by occupation, wealth, age, and sex.

Derisive humor was expressed most commonly in erotic posturing and grotesque grimacing, insulting language or song, and bodily imagery associated with eating and defecation. The body in marketplace culture . . . symbolized the material existence shared by all human beings. Representing fertility, nourishment, and renewal, the body was an image of the collective mass of humanity, a positive symbol of the festivity of the streets. In the fair theaters of the eighteenth century the characters were always defecating and copulating. They were usually hungry or thirsty. . . .

The satirical celebration of material existence and . . . the "grotesque realism" arising from folk humor were evoked most typically in *parades*. *Parades* were coarse farces using characters drawn from commedia dell'arte,[9] which were given by fair actors on balconies over the entrance to their shows. They were performed free of charge and were aimed at attracting people to the main production, usually an opéra-comique.[10] For those in the crowd with no money to spend on entertainment, *parades* were about the only kind of theatrical fare available. In *Le Marchand de merde*,[11] for example, which was typical of the genre, Léandre entreats Arlequin[12] to help him solve a problem: a mischievous rascal named Gilles defecates every morning on Léandre's doorstep. Arlequin's solution is to pose as a merchant of excrement and to persuade Gilles

---

[9]Improvised comedy (which came to France from Italy) with stock characters.
[10]Comic opera.
[11]*The Shit Peddler.*
[12]Arlequin was a stock character in comedy.

that he has hit upon a lucrative profession which no one had thought of before. When Arlequin dupes an apothecary into buying his barrel of excrement for seven écus, Gilles, who is seeking a trade that will enable him to marry his beloved Catin, is taken in by the ruse and resolves to be a marchand de merde. Offering his excrement for ten écus a barrel to the apothecary, Gilles cries: "Qui veut de ma merde? . . . c'est de la fraiche."[13] The apothecary's response, however, is to flail Gilles with his stick. Bemoaning the misfortunes of honest commerce, Gilles seeks consolation from Catin, but she rejects him as a hopeless fool. Léandre warns him to keep his merchandise to himself, while Arlequin will have nothing to do with a man so inept at business.

The conclusion of *Le Marchand de merde* seems to carry us out of the folk humor of the marketplace with its suggestions of charivari[14] where excrement was an image of renewal and fertility. We enter the world of eighteenth-century duplicity, commerce, and bourgeois convention. Yet enough billingsgate is preserved in the derisive mockery of the excrement dealer and in the popular cries and gestures of charlatans, porters, tumblers, and Arlequins to remind us that the eighteenth-century fairs and their entertainers still belonged to the familiar, regenerative culture of the streets.

But does the crude humor focusing on bodily necessities and deceit in social relationships which this *parade* captures so well suggest that the culture of the fairs was popular in the sense that it was for the lower ranks of society? Do the vulgarities and obscenities of fair theater, the jangling carnival atmosphere punctuated by the raunchy cries of street vendors, and the low cost of tickets to the fair *spectacles* point to an elite/popular distinction based on levels of taste and sophistication or on social composition, whether pegged to wealth, profession, or education? One thing seems clear: . . . [t]he fair entertainments were understood by most commentators of the age to be shows aimed at ordinary people, at the lower ranks of society. This understanding derived from the genre and the fair setting. But it does not mean that *spectacles* intended to appeal to "le bas peuple"[15] did not appeal to people of high rank, wealth, learning, and sophistication. . . .

. . . [B]y the late eighteenth century if not before, popular entertainment embraced all segments of society including the elite, however they are defined. . . .

The sources stress the mixed social composition of fair audiences and crowds. In his tourist guide *Le Voyageur fidèle*[16] (1716) Louis Liger spoke of "a great concourse of people from every social rank" at the

---

[13]"Who wants my shit? . . . it is fresh."

[14]A noisy mock serenade, usually for newlyweds.

[15]The lower ranks of society.

[16]*The Accurate Traveller.*

Saint-German fair, and . . . Rétif de la Bretonne[17] observed that a crowd watching a *parade* at the fair included workers, scrubbing women, gauze-makers, seamstresses, pickpockets, and prostitutes, but also uncorrupted apprentices, children of good families, and artisans' daughters. . . .

Further evidence is provided by the enormous success of the fair theaters compared with the privileged ones, which suffered a decline in audience. The Opéra from which Jean-Baptiste Lully[18] made a fortune in the seventeenth century was 500,000 livres in debt in 1747 and over a million by the 1780s. The Comédie-Italienne[19] floundered badly until it literally stole the Opéra-Comique in 1762. Both theaters blamed the little *spectacles* for corrupting morals and good taste and for stealing their audiences. As for the Comédie-Française,[20] it waged a relentless campaign lasting from 1700 until 1791 to suppress the Opéra-Comique and all of the theaters that came along after 1762 in the wake of the Comique's demise. It invoked its monopoly on plays in verse or prose to force the Comique to sing rather than speak, and to try to force later theaters to limit themselves to pantomime. Moreover, the Comédie-Française tried to make the little theaters unattractive to *le monde*.[21] Their censor reviewed every piece of the popular theaters to ensure that no serious work was ever given and that the overall dramatic unity and content be kept as poor as possible. They also got the crown to keep the ticket prices low at the popular theaters on the assumption that this would deter *le monde* from attending. None of these measures worked. Indeed, the theater of the marketplace had become so attractive to the upper ranks of Parisian society by the middle of the century that they brought it into their homes. It became fashionable for nobles to have private theaters in at least one of their residences, where they performed the bawdiest, most obscene *parades* and farces of the streets. The fair shows were not licentious enough . . . , so nobles hired writers . . . to compose erotic works especially for them, pieces that often turned into orgies.

Final proof that fair entertainments were not confined to the lower ranks is provided by the astonishing growth of popular entertainment in the second half of the century. New locations such as the Place Louis XV with its Foire Saint-Ovide opened up, and there was a vast array of *spectacles* along the boulevards of Paris. Finally, the aristocratic heart of Paris, the gardens of the Palais-Royal, became the hub of popular entertainment in the 1780s. . . .

[17]French novelist and chronicler of society, 1734–1806.

[18]French composer, 1632–1687.

[19]The Italian Comedy, composed of Italian actors who performed in Paris from the sixteenth to the eighteenth centuries.

[20]The French Comedy, the national theater established in 1680.

[21]High society.

If popular entertainment can not be defined through the social composition or taste of crowds and audiences, what meaning does it have? Perhaps the term itself should be thrown out of our vocabulary, or we should take a longer, more skeptical look at the fashionable popular/elite distinction. At the very least, I suggest that we ask different questions about marketplace entertainments. What sort of gratification were audiences seeking and receiving from them? What was their appeal? The fair *spectacles* themselves must provide the answers.

In addition to opéras-comiques, there were five main types of fair shows: acrobats, marionettes, exotic animals, freaks, and exhibitions of mechanical and optical devices. Acrobats, tumblers, equilibrists, and what were called *danseurs de corde* or funambulists[22] had been the principal showmen of the fairs since at least the sixteenth century. Their acts, often accompanied by music, included exaggerated postures, grimaces, and gesticulation. These were mute shows, depending on gesture and agility. The acrobats also frequently wore masks and were dressed as lions and tigers, thus enhancing both the comic and exotic aspects of their performance. Although there were many variations, in the standard leap one of the acrobat's legs was bent obliquely on the ground and the trunk of his body was twisted low to the ground. From this position he quickly contracted his muscles and sprang, uncoiling, into the air. A leaper named Grimaldi vaulted to the height of the chandelier at Saint-Germain in 1742.

Most of the acrobats did their handsprings, contortions, somersaults and cartwheels on platforms or planks extended across the *tréteaux*.[23] Some performed on ladders or chairs. Most of the leapers had a speciality: Du Broc did reverse somersaults from a springboard holding a torch in each hand; . . . Evince was the first *sauteur*[24] to leap over barrels in France. In 1726 Nemeitz reported seeing a two-year-old child whirling rapidly like a top while swords were pointed at her eyes, throat, and stomach. He expressed shock at these acrobatic shows, assailing "the indecent, lascivious postures of the girls who dance, shocking reason and decency." An acrobat known only as the Turk climbed a rope to the ceiling of the theater where he perched on a wooden disk attached to a mast. There, he executed contortions, spins, and headstands. In 1754 one of the troupes introduced a novelty—a company of "Femmes-Fortes."[25] These girls walked barefoot on hot iron or coals, held hot melted lead in their mouths after lining them with oil, and supported an anvil or rocks or several men on their stomachs while stretched out with their heads resting on one chair and their feet on another. The more any stunt

[22]Tightrope walkers.
[23]Trestles, supports.
[24]Jumper.
[25]Strong women.

seemed physically impossible, daring, and miraculous, the better the crowd liked it. For this reason, funambulism, an awesome physical feat, was especially relished. . . .

Like the *sauteurs*, the funambulists had their assortment of stunts. In one the performer flew around the rope holding himself by his hands or feet, while in others he raced back and forth on a horizontal rope, or climbed one stretched at an angle. The most spectacular trick was leaping and whirling from the rope. The funambulists also did their acts while playing violins behind their backs or over their heads. One notable performer, the Dutchman, did his contortions on the tightrope wearing iron shoes. He also swung from a slack rope to a tight one. . . . Laurent walked the rope with chains or baskets fastened to his feet, while Lavigne, costumed as Scaramouche,[26] danced on the rope without using a balancing pole, playing a violin over his head and between his legs. . . .

Speculating on why the public derived so much pleasure from such performers, Nougaret[27] and Rétif came up with this explanation: "To delight, to renew the people: an object more important than a young person can sense. Entertainments which are suited to them are necessary for the people, material *spectacles* like *danses-de-corde, tours-de-force.*[28] . . . " The key word here is "material." These were entertainments focused almost entirely on the human body, the symbol of material existence, the universal denominator of humanity. It was an affirmative symbol of the strength and renewal of life. The *sauteurs* and funambulists suggested the dexterity and power inherent in man's physical being.

But there is more to it. These exhibitions seemed to reach beyond the physically possible. They were daring, often death-defying, suggesting a miraculous dimension. They aimed to arouse astonishment and awe. It is not surprising, therefore, to find leaping, vaulting, and rope walking combined in the eighteenth century with other entertainments where the marvelous played a role. For example, funambulism was combined with pyrotechnics at one of the century's most spectacular pleasure palaces, the Colisée.

Located on the Rond-Point of the Champs-Elysées, the Colisée formed an extension of the Saint-Ovide fair, which was moved to the Place Louis XV (Place de la Concorde) in 1771. This mammoth structure capable of holding 8,000 people contained a rotunda eighty feet high and seventy-eight feet in diameter and was equipped with galleries, an amphitheater, cafés, and a basin usually full of six feet of water. Nautical jousts, dances, concerts, mimed tableaux, and other *spectacles* were presented at the Colisée. In August 1773 funambulism was joined to fireworks when the directors hired le Beau Dupuis from the Grands

---

[26]A stock character in Italian farce, depicted as a foolish and cowardly braggart.

[27]Pierre-Jean-Baptiste Nougaret, eighteenth-century writer.

[28]Feats of strength.

Danseurs de Corde and announced that this celebrated stunt man of the fairs "would make a grand ascent to the tightrope and would climb to the top of a magnificent decoration depicting in fire of diverse colors the splendid portal of Notre-Dame."

Long associated with royal pageantry, fireworks were introduced into the French theater by Giovanni Niccolo Servandoni and by a pyrotechnist named Torré who staged *spectacles pyrriques*[29] in his Waux-Hall on the Boulevard Saint-Martin in the 1760s. Torré fitted his fireworks onto a metal conductor and produced crackling explosions and sprays of bubbling fire. Fireworks always seem to have an extraordinary emotional impact on crowds who gather to watch them, whether in court pageantry, arenas like the Colisée, or in front of the Eiffel Tower on Bastille Day. They evoke a myriad of images and symbols. Their dazzling effects can inspire moods ranging from reverie to terror. Appearing to be alive and unpredictable, fireworks can plant in the imagination the ideas and sensations of violence, passion, luxury, joy, and hell. In the eighteenth century, pyrotechnics became an art, as its practitioners were able to produce specific images such as dragons, rivers, shooting stars, and erupting volcanoes. In combination with funambulism and military music, as they were on the occasion of le Beau Dupuis' performance at the Colisée, they must have filled the audience with wonder and fear.

What a sight to behold! After an explosion announcing the pyric show from the cupola at the top of the rotunda, Dupuis appeared at the bottom of a cable that sloped upward from the base of one side of the wall to the peak of the framework of the fireworks. As the snakes, rockets, and wheels broke into flame, Dupuis, dressed in a white satin costume and brandishing torches in both hands, made his ascent to the top of the cable where he was silhouetted like an apparition against the radiant flames. As he began his descent, someone in the crowd shouted that the rope was loosening. In the confusion that followed, a person dressed as a pyrotechnist began turning the cylinder around which the cable was wound. Disaster ensued. As the crowd screamed, the rope suddenly sagged, Dupuis tottered, tried to regain his balance, and then fell fifty feet to the tiles below.

If the physical strength and prowess of the fair acrobats could be successfully joined to the magical allure of fireworks, producing feelings of awe and astonishment in crowds, so too were they easily and naturally linked to the popular theater of the fairs. The early opéras-comiques were in fact presented by acrobatic troupes. Their farces, in which the action unfolded by means of magic carpets, talismans, demons, elixirs, and superhuman victories, were easily adapted to leaping and tumbling routines. Indeed, several years prior to the establishment of the Opéra-Comique, the fair *sauteurs* had already discovered the popularity of this

---

[29]Fireworks.

mix of real and fictitious marvels. In 1678 a team of 24 acrobats led by a Dutch *sauteur*. . . presented a piece at Saint-Germain called *Les Forces de l'amour et de la magie*,[30] which, the notices said, would "display perilous postures and somersaults in the Italian style." Merlin's opening monologue about his tribulations as the valet of the devilish, toad-eating magician Zoroastre was preceded by acrobatic stunts performed on pedestals and followed by the menacing contortions and "perilous" leaps of demons who came to fetch the shepherd girl, Grésinde, to a tryst with their evil leader. In subsequent scenes, Merlin failed to prevent Zoroastre from terrifying the girl with his black magic: a wave of his wand released somersaulting monkeys from a goblet and flying serpents from an unctuous paté. But while Merlin distracted Zoroastre, Grésinde appealed to the goddess Juno, who substituted a leaping demon for the girl just as the wicked magician was about to seize her. Zoroastre was compelled to acknowledge Juno's stronger magic. The play was little more than a vehicle for the acrobatics, but it enhanced the thrilling, suggestively magical aspect of the physical stunts. The opéra-comique genre launched by the fair acrobats just after the turn of the century embodied the same combination of bodily gyrations and farcical plots abounding in sorcery and metamorphoses with the added dimension of song and dance.

Marionettists, who for years had entertained fair crowds, also found the lyric comedy appropriate for their shows. . . . The enduring enthusiasm of Parisians for these springy puppets suspended from strings by a *saltimbanque*[31] working behind a curtain is indicated by a police report in May, 1763, stating that long after the other *spectacles* had closed for the season at Saint-Germain, indeed after the legal closing date, . . . marionettes were still performing. The patrol thought it advisable to let the show continue rather than risk angering the crowd. . . .

But the marionettes might have had their own special appeal, one that was more peculiar to Old-Régime Europe than to modern times. Magical power, especially when the wooden model possessed the traits of a real person, may have been attributed to these animated figures. Linked to black magic, specifically to voodoo, they were for a long time denounced by the Church. Persons accused of being witches were often charged with using dolls and puppets to work their maleficent, supernatural evils. Yet the Church did not always discourage credence in wooden statues crying or oozing blood. Even after they began to appear in Parisian salons and in public places, marionettes were still associated in popular belief with prodigies. No doubt most people by the seventeenth century saw them more as vehicles of amusement than as mysterious androides, but Paul Scarron[32] in 1643 noted that people believed

---

[30]*The Powers of Love and of Magic.*

[31]Showman, charlatan.

[32]Burlesque writer, 1610–1660.

the puppets of Pierre Datelin were enchanted, and in 1649 Datelin was still denounced as a magician working with devils. Audiences may also have been fascinated by the size of marionettes. Small figures, especially when they come to life in the make-believe world of the theater, appeal to the imagination. Like dwarfs and figurines, they evoke sympathy because they are fragile. To many, they probably seemed charmed.

Yet for others, it seems likely that the appeal of the marionettes lay in the salty pieces full of equivocation which were often performed at these shows. . . . Nicolas-Toussaint Le Moyne[33] expressed concern about the impression the puppet shows made on children: "Nearly all the farces that are played by the marionettes," he wrote, "are embroidered with equivocations, jokes, and indecent situations. Children who attend these shows retain all too easily the impressions they receive in these dangerous places. Parents are often astonished to find them informed about things they should not know about; they ought to blame the lack of prudence they have shown in permitting their children to be taken to shows that should have been forbidden them." On one occasion the Parisian guard intervened in the marionette show of Monsieur Ribier at Saint-Laurent to prevent him from showing "a little figure who was indecent, who pissed in front of the spectators, and who had all the bodily parts of a man, and very visible."

Throughout the century, fair crowds were attracted to exhibitions of exotic animals. Lions, bears, tigers, and leopards were unfamiliar sights to Parisians, among whom they generated considerable curiosity and excitement. Although elephants had been seen in Europe since the sixteenth century, they were certainly not common. One, eight or nine feet tall apparently, with toenails five inches long, was seen at Saint-Germain in 1698. . . . Perhaps the greatest sensation of the age was a rhinoceros at Saint-Germain in 1749. The animal, which became the subject of naturalist tracts and engravings, was brought from Asia to Holland and then transported by a horse-drawn van to Germany and France. . . .

Seals were still so rare in France that when one died in 1779 his cadaver was embalmed, and he remained on display. . . . Perhaps the most exotic menagerie at Saint-Germain and certainly one of the most successful was that of Monsieur Ruggieri, the celebrated pyrotechnist. The nature of his exhibition and of animal shows in general can be gleaned from the "Avis au Public"[34] which he sent to the newspapers:

Sieur RUGGERY [sic] . . . proposes to show a new menagerie consisting of 10 animals coming from foreign countries, among which are two which appeared in the year 1771. The first is L'OUISTITI who is commonly called the ladies' favorite, or the little monkey. The one that the said RUGGERY

[33]Eighteenth-century French writer.
[34]Public announcement.

sold in 1771 for 35 louis weighed 5 ounces; he was admired by the public. The one that he has this year will satisfy the curious even more; he weighs only 3 ounces. The second is the same leopard from the last fair; he is twice as large. He is going to perform some tricks which will surprise spectators. The third is L'ASPATULLE, an animal who lives entirely on fish. The fourth is a monkey called LE CAPUCIN[35] because of his beard. He cracks nuts with a stone with unusual skill. The fifth is a MAKIS;[36] he deserves to be seen; nothing equals his beauty and gentleness. The sixth and seventh are two PIERROTS[37] from China, male and female. The eighth is a very rare species of monkey; his name is not found in dictionaries of natural history. The ninth is a very little flying squirrel; he is not a quarter as large as ordinary ones. His wings are placed just like those of the bat; this animal deserves the attention of connoisseurs. The tenth is a very rare animal whose loss is greatly regretted; he died at Royes coming from Holland. Since this animal had never appeared in Europe dead or alive, the said RUGGERY has had him stuffed with the greatest care. . . .

The public was frequently lured into the animal exhibitions by posters promising exotic animals which turned out to be common ones or animals so strange as to defy belief. In 1698 one booth advertised beasts from India bearing unusual names which in reality were a leopard and a racoon. Two wild animals allegedly from the "mountain of Barbery" were displayed at Saint-Germain in 1748. One was described as having the head of a sheep, the back of a Spanish horse, the face and neck of a deer, the barbels of a goat, the ears and breast of a hind, a coat of fine wool, the croup of a horse, and the tail of a dog and front feet of a calf. It was reportedly six feet tall and ran with the speed of a horse. In actuality, however, the animal, just two and a half feet tall, had the appearance of a human being. It did acrobatic stunts and conjuring tricks. . . . Louis-Sébastien Mercier,[38] who scoffed at such deceptions as a giant wearing platform boots and a sultan's headdress, a shaved, depilated she-bear dressed in breeches, shirt, and jacket who was passed off as a "unique animal," and a large wooden dummy who could speak because a small boy hid in his stomach, understood, nevertheless, why such shows succeeded and were appealing: "People are so taken in," he wrote, "that they expect in advance that a fake marvel will transport them no less than if it were true."

Savant animals evoked even greater curiosity than bizarre ones. . . . Nemeitz was struck by a monkey dressed as a musketeer who executed military drills, danced a minuet, and did tricks on a dog's back. He also described a show in which pigeons turned roasting meat by pulling

[35]After Capuchin monks, who wore beards.

[36]Lemur.

[37]Sparrows.

[38]Dramatist, 1740–1814.

a chariot attached to a spit. In the 1770s there were birds who could count and tell time. . . . Finally, a "scholarly deer" guessed people's ages, played cards, charged cannons, and trotted like a Spanish horse, and a Dutch lady played with snakes . . . which wrapped themselves around her, caressed her, and put their heads into her mouth.

It was a short step from exotic animals to freaks. . . . In 1777 a twenty-eight year old Westphalian named Roose, who measured eight feet one inch, appeared at the fair. Earlier "la grande géante Algérienne,"[39] six feet eight inches tall, and a dwarf named Moreau, two feet four inches, were on display at Saint-Germain. Probably the most unusual of these people was the "giant dwarf,". . . described as "a four-year old child, who, formed as fortunately as the most vigorous man beyond the finest proportions in the viril organ, has the diverse abilities of it such as erection, ejaculation. . . . It is especially at the approach of a woman that his virility manifests itself. . . . " His age was verified by his birth record, teeth, and lingual ability.

There are no references to bearded ladies, but people with congenital deformities attracted the crowd's attention. A German without arms and legs, who performed at Saint-Germain in 1716, was able to write, play a drum, and make houses out of cards. A certain Paschal Discol, described as a handsome sixteen-year-old Venetian with hands growing from his shoulders and feet from his haunches, executed bodily gyrations at Saint-Laurent in 1752. In 1779 at Saint-Germain a Liègois schoolmaster who had no arms uncorked bottles, drank, smoked, tied knots, threaded needles, played cards, loaded a pistol, carried a chair, and hurled a baton forty feet behind his back.

In . . . 1665 Jean Loret[40] noted that he crossed himself several times while watching "flashes of bodies fleet like ghosts" twisting and dancing noiselessly on a wall. He was describing one of the first exhibitions of a magic lantern (invented by the Jesuit scientist Athanasius Kircher)—a box containing lenses which projected luminous, seemingly animated tableaux. Perfected in the eighteenth century by the Abbé Jean-Antoine Nollet, a physicist who invented an electroscope and improved the Leyden jar, the magic lantern was one of several devices used in what were called *cabinets de physique,* little booths or theaters in the fairs and boulevards where electrical, mechanical, and optical contraptions were used to amaze and fool audiences.

The aim of these sideshows was not really to clarify the laws of physics, but rather to make science mysterious and awesome. They must be put in the context of white magic, the art of producing the illusion of superhuman prodigies by natural means. Spectators often may have understood the phenomena they observed in the *cabinets de physique,*

[39]The great Algerian giant.
[40]Writer of weekly letters in verse describing current events.

though there is a human predilection to want to be fooled, and white and black magic were often confused in popular belief. There did not seem to be that much difference between the black arts of necromancy, mesmerism, and divination, and such mysterious natural phenomena as gravity, electricity, hypnotism, ventriloquism, and human flight in gas-filled balloons. The practitioners of white magic in the fairs took advantage of the mounting curiosity about natural science that developed among all levels of society in the eighteenth century. They took advantage not only of the lingering belief in sorcery and the occult but also of the human delight in being deluded and awed, just as those who wrote for the popular theater filled their shows with magic wands and sorcerers. . . .

Although mechanical gadgetry, especially *automates*,[41] had been shown at the fairs for years, their great vogue was in the eighteenth century. In 1727 Nemeitz described an "Invention Méchanique"[42] that represented the Opéra. The mechanism enabled paper figures of actors to move about on stage, a chariot to descend, and a conductor to beat time. In 1775 . . . the Droz brothers from Switzerland offered movable figures of a man taking dictation with pen and ink, a child painting portraits, and a clavecinist. . . . In the late 1770s the Abbé Mical used ventriloquism for his exhibition of talking *automates* which were later displayed in the Tuileries palace. Anton de Kempelin, a Hungarian, brought a chess-playing *automate* to the fairs, and in 1784 an *automate* funambulist was featured. . . .

The mechanical wizardry which made lilliputian figures and objects appear to be alive was most effective when combined with catoptrics, electricity, and prestidigitation. At Saint-Laurent a magic palace supposedly inhabited by "invisible spirits" was combined with electrified jumping jacks. The palace, containing several rooms, was set in a forest rigged up with optical devices. . . . The "invisible spirits" *were automates* who told the fortunes of people in the audience, answered questions, and read minds. Promising the crowd he would produce "terrifying sparks drawn from the surface of the water," the entrepreneur of this show, Blaise Lagrelet, made small figures from elder pith which he placed on metal plates. One was grounded; the other, connected to a machine, enabled him to vault the dolls or jacks from plate to plate. His *spectacle* was rivaled in 1750 by the *cabinet* of Monsieur Rabiqueau, who presented ships sailing in a pool of water in directions commanded by the audience; copper balls propelled into the air where they remained without apparent support. . . . In the 1780s a certain Monsieur Pinetti, billed as a physicist from Rome, brought his "bouquet philosophique" [43] to Paris. An orange

[41]Automatons.
[42]Mechanical invention.
[43]Philosophical bouquet.

tree enclosed in a bottle blossomed and bore fruit when sprinkled with Pinetti's special water. His specialty, however, was an act with a pigeon which he dangled alive by the head from a cord. A candle cast the bird's shadow on a piece of cloth. Sticking the shadow of the bird with his dagger caused its blood to drip into a plate leaving the impression that the bird itself had been stabbed. . . .

The shows featuring optical illusion were the most popular in the *cabinets de physiques*. Several types of magic lantern acts . . . were in use by the late eighteenth century. One . . . was a box about four feet high containing a mirror inclined at a forty-five degree plane and a double convex glass. This contraption enabled the entertainer to make objects appear very fat or thin and to invert objects. Yet another version of the optical box, one attributed to Louis Carrogis, known as Carmontel, made use of transparencies. Carmontel produced tableaux depicting landscapes, wild animals, genre scenes, flaming palaces, hurricanes, and caricatures. He unrolled long bands of these transparencies in front of an illuminated pane of glass, so that they appeared to the spectator as an animated drama. By mid-century, the streets of Paris were full of Savoyards, who made a speciality of these forms of optical magic, carrying their lantern boxes on their backs, which they exhibited whenever a small crowd could be lured by the sound of their hurdy-gurdies.

Two versions of optical magic found their way into the theaters of the fairs and boulevards: ombres Chinoises[44] and phantasmagoria. . . . Frédéric-Melchior Grimm[45] explained that in ombres Chinoises a piece of white linen cloth or tautly stretched oil paper was used as a curtain. Actors—later on cut-out figures—were placed behind the curtain, and the light from a candle seven or eight feet back projected their images onto the cloth, so the audience saw moving shadows. . . .

Phantasmagoria became the speciality of one of the century's most successful charlatans of science, Nicolas-Philippe Ledru, known as Comus. His show, billed as "Expériences Physiques et Mathématiques,"[46] combined fortune-telling and sleight-of-hand with mental telepathy, electrical healing, and optical magic. Catering to the popular taste for sound and light shows, Comus produced lightning by discharging Leyden jars, and thunder by lighting a mixture of saltpeter, sulfur, and tartar salt. He used electricity allegedly to extract powder from diamonds, and he claimed the ability to establish communication between two people separated by a barrier. Denis Diderot[47] wrote . . . that "Comus is a charlatan of the rampart who twists the mind of all our physicians; his secret consists of establishing communication between two people from one room

[44]Shadow-shows.

[45]A German (1723–1807) who reported on events in Paris.

[46]Physical and mathematical experiments.

[47]French philosophe, 1713–1784.

to another without the discernible assistance of any intermediary agent." In his phantasmagoria shows, Comus, working in a dark room, beamed a lantern around the walls or at a curtain from the audience side. A tiny needle of light appeared on the screen which suddenly grew larger, and a specter appeared to leap out at the audience, or hover over its head.

Comus' vogue was not confined to the streets, though he was a celebrated figure there. He conducted experiments in the decomposition of colors without the use of prisms for the Austrian Emperor Joseph II. . . . In 1783 his use of electrical shocks to cure epileptics was so well regarded that he was able to establish a sort of clinic for the treatment of nervous disorders in the residence of the Celestins. In 1784 Louis XVI conferred on him the title of Physician of the King and of the Faculty of Paris. Comus made the transition with crown support from street conjurer to electrotherapist. He was hailed by the Faculty of Medicine for "his marvelous cures." A contemporary of Pierre Mesmer[48] and only one of many self-proclaimed experts in science, Comus reminds us of the veritable craze for science on the eve of the Revolution . . . and of the fact that little distinction was made in the popular mentality between science and magic.

Eighteenth-century Parisians were fascinated by mechanical wizardry, magic lanterns, electrical healing, funambulism, fireworks, aerostatics, phantasmagoria, and the exotic, whether in the form of menageries of unusual animals and freaks or in the theater. All in one way or another became part of the entertainment world of the Parisian fairs. Why? What did crowds seek in these shows? Did they have something in common that explains their popularity? These, I believe, are the important questions that must be asked of popular entertainment and its place in popular culture.

All of the fair *spectacles* in one way or another appealed to the human fascination with the marvelous, the predilection to be awed by something incredible and fantastic. Playing on the senses and the imagination through what were largely visual media, the marvelous permitted an escape from reality into dream-like experiences. It was and is perhaps a projection into adult experience of the fanciful worlds all children create and play in. The wonderful moments of childhood revery in which the laws of nature and the constraints of society can be cast aside were rekindled in the entertainments of the fairs. The *spectacles* enabled people to accept the illusion of the incredible, to dream, and to marvel, if only for fleeting moments. Light, water, and fire, which figured in so many entertainments, caused people to marvel, as they still do. Electricity seemed miraculous, arousing astonishment and wonder not unlike that evoked by strange beasts from unseen regions of the earth and the frighten-

---

[48]German physician (1734–1815), creator of the theory of animal magnetism, known as mesmerism.

ing apparition of phantoms in the dark. The equilibrists, tumblers, and ropewalkers—the Wallendas and Evel Knievels of their day—performed amazing feats which raised the specter of crippling accident or death.

As for the popular theater, the settings and characters of most pieces were magical, bizarre, and exotic. Action occurred on flying carpets, clouds, stormy seas, or in crystal palaces, seraglios, or grottoes inhabited by demons. Spells were cast; figures disappeared; apparitions abounded. There were no limits of time and space. Everything suggested a fabulous realm probably rooted in peasant folklore. It was not such a great leap from superstitious peasant lore about werewolves, spells, and goblins to the seductive marvels of fair conjurers, illusionists, freaks, and tumblers. The appeal of popular entertainment was that it stirred the lingering childhood need to dream and fed a human desire to marvel. Yet its social setting in the marketplace and its retention of the real speech, gesture, chant, and derisive humor of marketplace existence made it fun, even credible, as well as wonderful. The *spectacles* of the fairs were appealing because they combined derisive humor and fairyland enchantment, the material and the magical. They joined the sense of renewal gained by physical imagery and derisive laughter at regimented society with the sense of escape from actual existence into a world of marvels, whether real or factitious.

The criticism of polite society and officialdom generated by the derisive humor of many fair shows, especially opéras-comiques, forms an intriguing counterpoint in popular culture to the criticism of the Old Régime by the philosophes. Intellectual and *forain*[49] were indifferent or hostile toward each other, yet both exposed to critical ridicule the society around them. Did Arlequin . . . rattle the foundations of a society vulnerable to criticism and upheaval? Or, did the fair shows, which the police eventually began to encourage, have the opposite effect of diverting *le bas peuple* from more dangerous pursuits? The remarkable expansion of marketplace entertainment all over Paris in the years immediately preceding the Revolution beckons the historian to seek answers to these questions.

[49]Strolling actor.

Finding Solace in Eighteenth-Century Newgate

W. J. SHEEHAN

In the eighteenth century, governments began for the first time to confine significant numbers of the population. Thus certain modern institutions—prisons, hospitals, and asylums—date from this period. Perhaps the most notorious of Europe's prisons was London's Newgate; its very name conjured up, as W. J. Sheehan notes, "misery, despair, wickedness and death." In this essay, Sheehan examines whether those images are accurate by describing the lives of prisoners, especially the means they employed to make their hell more tolerable.

How did Newgate gain its terrible reputation? What was prison life like? Just as wealth made a difference outside, it distinguished prisoners inside. What advantages did affluent inmates have?

Save for providing the ministrations of religion, the authorities made no effort at rehabilitation. Hence the daily routine left prisoners with quite a bit of leisure time. What did they do to relieve their boredom and misery? How exactly did they find solace? Which means proved to be the most popular or effective? One is impressed by the prisoners' ingenuity.

Two groups impinged on the prisoners' efforts to make their lives endurable. First, there were the keepers, the jailers, certainly not a social élite themselves, who watched and limited some of their charges' activities while trying to profit from them. What was the nature of the relationship between keepers and prisoners? Second, there were visitors. If Newgate was not a nice place to live, it apparently was an attractive place to visit. Who visited Newgate, and why did so many drop by or even sojourn there? After all, Newgate was overcrowded, filthy, and dangerous.

.　　.　　.

Newgate is a dismal prison . . . a place of calamity . . . a habitation of misery, a confused chaos . . . a bottomless pit of violence, a Tower of Babel where all are speakers and no hearers. There is a mingling of the noble with ignoble, rich with the poor, wise with the ignorant, and the [innocent] with the worst malefactors. It is a grave of gentility, the banishment of courtesy, the poison of honour, the centre of infamy, the quintessence of disparagement, the confusion of wit.

A. Smith, *A Complete History of the Lives and Robberies of the Most Notorious Highway-Men* (1719), I, p. 153

W. J. Sheehan, "Finding Solace in Eighteenth-Century Newgate," in *Crime in England, 1550–1800*. Ed. J. S. Cockburn (Princeton, N.J.: Princeton University Press, 1977), 229–245.

As the principal criminal prison for metropolitan London, eighteenth-century Newgate was synonymous with misery, despair, wickedness and death. 'The name of Newgate is a great terror to all', observed a prison officer in 1724, 'from its being a prison for felons . . . and the blackest sort of malefactors'; the gaol's sinister reputation was further enhanced by public-spirited citizens who reviled it as a 'tomb for the living', 'the mansion of misery' and even 'Hell itself'. To a great extent this repugnance towards Newgate stemmed from the gaol's squalor and unhealthiness. In warm weather a noisome stench drifted from the prison and permeated the surrounding neighbourhood, forcing local shopkeepers to close their businesses and persuading pedestrians to hold their noses as they passed through the gateway. Physicians flatly refused to enter Newgate and frequently warned that gaol fever, a virulent form of typhus, might spread from the prison and decimate the entire city. Indeed, in May 1750 this contagion did infect the Old Bailey sessions, killing forty persons, including the Lord Mayor, two judges and several other court officials. In the wake of this disaster, popular revulsion became so intense that in 1767 the City authorities finally razed the ancient prison.

Of course, prisoners in Newgate endured outrageous hardships. Early in the century a series of investigations by the Court of Aldermen and the Common Council, the City's two most powerful governing bodies, revealed that the Newgate officers had grossly mismanaged the gaol and had brutalized, robbed and starved the prisoners. Because of the squalid conditions, there was always sickness in the gaol and it was not unusual for thirty prisoners to perish in a year. Imprisonment in Newgate also had a depressing effect: in 1774 a keeper recalled that he had often observed 'a dejection of spirits among the prisoners . . . which had the effect of disease, and many had died broken hearted'. . . . Newgate prisoners welcomed any diversion that would alleviate their suffering. Some of these diversions provided real solace for the prisoners while others, as we shall see, simply added to Newgate's infamous reputation.

Outwardly, Newgate was an unimposing structure. Housed in the ancient gatehouse which spanned the junction of Holborn and Newgate streets near the Old Bailey,[1] the prison stood five stories tall and measured eighty-five by fifty feet. The ancient stone structure dated from the fifteenth century, although it had been completely refurbished after the Great Fire of September 1666. . . .

Newgate's ornate exterior concealed a dismal, warren-like interior that was divided into the 'Common Side' and the 'Master Side'. In turn, each of these sides included various rooms, or 'wards', where the prisoners lived. Newgate was divided into two sides because it was customary for the prisoners to pay the prison-keeper for their lodgings much as if

[1]The criminal court of London.

they were staying in an inn or hotel. Affluent prisoners paid as much as £3 6s. 8d. weekly to reside on the Master Side, while all destitute prisoners lodged in the charity wards on the Common Side. The cellar and the north section of the gatehouse together contained nine of Newgate's thirteen common wards, sparsely furnished with hammocks or wooden bunks, cupboards, tables, a fireplace and sometimes a privy. Gross overcrowding often made it necessary for several prisoners to share the same bunk, while those who did not have a bed simply slept on the floor covered with rags and verminous straw, 'huddled like slovenly dogs . . . so near the fires that they roasted their asses'. The high prices meant that the Master Side was much smaller, including only five wards, all located in the south section of the gatehouse along with the prison office, the taphouse, several community rooms and the chapel, situated on the uppermost floor.

Adjacent to this south section of the gaol was the Press Yard, a diminutive area which measured only nine by fifty feet and was overshadowed by the keeper's residence and a two-storey building that contained Newgate's most expensive lodgings. Legally, the Press Yard was not part of the prison, but was regarded as part of the keeper's residence. Nevertheless, the keepers did detain prisoners there, providing they were not security risks and could pay exorbitant prices for such luxuries as private rooms, gourmet meals and maid service. In 1717 one prisoner estimated that he had paid enough to rent 'the best house in St James or Piccadilly for several years', but felt that the money was wisely spent because it was 'better to pay the additional cost than to have thieves and villains for your associates and to be perpetually eaten up by insects and vermin' in the other wards. . . .

Newgate could comfortably accommodate about 150 prisoners at most, but this capacity was rarely observed and the gaol was chronically overcrowded throughout the eighteenth century. The prison records for a typical four-month period in 1735, for example, show that the prison population was never under 275; thirty years later a Newgate keeper told a parliamentary commission that there were always about 250 prisoners in the gaol and that it was necessary for thirty prisoners to occupy a ward measuring only thirty-two by twenty-six feet. This overcrowding became intolerable prior to each sessions when the gaolers from the surrounding metropolitan prisons transferred their serious offenders to Newgate for trial at the Old Bailey. . . . [I]t was not unusual for a thousand prisoners to pass through Newgate each year.

Since most persons were committed to Newgate to await trial at the Old Bailey sessions, the length of their imprisonment depended on the court's action. Generally, a prisoner's stay in Newgate lasted from a week to about three months, although there are isolated examples of debtors or State prisoners spending years in prison. Acquitted prisoners had the briefest stay in Newgate because they were discharged *en masse* on the last day of the sessions. On the other hand, the court remanded numerous prisoners back to Newgate pending further action. These remanded prisoners included 'respites' who were appealing their sentences, 'convicts' sentenced to be transported to the American colonies, 'fines' or lesser offenders who were to be pilloried or otherwise punished and condemned malefactors who were to be hanged at Tyburn. Together with the sundry debtors and State prisoners, these remanded prisoners comprised the more permanent element of Newgate's population and were, of course, most in need of consolation to alleviate the hardships of prison life.

For the most part, life in Newgate was loosely structured and varied little from day to day. The prison day began at 7 a.m. with the loud clanging of a bell and was soon followed by the noisy rattling of keys, locks and leg-irons as the turnkeys unlocked the wards and counted the prisoners. Each prisoner provided his own breakfast before beginning the onerous chores of emptying the chamber pots, carrying water and cleaning the rooms. Following these morning rituals there was little to do until mid-afternoon when the main meal was prepared. Food was usually plentiful on the Master Side where, according to one prison officer, 'the prisoners have every day a very good dinner either roasted or boiled in a decent manner a joint of mutton, veal, lamb or beef'. On the Common Side, however, food was much less abundant and the prisoners had to subsist on the City's meagre ration of bread and water supplemented by charitable donations and the sheriffs' weekly meat supply. 'The food ration on the Common Side', noted one keeper, 'has always been the bare allowance, and would probably be insufficient . . . a very poor subsistence, if not for the gifts and help of friends'. In fact, by the end of the century this diet was so inadequate that the keepers were often forced to provide meals out of their own pockets to keep the prisoners from starving.

After lunch the prisoners were again left on their own until about 7 p.m. when dinner was served. Newgate closed at 9 p.m. and the day ended with the turnkeys herding the prisoners back to their wards, 'like drivers with so many Turkish slaves'. All prisoners were supposed to be in bed by 10 p.m. and to maintain strict silence until the following morning but, as we shall see, these quiet hours were rarely enforced and raucous activities continued long into the night. . . .

. . . [T]he City did not devise an acceptable set of ordinances until 1816, so that throughout the eighteenth century daily life in Newgate was left to the discretion of the prison staff or, more importantly, to the prisoners themselves who had perfected their own remarkable system of self-government.

Prisoner autonomy had originated at Ludgate, the City's other gate-prison, in the mid fifteenth century and had functioned so smoothly there that in 1633 the Court of Aldermen ordered the Newgate prisoners to establish a similar form of government, 'in much the same manner as at Ludgate'. The prisoners were to hold monthly meetings to discuss their problems and then elect a Steward and wardsmen to deal with any difficulties. We know little of the workings of the Newgate constitution before the late seventeenth century when it becomes obvious that the prison staff callously subverted it for their own benefit. Instead of holding the monthly meetings to elect officers, the keepers simply named four of their favourites, derisively called the 'Partners', who assisted the turnkeys and, too often, brutalized the other prisoners.

The Partners' abuses were especially widespread throughout the 1720s. For example, in 1724 the prisoners complained that these officers had broken into one of the wards and taken the charity money. A few years later the Partners stole the prisoners' meagre bread ration to sell to local merchants and confiscated all gifts from visitors. When a prisoner died, the Partners immediately stripped the corpse and then made the deceased's relatives pay to claim the body for burial. Several prisoners who protested against these outrages were savagely beaten, 'confined in a stinking, wet dungeon . . . and loaded with irons'. Such oppressions continued until about 1730 when the City authorities finally curbed the Partners' powers and revived the original Newgate constitution; thereafter, the prisoners managed their own affairs.

There seems little doubt that the workings of the prisoners' government was one of the most notable features of life in Newgate. The elected officers played a major role in enforcing discipline in the gaol by establishing codes of conduct and then sitting as a tribunal to punish those who had violated the rules. In addition, the officers helped the Steward distribute the prisoners' charity funds as well as the rations from the City. In an effort to supplement the prisoners' charity income the officers also collected from each newcomer 'garnish money' which was used to buy candles, coal, soap and other prison supplies. Finally, the officers also named 'swabbers' to supervise the cleaning of the gaol. Since most Newgate prisoners remained in gaol for a fairly short time, there was a considerable turnover among the elected officers; nevertheless, conscientious involvement in prison government must have consumed much of the elected officers' spare time and helped to take their minds off their problems.

For the other prisoners the most frustrating thing about life in Newgate was that they had abundant spare time but few valuable activities with which to fill it. . . . [T]here was no organized prison labours in the gaol until the early nineteenth century, although some prisoners did busy themselves with such handicrafts as leatherworking, woodcarving and tailoring.

The religious services provided by the City to comfort the prisoners and, hopefully, to reform them were also of questionable value. There had been a full-time chaplain, or Ordinary as he was popularly known, at Newgate since the early seventeenth century and it was his duty to read prayers daily, attend all condemned prisoners and preach on Sundays, holidays and once during the week. Attendance at religious services was supposedly compulsory, but since the tiny chapel was unable to accommodate the entire prison congregation, the prisoners were permitted to miss services provided they stayed in their wards and did not create a disturbance. Prisoners who disrupted chapel services were to be ironed, put in solitary confinement and deprived of their food ration. By and large, however, these punishments were rarely enforced and the prisoners tended to be scandalously irreverent during the religious services. They wandered about the gaol and caused so much noise that the Ordinaries had to shout their sermons. In September 1716 the Ordinary protested that several prisoners 'were eating and drinking on the communion table and that it is now broken'. A decade later another chaplain recalled that the prisoners often sauntered through the chapel during services and relieved themselves in a corner so that 'there is always an evil smell'. . . .

Chapel services at Newgate took on an almost carnival-like atmosphere when the Ordinaries preached to the condemned prisoners on the day before their execution. The unfortunate prisoners sat in front of their black-shrouded caskets, while the turnkeys stationed themselves at the chapel entrance where they sold tickets to curiosity seekers wishing to view the morbid spectacle. 'For a full two months we have been hindered from going to chapel', grumbled the prisoners in December 1724, 'because the keepers . . . make a show of the condemned prisoners in the chapel by which they raise great sums of money'. . . . Although the Court of Aldermen forbade this custom in 1735, it was soon revived and continued into the nineteenth century. In 1750 Horace Walpole[2] wrote that over 3000 people had paid to view a notorious highwayman on the day before his execution. . . .

Since outsiders were permitted to come and go at Newgate virtually at will, visitors thronged into the gaol to comfort the prisoners and to supply them with food, money, drink and other necessities. . . . The prisoners' families were the most frequent visitors to Newgate and they often caused pitiable scenes at closing time. 'It was a most pathetic sight', recalled one gaoler, 'to see wives and children . . . so distressed at parting'. In 1765 a visiting clergyman recalled how one pregnant wife visited her husband daily 'to supply him with sufficient food and when they were together they rarely talked, but she simply sat at his side; throwing her arms around his neck, they would shed mutual and sympathetic floods of tears'. Rather than be separated from their families, prisoners often tried to conceal their spouses and children in the gaol. In 1815 one prison officer frankly admitted that although he was constantly

[2]English author, 1717–1797.

vigilant for prisoners who tried to hide their families 'many wives do manage to stay overnight'.

On the other hand, affluent prisoners did not have to conceal their families in Newgate but merely paid a fee to have them reside in the gaol. . . .

There were no nursery facilities in Newgate so children had to stay in the wards with the other prisoners. . . . 'We have a vast deal of difficulty with children', complained one keeper in 1811, 'to know how to dispose of them'. It goes without saying that Newgate was certainly no place for children to grow up for, as one prisoner put it, 'they are quickly debauched'.

In addition to their families, prisoners in Newgate were allowed to keep pets. In 1717 the prisoners actually staged a badger-baiting in the Press Yard. . . . The City authorities finally prohibited the keeping of dogs in the gaol in 1792 and forbade 'pigs, pigeons and poultry' in 1814.

Literacy was not high in Newgate but a few prisoners did find some comfort in reading. They were especially anxious to keep abreast of current news and paid the turnkeys to deliver the daily papers; some keepers even encouraged this newspaper reading by placing a literate prisoner in each ward to read to the others. Law books were also popular reading and prisoners pored over these volumes in order to prepare their defences, often with the assistance of law students preparing for the bar. There was also considerable inspirational reading, particularly among the condemned prisoners who spent their final hours seeking solace from Scripture and other religious works provided by the City and the Society for Promoting Christian Knowledge.[3] 'Prison was the best school that I ever went to', proclaimed one prisoner, because 'I read the Bible constantly . . . and my soul was delighted . . . experiencing a spiritual rejuvenation . . . and a return to Christian teaching'. . . . In 1717 a newcomer to the Press Yard was amazed to find that his colleagues were quite cultured, well-educated and read the classics; indeed, it was customary for these prisoners to end the day with a poetry reading. . . .

Writing materials were available in Newgate so that the prisoners spent part of their time writing letters or petitioning various governmental authorities. . . .

In the final analysis, however, the most famous literature from eighteenth-century Newgate were the many autobiographies of condemned prisoners. Condemned malefactors recognized the morbid fascination crime held for the popular imagination and often attempted to make a final, dying profit from this appeal. As soon as a condemned prisoner learned the day of his execution, he immediately turned his final hours to writing his autobiography which would be sold at

---

[3]Established in the late seventeenth century, the SPCK operated charity schools in England, produced religious tracts, and supported missionaries overseas.

Tyburn. . . . This gallows literature had such an enormous appeal that the authentic autobiographies often had to compete with gross forgeries and even the Ordinary's account of the dying man's last hours and final confession. Eventually, the Ordinary's accounts gained the greatest appeal and became one of the most profitable perquisites of that office. . . .

Because Newgate was so small, there was virtually no place for any worthwhile recreation, although the prisoners did use their ingenuity to get some exercise. Early in the century they converted a large room on the second floor into a sort of gymnasium where they jogged and did calisthenics until overcrowding made this impracticable. In addition, prisoners sometimes went up on the prison roof for air and exercise but even this was discontinued by mid century for security reasons and because the prisoners pelted neighbouring buildings with debris. For a price, prisoners could stroll about the Press Yard and some even tried to organize games in the tiny area. 'The prisoners were playing skittles', recalled one newcomer to the Press Yard, 'where there was scarce room to set up the pins'. . . . But after the completion of the new condemned cells in 1728, the Press Yard became useless because the new building encroached on the small space, cutting off air and filling it with 'ill-smells and dismal noises . . . all very offensive'. Of course, the lack of exercise facilities had a debilitating effect on the prisoners' health and morale. 'There should be room for games . . . and exercise', warned a physician who visited Newgate regularly late in the century, 'or spirits sink and the body turns to flab'.

All of the diversions we have discussed thus far made confinement in Newgate endurable to some extent, but it would be mistaken to think that they were the primary sources of solace for the prisoners. Instead, like so many other despondent inhabitants of Georgian London, the prisoners turned to excessive drinking in hope of forgetting their troubles. . . . Throughout the eighteenth century, then, the Newgate taphouse was the centre of prison life where the prisoners could get drunk night after night, or pass their time gaming, smoking or merely conversing.

The Newgate taphouse had always been a perquisite of the keeper's office. In turn, the keeper appointed a full-time tapster who expanded the enterprise into a sort of general store selling coal, candles, soap, tobacco and whatever else was marketable in prison. Usually a turnkey or his wife managed the taphouse, although prisoners sometimes held the post. During the eighteenth century there was increasing criticism of this trade in beer and spirits, but the Newgate keepers were able to devise some disingenuous arguments to justify their role as publicans. In 1730 William Pitt[4] argued that the taphouse played a vital role in the

---

[4]The keeper, or warden, at Newgate.

prison's security because the tapsters could overhear conversations in the taphouse 'where escapes were often contrived . . . but the turnkeys' wives being constantly there do often prevent their villainous designs by giving timely notice to their husbands'. The keepers also contended that drinking had medicinal value and in 1787 one keeper even suggested that drunkenness improved prison discipline because 'when the prisoners are drunk, they tended to be docile and quite free from rioting'. It would also seem that the £400 annual profit from the taphouse was an important reason for the keeper to encourage insobriety.

Since dishonest publicans were a common nuisance in eighteenth-century London, it is not surprising to find that the Newgate tapsters often resorted to unscrupulous frauds to increase their profits. The City records contain numerous petitions from Newgate prisoners complaining that the tapsters served short measures, diluted the beer or charged exorbitant prices. In 1724, for instance, the tapster refused to allow visitors to bring beer into the gaol; four years later the keeper moved the prisoners out of two wards and converted them into additional taprooms. . . . The City authorities took harsh action against the Newgate tapster in 1756 after the prisoners had protested that they were forced to pay exorbitant prices for watered-down beer which tasted like 'hog-wash'. . . .

Harassed by such petty frauds, it is no wonder that many prisoners refused to buy from the prison taphouse and had their friends bring them beer and spirits. It was common to see visitors enter Newgate with several bottles and even kegs under their arms. In 1737 a turnkey recalled that one prisoner had a local public house deliver his beer in a nine-gallon cask. Twenty years earlier Captain James Forster, a prisoner in the Press Yard, had accumulated such a fine assortment of French wines that he was often visited by the keeper, William Pitt. In the end, however, this relationship turned out disastrously for Pitt when Forster made an easy escape after the keeper had got drunk and Forster had sent a turnkey into the cellar for another bottle of wine. . . . By the end of the century the Newgate prisoners had organized a sort of co-operative to supply their drinking needs. In each ward the prisoners appointed one of their own number to purchase beer, wine and spirits from local public houses in large quantities to be sold among the prisoners of the particular ward. . . .

Tippling in Newgate was not confined solely to the prisoners. In 1717 a witness recorded that 'towards evening visitors began to flock in to take a bottle . . . and comfort the distressed inhabitants of the place'; among this group were an alderman's son, several wealthy merchants and a local vicar 'all enjoying considerable drink . . . and screaming out of the windows for the turnkeys to bring more bottles'. . . . In 1725 one observer objected that the visitors to Newgate consumed 'seas of beer'; and two years later two prisoners used the riotous drinking in the taphouse to cover the noise they made as they tore a hole in the prison roof and escaped. . . .

Drunkenness was so widespread in Newgate by the latter half of the century that the prisoners actually organized a drinking society called the 'Free and Easy Club'. They devised a farcical set of by-laws which proclaimed that the society had been formed to 'promote tumult and disorder' and held regular drinking bouts or 'hops'; the prisoners sold tickets, brought in vast quantities of beer and sometimes even provided music. One keeper counted over 150 revellers at such a party not long before the drinking society was prohibited in 1808. 'No visitors shall be permitted within the prison', ordered the City authorities, 'to dance or be present at any Free and Easy Club or other meeting of persons assembled for the purpose of tippling, singing songs or gaming'.

By and large the tippling in Newgate was convivial and good-humoured but a few prisoners did become violently drunk. On at least two occasions drunken prisoners murdered prison officers. . . . [V]isitors sometimes complained that they had been robbed or molested by drunken prisoners.

At times the riotous drinking in Newgate became a public nuisance. Pedestrians were often scandalized by the obscenities shouted at them from the prison grates, especially from foul-mouthed women prisoners who 'behaved like a troop of hell-cats . . . having no place to divert themselves but at the grate joining the foot passage . . . where they swear at passers-by'. Neighbours complained that the loud noise from the taphouse kept them awake all night. In addition, anyone passing near the prison had to be on guard because the prisoners enjoyed urinating out of the windows or dousing unsuspecting citizens with excrement and dirty water from their chamber pots.

The City authorities had long recognized the unfortunate effects of drunkenness in Newgate, but their efforts to halt these excesses were futile. . . . During the eighteenth century a series of statutes aided the City's temperance campaign in Newgate. . . . According to these statutes, only beer was permitted in the gaols and it had to be brought in by friends; anyone caught smuggling spirits into prison could be prosecuted. Unfortunately, this impressive legislation was laxly enforced at Newgate and the prisoners were able to buy whatever they wanted to drink. 'We cannot restrain them', declared a keeper in 1787, 'and their friends bring in [liquor] in great quantities'. Clearly, drunkenness was the primary source of solace for Newgate prisoners who, as one sheriff put it, perceived a certain 'infamy in living and dying drunk'.

Drunkenness and carousing naturally encouraged other vices at Newgate. Tobacco and pipes were available in the taphouse so that the prison's poorly ventilated wards were choked with evil-smelling smoke. Early in the century one prisoner wrote that the gaol reeked of 'mundungus tobacco' and made him sick to his stomach. The clouds of tobacco smoke were so thick in the taphouse that the prisoners were compelled to compare the drinking room with 'Hell itself'. . . . There is also some evidence which suggests that the prisoners' careless smoking may have caused several fires at Newgate. The City authorities had made numerous attempts to prohibit smoking in the prison, but all these efforts were unsuccessful and tobacco continued to be a vital part of Newgate life. Ironically enough, some physicians argued that smoking was helpful because the tobacco smoke tended to counteract the ever-present prison stench which was thought to transmit gaol fever.

Gambling was also widespread in Newgate. In 1717 a prison officer observed that the prisoners in the Press Yard spent most of their time at cards, dice or other games. . . .

Illicit sex offered a pleasurable diversion from the rigours of Newgate and enhanced the gaol's notorious reputation. In order to prevent sexual promiscuity, the sexes at Newgate had always been separated and were to come together only during religious services. At the same time, the prison officers were charged to scrutinize all female visitors. In 1617 the Lord Mayor ordered that no female could be alone with a male prisoner 'but only his wife, daughter, sister or niece'. . . .

Such restrictions notwithstanding, overcrowding and the physical shortcomings of the prison made effective separation impossible so that the sexes intermingled freely. According to a 1643 report presented to the Aldermen, one prisoner had 'eight or nine children by one woman' in Newgate and has recently 'taken another'. During the early decades of the eighteenth century the Newgate turnkeys charged 6*d*. to allow male prisoners to enter the female chambers. Indeed, in 1702 a group from the Society for Promoting Christian Knowledge visited the gaol several times and was scandalized to see the female prisoners openly soliciting in hope of becoming pregnant so that they could 'plead their belly' and be pardoned by the justices at sessions. In 1766 a visiting cleric was shocked to enter a condemned cell and find the condemned malefactor engaged in 'wanton intercourse' with a female prisoner. Even the chapel was sometimes the scene of the prisoners' sexual misconduct. . . . As late as 1818 a member of Parliament visiting the gaol saw 'the grossest scenes in daylight'.

Such debaucheries, of course, meant a profit for the Newgate staff. Early in the century one prisoner observed that it was 'common practice' for whores to pay the officers to enter the gaol. In fact, during the years 1700–1707 William Robinson, the deputy-keeper, virtually transformed the gaol into a brothel. The City authorities learned in July 1702 that Robinson permitted 'lewd women and common strumpets . . . to constantly lay there all night'. Moreover, whores were admitted to the condemned cells where they drank all night and 'wished that God would damn King William and Parliament'. When several investigations confirmed these allegations the keeper, James Fell, vowed to halt the excesses and later assured the City officials that Robinson and his cohorts had reformed and were now 'so sensible of their former wickedness . . . that they now take the sacrament frequently'.

As it turned out, however, Robinson's rehabilitation was short-lived and in 1707 he was again in business. In July the Aldermen visited Newgate and discovered that Robinson permitted male and female felons to spend all night together for 12*d*. or 'just visit' for half that price. Once again the gaol was swarming with whores and 'these lewd women caused much disturbance because of their drinking and boisterousness at night'. Moreover, Robinson encouraged the prostitutes to bring in stolen goods and actually made the gaol a clearing house for contraband items. When confronted by the City officials, Robinson pleaded his innocence and argued that all these women were, in fact, prisoners' wives. But this story collapsed when several prisoners testified that one 'Polly Pope' must have been a bigamist since Robinson permitted her to spend the night with several prisoners. Robinson lost his post but the whoring continued at Newgate. . . .

It appears that after 1730 the officers did less procuring, but illicit sex was still available for any prisoner who was willing to pay. As late as the nineteenth century objections were raised concerning the debaucheries in Newgate. In February 1810 one prisoner testified before an Aldermanic committee that he had frequently seen the turnkeys collect a shilling from the 'common women' so that they could remain overnight. Newgate is 'much like a bagnio' concluded another prisoner, while a frequent visitor noted in 1818 that 'the depravity of the Metropolitan prison is proverbial . . . since every man is visited by a woman . . . for the purposes of general prostitution. '

Undoubtedly the ultimate source of solace in Newgate was money. Wealthy prisoners paid to make their imprisonment tolerable in the Master Side or Press Yard where they enjoyed fine meals, choice wines and other amenities. 'Those offenders who have the means of purchasing the comforts of life', observed one sheriff in 1797, 'scarcely felt . . . the horrors of prison or the inconvenience arising from confinement . . . finding it so exceedingly ameliorated and softened down by the indulgences which are granted from money'. On the other hand, indigent prisoners in the Common Side were unable to buy a comfortable life. Surrounded by squalor and apprehensive of their future, they tried to forget their troubles in sex, drunkenness and gaming, activities which only confirmed Newgate's notorious reputation.

The Devils of Toulon: Demonic Possession and Religious Politics in Eighteenth-Century Provence

B. ROBERT KREISER

In Europe of the sixteenth and seventeenth centuries, courts executed perhaps 100,000 accused witches, most of them convicted for having allegedly signed a pact with the devil to cause evil and overturn Christendom. Both intellectuals and the populace were united in proclaiming the terrible danger that witches posed; only a few skeptics dared to protest the torture and execution of those hapless women designated as Satan's agents. The witch craze in France differed from that in other parts of Europe in having a number of spectacular trials involving sorcerer-priests accused of bewitching nuns. The trials regularly concluded with notoriety for the nuns' convent and flames for the priest. In this article, B. Robert Kreiser examines the last case of such a sorcerer-priest in the southern French town of Aix in 1730– 1731. Although social historians often study aggregate groups, sometimes a case study can illuminate collective mentalities. This witchcraft trial thus exposes popu- lar beliefs and politics and helps us understand the decline of witchcraft accusations.

Like the earlier trials of the seventeenth century, this one quickly gained notoriety. It had all the necessary ingredients: an accomplished priest, a beautiful and religious girl, sexual improprieties, and the involvement of outside groups that had more than a casual interest in the outcome of the trial. Kreiser's detailed look at the forces and issues at play raises several questions. What, for example, does the Cadière-Girard affair say about the nature of popular religion? How does one explain the difference between the view, on the one hand, of the judges and other educated persons toward the lurid accusations of witchcraft and the attitude, on the other, of the populace? Why did the priest, Jean-Baptiste Girard, not burn for his alleged crimes?

On the night of 17 November 1730 and continuing for much of the next day, the streets of the Provençal port city of Toulon buzzed with excitement over news that an exorcism was in progress at the apartment of the Cadière family. The dramatic ritual was being performed in the

B. Robert Kreiser, "The Devils of Toulon: Demonic Possession and Religious Politics in Eighteenth-Century Provence," in *Church, State, and Society under the Bourbon Kings of France*, ed. Richard M. Golden (Lawrence, Kansas: Coronado Press, 1982), 173–200.

presence of numerous awestruck witnesses by the abbé François Cadière, a novice priest, over the prostrate body of his younger sister, Marie-Catherine, the alleged victim of demonic possession. Although unauthorized by the bishop of Toulon, the ceremony was conducted in general conformity with the rules prescribed in the Roman Ritual and included the recitation of long, solemn prayers, the pronunciation of words from Scripture, sprinklings with holy water, repeated signs of the cross, adjurations addressed to the devil, and invocations to God for His protection against malign powers—all designed ostensibly to drive out the demonic personality from Mlle. Cadière and deliver her from her various torments. Between spells of unconsciousness and seizures of violent convulsions, Catherine rolled about the room and spat at the crucifix in her brother's hands; her face contorted, her eyes "fixed in a piercing and unnatural stare," she burst forth with loud screams and torrents of blasphemy and obscenity which could be heard by the huge throng gathered in the streets below. Upstairs, speaking in Latin (a language Catherine did not know), the abbé Cadière asked his sister to reveal the identity of the sorcerer presumed responsible for her condition. Replying in a mixture of Latin and Provençal, in a strange, almost disembodied voice, she repeatedly declared that the source of her possession was Jean-Baptiste Girard, a well-known Jesuit priest who until two months earlier had served as her confessor and spiritual director. This dramatic public accusation, which another Cadière brother took pains to announce from the window to the crowds outside, marked the final break in the bizarre relationship which had developed between the Jesuit and his young, hitherto socially obscure female penitent and launched the notorious Cadière-Girard affair on its way to becoming a major witchcraft trial—the last such trial in French history. . . .

The Cadière-Girard relationship had not always been so strained or irregular as it must have appeared on that mid-November night in 1730 when the exorcism was under way. At the outset their relationship had been perfectly innocent and proper. . . . The highly respected Jesuit priest had arrived in Toulon in April 1728. . . . His transfer to Toulon was intended to improve the position of the Society of Jesus in that city and to win back souls from the pro-Jansenist[1] Carmelites[2] and the Oratorians,[3] the Jesuits' chief rivals in the spiritual life of Provence. Girard was at this time aged forty-eight, gaunt, physically unattractive, but with a reputation as a celebrated preacher and talented confessor who had already directed several of his previous penitents on the path toward saintliness. Catherine Cadière, eighteen years old, "ravishingly beautiful," unedu-

---

[1]Jansenism was a Catholic theological and political movement that stressed the sinfulness of man.

[2]Members of a Catholic religious order established in the twelfth century.

[3]Members of the French Oratory, a Catholic order that emphasized the training of priests in seminaries.

cated, and extremely naive and impressionable, had been raised by her widowed mother in an atmosphere of almost obsessive religiosity and rigid moral discipline. With her family's encouragement she had determined from a very young age to devote herself to an intensive regime of strict observance—a decision she repeatedly confirmed and strengthened and eventually expanded into a resolve to lead a wholly ascetic life. . . . Catherine gradually came to believe that she was an "elect soul," particularly favored in heaven, and that she had received a divine command to serve and suffer for others. Her guiding ambition was to become a saint, and in her single-minded determination to achieve this goal she assiduously studied the lives of several celebrated mystics, endeavoring to emulate, if not to surpass, their spiritual feats. Her own exemplary piety and selfless acts of charity, her frequent religious transports and remarkable gifts of prayer, lent some credence to these pretensions to divine inspiration. But it was not until the arrival of Father Girard that she finally found a director of conscience sympathetic to her spiritual aspirations.

. . . Girard was just as eager to enhance his own reputation as a "maker of saints" as Cadière was to attain recognition for her holiness. Within a short time she had become the Jesuit's star adept, singled out from among his many penitents to be the object of his special attention. She also reportedly began to display gifts and perform feats—clairvoyance, divination, levitation, stigmata—which, though later shown to be of dubious authenticity, for a long time afforded further support for her claims to saintliness. . . . Indeed, under Girard's influence and guidance Catherine's fame and popularity spread rapidly throughout Provence. Once word of her remarkable religious achievements had reached the public, the people of Toulon, believing Catherine to be truly inspired, began to venerate her as a saint and to invoke her intercession with God in order to effect a variety of cures. Many persons, including a number of Jesuits besides Girard, testified to the "salutary effects" of her "holy prayers," But no one was more taken with the saintly ecstatic than the bishop of Toulon, . . . Louis de La Tour du Pin de Montauban. Anxious for the prestige which he and his diocese would gain from the presence of a future saint, he was quick to extol Catherine's virtues, publicize her marvels, and take her under his protection. By the middle of 1730, therefore, Catherine's status as a living saint and a celebrated local heroine appeared to be quite securely established—a fact which helps to explain much of the popular support she would later receive in her legal battles with Girard.

In the meantime, however, even while Girard was promoting Catherine as a would-be saint, and enhancing his own reputation in the process, their relationship had not remained entirely innocent. According to evidence brought out by the partisans of the Cadières during the course of the trial, toward the end of 1729 (after having served some eighteen months as her confessor) Father Girard began to display an unseemly interest in his young, attractive penitent, though he managed for a long time to keep his allegedly unholy designs and his illicit behavior discreetly hidden from the outside world, even from Catherine's own family. The Cadières naturally insisted that the responsibility for initiating this affair lay completely with Girard. They claimed that Catherine had been the reluctant victim of his sexual advances, coerced into immorality against her will. They alleged, in fact, that the "wanton Jesuit" had resorted to magic and sorcery in order to seduce and corrupt his innocent, unsuspecting penitent. According to the later testimony of Mlle. Cadière herself, Girard first bewitched her in November 1729, literally casting a spell by breathing into her mouth and blowing on her forehead, "in a way that had something very peculiar about it" — an act he was said to have performed frequently in the course of the following year. From that point on Catherine was completely infatuated with her confessor. She reported feeling strange sensations whenever she was in his presence, "something like a finger moving about my entrails and making me feel quite wet." To complicate matters even further, in March 1730, when Cadière feared she had gotten pregnant — a claim that was never actually substantiated — Girard reportedly forced her to drink a potion which resulted in an abortion.

By exploiting his position as a director of conscience and perverting the holy sacrament of confession for diabolic ends — at least according to the Cadières — Girard had violated the very laws of God and thus stood charged of the crime of "spiritual incest." Worse, to justify this irregular behavior and to overcome his penitent's often-expressed misgivings about her own "evil thoughts" and "shameful immodesties," Girard allegedly had recourse to the heretical mystical doctrines of Quietism,[4] which reportedly held that an individual filled with or illuminated by the Holy Spirit could not commit a sin and which also taught the total disregard of bodily acts in achieving a complete purity of soul. When Catherine continued to display great anxiety about the extraordinary abuses and "discipline" to which Girard was daily subjecting her body, the Jesuit sought to allay her fears, repeatedly reassuring her that it was "the will of God" that she endure such "humiliation" in order to advance on the path to saintliness. "My dear child," he supposedly told her, "I want to lead you to [the highest stages of] perfection; do not be disturbed by what happens to your body; banish your scruples, your fears and doubtings. By this means, your soul will become stronger, purer, more illuminated. It will acquire a holy freedom." In their private correspondence Father Girard frequently urged Catherine, "Do not have any will of your own, and do not feel the least repugnance. Do everything I tell

---

[4]A seventeenth-century French Catholic movement, condemned by the papacy, that stressed the inadequacy of human effort. Quietism held that a person should maintain complete passivity, including indifference toward salvation, and abandon himself to God.

you, like a good [little] girl who finds nothing difficult where her father asks for [something]." This combination of Catherine's complete and utter devotion to her extremely solicitous confessor and his insistence on her obedience and submission to his "paternal" authority had come to characterize their relationship by the summer of 1730. . . .

The last year of Mlle. Cadière's association with Father Girard was also marked by the onset of classic "hysterical" symptoms. From November 1729 onward, despite periods when she experienced a sense of spiritual peace and "an abundance of divine grace," she felt persistently besieged and harassed by demons, overwhelmingly powerful discarnate forces which troubled her imagination and disturbed her every action. During these prolonged periods of torment she heard sinister voices and was assaulted by sordid visions and erotic fantasies. In addition to these hallucinations, she suffered a variety of psychomotor disturbances and fell repeatedly into ecstatic trances, during which she suddenly gave out with howlings and unwonted profanity and blasphemed against the Eucharist, the saints, and the mysteries of the faith. On occasion she displayed a complete aversion to sacred things and an inability to pray or to take part in religious exercises. For many months Girard, apparently still convinced that his penitent was a likely candidate for eventual beatification, succeeded in convincing Catherine that she was suffering from only a temporary "state of obsession," which had actually originated with God as a way of testing her commitment and her faith. He also persuaded her that she would have to endure these demonic assaults for a period of a year. Before the year was over, however, Catherine had begun to interpret her torments—and her strange relationship with Girard—in a wholly different light.

Already increasingly ambivalent in her feelings toward Girard, Mlle. Cadière had a falling-out with the Jesuit in the late summer of 1730, owing in large part to his refusal to allow her to leave the gloomy, secluded convent at Ste.-Claire d'Ollioules in which he had placed her several months earlier. In September, after Girard had attempted to transfer his penitent to another convent outside the diocese, the bishop of Toulon, Catherine's self-appointed protector, decided to place her under a new spiritual guide. On the urging of Mlle. Cadière's Dominican brother, the bishop appointed to this position Father Nicolas Girieux, a virulently anti-Jesuit Carmelite priest and a prime mover in the subsequent developments in this affair. Following the break with Father Girard and the change of confessors, Catherine began to reveal the details of her association with her former director of conscience. These stunning revelations led Father Nicolas to conclude that Catherine's sensational physical and moral afflictions went far beyond a "state of obsession" and were, in fact, incontrovertible evidence that she was actually the victim of demonic possession. He also contended that Father Girard was responsible for sending the invading spirits which had been dominating her entire personality and impelling her to act contrary to her reason and against her will. According to Father Nicolas even the marvelous feats Catherine had claimed to perform and on which her reputation for saintliness had rested very likely came not from God, but rather from the devil.

But even under Father Nicolas's spiritual direction . . . fearsome demonic torments continued to plague Mlle. Cadière. . . . By mid-October, acting with episcopal authorization, Father Nicolas had privately exorcised Catherine and two other former penitents of Father Girard, both of whom claimed to have endured states of obsession and seduction experiences similar to Mlle. Cadière's.

In the meantime, however, Girard's numerous allies had managed to convince the bishop of Toulon that Cadière and her entire family were publicity-seeking impostors and that their attempts to discredit the virtuous Girard were motivated by revenge and were all part of an anti-Jesuit plot. On 10 November, therefore, the bishop suddenly revoked the priestly powers of Father Nicolas and Father Etienne Cadière, Catherine's Dominican brother, thus setting the stage for the dramatic events which took place in the Cadière apartment only a week later.

The nature and purpose of the spectacular, unauthorized, semi-public exorcism of Catherine Cadière on 17 November now become fully intelligible. When Catherine experienced a violent "hysterical crisis" on that day, her brothers and Father Nicolas were only too anxious to exploit it. Their main object in undertaking this theatrical ritual, which they apparently staged to achieve maximum publicity, was as much to indict Girard as to dispossess Catherine. Although they no doubt hoped to effect her "disenchantment," they also wished to demonstrate, supposedly out of the mouth of the devil himself, that the Jesuit priest was a sorcerer and that he had bewitched his former penitent into immorality and blasphemy.

In the days following the exorcism, Catherine and her family lodged a formal complaint with the civil authorities and delivered a barrage of charges—sorcery, "spiritual incest," Quietism, procurement of an abortion—against Father Girard. They spoke, in particular, of the numerous spiritual and physical torments Catherine had allegedly been forced to endure for over a year at the hands of her former confessor, whom they depicted as a depraved and hypocritical voluptuary and as a vainglorious, ambitious "monster of degradation." The fantastic revelations and titillating allegations of sexual exploitation, heresy, and bewitchment provoked a sensational scandal and piqued the curiosity of countless individuals. For at least a week the crowds in the vicinity of the Cadière house were so large as to render the nearby streets virtually impassable. The exorcism had thus brought the seamy affair into public view and stimulated a great deal of idle gossip about the "satanic immorality" and "evil reputation" of Father Girard, increasingly identified in the popular mind as a suspected agent of the devil. The portrait of Girard which had already begun to emerge in the writings of several pro-Cadière polemicists came more and more to involve the highly conventional, even stylized representation of a "type": the debased, smooth-tongued sorcerer-priest, instrument of Satan and traitor to God and to his conscience—a familiar figure in the history of French witchcraft. Indeed, in preparing their stereotyped portrait of Girard, his detractors combed through the records of previous French witchcraft trials and pored over the rich demonological literature in a conscious effort to establish direct parallels between Father Girard and such notorious sorcerer-priests as Louis Gauffridy (Aix-en-Provence, 1611), Urbain Grandier (Loudun, 1634), and Thomas Boullé (Louviers, 1647), all three of whom had been convicted of and executed for crimes similar to those alleged against Girard. . . .

The fact that a highly regarded member of the Jesuit order was now under such a cloud practically guaranteed that the affair would quickly become embroiled in the contemporaneous controversies of French ecclesiastical politics. To the Jansenists, self-proclaimed champions of a pure, uncorrupted form of Christianity who were fighting for their survival after a century-long conflict with the formidable Society of Jesus, Girard's "heinous crimes" offered a welcome opportunity to launch a major assault against the dominant theological and moral position of their powerful rivals. Although they questioned Catherine's innocence in the sordid affair, certain Jansenist controversialists eagerly took up her cause as a convenient vehicle for indicting the entire Jesuit order. In their view Father Girard exemplified the longstanding moral bankruptcy of his Society, which they held ultimately responsible for his perversions; in accomplishing the disgrace of Girard, therefore, they hoped to heap discredit upon all of his fellow Jesuits as well. . . .

Forced on the defensive, Father Girard and his Jesuit colleagues fought back. While the friends and relatives of Mlle. Cadière were carrying their charges to the police lieutenant of Toulon, Girard acted to save his honor and protect his order from further embarrassment by appealing Catherine's "vicious calumnies" to his bishop. At the same time the Jesuits closed corporate ranks and brought their considerable influence to bear in an effort to stifle the entire affair. . . .

On 16 January 1731, after parallel investigations by the civil and ecclesiastical authorities in Toulon had proved inconclusive, an *arrêt du conseil*[5] transferred the entire affair to the *Parlement*[6] of Aix, in the hope—and expectation—that the sovereign court would dispose of the matter with great dispatch. In turning the case over to the Parlement, however, the government was placing it in the hands of a judicial body that could be quite fractious and even unruly, especially where issues of religious

---

[5] A decree of the king's council.

[6] A sovereign judicial court.

politics were concerned. . . . As a precaution, therefore, the government, anxious for a favorable outcome in the case, placed the actual conduct of the inquest in the hands of two magistrates who were staunch allies of the Jesuits. . . .

. . . [T]he conduct of the investigations was far from even-handed. From the outset, in fact, the authorities appear to have countenanced a host of procedural irregularities designed to favor Girard. Alleged violations of the customary investigative process as well as abuses of ecclesiastical authority were already reported to have occurred during the preliminary inquest carried out by diocesan officials in Toulon. The Cadière family charged these officials with suppressing evidence, rehearsing and prompting many witnesses, suborning others into perjury, and taking down depositions only from persons who were predisposed to defend the conduct of Father Girard. Individual whom Mlle. Cadière called to testify on her behalf were faced with threats of reprisals; those who persisted in giving testimony later discovered that their remarks had not even been entered into the record. Several other former penitents of Girard who came forward to corroborate Catherine's allegations against the Jesuit faced harassment and intimidation. . . .

. . . Throughout the diocesan hearings and during the subsequent parlementary investigations, Catherine was treated as though she, and not Girard, were the accused. The authorities kept her interned in convents under Jesuit control, refused to allow visits from her family, and denied her access to a confessor of her own choosing. The *commissaires*[7] assigned to the Parlement's inquest subjected her to a series of relentless interrogations and allegedly went so far as to extort from Catherine a drug-induced retraction of all the charges pending against Father Girard. When she later withdrew the retraction, they reportedly threatened her with various forms of judicial torture if she did not recant. Even with all the official efforts at browbeating and coercion, she would manage to persist in her original accusations to the end of the trial. As for Girard, despite the seriousness of the allegations made against him, he not only remained free during most of the inquest, but was also allowed to perform his various priestly duties unimpeded. . . .

While the authorities did everything within their power to influence the proceedings, Girard's lawyers also mounted a strong counterattack on the Jesuit's behalf, categorically denying as unsubstantiated all the charges pending against him. They depicted Girard as a honorable priest of solid faith, exemplary virtue, and saintly piety—a far cry from the monster of degradation portrayed by the Cadières. His only faults during his two years as Catherine's director of conscience, they contended, had been an imprudent excess of credulity and zeal, as a result of which he had failed to act quickly and decisively to disabuse his penitent of

[7]Commissioners.

her monstrous delusions or to stifle her overwrought sensuality. His accusers, by contrast, were vengeful partisans and conniving schemers, who had deliberately distorted and even fabricated evidence, with the aim of publicly dishonoring the name and defaming the character of Father Girard. The Jesuit's partisans charged Catherine with having faked and cynically manipulated the various "supernatural" phenomena she had earlier claimed in trying to pass herself off as a saint. . . . In fact, they insisted, the charges of sorcery and bewitchment which the Cadières had brought against the maligned Girard were a tissue of lies and absurd inventions, designed to deflect attention from Catherine's own misdeeds and indiscretions. As for her exorcism, that had been staged by Catherine's brothers, who had carefully rehearsed their sister to act out a role, counterfeiting the signs of possession in conscious imitation of several notorious demoniacs before her.

Confronted by these countercharges, polemicists and lawyers on the Cadière side replied with a torrent of impassioned pamphlets and legal briefs of their own. Dozens of such works appeared in 1731 and served to arouse a general revulsion against Girard and the Jesuits and gave new life to the Jansenist cause. . . . Where the pamphleteers left off, the clever song writers and crude versifiers joined the fray, endlessly repeating one another in their caustic vilification of Girard and derisively chanting of his imminent conviction. Verses, epigrams, and songs circulated in manuscript and in print, frequently accompanied by explicitly pornographic *estampes*.[8] At the same time, the rumor mills were grinding out lurid stories about Father Girard's allegedly scandal-ridden past. A proliferation of allegorical fables and scurrilous lampoons contributed further to Girard's disgrace. Like some of the tracts, many of these other propaganda pieces exploited the theme of Girard as a sorcerer-priest and played on popular fears of the devil and of demonic forces operating in the world.

Where public opinion was concerned, the pro-Cadière propagandists seem to have correctly gauged the mood and temper of the time. If most of those in positions of authority favored Girard, the Cadière side could count on increasingly strong and vocal support from other levels of society, especially from among the *menu peuple*,[9] many of whom had come to revere Catherine as a saint. In taking their case to the streets, therefore, the proponents of Mlle. Cadiére found an extremely receptive audience, only too eager to rally to her cause. The people of Provence had been following the trial very closely and were ready to believe the allegations made against Father Girard, particularly those which portrayed the Jesuit as an instrument of Satan. Throughout the spring and summer of 1731 they held frequent demonstrations to show solidarity with their

[8]Prints.
[9]The "little people," the common people.

beleaguered saint and to express their indignation at Girard, whom they repeatedly denounced as a scoundrel, a devil, and a sorcerer. . . . By the end of August 1731 most of Provençal society, from the great *gens de qualité*[10] to the lowliest of the laboring poor, was caught up in the furious debates. With almost everyone forced to take sides, it became virtually impossible to remain neutral. What is more, growing agitation on behalf of Mlle. Cadière had begun to have an important impact on the conduct of the trial, as Catherine's ardent supporters came increasingly to look to the judges in the Parlement of Aix to save her and punish the accused sorcerer—already convicted in the court of public opinion.

It was in this highly volatile, intensely partisan atmosphere that the Parlement of Aix attempted to conduct its deliberations. . . . So sharp were the divisions and so heated were the discussions that several sessions erupted into shouting matches; some especially zealous and short-tempered magistrates traded insults with each other, and on more than one occasion a few judges almost came to blows. . . .

Similar tensions and differences of opinion existed within the *parquet*,[11] whose five members had responsibility for reviewing the collected evidence, determining guilt or innocence, and proposing appropriate penalties. . . . On 11 September 1731, speaking for a majority of three, the *procureur-général*,[12] Boyer d'Aiguilles, delivered a stunning pronouncement. He recommended that the court find Catherine Cadière, the initiator of the original complaint, guilty of false accusations, calumnious slander, abuses of religion, profanations of the faith, and the feigning of saintliness and possession—all the charges which Father Girard, the accused, had levelled against her. . . . Boyer further proposed that Catherine be subjected to "the question,"[13] both "ordinary" and "extraordinary," in order "to extract the complete truth concerning her accomplices," and that she then be turned over to the public executioner for hanging. Boyer also recommended a series of lesser punishments for the Cadière brothers, Father Nicolas, and Catherine's *avocat*,[14] Chaudon. Concerning the fate of Girard, the *procureur-général* was completely silent. After publishing his conclusions, he turned over the case to the *Grand'Chambre*[15] for final review and adjudication. A tumultuous four weeks were to pass—including final interrogations of and confrontations between Cadière and Girard—before the court was to deliver its verdict. . . .

. . . Fearing the worst, many of her partisans began pouring into

[10]People of quality.

[11]The collective name for the king's representatives in Parlement.

[12]The Attorney General, the king's primary representative in Parlement.

[13]Torture. "Extraordinary" was more intense than "ordinary" torture.

[14]"Advocate" or barrister.

[15]The most important chamber of the Parlement.

Aix from all over Provence to protest the *parquet*'s conclusions and to mount a campaign to dissuade the magistrates in the *Grand'Chambre* from upholding the *procureur-général*'s judgment. Some particularly ardent supporters, meanwhile, were even preparing to take up arms to save Catherine if that became necessary. With emotions and public suspicions running higher every day, rumors of Jesuit intrigues and plots were rampant. Reports began circulating that the Jesuits were planning to poison Father Girard and kidnap Mlle. Cadière in order to put an immediate end to the whole affair. Though unfounded, such reports prompted some of Catherine's alarmed partisans to establish an around-the-clock vigil near the convent in which she was being held captive. Any member of the Jesuit order seen on the streets could expect to be insulted, threatened, or even beaten.

On 10 October, the day the Parlement was at last to render its verdict, the magistrates of the *Grand'Chambre* entered the Palais de Justice[16] around 7:00 a.m. Even as the judges were filing into the court, huge, noisy, increasingly restive crowds, no doubt hopeful of influencing the Parlement's deliberations, had begun to gather in the public square outside. . . . The judges finally published their verdict just before nightfall. And a confusing and paradoxical verdict it was! To begin with, none of the magistrates, not even the most ardent partisans of the Jesuits, was prepared to follow the harsh conclusions of the *procureur-général*. But beyond general agreement on that point, the judges voting on the case were sharply divided. Twelve held that Father Girard should be burned and Catherine Cadière released; twelve others voted to acquit the Jesuit while condemning his former penitent to penalties ranging from two years confinement in a convent to life imprisonment. Forced to break the tie and cast the deciding vote, First President Lebret (who was also the intendant[17] of Provence) determined on what essentially amounted to a double acquittal, returning Girard to the ecclesiastical authorities for judgment of his irregular conduct as a priest and sending Mlle. Cadière back to her mother. The court voted to drop the charges against Father Nicolas and the brothers Cadière, though the Cadière family was left to pay all court costs.

The Parlement rendered its verdict without publicly commenting on any of the various charges which had been raised during the course of the trial. It is nevertheless clear that, at least where Girard was concerned, the decision as to his guilt or innocence rested not on the accusations of demonopathic sorcery, but rather on the charges of priestly malfeasance. Indeed, the allegations of sorcery and bewitchment, which had seemed so central to the case against the Jesuit (at least in the public's mind), did not even figure in the court's final deliberations, since the judges,

---

[16]The Palace of Justice, the seat of the Parlement.

[17]The chief royal agent in a province.

adhering to strict standards of evidence, and skeptical about charges that were predicated on the unacceptable premise of diabolic intervention or possession by an evil spirit, set them aside as not proved. Even among the dozen magistrates who voted to convict Girard there was no willingness to give any credence to these charges, which several of the pro-Cadière jurists openly disparaged. In declining to sanction the accusations of sorcery and possession, the court was explicitly acknowledging its acceptance of the royal edict of 1682. That decree, which was designed to establish judicial uniformity throughout the kingdom for such alleged offenses, had marked the monarchy's official abandonment of criminal prosecutions for witchcraft. It was this point of view which the Parlement's verdict of 10 October 1731 had thus reaffirmed.

But the announcement of the court's highly equivocal verdict produced a mixed reaction. The decision satisfied neither the Jesuit partisans of Father Girard, eager to see their colleague completely exonerated and his accusers convicted for their "vicious calumnies," nor the supporters of Catherine Cadière, convinced of their saintly heroine's total innocence and equally certain of Girard's guilt. To be sure, the allies of Mlle. Cadière, having come to expect that her execution might be imminent, were overjoyed at her acquittal. The crowds stationed outside the Parlement burst into loud applause for the twelve judges who had voted to set her free and raised her lawyer on their shoulders in triumph. When Catherine was released from her convent prison, hundreds of her supporters rushed to touch and embrace her or to kiss the hem of her dress. Others had to be satisfied with catching only a glimpse of their heroine as she was escorted through the streets of Aix. Similar celebrations went on in every corner of Provence. But the indignation many of Catherine's adherents felt over Girard's virtual acquittal soon overcame much of the joy they experienced on hearing of her release.

All over France—and beyond—pamphleteers and songwriters joined in the chorus of criticism. . . . The protests sometimes became quite unruly. In Aix crowds of Cadière's supporters hurled rocks at the carriages of pro-Girard magistrates and hooted and jeered at Girard himself when he appeared in public for the first time in months. In Toulon the local agitation went on for three days and nights. Effigies of Father Girard were dressed to represent the figure of the devil, paraded around town, and then burned in a spectacular ceremony. Royal troops had to be called in to prevent one aggressive mob from setting fire to a Jesuit religious house. Similar acts of vandalism and minor riots occurred throughout Provence. This violent behavior served not only as a means of venting the public's anger at the Parlement's "craven action" in allowing Girard to go unpunished, but also as a ritualized expression of popular justice and as a symbolic purging of the demonic influences and polluting elements in their midst; for to their way of thinking the court's release of the Jesuit priest had let loose on the community a potentially dangerous sorcerer.

In an effort to quell these disturbances the intendant Lebret ordered a regiment of royal troops into Aix. In addition, he secured scores of *lettres de cachet*[18] which authorized the arrest or exile of Cadière partisans in Toulon, Aix, and Marseille, including a significant number of magistrates, lawyers, merchants, and clergy. Others suffered the loss of royal pensions. The harshest treatment was reserved for members of the Cadière family, all of whom were subjected to intense persecution and harassment. Catherine herself, within a short time of her release, had been ordered to leave the city of Aix at once or face arrest. From that day on she mysteriously disappeared from sight, never to be heard from again.

As for Father Girard, he made haste to escape from Provence entirely. . . . [H]e retired to his native Dôle in February 1732. That same month the ecclesiastical authorities in Toulon formally absolved him of all the crimes imputed to him. In the meantime, the Jesuits, determined on a clear-cut vindication, had embarked on a vigorous campaign to rehabilitate the reputation of Girard and refurbish the image of the Society of Jesus. Several writers concentrated their efforts on extolling Girard's heretofore neglected merits. One apologist went so far as to compare Father Girard to Jesus Christ, since they had both allegedly suffered similar trials and tribulations. By the time Girard died, on 4 July 1733, allegedly in "the odor of sanctity," his colleagues already deemed him worthy of veneration as a future saint and were even preparing to propose him for beatification. In the long run, however, their efforts proved unsuccessful.

Although the authorities had managed to restore relative calm in Aix and Toulon by the end of 1732, the memory of the Cadière-Girard affair would linger on long after all the protagonists in the case had passed from the scene. Despite Girard's apparent "rehabilitation" the notorious scandal had badly tarnished the image and reputation of the Society of Jesus and would continue to plague the order until its expulsion from France in 1764. No amount of influence, corporate solidarity, or casuistry had been able to deliver the Jesuits from the embarrassment, popular distrust, and increasingly low public esteem which their colleague's alleged improprieties had brought them. In large part this situation resulted from the fact that the Jansenists had conducted a very successful campaign to exploit this episode to their own advantage. . . . Portraying Mlle. Cadière—and themselves—as innocent victims of injustice and arbitrary authority, they managed not only to mobilize public opinion behind her, but at the same time to attract considerable popular support for their own cause as well. In the process they contributed much to bringing the larger debates of religious politics within the public's purview and to raising the political consciousness of

---

[18]Sealed letters addressed to private persons that usually ordered imprisonment or banishment.

groups and individuals who were not ordinarily or traditionally "political."

The Cadière-Girard affair . . . thus reveals the deep divisions which were beginning to rend the very fabric of the Gallican Church and which were to undermine public respect for and confidence in the established authorities. Equally important, however, the Cadière-Girard case also discloses the growing cultural cleavage in early eighteenth-century France between the two traditions of belief in witchcraft, the popular and the learned, whose convergence in the late Middle Ages had been a significant precondition of the great sixteenth- and seventeenth-century witch hunts. Since the mid-seventeenth century an increasing proportion of the educated had come to display a more sophisticated understanding of and a greater sensitivity to the basic psychological and physiological processes which lay behind the unusual manifestations and abnormal organic and mental states displayed by Catherine Cadière and others. Ever greater numbers of learned doctors, lawyers, judges, philosophers, and theologians were directly challenging the very notions of sorcery and demonic possession, ascribing the strange phenomena and deviant behaviors which were usually associated with diabolic intrusions to various natural causes: hysterical passions, vapors, melancholia, derangement, insufficiently controlled imagination, or pure trickery. For these critics the alleged demoniac was more in need of medical attendance and/or incarceration than exorcism or the prayers of the Church. Although their "natural" explanations remained tentative and uncertain, their vision of the world and of man had reduced dramatically, if not completely, the domain of the supernatural.

But this "structural change in human mentality" among the learned elite still had not, of course, penetrated to the uneducated masses. While skepticism was becoming the dominant view among the educated, popular mental structures and traditional habits of belief remained essentially untouched. The terrifying fantasies and hallucinations reported by Catherine Cadière made a strong impression on these people, for whom the world was still dominated by innumerable benign and malevolent forces. Intervention by unseen powers in the natural order of things remained for them an ever-present reality and a constant source of apprehension. Along with their belief in the devil's continual surveillance over and intrusion in their daily lives, they continued to place great credence in the reality of human witches and sorcerers who willfully chose to act as agents of a lustful, destructive devil in order to cause the possession of their helpless victims. For the people of Provence the traditional stereotype of the sorcerer-priest was still very much alive, and they were thus quite prepared to believe that Jean-Baptiste Girard had had "commerce with demons" and ought therefore to have been executed for his despicable and dangerous crimes. But despite the tenacity and continued vitality of these traditional beliefs, especially among the unlettered, the view embodied in the royal edict of 1682 was the one which came to prevail.

Even more than the declaration of 1682, however, it was the Cadière-Girard case which, as the first (and only) major test of this decree . . . , clearly marks the end of witchcraft as a justiciable crime. The refusal of the Parlement of Aix to convict Father Girard for sorcery and bewitchment, and its outright dismissal of these charges as not proved and not credible, reaffirmed the official view—gaining strength since at least the middle of the seventeenth century—that witchcraft no longer represented a threat to the established religious, political, or social order. In the last analysis, it is far less important whether Girard was actually guilty of any of the numerous crimes of which he stood accused or, for that matter, whether he died "in the odor of sanctity" or in disgrace. What is significant is that, unlike Urbain Grandier and other accused sorcerer-priests of the previous century, Jean-Baptiste Girard died in his bed, and not at the stake.

Death's Arbitrary Empire

JOHN McMANNERS

The eighteenth century is known as the Enlightenment, the Age of Reason, or the Age of Voltaire. John McManners reveals the underside of that epoch of cultural achievement, a world where, for most people, death triumphed early. When McManners reviews the history of eighteenth-century France in terms of medicine, disease, and mortality, he finds ill health, violence, and misery to have been as characteristic of the age as enlightened reason and Voltarian wit.

How long could one expect to live in the eighteenth century? The high rate of infant mortality was the primary reason for such a low life expectancy. Why did so many infants and children die? Did people do all they could to ensure their children's health and long lives? Orphans were less likely to survive childhood than any other group. The presence of orphanages suggests that society attempted to care for orphans. If that is true, why did so many die so young?

Which diseases were most deadly? McManners paints a bleak picture of physicians and their ability to treat illness and disease. Why were medical doctors so ineffective? Surely we can not place the blame on physicians, for their patients, even in the best of times, were models of poor health. Living conditions in towns (such as overcrowding and the lack of sanitation), an insufficient and poor diet, the dangers of the workplace, even the clothing, all made people easy prey for disease. And where could one be safe? Not in an institution, for hospitals, army barracks, and asylums, for example, were dangerous places.

Nothing, not even youth and robust health, could give security from suffering or early death, for eighteenth-century France was a violent society. Highwaymen, domestic violence, wild animals, and rural conflicts were omnipresent. Often hungry, cold, sick, and frightened by forces seemingly beyond their control, the overwhelming majority of people had little time to marvel at Voltaire's wit.

In eighteenth-century France, 'death was at the centre of life as the graveyard was at the centre of the village'. Speaking in averages, and confounding in one the diversity of the whole country and the fortunes of all classes, we find that something like a quarter of all babies born in the early years of the century died before reaching their first birthday, and another quarter before reaching the age of eight. Of every 1,000 infants, only 200 would go on to the age of fifty, and only 100 to the

John McManners, *Death and the Enlightenment* (Cambridge, Engl.: Oxford University Press, 1981), 5–23.

age of seventy. A man who had beaten the odds and reached his half-century would, we may imagine, have seen both his parents die, have buried half his children and, like as not, his wife as well, together with numerous uncles, aunts, cousins, nephews, nieces, and friends. If he got to seventy, he would have no relations and friends of his own generation left to share his memories. If this is a description of the average, what can we say of the unfortunates whose sombre ill luck weights down the figures to this mean? . . .

A new understanding of the eighteenth century comes to us when we review its history in terms of disease and mortality. In narrow fetid streets and airless tenements, in filthy windowless hovels, in middens and privies, in undrained pools and steaming marshes, in contaminated wells and streams—and, for that matter, in the gilded corridors of Versailles, where excrement accumulated—infections of every kind lurked. The files of the administrators, more especially those of the Royal Society of Medicine at the end of the *ancien régime*,[1]Old Régime, the period before the French Revolution of 1789. are full of information sent in by medical experts about local epidemics and peculiar illnesses, but it is often difficult to deduce from their accounts what the specific diseases were. They spoke essentially of symptoms. Fevers were 'bilious', 'putrid', 'autumnal', 'red', 'purple', 'intermittent', 'malignant', 'inflammatory'. The spitting of blood so often mentioned could have been the result of cancer of lungs or larynx, infection of the trachea, or pulmonary tuberculosis; their 'scurvy', deduced from bleeding gums and painful joints, could include arthritis and pyorrhoea. An autopsy frequently produced a report of 'worms' in lungs or stomach, without any other evidence to bring precision. . . . 'With their bodies assaulted on all sides, these people were carried off before the more subtle disorders had a chance to strike.' The main killers were influenza and pulmonary infections, malaria, typhoid, typhus, dysentery, and smallpox, striking in waves across a debilitating pattern of routine afflictions—mange, skin disorders, gout, epilepsy. The grimmest scourge of all was smallpox, which seems to have become a more common and more virulent disease from the late seventeenth century. A doctor of Montpellier in 1756 described it as being 'everywhere', as it were 'naturalized' and 'domesticated', especially at Paris, 'where it never relaxes its grip'. . . . Not surprisingly, then, the army records on new recruits continually speak of marked faces. . . . This was, indeed, a disease which destroyed the beauty of so many of those it did not slay. . . .

. . . There were two seasons when mortality was at its highest, winter and early spring on one hand, and autumn, especially the month of September, on the other. In some places, winter was the cruellest season,

---

[1]Old Régime, the period before the French Revolution of 1789.

in others autumn. From December to March, pneumonia and pulmonary afflictions abounded, and the sheer cold took its toll of those who were ill-clothed and lacked the means to keep warm. And these were numerous. Wood was in short supply in the cereal-growing plains and in the cities. Heating arrangements were rudimentary; even in Versailles, wine froze at the royal table in winter, and the heavily padded and decorated coats of courtiers were not just for display. Clothing passed from upper to lower classes and from older to younger generations, getting more and more threadbare on its journey. The poorer streets of cities were a motley pageant of rags, anonymous or with prestigious social origins. There were peasants who never changed their linen, and when they discarded it, it was too worn to be sent to the papermills. Even the more prosperous peasants . . . made do with two shirts and two coats a year, and a cloak every five. There was not much in the wardrobe to keep them warm and dry in the snow or rain of winter. In August, September, and October, dysentery would strike, and before illnesses encouraged by the excessive heat had declined, there would come the onset of those which flourished in the ensuing dampness. . . . These were fevers—malaria (coming, as contemporaries noted, with the floods), typhoid, and 'purple fever' which was often confused with the ubiquitous scarlatina or measles. Generally, it was adults, especially the aged, who succumbed in winter, and the younger children in the autumn—though there were exceptions: the cold in some places carried off more babies under the age of one than the intestinal infections of the hotter weather. Superimposed upon this yearly cycle of menace was the arbitrary onslaught of great epidemics, sometimes driving the death rate up to double and treble the monthly average; there was the dysentery in Anjou in 1707 and 1779, highly infectious and lethal within two or three days, the influenza in the same province which caused devastation in 1740, the typhoid and enteric fever in Brittany from 1758 onwards which was largely responsible for reducing the population of that province by 4 per cent; there were more localized outbreaks, like the military fever in Pamiers in 1782 which killed 800 people.

Being born was a hazardous business for both mother and child. 'Don't get pregnant and don't catch smallpox' was Mme de Sévigné's[2] advice to her married daughter . . . although she had only simple ideas of how to avoid either. The proverbial pride in pregnancy of primitive societies was overwhelmed, in eighteenth-century France, by fear. Medical manuals considered a pregnant woman to be suffering from an illness, and even cited Scripture in ascribing the pains of childbirth to the transgression of Eve. Many women, especially those of the poorer classes, came to their ordeal in wretched health, and the prevalence of rickets

[2]Famous writer of letters, 1626–1696.

caused deformities which made delivery difficult. There were hardly any hygienic precautions, the technique for arresting haemorrhages was not yet developed, and the manipulation of forceps (supposed to be limited to qualified surgeons alone) was clumsy. Until the reign of Louis XVI, there was hardly any attempt to train midwives. In reporting to their bishops or to the secular authorities, parish priests described how the office of midwife came to be filled in their parish. . . . A *curé*[3] in the diocese of Boulogne in 1725 said that his midwife inherited the job from her mother—'the women have a reasonable amount of confidence in her.' Another *curé* said that 'ours has worked here for thirty years: she took up the office of her own accord, the women of the parish accepted her, and it has not been thought fitting to oblige her to undergo further training.' Horror stories about midwives abound—beating on the stomach to 'hasten delivery', cutting the umbilical cord too close or failing to tie it, forgetting the placenta, crippling babies by rough handling, and—even—showing off by turning the infant round so that the feet emerged first. Louis XIV made a clean break with tradition when he called in a man, the surgeon Jacques Clément, to the *accouchement*[4] of the Dauphine in 1686. . . . But were surgeons much more use than midwives? Clément bled his patient, wrapped her in the skin of a newly flayed sheep, and kept her in a dark room for nine days without so much as a single candle. And how good was the gynaecologist whose advertisement in Paris has been preserved as a curiosity?—'Montodon, ci-devant pâtisseur, boulevard Bonne Nouvelle, est actuellement chirurgien et accoucher.'[5] In fact, there was little that even the most expert practitioner could do if things went wrong. If the baby's head stuck, there would be a week of agony and the vileness of gangrene before inevitable death. The Caesarian section without anaesthetics left one chance in a thousand for the women. . . . Many babies were stillborn, or died within a few days, or were maimed for life. A memoir to an intendant in 1773 describes young people coming out of a parish mass, marked by inexpert deliveries—atrophied, hunchbacked, deaf, blind, one-eyed, bandy-legged, bloodshot of eye, lame and twisted, hare-lipped, 'almost useless to society and fated for a premature end'. Many women too were killed, or crippled, or mentally scarred; a *curé* blames the rise of contraceptive practices in his parish on the neurotic determination of so many women never to undergo the experience of childbirth again.

. . . Between 20 and 30 per cent of babies born died in their first year: in a particularly wretched hamlet in the early part of the century,

[3]Chief parish priest.

[4]Parturition.

[5]Montodon, former pastry-cook, boulevard Bonne Nouvelle, is currently a surgeon and obstetrician.

over 32 per cent died in their first year and over 22 per cent in their second. There were, of course, healthy and unhealthy areas, depending on the peculiar combination of advantages and disadvantages in food supplies, geographical features, and climate. The national average in the eighteenth century for children surviving to the age of ten was, roughly, 55 per cent; at Crulai in Normandy it was 65 per cent; in poverty-striken villages amidst the stagnant malarial pools of the Sologne or of the Mediterranean littoral, it was 40 per cent. . . . The deadly season of the year for infants was early autumn, when heat, humidity and flies, and unhygienic ways of living brought the intestinal infections for which no remedy was known. These visitations were facilitated by the custom, prevalent among richer people and town dwellers, of sending infants away to be nursed by foster mothers. Towards the end of the century, of the 21,000 babies born each year in Paris, only 1,000 were fed by their mothers, another 1,000 by wet-nurses brought into the home, 2,000 to 3,000 were sent to places near the city, and the rest to more distant localities—concentric circles within which the proportion of deaths became higher as the distance from home increased. . . . For families of the urban working class, like small shopkeepers or the silk workers of Lyon, it was an economic necessity to get the wife back to counter or loom quickly. For the leisured class, a satisfactory explanation is harder to find; a certain harshness of mind, an unwillingness to become too attached to a pathetic bundle whose chances of survival were so limited, the desire to resume sexual relationships as soon as possible, the belief that loss of milk diluted the quality of the blood of the mother, a reliance on the therapeutic qualities of country air to give the baby a good start or (very doubtfully) some subconscious reaction against an infant's 'oral sadism'—whatever the reasons, a compelling social custom had arisen. In 1774, a reformer, appealing to have children 'brought up in the order of Nature', described the sensation when a mother declares her intention of breast-feeding her first child: protests from her parents, and all the ladies lamenting to see her risking her life for a new-fashioned theory. Given the demand, around the cities a wet-nursing 'industry' had arisen. In some villages near Limoges, girls married earlier to qualify. Such glimpses as we get of this peculiar interchange between town and country show an unfeeling and mercenary world—women who take on two or three babies in addition to their own, knowing that there will be competition for survival, who go on drawing their pay when they know their milk is drying up and their client's infant will have no chance. . . . These practitioners are preying on legitimate children, with parents to look after their interests and hoping against hope that they will be trundled back home in nine months' time. What then of the illegitimate ones, the multitude of foundlings, the *enfants trouvés*?[6]

[6]Orphans, foundlings.

The fate of these unhappy infants throws a harsh, cold light on the cruel underside of the century of crystalline wit and rococo delicacy. Increasing numbers of children were being abandoned. An average of 2,000 a year came to the Enfants Trouvés of Paris in the 1720s, rising to a record total of 7,676 in 1772; thereafter, royal edicts forbade the bringing-in of foundlings from the provinces, and the Parisian total stabilized at about 5,800 a year. In Bordeaux at the mid-century, there were about 300 admissions annually; in Metz, in the winter of 1776, no less than 900. . . . These numbers swamped the organizational abilities of the *ancien régime*, . . . and the hopeless problem they presented deadened the charitable instincts of those who cared. A Genevan doctor reports a nun of the Parisian foundling hospital taking refuge in the reflection that these innocent souls would go straight to eternal bliss, since the revenues of her institution could not feed any more of them anyway. There was a prejudice against making immoral conduct easier by spending money on those 'unhappy fruits of debauchery' (though it is true that some children were abandoned by married parents who were too poor to maintain them). Many illegitimate children were doomed before ever they reached the shelter of an institution—physically impaired by the mother's attempts to conceal her pregnancy or to produce an abortion, infected with venereal disease, or hopelessly weakened by a journey from some distant place, crowded in baskets on the back of a donkey, or of a porter travelling on foot, or jolting in a wagon. The infants who got through the crucial first week in which so many died had to survive the grim and crowded conditions in the hospital, and the rigours of the system of putting out to nurse (with private families paying more to pre-empt the healthiest and most reliable foster mothers). Only one foundling in ten lived to reach the age of ten: nine had perished. Such survivors as there were would live gloomily learning a trade in some institution full of prostitutes, layabouts, and madmen, or in some ruthlessly disciplined orphanage; a very few might be found again by their parents or left with some sympathetic country family—but the chances of a decent existence were infinitesimal. One who did get through the hazards and succeeded was the *philosophe* and mathematician d'Alembert,[7] left as an infant on the steps of the church of Saint-Jean-la-Ronde. An expert on the calculus of probabilities, he must often have reflected on the odds that he had beaten.

Driven to despair by poverty, some parents abandoned their children: there were suspicions that others did not strive officiously to keep them alive. The synodal statutes of various dioceses ordered the *curés* to warn their flocks against the dangerous practice of putting children to sleep in the beds of their parents, where so often they were suffocated. . . . A surgeon described the injuries suffered by babies in the

[7]Jean le Rond d'Alembert, 1713–1783.

vineyard country around Reims: while their mothers toiled among the vines they were sometimes attacked by animals—eyes pecked by turkeys, hands eaten off by pigs. And for the healthy grown-up, the ordinary routines of life were precarious. Society was ill-policed, unable to take effective measures to suppress highwaymen and discipline vagabonds. Rural life was violent. Wife-beating was common. Unpopular *curés* were kept awake by nocturnal *tapages*[8] which could degenerate into riots. There were affrays with cudgels and clubs at fairs. In Languedoc, where the hunting rights of the lords had been bought off, peasants went around with guns; poachers returned the fire of gamekeepers; and pot-shots were taken at *seigneurs*[9] and other unpopular local worthies. The youths of villages were organized, quasi-officially, into bands, the *'garçons de paroisse'*,[10] who fought pitched battles with those from other places at fairs, marriages, and the draw for the *milice*,[11] or when communities quarrelled over boundaries or grazing rights. . . . In towns, the police force was inadequate to maintain order at festivals or to organize precautions against accidents. A panic at the fireworks in Paris for the marriage of the Dauphin in 1770 led to more than 1,000 being trampled to death; two years later, the great fire at the Hôtel-Dieu claimed many victims. There were, indeed, few precautions against fire—for long the only Parisian fire brigade was the Capuchin friars, swarming into action in frocks and cowls, with axes and ladders. Narrow streets, ramshackle buildings, and an abundance of wooden construction made the old parts of cities hopelessly vulnerable, tinder dry in summer, and underpinned with extra fuel in winter when the cellars of the rich were crammed with firewood and grain. . . . Buildings, especially the parish churches for whose maintenance a local rate had to be levied, were often left unrepaired and dangerous; every year there were floods from unbanked rivers, wreaking devastation and leaving legacies of fever. In the streets and in the countryside, savage dogs, some with rabies, wandered; in remote areas wolf packs hunted—there was a government bounty for each one killed, the parish priest to issue a certificate on the production of the ears; in 1750, 126 were killed in the province of Anjou alone. Our modern concept of 'accident' as some technical failure—burnt-out wire, slipping flange, broken lever—obtruding into well-organized habitual comfort, was almost unknown in the eighteenth century. Life was hazardous throughout. . . .

Up to the last two decades of the *ancien régime*, hardly anything was done to regulate dangerous trades or to prevent industrial accidents. . . . Even so, though nothing was being done, contemporaries

[8]Rows.
[9]Lords.
[10]Boys of the parish.
[11]Militia.

were becoming aware of the terrifying hardships which crippled industrial workers and abbreviated their lives. . . . Conditions in French mines
were grim enough: twelve hours a day underground, in continual danger from explosions (because fires were burning to suck air along
the galleries) and from flooding (if the horse-turned pumps failed).
The workers who polished mirrors, their feet continually in water
and hands continually getting cut, were worn out by the interminable pushing to and fro of the heavy weight; printers received
fractures and bruises from the levers of their presses; candle
makers stifled in the heat around the furnaces; hemp crushers
invariably got asthma; gilders became dizzy within a few months
from the mercurial fumes which eventually poisoned them; workers who handled unwashed wool were recognizable by their pale and
leaden countenances, upon which would be superimposed the permanent stains of the colours used in dyeing. Alarming examples of the effect
of bad conditions of working and living on mortality rates can be studied
in the armed forces. In war, few sailors were killed by cannon-balls. The
seventy-four-gun ship *Ajax* patrolled in the Atlantic and Indian Oceans
from February 1780 to June 1784; during that period 228 of her crew of
430 died. Battle accounted for only thirty (and of these half perished from
the explosion of one of the ship's own cannon); nine were drowned . . . ;
no less than 185 were killed by diseases: scurvy, dysentery, malaria—
infections that ran riot among men cooped below decks for most of their
time afloat, and living on food lacking in indispensable vitamins. . . . It
could be said that war killed soldiers, but essentially indirectly. The mortality rate in a particular regiment from 1716 to 1749 was five times higher
in war years than in those of peace, but the deaths occurred principally
from December to April, when the troops were in winter quarters. In
the barracks built in the eighteenth century (always at the expense of
the local authorities, not of the Crown), the standard size for a room
was 16 by 18 feet, to contain thirteen to fifteen men crammed into four
or five beds. These stifling conditions, rampant epidemics, the cold outside, and venereal disease killed many more in winter quarters than the
shot and steel of the enemy in the summer campaigning season. It was a
rule under the *ancien régime* that life in State institutions was abbreviated.
When *dépôts de mendicité*[12] were set up in 1767 to clear vagabonds off the
roads, the inmates died off rapidly. . . . At Rennes, of 600 initially arrested, 137 died within a year, though it is true there were a lot of infections
about at the time. At Saint-Denis, the death rate in the *dépôt* was consistently double that for the town, not excepting the high infant mortality
from the latter total.

. . . [D]eath was not without deference to rank and possessions, to
the well-to-do with their log fires, warm clothing, protein diet, and

[12]Workhouses.

spacious houses. . . . True, in this age of multitudinous servants, it was difficult to erect effective barriers of unofficial quarantine—in the last resort, infections got through. . . . No doubt there were special afflictions to descend upon the self-indulgent; moralists (with some injustice to the sufferers) liked to instance apoplexy, paralysis, and gout. Cynics would add the dangers from the medical profession; the peasant, who distrusted blood-letting and could not afford to pay the surgeon to do it, was at least free from his attentions. Even so, the life expectancy of the rich was much better than that of the poor, and the men of the eighteenth century knew it. In statistical terms, we might guess that the advantage was something like ten years above the average and seventeen years above that of the very poor. Peasants, living crowded together in single-roomed cottages, were very vulnerable, and even more so were the poor of the towns, whose debilitating conditions of working were allied to crowded, insanitary accommodation. Disease spread quickly where there was only one bed for a family. A doctor in the countryside complained of the way in which people 'occupy the beds of those who are dead of the malady [typhoid] on the same day the corpse is taken out of it', and it was well known that the communal bed was one of the reasons why the great plague of 1720 in Provence so often swept off a whole family. . . .
The churchwardens of the poverty-stricken parish of Saint-Sauveur in Lille complained that the death rate of their parishioners in the epidemic of 1772–3 had been much higher than in the wealthy parish of Saint-André. 'The higher numbers here', they said, 'can only be because the inhabitants are poor, more numerous and crowded into little houses, often occupied by many families, and situated in very narrow streets called alleyways . . . , they breathe the less pure air here, and because of the dirt which is virtually inseparable from poverty, they propagate all the diseases which catch a hold among them.' In Lyon, the silk workers lived twelve to fifteen in a garret, forty to fifty families in a house in the tall buildings around sunless courts, stinking of the chickens, pigs, and rabbits that they reared, and of latrines. . . .

When the Royal Council on 29 April 1776 set up its commission to investigate epidemic diseases in the provinces, one of the questions it posed was: 'Why do epidemics sometimes seem to spare a particular class of citizens?' Probably, the intention was not to look at the obvious overcrowding of the slums, but at the food and water supplies and at the dietary habits of the different classes. Seventy years earlier, during the misery at the end of the reign of Louis XIV, the economist Boisguilbert, in a burning tirade, had censured the maldistribution of food supplies which cut short so many lives. There are men, he said, who sweat blood in their toil, with no food other than bread and water, in the midst of a land of abundance, who 'perish when only half their course is run', and whose children are 'stifled in their cradles'. . . . Estimates . . . —at Arles in 1750, by the agricultural society of La Rochelle in 1763, by the owner of a carpet factory in Abbeville in 1764—show that the poorer peasants and urban workers, though far from being reduced to bread and water, lived all their lives on the margins of danger: any loss of working days had to be paid for by starvation later. There was a cycle of illness, debt, and hunger which made death almost certain on the next round of visitation, and it was not unusual for wretches who had struggled fiercely against starvation to give up on hearing that they had caught some disease, knowing that the future had little hope.

Most people in France lived on cereals, because this was what they could afford. A modern attempt to work out a typical budget for a family of the poor majority in an ordinary year, suggests 50 per cent of expenditure on bread, 16 per cent on fats and wine, 13 per cent on clothing, and 5 per cent on heating. So far as the proportion on bread is concerned, eighteenth-century estimates studied more recently confirm the generalization. The ration in hospitals was one and half *livres* a day, and this was the amount an employer generally allowed to a servant in Paris. . . . Judged on the scale of calories, in a fair year, the workers of France were fed efficiently, so far as potential energy was concerned, but, as more than 90 per cent of these calories came from cereals (including maize porridge in the south and beer in the north), the dietary deficiencies are obvious. The food consumption of the inmates of the hospital of Caen (bread, and the unusual advantage of plenty of Norman cider), of the conscripts doing guard duty at the citadel of Saint-Malo in the mid-century (unimaginative bread, biscuits, and salt meat, with none of the coastal fish which ought to have diversified their diet), of the peasants of Périgord (chestnuts and maize in fearful stews kept simmering all day), of the peasants of Basse-Auvergne (bread, soup of nut oil, and water tinctured with wine) — all show the same deficiencies: a lack of meat, fish, dairy produce, and fresh vegetables. That meant a deficiency of vitamins, animal fats, calcium, and trace elements, leaving the way open for rickets, scurvy, skin eruptions, loss of teeth, the breaking down of the natural power of resistance to cold, and the stunting of growth, both physical and mental. It was a matter for wonder that men from mountain areas (where the pastures offered milk and meat) were so tall—as in Auvergne, where they towered over the puny inhabitants of the cereal-growing plain. . . . The ill effects of the inevitable deficiencies were increased by ignorance. . . . [T]here was little knowledge of what constituted a balanced diet. Even the rich did not know what was good for them. They ate a large amount of meat. . . . But an analysis of the meals eaten by a magistrate of Toulouse and of the pupils at a boarding-school for young nobles show, even so, a lack of calcium and some vitamins. The food available to ordinary people was not always wisely used. The regulation stew-pot of the peasants boiled away the vitamins. . . . Fresh bread was unusual, since for economy, huge loaves which lasted for two or three months were baked in communal ovens.

The oft-recorded obstinacy of peasants in refusing to eat unusual food like potatoes, even when starving, is paralleled by the refusal of the Parisians to accept the government economy bread of wheat, rye, and barley, invented during the dearth of 1767. And of course, the people were spendthrift; living on crusts and onions all week, they would go to drinking booths on Sunday night, or swig a tot of *eau-de-vie*[13] on their way to work in the mornings. But statistics of vitamin, calcium, and trace-element deficiencies can prove too much. Like the analysis of wages in eighteenth-century France, they go to show that half the population ought not to have been alive at all. Life, for these people, was 'an economy of makeshifts', patching up a living by all sorts of incongruous combinations of earnings; no doubt they supplemented their food supplies by tilling odd corners, keeping animals in hutches, gleaning in hedgerow and common, begging, poaching, and pilfering. That was why it was so dangerous to become institutionalized, whether shut up in a *dépôt de mendicité*, a hospital, a madhouse, or on shipboard. Survival became difficult when there was no scope for enterprise.

Whatever mysterious and useless medicines they prescribed, the doctors of eighteenth-century France knew the primary importance of sound nourishment to aid the sick to recovery. Meat soup was the standard prescription for all convalescents. . . . 'Remedies and advice are useless unless there is a foundation of solid nourishment,' said a physician called in to investigate the outbreak of dysentery in Anjou in 1707, and he asked for 'bouillons' to be dispatched daily to all who had been afflicted. 'Bread, wine, and blankets' were the prescriptions of the doctors of Anjou who dealt with epidemics of dysentery in 1768 and typhus in 1774. In times of dearth, the poor were driven to eat contaminated or unripened grain, and were poisoned in consequence. . . . Officials in Brittany in 1769 and 1771 reported diseases (one called them of an 'epileptic' kind) which were sweeping the provinces because the crop failures had driven the people to eat grain that had been damp when stored and had fermented and grown musty. . . . In the Sologne, there were outbreaks from time to time of ergotism caused by infected grain—the disease was called 'St. Anthony's fire' and 'dry gangrene': it led to the loss of fingers, noses, or whole limbs, and eventually to madness. And the greatest killer of all was contaminated water. Springs and wells would become infected as they dried up or floods overflowed them from dubious catchment areas, or were permanently dangerous because of defective masonry in cisterns, or because animals had access to them. Typical complaints concern effluent from flax-crushing or animal manure getting into drinking supplies, or froth from the oxen's mouths still floating on the top of buckets brought in for domestic consumption. In some villages without a well, water was collected in shallow holes dug here and there and had

---

[13]Brandy.

to be filtered through linen. And any Parisian who gave a thought to where his water supply came from would confine himself to drinking wine always—if he could afford it.

Certain seasons of the year brought the shadow of food shortages. There were the dangerous months . . . from April to July, when the previous year's grain was being used up, and before the new crop was harvested. There was a danger period too in winter, especially for townspeople, for freezing weather might ice up the canals along which the supply barges came, or stop the water-mills from grinding the flour. And, worst of all, the crop might fail, damaged by unseasonable cold or rain or hail; rumour would race ahead of truth, encouraging the hoarding which transformed fear into the first instalment of grim reality.

It is generally said that the era of great famines ended in 1709; thereafter came shortages, serious indeed, but not deadly. . . . 'In the seventeenth century people died of hunger: in the eighteenth they suffered from it.' This is true so far as dying as a direct result of starvation is concerned, though local historians can always find a catastrophic year to form an exception worthy to qualify as the last of the crises. . . . A common-sense review of the probabilities of dying might suggest a logical sequence: famine, hunger weakening the resistance of the population, the resort to contaminated food causing illness, the onset of some killing disease, and the starving poor forced into vagabondage acting as carriers for the infection. In practice, in the eighteenth century this proposed pattern of death's operations is only occasionally borne out by comparisons of the graphs of corn prices, illness, and mortality. At Dijon in the 1740s, it seems clear that famine must have been the essential cause of the increase in the number of deaths, though an epidemic could strike at a particular place with an overwhelming impact only explainable by its own virulence. . . .

It has been argued, with eighteenth-century England as the example, that malnutrition does not weaken resistance to disease, except in the case of afflictions arising directly from deficiencies of diet, and tuberculosis and dysentery. A historian who has never known what it is to be hungry for very long instinctively feels inclined to doubt this assertion. True, studies of the Third World today show how deprived peoples can sometimes maintain themselves in calorific and protein balance on a diet that would mean starvation to the inhabitants of advanced countries. While bodily size and appearance are affected by the food supply, the same does not necessarily apply to resistance to infection. But there is a distinction to be made. While the nutrition taken by individuals seems not to have much effect on their chance of becoming infected with most diseases, it is of the utmost importance in deciding what their ultimate fate will be. 'Malnutrition does not particularly favour or impede the acquisition of infection, but it goes a long way to determine the course of the resulting disease.' The relationship between dearth and epidemic among the poorer classes of eighteenth-century France is not so much a short-term correspondence, but a general pattern of attrition by the alternations and the accumulated onslaughts of hunger and disease. The point may be taken, however, that pathogenic bacteria and viruses do not need to wait to find a human population weakened by famine before they strike; some apparently hopeless human groups may have built up an immunity, while some apparently flourishing ones may be unprotected. One disease may fade out, leaving the weak as predestinate victims for another; thus the plague vanished from Languedoc after 1655, and malaria took over, its victims forming a new reservoir of infection to pass on to future generations. We may picture death as vigilant but unhurried and patient. Sometimes hunger served its purposes, as in the terrible dearth in the spring of 1740 in Auvergne, where a *curé* reported that the women let their children die so that the adults could live, and the men, to avoid conceiving children, resorted to unnatural practices with animals. Sometimes some overwhelming contagion, like the plague of Marseille, swept away all human defences. It could be, in these disasters, that the swift succumbing of the physically weak was a precondition for a widespread pattern of infection which trapped the rich, who might otherwise have escaped. . . . More often, the continuing cycle of disease, hunger, renewed disease, and despair brought life to an end. There is a story of Louis XV encountering a funeral procession and asking what the man had died from. 'Starvation, Sire.' It was an indictment of his government, and the answer would have been true, indirectly, of many other deaths from infections and accidents. 'C'est de misère que l'on meurt au dix-septième siècle". . . . [14] Though the situation was changing in the eighteenth century, this grim generalization was still broadly applicable. Particular diseases were the indispensable infantry in Death's dark armies, but his generals were Cold and Hunger.

[14]"It was destitution that brought on death in the seventeenth century."

The Sans-Culottes

ALBERT SOBOUL

One of the great watersheds in history, the French Revolution signaled the passing of the Old Régime. Monarchy, hierarchy, and privilege, all pillars of the social order, came under attack, not only in France, but through much of Europe. French armies crisscrossed the continent, attempting to spread revolutionary ideals of "liberty, equality, and fraternity," and in the process inadvertently awakened the most potent of nineteenth-century ideologies, nationalism. Historians have entered seemingly interminable debates concerning the French Revolution, questioning, among other things, whether or not it was favorable to liberty, or to capitalism, and which social groups benefited the most from the Revolution.

Albert Soboul was a Marxist historian. As such, he argued that the Revolution opposed what was a feudal society, virtually destroying the old nobility, and so prepared the triumph of a capitalist economy. For Soboul, class conflict was an integral part of the Revolution. Soboul gained fame with his magisterial study of the Parisian sans-culottes, *a fascinating, if ephemeral social group that influenced political events in Paris and supported vociferously the Terror of 1793–1794.*

The sans-culottes *were workers, artisans, and shopkeepers, distinguishable, according to Soboul, by their dress, behavior, and attitudes (political, economic, and social). Why did the* sans-culottes *detest aristocrats, abhor merchants, and loathe the rich? What did the* sans-culottes *want from the Revolution? What political ideas did they espouse? We should not romanticize the* sans-culottes *as virtuous workers out to cleanse society of oppressive noblemen, exploitative businessmen, and other enemies of the "people," for the* sans-culottes *often resorted to pillaging, frequently hailed violence, and cheered the guillotine as it lopped off thousands of heads. Why did they favor execution—so many executions—as an instrument of state policy? Ironically, many of the* sans-culottes *themselves fell victim to the guillotine.*

Soboul's study is valuable not only as an example of Marxist historiography but as a thorough examination of the sans-culottes, *as well. Thus he depicts their violent behavior without neglecting what motivated them to indulge in it.*

If we are to attempt to discern the social characteristics of the sans-culottes, it is important first to draw attention to the manner in which they defined themselves. . . .

Albert Soboul, *The Sans-Culottes* (Garden City, N.Y.: Doubleday and Company, Inc., 1972), 2–10, 13–20, 158–162.

Ostensibly, the sans-culottes were recognizable by their costume, which set them apart from the upper strata of the former Third Estate. Robespierre[1] used to differentiate between *golden breeches* and *sans-culottes*. The sans-culottes themselves made the same distinction. Noting the intrigues that undermined the Sceaux Committee of Surveillance, the observer Rousseville, in his report on 25 Messidor, year II,[2] stresses the antagonism between the "silk-stockings" and the sans-culottes. Conventions of dress also pitted sans-culottes against the *muscadins* [royalist sympathizers]. Arrested on 4 Prairial, year III, for having said that "the blasted muscadins'll soon have a spade up there . . . ", and questioned as to what he meant by these words, Barack, a clockmaker's assistant of the *Lombards* section, replied that "as far as he was concerned, muscadins were those who were well dressed.". . .

Costume was accompanied by particular social behavior. Again, on this subject, the sans-culottes declared their stand through opposition. In the year II, the manners of the ancien régime were no longer acceptable. The sans-culottes refused to adopt a subordinate position in social relations. Jean-Baptiste Gentil, timber merchant, arrested on 5 Pluviôse, year II, for not having fulfilled his duties toward the Republic, was reprimanded for his public demeanor: "One had to approach him with hat in hand, the word *sir* was still used in his household, he retains an air of superiority.". . . The principal charge against Gannal, iron merchant from the *Réunion* section,[3] arrested on 7 Frimaire, was his "haughty manner toward his workers.". . .

The sans-culottes often estimated a person's worth by external appearance, deducing character from costume and political convictions from character; everything that jarred their sense of equality was suspect of being "aristocratic." It was difficult, therefore, for any person of the old regime to find favor in their eyes, even when there was no specific charge against him. "For such men are incapable of bringing themselves to the heights of our revolution; their hearts are always full of pride and we shall never forget their former grandeur and their domination over us."

. . . The sans-culottes tolerated neither pride nor disdain; those were aristocratic sentiments contrary to the spirit of fraternity that existed between equal citizens and implied a hostile political stand toward democracy as practiced by the sans-culottes in their general assemblies and in their popular societies. These character traits appeared frequently in reports justifying the arrest of suspects.

On September 17, 1793 (Fructidor, year I), the committee of the

[1]Maximilien Robespierre (1758–1794), leader of the most extreme political faction during the Terror of 1793–1794.

[2]The French Revolution introduced a new calendar on 5 October 1793 and dated the year I from 21 September 1792, the beginning of the Convention.

[3]In June 1790, Paris was divided into 48 sections, which held regular meetings.

Révolutionnaire section decided to arrest Etienne Gide, clock merchant, who had supported the Brissotins;[4] he was also accused of being haughty and proud and of often speaking *ironically.* On October 12, one bourgeois, a solicitor, was arrested by the revolutionary committee of *Réunion*: he had risen to support aristocrats in the general assemblies; more particularly, he demonstrated a "haughty manner toward the sans-culottes.". . . .

Even more serious, according to the sans-culottes, than a haughty or disdainful manner toward themselves or straightforward indifference were statements referring to them as being of a lower social order. In its report of 8 Frimaire on Louis-Claude Cezeron, arrested for being a "suspect," the committee of the *Poissonnière* section made a particular case of a statement made during a meeting of the general assembly on the preceding May 31 (12 Prairial): "that the poor depended on the rich and that the sans-culottes were never any more than the lowest order possible." Bergeron, a skin merchant from *Lombards,* said that "although he understood that the sans-culottes were fulfilling their duty as citizens . . . it would be better for them to go about their work rather than meddle in politics." He was arrested on suspicion on 18 Pluviôse.

The sans-culottes refused to tolerate others taking advantage of their social or economic status to impose upon them. . . . Anthéaume, a former abbé, . . . was arrested on 16 Brumaire: he was reprimanded for "pride and intolerable pedagogy contrary to equality and the simplicity of a good republican."

The sans-culottes had an egalitarian conception of social relations. Their behavior also concealed realities which were more specific. To what extent were they seized upon and expressed?

The most clearly stated social friction in popular awareness was that which pitted aristocrat against sans-culotte: it was against the aristocrats that the sans-culottes addressed themselves from July 14[5] to August 10,[6] and against whom they continued to battle. The address of the sans-culottes society of Beaucaire before the Convention[7] of September 8, 1793, is significant: "We are sans-culottes . . . poor and virtuous, we have formed a society of artisans and peasants . . . we know who our friends are: those who freed us from the clergy and from the nobility, from feudalism, from tithes, from royalty and from all the plagues that follow in its wake. . . . "

The nature of the class struggle was even more clearly stated in the address of the Dijon Popular Society on 27 Nivôse, year II: "We must be

---

[4]Followers of Jacques-Pierre Brissot de Warville, who in 1791 advocated that France go to war against European monarchies.

[5]14 July 1789, fall of the Bastille in Paris.

[6]10 August 1792, overthrow of the French monarchy.

[7]Name of the governmental assembly that first met on 21 September 1792 and established a republic.

one people, and not two nations, opposed . . . all recognized aristocratic individuals without exception should be condemned to death by decree." According to mechanic Guyot . . . , "all the nobles, without exception, deserve to be guillotined."

At this point, the aristocracy was the main enemy of the sans-culottes. Ultimately, they managed to include in this term all their adversaries, although these might not necessarily belong to the quondam nobility, but to the upper echelons of the former Third Estate. In this way the role of the sans-culottes is imprinted upon the Revolution, and further demonstrates the autonomy of their action.

On July 25, 1792, the *Louvre* section announced the fall of the King, at the same time denouncing the hereditary aristocracy, "the ministerial, financial and bourgeois aristocrats, and particularly the hierarchy of recalcitrant priests." By the year II, the meaning of the word "aristocrat" was extended to embrace all the social classes against which the sans-culottes were struggling. . . . Hence the specifically popular definition, coined by an anonymous petitioner in the year II, which has both political and social connotations: the aristocrat was one who regretted the passing of the ancien régime and disapproved of the Revolution, did nothing to further its cause, did not swear his allegiance to it, did not enlist in the National Guard,[8] one who did not purchase expropriated land, although he might have had the means to do so; one who left land uncultivated without selling it at its true value, or leasing it, or giving a half share in the produce. The aristocrat was also he who did not give work to laborers or journeymen, although he might be in a position to do so, and "at a wage commensurate with food prices"; did not subscribe to contributions for the volunteers; and had done nothing to improve the lot of his poor and patriotic countrymen. The real patriot was he who took a contrary attitude on every possible occasion. The term aristocrat in the end, therefore, designated all the opponents of the sans-culottes, bourgeois as well as noble, those who formed "the class of citizens from whom one should take the billion we have to levy throughout the Republic." The most extreme sans-culottes did not use the term "aristocrat" for the old nobility, but for the bourgeoisie. On May 21, 1793, a popular orator from the *Mail* section declared that "aristocrats are all the people with money, all the fat merchants, all the monopolists, law students, bankers, pettifoggers and anyone who has something."

The economic crisis had contributed to bringing social clashes to a head: to the fundamental hostility between sans-culotte and aristocrat was added that of the sans-culottes and the upper sectors of the Third Estate. . . . A note sent to the Public Safety Committee in Pulviôse, year II, pointed out the existence of two parties in the *Brutus* section: that of the people, the sans-culottes, and the other consisting of "bankers,

[8]Citizen militia organized in Paris after the fall of the Bastille.

money changers, rich people." An address delivered before the Convention on 27 Ventôse mentioned the brave sans-culottes, who were opposed not only to the clergy, the nobility, royal coalitions, but also to attorneys, lawyers, notaries and also all "those fat farmers, those egotists, and those fat, rich merchants: they're at war against us, and not against our tyrants."

Was this the "haves" against the "have-nots"? Not precisely. As far as the sans-culottes were concerned, artisans and shopkeepers belonged to the propertied classes. More particularly, the friction was between those who believed in the notion of limited and controlled ownership and the partisans of total ownership rights such as were proclaimed in 1789. Or the opposition between those who believed in controls and taxation, and those in favor of economic freedom; the opposition between consumer and producer.

Contemporary documents, over and beyond these basic reactions or distinctive statements, also allow us to explore the nuances of the social antagonisms expressed by the sans-culottes with some accuracy. They denounced "respectable people," meaning by this those who possessed, if not riches, then at least leisure and culture, the better-educated citizens, the better-dressed, those conscious if not proud of their leisure and their education. They denounced the propertied classes, that is to say, those who had unearned incomes. Finally, they denounced the rich in general, not only the propertied classes or the "haves," but also the "big men" as opposed to the "little men," which they were. The sans-culottes were not against property already owned by artisans and shopkeepers, and which journeymen aspired to possess, provided that it was limited.

The expression "respectable people" was first heard after June 2 (13 Prairial), when sans-culottes and moderates opposed one another on political and social platforms. The term was first applied to the bourgeoisie opposed to equality, but ended by having as wide a connotation as the term "aristocrat," and embracing all the enemies of the sans-culottes. . . . A certain Lamarre, lemonade vendor from the *Bon-Conseil* section, was arrested on 5 Prairial, year III; he consistently raised his voice against "respectable people," demanding before the assembly that they all be guillotined. As for washerwoman Rombaut, she stated that every single one of those so-called "respectable people" should be guillotined.

If the sans-culottes ironically called their adversaries "respectable people," the latter did not fail to treat them as rabble; thus, with two expressions, the lines for social clashes were drawn. On September 25, 1793 (4 Vendémiaire, year II), carpenter Bertout was arrested on the orders of the committee of the *République* section: he had declared a desire for "another government being established to oppose the rabble, because respectable people were lost.". . .

This opposition was further expressed in the animosity between the sans-culottes and those who possessed unearned incomes, a situation that came to a head during the autumn of 1793, when the economic crisis and the difficulties of daily living resulted in increased class antagonism. The fact of being independently wealthy gave cause for suspicion. On September 18, 1793 . . . , the revolutionary committee of *Mucius-Scaevola* ordered the arrest of Duval, first secretary of the Paris Police, on two counts: for contempt toward the assemblies of that section, and for enjoying an income of 2,000 livres. . . . On 2 Germinal, the revolutionary committee of the *Mont Blanc* section issued a warrant for the arrest of Jean-François Rivoire, formerly a colonist in Santo Domingo: he had not signed the Constitution, he had never contributed to the funds, nor had he served in the Guard. Further, he had an income of 16,000 livres. In one extreme case a certain Pierre Becquerel from *Guillaume-Tell* was arrested on 19 Ventôse during a raid by the police in the Gardens of Equality, simply for having said he had a private income. On the preceding 2 Frimaire, the *Lepeletier* popular society adopted a petition to exclude from all government posts not only former nobles, the sons of secretaries to the king, brokers and dealers, but also all persons known to possess incomes of more than 3,000 livres. Posts vacated by this measure would be reserved for sans-culottes. These latter were not therefore opposed to all forms of income from investments, but only to the very wealthy. . . .

The sans-culottes' hostility toward those with large private incomes was merely one particularly stressed aspect of their instinctive opposition to the rich. Extreme sans-culottes like Babeuf[9] in the year IV were not far from considering the Revolution as a declared war "between the rich and the poor." The nature of this clash to a large extent characterized Terrorist sentiments. . . . When sectional power was in the hands of the sans-culottes, full of animosity or hatred toward the rich, they did not fail to take discriminatory action against them. Wealth was often the motive for suspicion. Although wealth was rarely the only motive invoked, it often lent support to vague accusations. . . .

This deep-rooted tendency among the sans-culottes to speak against the rich was encouraged in the year II by the ruling politicians of the time. "Herein lies the revolution of the poor," wrote Michel Lepeletier in the National Education Project which Robespierre read before the Convention on July 12 and 29 of 1793 (Messidor/Thermidor, year I). . . . Saint-Just[10] said: "The unfortunate are the powerful on earth; they have the right to speak as masters to governments who neglect them.". . . The crisis of the Revolution from the spring to the autumn of 1793 made the popular alliance necessary: the sans-culottes formed the cadre that was to permit the most advanced faction of the bourgeoisie to quell the

[9]François Babeuf (1760–1797), firebrand who formed the "Conspiracy of Equals" and attempted to overthrow the government in 1797.

[10]Louis-Antoine Saint-Just (1767–1794), a revolutionary leader during the Terror.

aristocracy and its allies. "The hidden danger," wrote Robespierre in his diary during the June 2 insurrection, "lies in the bourgeois; in order to conquer the bourgeois, it will be necessary to rally the people.". . . Those who did not belong to the government openly exploited the antagonism between the rich and the sans-culottes for political ends. . . .

The differences between the sans-culottes and the rich were rounded out by the former's hostility toward business enterprise, and this hostility constituted one of the fundamental currents of popular opinion during the year II.

Being urban consumers, the Parisian sans-culottes were naturally against those who controlled staple food supplies. Retailers, they blamed the wholesalers. Artisans or journeymen, hardly workers in the actual meaning of the word, they remained essentially small independent producers, hostile toward those who had interests in commercial capital. The economic crisis and political struggles intensified this inherent antagonism among the sans-culottes. Scarcity and high prices spiraled, and every merchant was soon suspect of being a monopolist or a shark. The struggle against the Girondins[11] and subsequently, after May 31, against the moderates, was often, at least on the sectional level, turned into a struggle against the merchant bourgeoisie. The sans-culottes were insistent upon taxation and controls, and the conflict deepened; to the extent that they defended freedom of enterprise, the merchants became suspect. Henceforth, the sans-culottes included with the noble aristocracy and the religious hierarchy the mercantile aristocracy as well. . . .

In 1793 and in the year II, popular hostility against the merchants was marked, in its moments of paroxysm, by violence and pillage. It was also marked by a constant desire for repression. . . . In March of 1793 (Ventôse/Germinal, year I), during the recruitment of troops for the Vendée campaign, collections for volunteers were often an occasion for the sans-culottes to confirm their hostility toward the merchants. In *Lombards*, Jean-Baptiste Larue, journeyman mason and member of the revolutionary committee, declared that the volunteers were "idiots if they left without each having a hundred pistoles in their pockets, that we should cut off the heads of all these buggers, those merchants, and that after this operation, the sums of money required would soon be found."

Once popular power was on firm ground, the title of merchant alone was often reason enough for suspicion on the part of revolutionary committees. They were encouraged by the Commune,[12] whose arrests of the nineteenth of the first month ranged among their suspects "those who felt sorry for needy farmers and merchants, against whom

[11]Name given to a group of moderate republican deputies. They were purged in 1793 from the Convention.

[12]Government of the city of Paris, 1789–1795, divided into 48 sections and dominated by radical factions.

the law must take measures." Certain committees had not expected this encouragement. After September 14, the committee of *Lombards*, where hostility toward the merchants was particularly strong, arrested a certain Dussautoy; he was reprimanded simply for being a wholesale grocer. . . . In *Bon-Conseil*, the committee justified the arrest on 25 Brumaire of Jean-Louis Lagrave, wholesale grocer, merely because of his social behavior: "He spends his time among business people, snobs like himself, not consorting with any patriot . . . always flaunting his rank among the wholesalers, censuring and even molesting citizens, like most wholesalers.". . .

The hostility of the sans-culottes toward business was not restricted to measures against individuals; this was a war against an entire social class that, although it did not seek to eliminate that class from politics, at least sought to curb its powers, to put a halt to its prejudicial activities. . . .

The reaction set in finally after the year III, and the merchants made the most of their revenge against former Terrorists for the maltreatment to which they had been subjected. During Germinal and Prairial, a simple remark was sufficient motive for arrest. The food shortage, worse because the "maximum"[13] had been abolished, once again increased hostility toward commerce among the sans-culottes. The dossiers of the anti-Terrorist repression offer ample evidence, allowing us to determine the precise nature of public opinion on this subject; this varied, circumstances permitting, from a simple expression of hostility to a suppressed desire for the elimination of a social class.

For having said, in year II, "Neither the merchants nor the rich are worth sparing," Davelin, a feather dealer from *Amis-de-la-Patrie*, was disarmed on 5 Prairial, year III. Jacques Barbant, from *Arsenal*, was arrested: he had made certain vague derogatory remarks about merchants. . . .

From hostility toward commerce, the more aware or the more violent among the sans-culottes went on to justify pillage. . . .

During the upheavals of February 25 and 26, 1793 (Ventôse, year I), cobbler Servière, revolutionary commissar of the *Muséum* section in the year II declared before the general assembly, in what was formerly the Germain church, "that he thoroughly approved of pillage and would be very much against having to oppose it.". . . In *Bonne-Nouvelle*, water carrier Bergeron was arrested on 6 Pluviôse, in the year III, when "as a result of his provocations he incited the pillaging of the wood merchants." In some ways . . . , pillage corresponded to the fundamental egalitarianism of the sans-culottes: individual action was legitimated by the inequality of living conditions.

Beyond the offensive remarks or the exhortation to pillage, Terrorist

---

[13]Name applied to two laws in 1793 that set maximum levels for wages and prices. The ceiling on wages, but not that on prices, was stringently enforced. Thus the *sans-culottes* were not satisfied.

exaltation and the desire for punitive measures show the deep-rooted hostility of the sans-culottes toward the commercial bourgeoisie. Many militants considered the threat of the guillotine in times of shortages an excellent remedy. To oblige farmers to sell their grain according to the official price, they insisted upon the creation of a revolutionary army. When this army was created, the sans-culottes constantly demanded that it be accompanied by a mobile guillotine, in order further to insure its efficaciousness. This outlook can be traced throughout all the Terrorists' abusive remarks made in the year II against the merchants. Widow Barbau, from *Indivisibilité*, a veritable harridan according to her denunciators, had the habit of declaring "that until the snobbish merchants, the aristocrats, the rich, etc., are guillotined or dispatched en masse, nothing will work out properly." Widow Barbau quite naturally placed the merchants before the aristocrats. In *Unité*, a certain Roux asked for the erecting of guillotines "on every street corner in Paris, on the doorsteps of every merchant, so that, he said, we can have cheap merchandise.". . . In *Invalides*, the clockmaker Fagère declared that "when the aristocrats are finished, we'll take up with the merchant class again. . . . "

In the year III, shortages and misery still exacerbated sans-culottes' hatred of the merchants. Terrorist remarks abound in the dossiers of the repression. On 19 Ventôse, Jacques Rohait, a job printer from the *Panthéon-Français* section exasperated by the high cost of meat, said that "all those wretched merchants deserve to swing.". . .

During those Prairial days, frenzied offensive remarks were not unusual. Nicolas Barrucand, dyer, former revolutionary commissar of *Arsenal*, declared that on the feast day of Corpus Christi "the streets should be carpeted with the heads of merchants.". . .

The still vivid memories of the year II suggested to many sans-culottes the need for a return to organized terror in order to put an end to the merchants, as they had done to the aristocrats. Ferrier, a hatter from *Gardes-Françaises*, remembering the uprisings in Lyons, Marseilles and Bordeaux in 1793, and the repression which followed, declared that "the large communes composed entirely of merchants and the wealthy must be destroyed, their inhabitants humbled and put down.". . .

These texts reveal that the sans-culottes identified themselves by opposition to the aristocracy, riches, and to commerce—antagonisms that account for the imprecise nature of the social distinctions within the former Third Estate and the difficulty of defining the sans-culottes as a social class. The sans-culottes can be clearly defined only when compared to the aristocracy; when compared to the bourgeoisie, the distinction becomes less clear. Composed of many socially disparate elements, the sans-culottes were undermined by internal dissent, which explains both their inability to establish a coherent program and, in the last analysis, their political defeat. . . .

The sans-culottes considered violence to be the ultimate recourse against those who refused to answer the call of unity. This stand was one of the characteristics of their political behavior. Popular violence had allowed the bourgeoisie to carry out its first attacks against the ancien régime; indeed, the struggle against the aristocracy would not have been possible without it. In 1793 and in the year II, the sans-culottes used that violence not solely against the aristocrats, but also against the moderates who were opposed to the establishment of an egalitarian republic.

Doubtless we should at times seek the biological roots of this recourse to violence, of this exaltation. Temperament offers some explanation. The reports of Prairial, year III, on the former Terrorists often mention their irascible, passionate nature and their tendency to fits of rage; "Their outbursts were usually the result of being in a position to make malicious remarks without thinking of the consequences." Their reactions were the stronger because the sans-culottes were often frustrated, poor, uneducated, inflamed by awareness of their misery.

In the year III the reactionaries indiscriminately labeled all Terrorists drinkers of blood. Although one must be careful not to generalize and take denunciations and police reports literally, one must nevertheless concede that, for certain individuals, violence did mean the spilling of blood. . . . Bunou, from the *Champs-Elysées* section, who was arrested on 5 Prairial, demanded in the year II that a guillotine be erected in the section, "and that he would act as executioner if there was none to be found." Lesur, from the *Luxembourg* section, was arrested on 6 Prairial for having made a similar suggestion: "that the guillotine was not working fast enough, that there should be more bloodletting in the prisons, that if the executioner was tired, he himself would climb the scaffold with a quarter loaf to soak up the blood." In the *Gardes-Françaises* a certain Jayet was arrested on 6 Prairial for having declared in the year II, "that he would like to see rivers of blood, up to the ankles." On leaving the general assembly of the *République* section, another declared: "The guillotine is hungry, it's ages since she had something to eat." Women shared this Terrorist exaltation. A certain Baudray, a lemonade vendor from the *Lepeletier* section, was arrested on 8 Prairial for having said "she would like to eat the heart of anyone opposed to the sans-culottes"; she intended to raise her children on the same principles: "You hear them talk of nothing but cutting, chopping off heads, not enough blood is flowing."

Nevertheless, temperament alone does not sufficiently explain the fact that the majority of the popular militants approved of if they did not exalt violence and the use of the guillotine. For many, brute force seemed the supreme recourse when a crisis had reached its paroxysm. These same men, who did not hesitate to make blood flow, were more often than not ordinarily quite calm, good sons, good husbands and good fathers. Cobbler Duval from the *Arsenal* section was condemned to death on 11 Prairial, year II, for his role during the uprising of the first;

his neighbors testified that he was a good father, good husband, good citizen, a *man of probity*. The feeling that the nation was threatened, the belief in the aristocratic plot, the atmosphere of turbulent days, the tocsin and the issuing of arms made these men beside themselves and created in them something like a second nature. According to the civil committee of the *Faubourg-du-Nord* section, Josef Morlot, a house painter, arrested on 5 Prairial, year III, was a man with two distinct personalities. "One of these, guided by his natural bent, was gentle, honest and generous. He has all the social virtues, which he practices in private. The other, subjugated by present threats, manifests itself in the bloody colors of all the conjoined plagues in their utmost virulence."

This violence was not gratuitous. It had a political aim and a class content; it was a weapon which the sans-culottes were forced to use in their resistance to the aristocracy. A teacher by the name of Moussard employed by the Executive Commission of Public Instruction, was arrested on 5 Prairial, year III. "Yes, I was carried away," he wrote in his defense. "Who wasn't during the Revolution? . . . They say I am fanatical: yes; passion burns within my breast, I am intoxicated with the idea of liberty and I shall always rage against the enemies of my country."

The guillotine was popular because the sans-culottes saw in it an instrument whereby they could avenge the nation. Hence the expressions *national cleaver, national ax*; the guillotine was also known as the *scythe of equality*. Class hatred of the aristocracy was heightened by the belief in an aristocratic plot which since 1789 had been one of the fundamental reasons behind popular violence. Foreign war and civil war further strengthened the popular notion that the aristocracy would only be exterminated by the Terror and that the guillotine was necessary for consolidating the Republic. Becq, a clerk in the Navy Department, a good father, a good husband and well thought of, but extraordinarily impassioned according to the civil committee of the *Butte-des-Moulins*, turned his impassioned nature against priests and noblemen, whom he *usually* recommended for assassination. Jean-Baptiste Mallais, cobbler and revolutionary commissar of the *Temple* section, was the same: he did not hesitate to use clubs when arguing with noblemen and priests considered enemies of the people; he spoke of arming the wives of patriots "so that they in turn can slit the throats of the wives of aristocrats.". . . Even more indicative of the political aims which the sans-culottes hoped to achieve through violence and through the Terror were the words recorded by the observer Perrière on 6 Ventôse, year II: "Is the guillotine working today?" asked a dandy. "Yes," replied an honest patriot, "there is always somebody betraying somebody or something."

During the year III violence became even more important for the sans-culottes. The Terror had also been an economic aspect of government; it had sanctioned the application of the "maximum," which had guaranteed the people their daily bread. Whereas the reaction coincided with the abolition of price-fixing and the worst shortages, certain among them came to identify the Terror with abundance, in the same way as they associated popular government with the Terror. Cobbler Clément from the *République* section was denounced on 2 Prairial for having declared "that the Republic cannot be built without blood flowing.". . . Mistress Chalandon from the *l'Homme-Armé* section declared, "Nothing will really work properly until permanent guillotines were erected at every street intersection in Paris." Carpenter Richer, from the *République* section, touched the heart of the matter when he said, on 1 Prairial: "There will be no bread unless we spill some blood; under the Terror we didn't go without."

Whatever specific aims the Parisian sans-culottes had in mind, the Terror and popular violence to a great extent swept away the remnants of feudalism and absolutism for the bourgeoisie. They nevertheless corresponded to a different form of behavior, in the same way as popular political practices, essentially characterized in 1793 and in the year II by voting by acclamation and by fraternity, expressed a concept of democracy that was fundamentally different from that of the bourgeoisie, even of the Jacobins.[14]

Doubtless the revolutionary bourgeoisie, during the critical moments of its struggle against the aristocracy, also resorted to violence; they, too, made use of certain popular practices; for example, during the course of the Convention elections, in Paris, they used the roll-call vote. Events justified this departure from the usual concepts of liberal democracy, and also class interests. Once the revolutionary government was in power, neither these interests nor the events would allow these practices to continue. Although these practices were in accord with the popular temperament, they were incompatible with the behavior and political ideas of the bourgeoisie. They also threatened its sovereignty. . . .

---

[14]Members of republican political clubs during the French Revolution. Originally containing moderates, the Jacobins became increasingly radical and dominated the government during the Terror.

THE NINETEENTH CENTURY

Historians generally count the nineteenth century as lasting from the end of the Napoleonic Wars (1815) to the beginning of World War I in 1914. Nineteenth-century Europeans appeared to possess a confident optimism, if not arrogance, that rested on European scientific achievement, industrial advance, and imperial conquest. The great world fairs of the period—London, 1851; Paris, 1900—which displayed all the world's art and manufactures, and which asserted European superiority over the rest of the world, suggest how rich, powerful, self-assured, and nation-proud were the times. In short, the nineteenth century was an era of seeming greatness as Europe flexed its industrial and political muscles, until World War I, the "war to end all wars," demonstrated the terrible consequences of modern technology joined with rampant nationalism and militarism.

Not all Europeans, of course, could revel in the power exercised by the leaders and the social élite of various nations. The power and wealth were not evenly distributed, and most people continued their never-ending struggle for food, work, and a modicum of security.

The major socio-economic development in this century was the Industrial Revolution, whose effects were felt throughout society. The factories and machines of the Industrial Revolution altered relations among social classes, gave rise to new types of work and workers' organizations, inspired original ideas about the reorganization of society, raised the standard of living, contributed to the formation of immense urban centers, and made change rather than stability the expected fact of life. This unequal distribution of the new riches helped to spawn class conflict, manifest in the programs of socialists, communists, and anarchists, as well as in mass political parties that gathered in the laboring poor.

One of the themes of nineteenth-century history is the development of worker consciousness (aided perhaps by growing literacy and the penny press) and the increasing politicization of the masses, who could easily resent the lifestyles and power of the bourgeoisie. These changes occurred in the midst of the new urban landscape, transformed by technological wonders such as steel and electricity. Great new industries arose in chemicals, oil, and pharmaceuticals. At the same

125

time, millions of Europeans left their homes to colonize and rule other cultures. The nineteenth century was the heyday of European imperialism and the great age of European power. Textbooks might stress ninteenth-century intellectual and cultural movements such as Romanticism or political developments such as the unification of Italy and of Germany, all important in their own right, but these must be set against the background of rapid and unsettling change in the human relationships, values, and beliefs that concerned the vast majority of the population.

Factory Discipline
in the Industrial Revolution

SIDNEY POLLARD

The nature of work and leisure time changed dramatically with the Industrial Revolution. Previously, workers could proceed at their own pace, determining when to rest or to cease their labors for the day. After all, who would care if a woman at a loom in her own home suddenly decided to take a fifteen-minute break? But, as Sidney Pollard shows, the entrepreneurs who were the early factory owners consciously endeavored to change the more relaxed work habits of pre-industrial England. In the process, they aimed at nothing less than the reformation of the workers' morals and character.

What exactly was the new factory discipline? How did it operate? The need to alter the employees' concept of work derived from the machinery. In what ways did machinery make it imperative for workers to conform to factory discipline? What does Pollard mean by the concept of "time-thrift"?

For the owners to demand factory discipline was not enough; they had to force or cajole their workers to relinquish patterns of behavior that were, after all, centuries old. The owners used three methods: the carrot, the stick, and "the attempt to create a new ethos of work order and obedience." What did each of these methods consist of? How effective were they? Surely some of the problems of factory-operative behavior—problems from the owners' point of view, that is—still persist today. Child workers presented a special problem for the owners. What methods helped insure that the very young would become accustomed to factory discipline?

It is interesting that Pollard claims that the carrot, a favored method of enlightened factory owners, was successful, but was not copied very much. Why? What did the owners think of the workers' character? How do you explain the owners' great concern to prohibit swearing and indecent language? Did they usually treat their workers with respect, or did they view them as mere cogs in the wheels of production? What conclusions does Pollard draw about the imposition of factory discipline?

It is nowadays increasingly coming to be accepted that one of the most critical, and one of the most difficult, transformations required in an industrializing society is the adjustment of labour to the regularity and discipline of factory work. . . . [T]he first generation of factory workers will be examined, irrespective of its appearance at different times in different industries.

Sidney Pollard, "Factory Discipline in the Industrial Revolution," *Economic History Review* 16 (December 1963): 254–71.

The worker who left the background of his domestic workshop or peasant holding for the factory, entered a new culture as well as a new sense of direction. It was not only that 'the new economic order needed . . . part-humans: soulless, depersonalised, disembodied, who could become members, or little wheels rather, of a complex mechanism'. It was also that men who were non-accumulative, non-acquisitive, accustomed to work for subsistence, not for maximization of income, had to be made obedient to the cash stimulus, and obedient in such a way as to react precisely to the stimuli provided.

The very recruitment to the uncongenial work was difficult, and it was made worse by the deliberate or accidental modelling of many works on workhouses and prisons, a fact well known to the working population. Even if they began work, there was no guarantee that the new hands would stay. 'Labourers from agriculture or domestic industry do not at first take kindly to the monotony of factory life; and the pioneering employer not infrequently finds his most serious obstacle in the problem of building up a stable supply of efficient and willing labour'. Many workers were 'transient, marginal and deviant', or were described as 'volatile'. It was noted that there were few early manufactures in the seaport towns, as the population was too unsteady. . . . Thus it was not necessarily the better labourer, but the stable one who was worth the most to the manufacturer: often, indeed, the skilled apprenticed man was at a discount, because of the working habits acquired before entering a factory. . . .

. . . [I]n Scotland even the children found the discipline irksome: when the Catrine cotton mills were opened, one of the managers admitted, 'the children were all newcomers, and were very much beat at first before they could be taught their business'. At other mills, 'on the first introduction of the business, the people were found very ill-disposed to submit to the long confinement and regular industry that is required from them'. The highlander, it was said, 'never sits at ease at a loom; it is like putting a deer in the plough'.

In turn, the personal inclinations and group *mores* of such old-established industrial workers as handloom weavers and framework knitters were opposed to factory discipline. 'I found the utmost distaste', one hosier reported, 'on the part of the men, to any regular hours or regular habits. . . . The men themselves were considerably dissatisfied, because they could not go in and out as they pleased, and have what holidays they pleased, and go on just as they had been used to do. . . . '

As a result of this attitude, attendance was irregular, and the complaint of Edward Cave,[1] in the very earliest days of industrialization, was later re-echoed by many others: 'I have not half my people come to work to-day, and I have no great fascination in the prospect I have to put

[1]Printer, 1691–1754.

myself in the power of such people.' Cotton spinners would stay away without notice and send for their wages at the end of the week, and one of the most enlightened firms, McConnel and Kennedy, regularly replaced spinners who had not turned up within two or three hours of starting time on Mondays, on the reasonable presumption that they had left the firm: their average labour turnover was 20 a week, i.e. about 100 per cent a year.

Matters were worse in a place like Dowlais, reputed to employ many runaways and criminals, or among northern mining companies which could not guarantee continuous work: 'the major part of these two companies are as bad fellows as the worst of your pitmen baring their outside is not so black', one exasperated manager complained, after they had left the district without paying their debts. Elsewhere, ironworks labourers, copper and tin miners and engineering labourers deserted to bring in the harvest, or might return to agriculture for good if work was slack.

'St Monday' and feast days, common traditions in domestic industry, were persistent problems. The weavers were used to 'play frequently all day on Monday, and the greater part of Tuesday, and work very late on Thursday night, and frequently all night on Friday'. Spinners, even as late as 1800, would be missing from the factories on Mondays and Tuesdays, and 'when they did return, they would sometimes work desperately, night and day, to clear off their tavern score, and get more money to spend in dissipation', as a hostile critic observed. In South Wales it was estimated as late as the 1840's that the workers lost one week in five, and that in the fortnight after the monthly pay day, only two-thirds of the time was being worked.

As for the regular feasts, 'our men will go to the Wakes', Josiah Wedgwood[2] complained in 1772, 'if they were sure to go to the D—l the next. I have not spared them in threats and I would have thrash'd them right heartily if I could'. . . .

Employers themselves, groping their way towards a new impersonal discipline, looked backwards sporadically to make use of feasts and holidays, typical of the old order in cementing personal relationships and breaking the monotony of the working year. . . . The Arkwrights and the Strutts, standing on the watershed between the old and the new, had feasts in Cromford in 1776, when 500 workers and their children took part, and annual balls at Cromford and Belper as late as 1781, whilst in 1772 the Hockley factory had an outing, led by the 'head workman' clad in white cotton, to gather nuts, and be regaled to a plentiful supper afterwards.

Other examples from industries in their early transitional stages include Matthew Boulton's[3] feast for 700 when his son came of age,

---

[2]Owner of a pottery factory, 1730–1795.

[3]Inventor (1728–1809), along with James Watt, of an efficient steam engine.

Wedgwood's feast for 120 when he moved into Etruria, . . . and the repast provided by the Herculaneum Pottery at the opening of its Liverpool warehouse in 1813. Conversely, the Amlwch miners organized an ox-roast in honour of the chief proprietor, the Marquis of Anglesea, when he passed through the island on his way to take up the Lord-Lieutenancy of Ireland. 600 workmen sat down to a roasted ox and plenty of liquor at the Duke of Bridgewater's expense to celebrate the opening of the canal at Runcorn, and feasts were usual thereafter at the opening of canals and railways, but within a generation it was the shareholders that were being feasted, not the workers, whose relationship with the employers had by then taken on an entirely different character.

Once at work it was necessary to break down the impulses of the workers, to introduce the notion of 'time-thrift'. The factory meant economy of time and . . . 'enforced asceticism'. Bad timekeeping was punished by severe fines, and it was common in mills such as Oldknow's or Braids' to lock the gates of the factory, even of the workrooms, excluding those who were only a minute or two late. 'Whatever else the domestic system[4] was, however intermittent and sweated its labour, it did allow a man a degree of personal liberty to indulge himself, a command over his time, which he was not to enjoy again.'

By contrast, in the factories, Arkwright,[5] for example, had the greatest difficulty 'in training human beings to renounce their desultory habits of work, and identify themselves with the unvarying regularity of the complex automaton'. He 'had to train his workpeople to a precision and assiduity altogether unknown before, against which their listless and restive habits rose in continued rebellion', and it was his great achievement 'to devise and administer a successful code of factory diligence'. 'Impatient of the slovenly habits of workpeople, he urged on their labours with a precision and vigilance unknown before'. The reasons for the difference were clear to manufacturers: 'When a mantua maker chooses to rise from her seat and take the fresh air, her seam goes a little back, that is all; there are no other hands waiting on her', but 'in cotton mills all the machinery is going on, which they must attend to'. It was 'machinery [which] ultimately forced the worker to accept the discipline of the factory'.

Regular hours and application had to be combined with a new kind of order in the works. Wedgwood, for example, had to fight the old pottery traditions when introducing 'the punctuality, the constant attendance, the fixed hours, the scrupulous standards of care and cleanliness, the avoidance of waste, the ban on drinking'. . . .

Finally, 'Discipline . . . was to produce the goods on time. It was

[4]Also known as the domestic system, whereby a merchant provided raw materials to workers, who then worked in their own homes.

[5]Richard Arkwright (1732–1792), inventor of the water-frame, a spinning machine that led to the creation of large cotton mills.

also to prevent the workmen from stealing raw materials, putting in shoddy, or otherwise getting the better of their employers'. It allowed the employer to maintain a high quality of output. . . .

Works Rules, formalized, impersonal and occasionally printed, were symbolic of the new industrial relationships. Many rules dealt with disciplinary matters only, but quite a few laid down the organization of the firm itself. 'So strict are the instructions,' it was said of John Marshall's[6] flax mills in 1821, 'that if an overseer of a room be found talking to any person in the mill during working hours he is dismissed immediately—two or more overseers are employed in each room, if one be found a yard out of his ground he is discharged . . . everyone, manager, overseers, mechanics, oilers, spreaders, spinners and reelers, have their particular duty pointed out to them, and if they transgress, they are instantly turned off as unfit for their situation.'

While the domestic system had implied some measure of control, 'it was . . . an essentially new thing for the capitalist to be a disciplinarian'. 'The capitalist employer became a supervisor of every detail of the work: without any change in the general character of the wage contract, the employer acquired new powers which were of great social significance.' The concept of industrial discipline was new, and called for as much innovation as the technical inventions of the age.

Child work immeasurably increased the complexities of the problem. It had, as such, been common enough before, but the earlier work pattern had been based on the direct control of children and youths, in small numbers, by their parents or guardians. The new mass employment removed the incentive of learning a craft, alienated the children by its monotony and did this just at the moment when it undermined the authority of the family, and of the father in particular. It thus had to rely often on the unhappy method of indirect employment by untrained people whose incentive for driving the children was their own piece-rate payment.

In the predominantly youthful population of the time, the proportion of young workers was high. In the Cumberland mines, for example, children started work at the ages of five to seven, and as late as 1842, 200–250 of the 1,300–1,400 workers in the Lonsdale mines were under eighteen. At Alloa collieries, 103 boys and girls of under seven were employed in 1780. In the light metal trades, the proportion was higher still. Josiah Wedgwood, in 1816, had 30 per cent of his employees under eighteen, 3.3 per cent under ten years of age. The greatest problems, however, were encountered in the textile mills.

The silk mills were dependent almost exclusively on child labour, and there the children started particularly young, at the ages of six or seven, compared with nine or ten in the cotton mills. Typically from two-thirds to three-quarters of the hands were under eighteen but in some

[6]Textile magnate.

large mills, the proportion was much higher: at Tootal's for example, 78 per cent of the workers were under sixteen. Adults were thus in a small minority.

In the cotton industry the proportion of children and adolescents under eighteen was around 40–45 per cent. In some large firms the proportions were higher: thus Horrocks, Miller and Co. in 1816 had 13 per cent of their labour force under ten years of age, and 60 per cent between ten and eighteen, a total of 73 per cent. The proportion of children under ten was mostly much smaller than this, but in water mills employing large numbers of apprentices it might be greater: New Lanark, under David Dale in 1793, had 18 per cent of its labour force nine years old or younger.

In the flax and the woollen and worsted industries, the proportions of workers under eighteen were rather higher than in cotton, being around 50 per cent. Again individual large works show much higher figures. In John Marshall's Water Lane Mill in 1831, for example, 49.2 per cent were under fifteen, and 83.8 per cent altogether under twenty-one. Further, in all the textile branches the children were largely concentrated in certain sections, such as silk throwing and cotton spinning. In such departments, the difficulties of maintaining discipline were greatest.

These, then, were the problems of factory discipline facing the entrepreneurs in the early years of industrialization. Their methods of overcoming them may be grouped under three headings: the proverbial stick, the proverbial carrot, and, thirdly, the attempt to create a new ethos of work order and obedience.

Little new in the way of the 'stick', or deterrent, was discovered by the early factory masters. Unsatisfactory work was punished by corporal punishment, by fines or by dismissal. Beatings clearly belonged to the older, personal relationships and were common with apprentices, against whom few other sanctions were possible, but they survived because of the large-scale employment of children. Since the beating of children became one of the main complaints against factory owners and a major point at issue before the various Factory Commissions,[7] the large amount of evidence available is not entirely trustworthy, but the picture is fairly clear in outline.

Some prominent factory owners . . . prohibited it outright, though the odd cuff for inattention was probably inevitable in any children's employment. More serious beatings were neither very widespread, nor very effective. . . . [L]arge employers frowned on beatings, though they might turn a blind eye on the overlookers' actions. 'We beat only the lesser, up to thirteen or fourteen . . . we use a strap', stated Samuel Miller, manager of Wilson's mill in Nottingham, one of the few to admit to this to the Factory Commission, 'I prefer fining to beating, if it answers . . . (but) fining does not answer. It does not keep the boys

[7]Royal commissions established to investigate working conditions.

at their work'. The most honest evidence, however, and the most significant, came from John Bolling, a cotton master. He could not stop his
spinners beating the children, he stated, 'for children require correction
now and then, and the difficulty is to keep it from being excessive. . . . It
never can be in the interest of the master that the children should be
beaten. The other day there were three children run away; the mother
of one of them brought him back and asked us to beat him; that I could
not permit; she asked us to take him again: at last I consented, and then
she beat him.'

Dismissal and the threat of dismissal, were in fact the main deterrent
instruments of enforcing discipline in the factories. At times of labour
shortage they were ineffective, but when a buyers' market in labour
returned, a sigh of relief went through the ranks of the employers at
the restoration of their power. Many abolished the apprenticeship system in order to gain it, and without it others were unable to keep any
control whatsoever. Where there were no competing mill employers, as
at Shrewsbury in the case of Marshall and Benyon's flax mills, it was a
most effective threat.

In industries where skill and experience were at a premium, however, dismissals were resorted to only most reluctantly. . . .

Fines formed the third type of sanctions used, and were common
both in industries employing skilled men, and in those employing mostly
women and children. They figure prominently in all the sets of rules
surviving, and appear to have been the most usual reaction to minor
transgressions. Where the employer pocketed the fine there was an additional inducement to levy it freely, and in some cases, as in the deductions and penalties for sending small coal or stones up in the corves from
the coal face, these became a major source of abuse and grievance.

Their general level was high and was meant to hurt. Typically, they
were levied at 6d. to 2s. for ordinary offences or, say, two hours' to a
day's wages. Wedgwood fined 2s. 6d. for throwing things or for leaving
fires burning overnight, and that was also the penalty for being absent
on Monday mornings in the Worsley mines. At Fernley's Stockport mill,
swearing, singing or being drunk were punished by a fine of 5s. and
so was stealing coal at Merthyr. Miners were fined even more heavily:
average weekly deductions were alleged to be as high as 1s. or 2s. out of
a wage of 13s.

Deterrence as a method of industrial discipline should, strictly, also
include the actions taken against workers' organizations. . . . The law
could usually be assumed to be at the service of the employer, and
was called into service for two types of offence, breaches of contract
and trade-union organization and rioting. Workmen's combinations were
widely treated as criminal offences in employers' circles, even before the
law made them explicitly such, and in turn, the legal disabilities turned
trade disputes easily towards violence, particularly before the 1790's. In
the Scottish mines, serfdom was only just being eradicated, and in the

North-East the one-year contract, coupled with the character note, could be used also to impose conditions akin to serfdom; opposition, including the inevitable rioting, was met by transportation and the death penalty not only in the mines, but even in such advanced centres as Etruria as late as 1783.

Where their powers permitted, employers met organization with immediate dismissal: 'any hands forming conspiracies or unlawful combinations will be discharged without notice' read one rule as late as 1833. More widespread, however, was the use of blacklists against those who had aroused the employer's disfavour. Little was heard of them, even in contemporary complaints by workmen, but their importance should not be underrated: . . . it is increasingly obvious that they were a most important prop of that reign of terror which in so many works did duty for factory discipline.

By comparison with these commonly used examples of the 'stick', more subtle or more finely graded deterrents were so rare as to be curious rather than significant. John Wood, the Bradford spinner, made the child guilty of a fault hold up a card with his offence written on it; for more serious offences, this punishment was increased to walking up and down with the card, then to having to tell everyone in the room, and, as the highest stage, confessing to workers in other rooms. Witts and Rodick, the Essex silk-mill owners, made their errant children wear degrading dress. These measures presuppose a general agreement with the factory code on the part of the other workmen which today few would take for granted. . . .

Employees were as conservative in the use of the carrot as they were in the use of the stick. For a generation driving its children to labour in the mills for twelve to fourteen hours a day, positive incentives must indeed have been hard to devise and, for the child workers at least, were used even less than for adults. Much better, as in the case of at least one flax mill, to give them snuff to keep them awake in the evenings. The extent of the predominance of the deterrent over the incentive in the case of the factory children is brought out in the returns of the 1833 Factory Commission, in replies to item 57 of the questionnaire sent out: 'What are the means taken to enforce obedience on the part of the children employed in your works?'. . . Bearing in mind that most respondents were merely concerned to deny that they beat their children, and that many replied with the method they thought they ought to use, rather than the one actually in use, the following proportion may appear even more surprising:

*Number of firms using different means to enforce obedience
among factory children, 1833*

Negative		Positive	
Dismissal	353	Kindness	2
Threat of dismissal	48	Promotion, or higher wages	9

Fines, deductions	101	Reward or premium	23
Corporal punishment	55		
Complaint to parents	13		
Confined to mill	2		
Degrading dress, badge	3		
Totals	575		34

The contrast is surely too strong to be fortuitous, especially since the bias was all the other way.

For adults, there were two positive methods which formed the stock-in-trade of management in this period. One was sub-contract, the transference of responsibility for making the workers industrious, to overseers, butty-men, group leaders, first hands and sub-contractors of various types. But this solution, which raises, in any case, questions of its own, was not a method of creating factory discipline, but of evading it. The discipline was to be the older form of that of the supervisor of a small face-to-face group, maintained by someone who usually worked himself or was in direct daily contact with the workers.

The other method was some variant of payments by results. This provided the cash nexus symbolic for the new age. It was also a natural derivation from the methods used in earlier periods in such skilled and predominantly male trades as iron-smelting, mining, pottery or the production of metal goods. In 1833, of 67,819 cotton-mill workers in 225 mills, 47.1 per cent were on piece-work and 43.7 per cent were paid datally,[8] the method of payment for the remainder being unknown. Labourers, children and others under direct supervision of a skilled piece-worker, and some highly skilled trades in short supply, such as engineers and building craftsmen, did, however, remain on fixed datal pay.

In many enterprises the 'discovery' of payment by results was greeted as an innovation of major significance, and at times the change-over does seem to have led to marked improvements in productivity. . . .

Many of the older systems of payment by results, as in copper or tin mines, or in sinking colliery shafts, consisted of group piece-work, in which the cohesion and ethos of the group was added to the incentive payment as such to create work discipline. The newly introduced systems, however, were typically aimed at individual effort. As such, they were less effective . . . and they were often badly constructed, particularly for times of rapid technological change. There were many examples of the usual problems of this type of payment, such as speed-up and rate cutting, as at Soho and Etruria, loss of quality, and friction over interpretation and deductions. Nevertheless, it represented the major change and forward step in the employer's attitude towards labour, not only because it used cash as such but more specifically because it marked the end of the belief that workers were looking for a fixed minimum income, and a

[8]Daily.

rate of earnings beyond this would merely lead to absenteeism . . . and the beginning of the notion that the workers' efforts were elastic with respect to income over a wide range.

The rise in the belief in the efficacy of incentive piece payments coincided with a decline in the belief in the efficacy of long-term contracts. These contracts were largely a survival of the pre-industrial age, adopted by many employers even during the Industrial Revolution at times of acute shortages of labour. In the north-eastern coalfield, the one-year binding had become almost universal since the beginning of the eighteenth century and it had spread to salters, keelmen, file-workers and others. Ambrose Crowley[9] bound his men for six months, Arkwright for three months, . . . some potteries for seven years, some cotton mills for five up to twenty-one years and the Prestonpans chemical works for twenty-one years. But any hope that these indentures would ensure discipline and hard work was usually disappointed, and the system was quickly abandoned as a disciplinary method, though it might be continued for other reasons.

A few employers evolved incentive schemes with a considerable degree of sophistication. In their simplest form, overseers bribed children to work on for fourteen or fifteen hours and forgo their meal intervals, and John Wood[10] paid them a bonus of 1*d*. weekly if they worked well, but hung a notice of shame on them if they did not. At Backbarrow mill, apprentices received a 'bounty' of 6*d*. or 1*s*., to be withdrawn if offences were committed, and in silk mills articles of clothing were given to the children as prizes for good work; at one silk mill, employing 300 children aged nine or less, a prize of bacon and three score of potatoes was given to the hardest working boy, and a doll to the hardest working girl, and their output then became the norm for the rest. Richard Arkwright, in his early years, also gave prizes to the best workers.

Later on, these bonuses were made conditional on a longer period of satisfactory work, or modified in other ways. In the early 1800's the Strutts introduced 'quarterly gift money'—one-sixth of wages being held back over three months, and paid out at the end only after deductions for misconduct. At John Marshall's the best department received a bonus each quarter, amounting to £10 for the overlooker and a week's wage for the hands, and some Dowlais men, at least, also received a bonus of £2 every quarter, conditional upon satisfactory performance. At the Whitehaven collieries, the bonus to the foremen was annual and was tied to net profits: when these exceeded £30,000, the salary of the two viewers was nearly doubled, from £152 to £300, and those of the overmen raised in almost like proportion from a range of £52–82 to a range of £90–170— a particularly effective and cheap means of inducing industry. In other

[9]Iron smelter who pioneered the large-scale importation of Swedish ores.
[10]A worsted manufacturer who began the movement for a ten-hour day.

coal mines, the ladder of promotion to overmen was used effectively as an incentive. . . .

Compared with the ubiquity of financial rewards, other direct incentives were rare and localized, though they were highly significant. Wedgwood at times appealed directly to his workers, in at least one case writing a pamphlet for them in which he stressed their common interests. . . . Arkwright gave distinguishing dresses to the best workers of both sexes and John Marshall fixed a card on each machine, showing its output. Best known of all were the 'silent monitors' of Robert Owen.[11] He awarded four types of mark for the past day's work to each superintendent, and each of them, in turn, judged all his workers; the mark was then translated into the colours black-blue-yellow-white, in ascending order of merit, painted on the four sides of a piece of wood mounted over the machine, and turned outward according to the worker's performance.

There is no doubt that Owen attached great importance to this system, entering all daily marks in a book as a permanent record, to be periodically inspected by him. There is equally no doubt that, naive as they might seem to-day, these methods were successful among all the leading manufacturers named, Robert Owen, in particular, running his mills, both in Manchester and in Scotland, at regular high annual profits largely because he gained the voluntary co-operation of his workers. Why, then were these methods not copied as widely as the technological innovations?

The reasons may have been ignorance on the part of other masters, disbelief or a (partly justified) suspicion that the enlightened employers would have been successful with or without such methods, enjoying advantages of techniques, size or a well-established market; but to limit the reasons to these would be to ignore one of the most decisive social facts of the age. An approach like Owen's ran counter to the accepted beliefs and ideology of the employing class, which saw its own rise to wealth and power as due to merit, and the workman's subordinate position as due to his failings. He remained a workman, living at subsistence wages, because he was less well endowed with the essential qualities of industry, ambition, sobriety and thrift. As long as this was so, he could hardly be expected to rise to the baits of moral appeals or co-operation. Therefore, one would have to begin by indoctrinating him with the bourgeois values which he lacked, and this, essentially, was the third method used by employers.

In their attempts to prevent 'Idleness, Extravagance, Waste and Immorality', employers were necessarily dealing with the workers both inside the factory and outside it. The efforts to reform the whole man were, therefore, particularly marked in factory towns and villages

[11]Industrialist and social reformer, 1771–1858.

in which the total environment was under the control of a single employer.

The qualities of character which employers admired have, since Weber's[12] day, been to some extent associated with the Protestant ethic. To impart these qualities, with the one addition of obedience, to the working classes, could not but appear a formidable task. That it should have been attempted at all might seem to us incredible, unless we remember the background of the times which included the need to educate the first generation of factory workers to a new factory discipline, the widespread belief in human perfectibility, and the common assumption, by the employer, of functions which are to-day provided by the public authorities, like public safety, road building or education. . . . [O]ne of their consequences was the preoccupation with the character and morals of the working classes which are so marked a feature of the early stages of industrialization.

Some aspects of this are well known and easily understandable. Factory villages like New Lanark, Deanston, Busby, Ballindaloch, New Kilpatrick, Blantyre, and . . . Antrim, had special provisions, and in some cases full-time staff, to check the morals of their workers. Contemporaries tended to praise these actions most highly, and it was believed that firms laying stress on morals, and employing foremen who 'suppress anything bad' would get the pick of the labour. Almost everywhere, churches, chapels and Sunday Schools were supported by employers, both to encourage moral education in its more usual sense, and to inculcate obedience. Drink and drunkenness became a major target of reform, with the short-term aim of increasing the usefulness of scarce skilled workers . . . who were often incapacitated by drink, and the long-term aim of spreading bourgeois virtues.

In this process much of the existing village culture came under attack. 'Traditional social habits and customs seldom fitted into the new pattern of industrial life, and they had therefore to be discredited as hindrances to progress.' Two campaigns here deserve special mention.

The first was the campaign against leisure on Saturdays and Sundays, as, no doubt, examples of immoral idleness. 'The children are during the weekdays generally employed', the Bishop of Chester had declared solemnly in 1785, 'and on Sunday are apt to be idle, mischievous and vitious.' This was not easily tolerated. Thus Deanston had a Superintendant of streets to keep them clear of immorality, children and drink. Charles Wilkins of Tiverton formed an 'Association for the Promotion of Order' in 1832 to round up the children and drive them to school on Sundays. All the hands at Strutt's and Arkwright's under twenty had to attend school for four hours on Saturday afternoons and on Sundays to 'keep them out of mischief'. Horrocks' employed a man 'for many years,

[12]German sociologist (1864–1920), author of *The Protestant Ethic and the Spirit of Capitalism.*

to see that the children do not loiter about the streets on Sundays'. At Dowlais the chapel Sunday school teachers asked J.J. Guest in 1818 to order his employees to attend, otherwise there was the danger that they might spend the Sabbath 'rambling and playing'. Even Owen expressed similar sentiments: 'if children [under ten] are not to be instructed, they had better be employed in any occupation that should keep them out of mischief', he asserted.

The second was the prohibition of bad language. At the beginning of the eighteenth century, Crowley's 'Clerk for the Poor', or teacher, was to correct lying, swearing, 'and suchlike horrid crimes'; while at the same time Sir Humphrey Mackworth, at Neath, fined 'Swearing, Cursing, Quarrelling, being Drunk, or neglecting Divine Service on Sunday, one shilling', and the Quaker Lead Company, at Gadlis, also prohibited swearing in 1708. Later this became quite regular, wherever rules were made: at Darley Abbey, in 1795, the fine was 9*d* or 1*s.*; at Mellor, 1*s.*; at Nenthead, 6*d.*; at Galloway's where 'obscene and vulgar language' was prohibited, the men themselves levied the fines. At Marshall and Benyon's also, according to Rule 4 of 1785, a jury of seven was to judge the offence of striking, abusing or harming another workman.

Again, the rules of Thomas Fernley, Jr., Stockport, cotton mills, stated: 'while at work . . . behaviour must be commendable avoiding all shouting, loud talk, whistling, calling foul names, all mean and vulgar language, and every kind of indecency'. Swearing, singing, being drunk were fined 5*s.*; overlookers allowing drink in the mills were fined 10*s.* 6*d.* . . .

This preoccupation might seem to today's observer to be both impertinent and irrelevant to the worker's performance, but in fact it was critical, for unless the workmen *wished* to become 'respectable' in the current sense, none of the other incentives would bite. Such opprobrious terms as 'idle' or 'dissolute' should be taken to mean strictly that the worker was indifferent to the employer's deterrents and incentives. According to contemporaries, 'it was the irrationality of the poor, quite as much as their irreligion, that was distressing. They took no thought of the morrow. . . . The workers were by nature indolent, improvident, and self-indulgent.'

The code of ethics on which employers concentrated was thus rather limited. Warnings against greed, selfishness, materialism or pride seldom played a large part, sexual morals rarely became an important issue to the factory disciplinarians (as distinct from outside moralists) and, by and large, they did not mind which God was worshipped, as long as the worshipper was under the influence of some respectable clergyman. The conclusion cannot be avoided that, with some honourable exceptions, the drive to raise the level of respectability and morality among the working classes was not undertaken for their own sakes but primarily, or even exclusively, as an aspect of building up a new factory discipline.

Any conclusions drawn from this brief survey must be tentative and hesitant, particularly if they are meant to apply to industrial revolutions in general.

First, the acclimatization of new workers to factory discipline is a task different in kind, at once more subtle and more violent, from that of maintaining discipline among a proletarian population of long standing. Employers in the British Industrial Revolution therefore used not only industrial means but a whole battery of extra-mural powers, including their control over the courts, their powers as landlords, and their own ideology, to impose the control they required.

Secondly, the maintenance of discipline, like the whole field of management itself, was not considered a fit subject for study, still less a science, but merely a matter of the employer's individual character and ability. No books were written on it before 1830, no teachers lectured on it, there were no entries about it in the technical encyclopaedias, no patents were taken out relating to it. As a result, employers did not learn from each other, except haphazardly and belatedly, new ideas did not have the cachet of a new technology and did not spread, and the crudest form of deterrents and incentives remained the rule. Robert Owen was exceptional in ensuring that his methods, at least, were widely known, but they were too closely meshed in with his social doctrines to be acceptable to other employers.

Lastly, the inevitable emphasis on reforming the moral character of the worker into a willing machine-minder led to a logical dilemma that contemporaries did not know how to escape. For if the employer had it in his power to reform the workers if he but tried hard enough, whose fault was it that most of them remained immoral, idle and rebellious? And if the workers could really be taught their employers' virtues, would they not all save and borrow and become entrepreneurs themselves, and who would then man the factories?

The Industrial Revolution happened too rapidly for these dilemmas, which involved the re-orientation of a whole class, to be solved, as it were, *en passant*.[13] The assimilation of the formerly independent worker to the needs of factory routine took at least a further generation, and was accompanied by the help of tradition, by a sharply differentiated educational system, and new ideologies which were themselves the results of clashes of earlier systems of values, besides the forces operating before 1830. The search for a more scientific approach which would collaborate with and use, instead of seeking to destroy, the workers' own values, began later still, and may hardly be said to have advanced very far even today.

[13]Casually, in passing.

Urban Man

HUGH THOMAS

When one thinks of great civilizations, cities come immediately to mind: Babylon, Athens, Rome, Alexandria, Paris, London, to name a few. Yet, until recently (1851 for Great Britain, 1920 for the United States), the great majority of the world's population lived in rural areas. Population increase, affirms Hugh Thomas, "created modern life," and much of the demographic growth occurred in cities, largely as a result of the influx of workers from the countryside. Furthermore, the Industrial Revolution was in large part responsible for our modern urban civilization. How did nineteenth-century technological developments in construction and transportation change cities? How did the post-industrial differ from the pre-industrial city or, for that matter, from nineteenth-century cities located in countries that did not industrialize rapidly?

Thomas moves from a discussion of technological changes to the new commercial patterns in urban life, found principally in the development of the modern shop. He then focuses at length on the quality of life, notoriously unhealthful because of the incredible filth and loathsome diseases that were omnipresent. Why did these conditions persist? What was the role of the state in improving the urban environment? Thomas rightly stresses the importance of good water and hygiene in the modern city; it was essential that clean water go into the city and that sewage go out. Perhaps the accomplishment of those two tasks most distinguishes the modern city from the earlier urban hell.

One disturbing consequence of the appearance of the industrial city has been a rise in crime. Why does Thomas believe that crime has increasingly become an urban problem? The tremendous growth of cities, then, has had both positive and negative effects.

The age of industry transformed the place of living of the majority of the world's population. This was seen most evidently in the growth of cities. Half the population of England was urban in 1851: a predicament never before found in a great nation. By 1900, agriculture only occupied ten per cent of the English population.

The rise in population, rather than industrialisation, created modern life. Urbanisation is not the same thing as industrialisation. Egypt, for example, is now as urbanised as Switzerland, more so (on the basis of the percentage of the population living in cities of 100,000 or more) than France, but not nearly so industrialised.

Hugh Thomas, *A History of the World* (New York: Harper & Row, 1979), pp. 410–421.

The fact that people live in cities has often been regretted as if it were in itself a source of major decline in the quality of life. Of this, it is possible to be sceptical. Urban life makes for easier access to schools and to professions linked to literacy. In every country in the world where illiteracy exists, and where statistics are reliable, those who live in cities are more likely to be able to read and write than those who live in the country. . . .

The Industrial Revolution found the world's population living in wood, mud, brick and stone. It is leaving it in cement, glass and steel. In the eighteenth century, there were places where living conditions were far worse than those which obtained in the days of Babylon. Even in England, in the early nineteenth century, there were many houses with mud floors, many turf houses with squatters. Some farm labourers lived in one-roomed hovels, sometimes below ground, usually damp. In Russia, many houses showed scarcely any improvement on the huts of hunters of the days before 10,000 BC. One of the first coherent observers of Russian life . . . described a typical house between St. Petersburg and Moscow in about 1770 thus: 'the upper half of the four walls and the whole ceiling were covered with soot; the floor was full of dust and covered with dirt at least two inches thick; the oven [was] without a chimney but their best protection against the cold; and smoke filled the hut every morning, winter and summer. Window holes . . . admitted a dim light at noon time; [there were also to be seen] two or three pots . . . a wooden bowl and round trenchers . . . a table, hewn with an axe, which they scrape clean on holidays . . . a trough to feed pigs and calves, if there are any. . . . If they are lucky, a barrel of *kvass* [the drink made from fermented bread, much drunk by Russian peasants] that tastes like vinegar and, in the yard, a bath house in which the cattle sleep if people are not steaming in it'. To those who lived in such places, the 'rough brick houses' of Babylon would have seemed a luxury. Yet, of course, those Russians had the countryside in which to breathe; and it is not clear beyond all doubt that they would have preferred to have lived in the London of the 1880s with what for Matthew Arnold[1] seemed 'its unutterable external ugliness'. It also seems possible that half the population of Asia and Africa still live in conditions worse than those which pertained in eighteenth century England.

The first impact of the Industrial Revolution on cities and on building everywhere, was to increase the quantity of brick used. Unless the building was of exceptional importance, stone was only used in regions where it could easily be quarried. That ruled out much of England and the east of the US. Wood was also scarce because of the need for it in shipyards and in charcoal burning, or because the country concerned had already used up the forests. Subsequently, John Nash, a Welsh architect, popu-

[1]English poet and essayist, 1822–1888.

larised anew the ancient practice of covering inferior brickwork with the stucco which has subsequently marked so much of northern European architecture.

Nash was still at the height of his popularity when, in 1824, Portland cement was invented. . . . Cement came into general use after 1850, with big demands made for it for sewers in modern cities. Cast iron was also added to possible new building materials, first to support columns, then to replace wooden beams, later still to give large frames for large buildings, as in the new apartment blocks of New York. Reinforced concrete (cement with steel or iron rods embedded, with the strength of steel and stone combined) began to be introduced from the 1850s. . . . [S]uch material could be laid under fifteen feet of earth, for sewers. Concrete bridges also began to be made. Subsequently, steel enabled large buildings, and bridges, to be prefabricated. The most striking consequence was the skyscraper, the demand for which derived from the rise of land values in New York and Chicago, about 1880. Wrought iron skyscrapers could be built to the height of fourteen floors, but they had to have greater thickness at the base than at the top. The steel frame could be raised almost to any height without an increase in the size at the bottom. Thereafter, the function of walls was only to give privacy and shelter. The first steel skyscraper went up in Chicago in 1890, in New York in 1894. There were twenty-nine there by 1900. Europe, however, was restrained. It was only after 1945 that steel framed skyscrapers began to be built there. London was earlier saved from these developments by the theory, which turned out unfortunately to be an illusion, that the ground under it was soft.

Long before that, another invention had made the skyscraper a practical, as opposed to a theoretical, possibility: the hydraulic lift was devised in 1854 by Elisha Graves Otis, a Vermont inventor. . . . Otis's elevator worked by steam and had safety appliances. The passengers were carried in a case with pawls which were forced by springs to engage in ratchets at the side should the rope fail. A hydraulic lift reached to the top of the Eiffel Tower. An electric version was soon introduced. The curious artistic sect who called themselves futurists later conceived of houses as being built with lifts and no stairs—an idea which palls now that futurists are men of the past.

By the time of the futurists, about 1910, prefabricated building of houses had indeed been started in, for instance, Chicago, where balloon frames, roofs, floors, walls were supplied in factories and put together by amateurs. Ready-made doors and windows were fitted into the prefabricated structures. This was the first concession to mechanisation in a business which had until then been resistant to it.

Then there was glass. Optical glass had been improving throughout the eighteenth century. Most glass made for windows, however, consisted of small round sheets, with bulls' eyes in the middle, constructed from a globe of glass attached by molten metal to an iron rod. But plate glass had been achieved in France in the days of Louis XIV (the Hall of Mirrors in Versailles was an early use of that). From the 1770s, plate glass could be made by steam power. That transformed the history of the window. In the nineteenth century, the demand for window glass in Europe, with so much new building, exceeded all expectations. . . . Subsequently, the use of glass, with iron and steel, enabled engineers to make both roofs and walls transparent.

But it was not only technology which made the modern cities. As suggested earlier, those conglomerations could not have survived had their supplies not come from old methods of grinding corn, in local windmills or water mills, baking it at home, bringing meat on foot, and gaining milk from suburban cattle keepers. Railways, refrigeration and tins were needed to ensure the food of the new urban millions.

The modern city saw, too, changes in the commercial exploitation not only of these foods but of everything saleable. In the seventeenth century, some public markets and producers' shops dating from the Middle Ages were converted into specialised shops under continuous operation. . . . Soon after 1815, the modern shop came into being, with fixed prices, low margins of profit, commissions on sales for the staff, sales at intervals and a social security system for the employees. This was developed in France with the Bon Marché, directed by Boucicaut, the Magasin du Louvre, managed by Chauchard, or the Samaritaine, and in Germany too after 1830. Street lamps and lighted windows also caused a change in the mid-nineteenth century, as did the department store in the US, invented in 1862 in New York by Alexander Stewart, an Irish protestant in origin, but brought to its culmination by John Wanamaker of Philadelphia, who began life as an errand boy and first thought up the one-price system, the marked prices in clear figures, and the money-back guarantees, which characterise shopping in the twentieth century. Mail orders began in 1872 with Montgomery Ward in Chicago, and the chain store with Frank W. Woolworth's 'Five-and-Ten Cent' store at Utica, New York in 1879. These innovations led to the swift end of the old fairs as major commercial enterprises. Even in Germany, fairs were in decline after 1840.

All capital cities grew at the expense of the rest of the country. Louis XIV tried to check the growth of Paris six times without success. Even before the Revolution, many provincial printing presses and other critical small businesses closed down in France. In the nineteenth century, similar efforts to cut the size of cities were even more unsuccessful. In democracies and tyrannies alike, all cities grew. Big cities grew faster than others. In the US in the nineteenth century, cities of over 8,000 inhabitants grew five times faster than the country as a whole. The reason was not so much the rise in population in the towns themselves, though that could not be ignored, as the influx from country-born workers. In

1851, out of 3,336,000 people aged twenty or over living in London, less than half had been born there. Much the same was true of New York, Chicago, Barcelona, Essen and Lyons, or other large English or Welsh towns, and soon would be of Moscow. Then, as the masses moved into the centre of the cities, the leaders of the society concerned moved out, living more and more in suburbs, often with separate municipal authorities, but linked with the city to which those same leaders began to 'commute', in order to work, travelling in daily, on horse or in coaches, before the railways, or the cars.

On the whole, the growth of the new industrial cities, particularly in Britain, denoted a major failure of imagination. In most such cities, there were, indeed in some cases there still are, long and dreary streets, street after street with the same formations, the same alleys filled with rubbish and the same lack of open spaces for children to play in. Little effort was made to plan the pattern of the streets according to sun and wind. The more respectable quarters, where 'artisans' or clerks lived, were almost as depressing as the straightforwardly shabby slums.

These cities were products of the managers of the railway, the factory and the coal mine. The slums served those institutions. They had, to begin with, no social heritage. All was subordinate to the factory concerned, including public services (police, fire services and water services, not to speak of hospitals, food inspection, education and church which came later). The early factory would usually be set on the best site, on the river, for it needed water for its boilers, for cooling and for dyeing, and it also provided the worst waste (thus ruining the bathing and fishing). The factory chimneys, magnificent though they were, polluted air and water. The railway was often driven into the centre of the town, severing such natural arteries as the place might once have had. Huge piles of waste metal stood untended for years. Workers' houses were built up against the 'works' and so were often bathed in dust. In many pioneering cities of the Industrial Revolution, back-to-back houses opened on to a yard and that meant that two rooms out of four had no direct daylight at all. Lavatories were inadequate. Manchester in 1845 had 33 per 1,000 inhabitants—a proportion which would now be thought bad in a prison. Rubbish was often thrown into the street. Cellars might sometimes house pigs, a sad reminder of happier rural days, but there was also a large human cellar population. Bedbugs, lice, fleas, rats and flies bred in the plaster walls. Plumbing was rotten, drains open, water bad. Even so, the building trades employed more men than any other profession. Reformers concentrated upon the need for good prisons and a state monopoly of sewage and failed to devote adequate attention to how people were housed. As Lewis Mumford points out, the nineteenth century was an age of rising nationhood, but the municipal councils did not rise to the occasion and built town halls only. London, for example, was ill managed in the mid-nineteenth century: some seventy-eight 'vestries'[2] shared local power, their nomination varying from co-option to election, and they had control of everything, from drains to poverty. Only in 1888 was there a Local Government Act which created a London district council to cover the whole city.

Several things need to be said. First, the changes in the size of populations were unprecedented. Second, the worst conditions were to be found in the boom towns, then as now. Third, horrible though mid-nineteenth century London no doubt was, with its fog, tuberculosis and rickets, it began to be radically improved from the middle of the century and, for all its evils, the expectation of life was higher than it had been a century before. Fourth, the errors in planning showed a failure to think carefully enough what should be the role of the State. Victorian reformers in both the US and Britain, as well as elsewhere, insisted upon a role for the State in such things as the postal service which could have been well managed by private companies. They sometimes neglected to give a role to the State, or the community, in matters such as town planning where the commodity at stake was finite such as land. Fifth, when all is considered, many slum cities of the nineteenth century were able to achieve a greater humanity than has proved possible in the futuristic cities of the twentieth century.

In comparison, cities in countries which were slow to industrialise seemed oases of peace. Vienna in 1848 still had walls and a moat. Green slopes lay between it and the suburbs. At night, the gates were closed. Even during the day, they were sometimes locked in the event of disturbances. The workers of Vienna lived outside the city, while students, nobility and middle classes lived inside. In general, cities which industrialised later had better services than those which did so early. Still, benefits in the form of better shops, department stores, internal city transport and vast numbers of salesmen followed industrialisation everywhere, and Vienna, like other such traditional cities was the battleground of class wars as much as more modern ones.

Modern cities of the poorer world, from South America to Africa, are also all surrounded by shanty towns so neglected as to make nineteenth century industrial cities seem prosperous. Africa, for example, has seen a more rapid industrialisation than anywhere in the world, specially confusing to those who live there since there is no real urban tradition on which to build. Instead, there is a juxtaposition of foreign investment with a population the majority of which are tribal people full of traditional fears, loyalties and prejudices. Usually populated by squatters, the urban areas of, say, Mexico, India, and Egypt, represent the most complicated of modern political problems. Still, the cities of Europe in the nineteenth century were marked by riots and, on the whole, are now at least polit-

---

[2]The governing body of a parish, elected by taxpayers, which has jurisdiction over civil as well as ecclesiastical matters.

ically tranquil and perhaps, when the pressure of population in Mexico City or Caracas has been alleviated, the intensity of their difficulties may diminish too. But will that happen?

It is hard to do other than compare unfavourably the lot of those who live in such new cities at present with those who lived, say, in Merthyr[3] when it was the largest town of the British iron trade in 1820. Tough, rough, overworked though the life there must have been, its population, when its four iron works were the largest in the world, was still only 20,000. The city was in easy walking distance of green valleys. There has always been some safety in such relatively small numbers.

Though, in many modern cities, history seems forgotten or remote, the past often remains close in spirit. A comparison between the towns of France and of Britain makes that point clearly. Freed from the likelihood of invasion, England is a country whose towns have outgrown the need for walls long ago. Invaded four times since 1800, France held back her cities at the walls where she could. Thus, where London sprawled, Paris grew upwards. In Britain, only Edinburgh has a tradition of blocks five, six or ten stories high. Then, in nineteenth century politics on the continent, unlike the eighteenth, there were numerous internal troubles. Barricades were easier to put up in old cities. Most streets were only six to eight feet wide with tall buildings. The pattern of a mediaeval town life seemed to impose itself in Germany even during industrialisation. Under the Nazis, the mediaeval city of Nuremberg was a national symbol. The party rallies were deliberately held there in order to create a mood of national renaissance as well as one of nostalgia.

Another tendency in the life of cities was to begin with more marked in the US. In the 1950s, in all but one (Los Angeles) of the largest US cities, there was a decrease in population. Only in the south in what were, in effect, new cities (Dallas and Houston, in Texas, or Birmingham, in Alabama) did the urban population keep growing. Yet the countryside also continued to lose population. In place of both, the suburbs became, in the 1960s, the preferred living place of the successful family, first in the US, then elsewhere. The political consequences of this have been quite negative for cities.

In most countries, capital cities have become more and more important, as the pretensions of governments have grown. Networks of communication radiate from capitals often, as with airways, to serve the nation's bureaucrats, rather than the vital members of the society concerned. Hence the revival of nationalist or regional movements, though both the growth of the capital and of regionalism derive from the single cause of the increased power of the State.

No modern city, however, would be able to survive for a week if it were not for an elaborate system of hygiene beneath it. A modern city

[3]Town in south Wales.

may be built of stone, steel, glass or brick. But it has to be built primarily upon water: which is needed against fire, for drinking, washing, sewage, and for most industrial processes.

At the beginning of modern times, the water supplies and the hygiene of cities alike had declined not only since *Roma antiqua*,[4] but since the Middle Ages. The ancient Persians never polluted rivers, for they worshipped them, while the Egyptians bathed twice a day in cold water and washed their clothes often. But, even in a rich country such as England, there was, in 1800, rarely a distinction made between sewers and water mains. All rivers were contaminated by both domestic and industrial waste. Ditches in cities were everywhere used as latrines. Dead animals were left to rot where they lay. The decomposing bodies of the poor in common graves stank. Bed sheets were changed at most three times a year. Women wore quilted petticoats and stays of bone or leather which they never washed. The public baths of Rome, or Constantinople, the vast *cloaca maxima*[5] and other Roman sewers copied from the Etruscans, the 1,352 public fountains which Rome had had in the fourth century, the dozen Roman aqueducts—all seemed inconceivable in England, much less in Rome, even in the time of Rome's greatest historian, Edward Gibbon.[6] The hygienic arrangements of Babylon would have strained the imagination of an ordinary citizen of eighteenth century Paris, as they might that of many citizens of Mexico or Calcutta today. True, Muslims maintained the tradition of baths even more effectively than they did that of mathematics. They also had baths of hot air . . . most extensively. Steam baths were also widely used in Russia, following Muslim patterns.

A mediaeval town in Europe was also often in advance of the nineteenth century there, or the twentieth in some continents. Then, the provision of water was an established collective function, arranged by a spring or a public fountain, and sometimes still conveyed in old Roman lead pipes. The public fountain remained, until the present generation in many Mediterranean places, a centre of gregariousness (or gossip), a work of art in construction, an inspiration for poets. As García Lorca[7] put it:

A village without a public fountain
Is closed, dark, every house is an isolated world.

. . . .

[4]Ancient Rome.
[5]Main sewer.
[6]1737–1794.
[7]Spanish poet and dramatist, 1898–1936.

In fact, therefore, the most enviable people from the point of view of hygiene in the late eighteenth century seem, from the point of view of statistics, those who did not live in modern towns. Yet visitors to many old towns would have challenged that view. Goethe,[8] in his famous journey in Italy, complained at the absence of a public cleansing service, of any sort, in Venice. Rubbish, including excrement, was pushed into corners, and irregularly carried away in flat-bottomed boats, as manure to the mainland, or thrown into the sea. Everywhere in Italy, Goethe found majestic colonnades which were simply 'made for people to relieve themselves whenever they felt the urge'. In an inn at Torbole, he found no lavatories: a valet pointed to the courtyard. 'Where?' 'Anywhere, wherever you like,' was the reply. But it was not simply the decadent south which seemed unhygienic. When Charles I's[9] court was at Oxford, courtiers left behind excreta in every corner of every college. In Edinburgh, in 1760, there were no latrines, public or private; all emptied excreta into the street at 10 p.m. When Mrs Pepys[10] was seized with diarrhoea at the theatre, she had no option but to go to a corner of Lincoln's Inn Fields. Even 'on the marble staircases of the Louvre, the natural necessities were performed daily'. . . .

There was also in the past no means of keeping water fresh. So, water carriers were essential. Even in the nineteenth century, most districts would count themselves fortunate if their population could go to a standpipe at the street corner once a day for an hour or so; though, by then, the rich were starting to be able to obtain running water in their basements.

A few other improvements began, however, in what seemed a dark time. Soap, for example, which started to be produced in France under Rome, continued to be made spasmodically during the Middle Ages and liquid soap, from potash, was used for laundry from the sixteenth century. Soap from palm oil was a possible alternative to the slave trade from Africa for many Liverpool merchants in the early nineteenth century. Sir John Harington, a Somerset squire who married an illegitimate daughter of Henry VIII, invented the water closet in 1596, but, for 300 years, there were few of them. Chamberpots continued to be emptied out of windows into the streets. Parisians went on relieving themselves in the Seine. Even the invention of an interior dry lavatory in the eighteenth century had no success. At Versailles, at the King's Court, there were little lavatories made as commodes on wheels. Mass-produced and, therefore, individual plates, knives and forks and cups, the decline of spitting, the custom of shaving heads under wigs, the

[8]Johann Wolfgang von Goethe (1749–1832), German intellectual.
[9]King of England, 1625–1649.
[10]Wife of the diarist, Samuel Pepys.

fashion for changing underclothes every day (defined as elegance itself by Beau Brummell[11] about 1820), all had certain good effects.

The problem of sewage became urgent in the nineteenth century, as towns grew yearly so big and so fast. The system of the 'privy bucket' meant endless emptying and removal of contents. Even so, where should it be emptied? The first solution found in London was the cesspool, of which there were about 250,000 in London by 1850. But this had an adverse effect on water from wells, at a time when most water in capital cities came from those ancient sources.

Two changes came to rich cities in the nineteenth century and then were copied elsewhere. Both were based on the false assumption that dirt causes disease. In the nineteenth century in northern Europe, it was believed that cleanliness was next to godliness. Not for the first time, a wrong concept led to a revolution in habits. The pioneer in most of these changes was a German, Josef Franach, who first suggested, in the six volumes of his *Complete system of medical polity,* that ideally there should be a complete system of state management of hygiene.

The practical initiative in these matters was, as usual by then, taken in the US. New York was the first big city to arrange for its citizens an ample supply of pure water, by means of a system of reservoirs and aqueducts opened in 1842. By the twentieth century, New York was stretching out in its demands for water into the Catskill mountains a hundred miles away. In London, the two or three large private water companies were taken over by the municipal authorities in 1902. There is nothing to prove that free enterprise could not have performed these tasks adequately and cheaply; but they did not do so and, from the mid-nineteenth century, the provision of water in nearly every country came to be a national enterprise. Huge dams, aqueducts comparable to the Roman ones, fifty-mile-long pure water canals, and long tunnels were all soon built. Wild valleys in romantic countrysides found themselves placed under water to serve the need for water of some distant manufacturing town.

The appropriate treatment of sewage had a similar outcome. The career here of Edwin Chadwick, a many-sided reformer in England, is illuminating. He insisted in 1837 on the establishment of a sanitary commission. Appointed to head it in 1839, it became, in 1842, a general board of health. Chadwick then recommended that cesspools should be abolished and that sewers should cease to be merely bricked-over watercourses. His idea was that they should become established as great arteries in their own right to be cleaned by regular water supplies. Those arteries would carry all rubbish by long underground routes to be disposed of at places remote from the city. Hamburg was the first to build sewers of that sort (because of a big fire there) and Paris began sooner

---

[11]English dandy, 1778–1840.

than London, whose problems were affected by a tangled web of local private and political interests. But the realisation that the cholera epidemic of 1850 was connected with pollution by excreta awoke the English to a serious appreciation of what should be done (the usual method of transmitting cholera is by water contaminated by discharges from the bowels of those suffering from the disease). Sir Joseph Bazalgette, a civil engineer of French origin, devised a system based on five huge sewers running parallel to the Thames which would be capable of dealing with all normal sewage and rain water. Only in stormy weather would it thereafter be necessary to use the old sewers connected with the rivers. The sewers discharged their vast quantities of refuse twelve miles from London Bridge at a place where it could be chemically clarified. Elsewhere, liquid sewage continued for a long time to be discharged into rivers or lakes. Various other methods of disposal developed: iron hydroxide, for example, and, in the twentieth century, chlorination. Here was an effective system of public works plainly superior to the negligent ways of the past.

At the same time, Europeans and North Americans, began to cease their fear of contact with water in other ways. Swimming began to seem again a practical part of education. Public baths began, from the 1840s, to be built again. Slowly, the idea of the private bath captured the imaginations of rich countries. The shower seems to have been devised in the 1880s. All these innovations, or revivals, depended not only upon running water attached to the houses—that immensely important innovation of the mid nineteenth century—but on the availability of heating it too— a possibility made easy after the gas heater of the 1860s and electricity a little later. Enamelled white baths began to be made about 1910 and to be mass-produced in the US and Britain by 1920. By 1939, the compact bathrooms of modern times (bath, basin, lavatory) were everywhere being constructed. The ideal of one such bathroom to every bedroom was beginning to be expressed as a goal by modern builders. These ideals were quickly passed on to a world which was anxious to copy US technology without copying their political ideals. The achievement of even the first of these aims was, however, far from complete even in rich countries before 1939 and, even in the 1970s, there are still many houses without baths—though all prejudice against them, like the old prejudice against tomatoes and potatoes, has vanished.

By the year 2000, a third of the world's population are expected to be living in cities of over 100,000 inhabitants in size. Tokyo with Yokohama, with about 17 million in 1980, may, by 2000, have 26 million. Cairo may have 16 million, Lagos 9.4 million, and Mexico, 31.6 million. São Paulo may rival Tokyo. The implications of these developments are enormous. We should recall that London only reached a million in 1800, and that Paris did not join her in that till 1850. Berlin and Vienna did not top a million till nearly 1880, and no Russian city except for St Petersburg reached a million before about 1870. Today, however, the cities of the world larger than one million number a hundred. Think of it, a hundred cities which are the size of Rome at her height, many of them larger!

One consequence of this extraordinary tendency has been, apparently, a vast increase of crime. From the evidence of primitive or hunting tribes surviving into historical memory, crime, as we know it, among those peoples, was both rare and severely punished. Still, the codes of law of ancient agrarian civilisations make clear that, in those early settled states, urban crime's long history had begun. In great cities such as Rome or Constantinople, or in Eastern cities, the growing semi-slave, rootless urban proletariat which did not accept, or even know, the customs of the dominant people, looked on robbery as part of their private war against the occupiers. Where peoples were insecure, or lived in a state of perpetual war, the distinction between crime and self-preservation was often ill marked. Of course, thefts and murders, rapes and minor acts of violence occurred often in the pre-industrial countryside. Figures recently analysed suggest that mediaeval Kent had a far worse record than anywhere in the US in the twentieth century. Two-thirds of all convictions in England in some years during the nineteenth century were under the game code.[12] But crime in industrial society seems today more and more an urban problem. . . . The absence of rewarding work or stimulating play; the charmlessness of many modern dwellings—above all, alas, those provided by the community; the loose or non-existent scale of values in societies materially richer than those which existed in the past, and the conversion of many who live in cities to a mentality utterly opposed, or indifferent, to the community in which they have full rights as citizens, all contribute. In some cities of the US, murder has been said to have been the most common cause of death among male black people in their prime of life. In other ways too, sometimes, modern cities recall Juvenal's[13] injunction: 'If you go out to dinner, first make your will'. That, of course, recalls the undoubted truth that all cities have been infested with crime since the earliest days. It is the increase in the cities which has offered greater opportunities.

The world of the future will be a world of cities. Older than nations and states, their history is as long as any other viable organisation of men. The errors of planning of the twentieth century have created worse asphalt jungles than the errors of neglect in the nineteenth. Communist cities, such as East Berlin or the new Moscow, do not suggest that there a new world functions better than capitalist ones.

[12]Laws that limited the hunting and trapping of game birds and animals to the landed gentry and that imposed severe penalties on poachers.

[13]Roman satirist, 60?–140? A.D.

Popular Anti-Catholicism in England, 1850–1851

D.G. PAZ

*Surely one of the most enduring legacies of Western Civilization is religious prej-
udice, sometimes covert, sometimes bursting forth in waves of persecution. What
religious toleration can be found has been, until very recently, the expression of isolated individuals or oppressed minority groups. In this selection, D.G. Paz examines
a famous outburst of popular fanaticism and religious intolerance in the furor over
the so-called Papal Aggression of 1850.*

*What had the pope done that so threatened English freedoms? He had merely
designated a Roman Catholic hierarchy for England, one that had existed two
centuries previously and is present today. Why did the populace object so vehemently
to the papal action? In seeking an explanation, Paz refers to the sources of increased
religious tension after 1830, including political, religious, and social developments.
But he does not exclude personalities from blame. What then were the reasons
for anti-Catholic prejudices among the English? Feelings of fear and hatred of
Roman Catholics were widespread. There were no Gallup Polls in nineteenth-century
England, so Paz examines the public protests of 1850 and 1851. During three
months in 1850, there were almost 900,000 signatures gathered on petitions against
the papal act and another 348,000 during five months in 1851. Did different
Protestant groups react differently to the Papal Aggression? How were Roman
Catholics popularly stereotyped? What role did the Irish play in the English opinion
of Roman Catholicism? Does Paz discuss any elements of English society that aimed
for tolerance and the abolition of national and religious stereotypes?*

Traditional religious distinctions gradually eroded in eighteenth-century
England under the impact of enlightenment rationalism: reason replaced
revelation as the criterion for belief, order ousted enthusiasm in worship, and interdenominationalism blurred sectarian boundaries in phil-
anthropic endeavors. But the French Revolution, economic troubles and
radical political activity after 1815, and intellectual Romanticism put an
end to co-operation and encouraged the growth of denominational self-
consciousness. That rise of denominationalism led to the greatest

D.G. Paz, "Popular Anti-Catholicism in England, 1850–1851," *Albion 77* (Winter 1979):
331–357.

conflict between the sects and the Establishment[1] since perhaps the mid-seventeenth century. The clash began on the local level in the 1820s when the Church attempted to use its legal powers to collect rates,[2] the events of 1828–1829[3] ushered in a period of conflict on the national level, as well. The Church turned to the state for support, only to find that Whigs and Liberals, in power for most of the period before 1874, were erastians and latitudinarians.[4] So the Church in its turn became militant; high-churchmen in particular came to distrust Parliament and to emphasize the independent sources of clerical authority in sacerdotalism[5] and the apostolic succession.[6]

The period from roughly 1830 to 1870 was one of heightened religious tension. Nonconformists,[7] having gained civil equality, now attempted to eliminate other symbols of the Anglican hegemony. Roman Catholics . . . asserted their spiritual claims and talked of converting England. The Church continued to insist upon its establishment rights and . . . tended its claims. Such tension reached the local and personal levels. This paper discusses one aspect of that tension—anti-catholicism—and focuses on one particular event in the heritage of Victorian religious animosities—the Papal Aggression of 1850.

The Papal Aggression is the story of an ebullition of anti-catholic prejudice in the winter of 1850–1851. On 29 September 1850 Pope Pius IX created a territorial hierarchy for English Roman Catholics; their bishops now ruled dioceses styled after English placenames rather than after points of the compass and bore titles derived from their sees rather than from extinct Levantine cities. Although England remained a missionary area in the Vatican's eyes, this change marked the coming of age of its Roman Catholic community. A day later, Pius elevated Nicholas Wiseman, one of the vicars apostolic, to head the new English hierarchy as the first Cardinal Archbishop of Westminster. When news of these events reached London, *The Times'* leader-writers reflected for five days, then launched a series of attacks against the new hierarchy. Since Westminster, the seat of Parliament, symbolized British liberties, Wiseman's use of that title was an insult. The hierarchy, moreover, would encourage "the wanton interference of a band of foreign priests" in domestic affairs. Although a few "weak minds" had converted, the Pope was mistaken in

[1]The Church of England, established by law as the state religion.

[2]Taxes for the upkeep of Church of England property.

[3]The repeal of laws that forbade Nonconformist Protestants and Roman Catholics from voting, serving in the House of Commons and in local government, and holding public offices under the crown.

[4]People who believed that the Church should be subordinate to the state and that points of doctrine were unimportant.

[5]The priesthood.

[6]The belief that bishops derive their spiritual powers from the apostles.

[7]Protestants, sometimes called Dissenters.

believing that England would ever return to "Romish bondage." Thus Pius' illegal exercise of spiritual power would be to no avail.

Roman Catholics themselves added fuel to the protestant fire. The London press took the text of the papal decree, published between 22 and 26 October, to be both an assumption of supreme spiritual authority over the nation and a denial of the validity of Anglican orders. On the 27th, John Henry Newman[8] preached what can only be described as an inflammatory sermon at the enthronement of the new Roman Catholic Bishop of Birmingham. (Newman believed that God was leading England back to the true church, which possessed both "divine prerogatives and . . . high destiny.") But Wiseman's first pastoral letter to his flock caused the most serious damage. The document was read in London chapels on Sunday 28 October and appeared in the newspapers the next day. "We govern, and shall continue to govern," the new archbishop affirmed, "the counties of Middlesex, Hertford, and Essex as ordinary thereof, and those of Surrey, Sussex, Kent, Berkshire, and Hampshire . . . , as administrator with ordinary jurisdiction." Turning to the hierarchy's significance, he declared:

> The great work, then is complete. . . . Your beloved country has received a place among the fair Churches, which . . . form the splendid aggregate of Catholic Communion; Catholic England has been restored to its orbit in the ecclesiastical firmament, from which its light had long vanished, and begins now anew its course of regularly adjusted action round the centre of unity, the source of jurisdiction, of light and vigour. . . .
>
> Then truly is this day to us a day of joy and exhaltation of spirit, the crowning day of long hopes, the opening day of bright prospects. How must the Saints of our country, whether Roman or British, Saxon or Norman, look down from their seats of bliss, with beaming glance, upon this new evidence of the faith and Church which led them to glory, sympathising with those who have faithfully adhered to them through centuries of ill repute for the truth's sake, and now reap the fruit of their patience and longsuffering. And all those blessed martyrs of these latter ages, . . . who mourned . . . over the desolate ways of their own Sion, and the departure of England's religious glory; oh! how must they bless God, who hath again visited his people. —how take part in our joy . . . , as they behold the silver links of that chain which has connected their country with the see of Peter in its vicarial government changed into burnished gold; not stronger nor more closely knit, but more beautifully wrought and more brightly arrayed.

It was unfortunate that this document transpired only a week before Guy Fawkes Day.[9] The press vigorously attacked Wiseman's pastoral

[8](1801–1890), convert to Roman Catholicism, cardinal, and a founder of the Oxford Movement.

[9]A popular holiday commemorating a Roman Catholic plot to blow up Parliament in 1605.

and Newman's sermon, damning their language as arrogant and their appraisal of English religious conditions as unrealistic. On the day itself the new hierarchy replaced "gunpowder, treason, and plot." Londoners awoke to see slogans such as "No Popery" and "No Wafer Gods" painted on walls. At noon, a large procession, centered about an effigy of Wiseman and escorted by men dressed as monks and nuns, marched through the metropolis. Throughout England many parishes held services commemorating the day, and effigies of Wiseman often replaced the usual straw "guys."[10]

Two days later the press published the text of Lord John Russell's notorious open letter to the Bishop of Durham. The prime minister attacked the "insolent and insidious" Papal Aggression because it challenged the royal supremacy and the Established Church by implying that Rome held authority over England. Russell did not fear this "outward attack," for a nation that had enjoyed freedom of speech and religion for so long had nothing to fear from a foreign ruler. Roman Catholics, therefore, were not nearly so great a threat as were the Tractarians,[11] who were leading their flocks to Roman "mummeries of superstition."

> Clergymen of our own Church . . . have been most forward in leading their flocks "step by step to the very verge of the precipice." The honours paid to saints, the claim of infallibility for the Church, the superstitious use of the sign of the cross, the muttering of the liturgy so as to disguise the language in which it is written, the recommendation of auricular confession, and the administration of penance and absolution, all these things are pointed out by clergymen of the Church of England as worthy of adoption.
>
> What then is the danger to be apprehended from a foreign ruler of no great power compared to the danger within the gates from the unworthy sons of the Church of England herself?

.   .   .

These pronouncements and counter-pronouncements resulted in nationwide protest meetings during the last two months of 1850. The clergy of Westminster and the parishioners of St. George's, Hanover Square, petitioned their bishop only a few days after Pius' decree had appeared in the press. The Anglican hierarchy denounced the assumption of titles, urged their clergy to circulate protest petitions, and themselves petitioned the Queen, contending that the creation of a rival hierarchy "unchurched" the Church of England and usurped the royal supremacy. Clergy, following their episcopal leaders, sponsored parish meetings; by the middle of November the movement had

---

[10]Effigies of Guy Fawkes.

[11]Anglicans who emphasized the Catholic elements in the Church of England; sometimes called Puseyites, after E.B. Pusey (1800–1882), professor of Hebrew at Oxford University.

grown to include town and county assemblies. Societies and corporations, municipal, professional, and educational, also protested the Papal Aggression. . . . Some protests resulted in violence. A crowd disturbed the Sunday service at the ritualist parish, St. Barnabas', Pimlico, with hisses and cries of "No Popery!" and actual riots occurred in Cheltenham, Birkenhead, and Liverpool. (The Birkenhead rioters attacked the police before a detachment of troops could disperse them and one person may have died.)

Certainly the Papal Aggression had summoned up energies and feelings in an unexpected way. A vicar near East Retford, Notts, reported on the mood in his parish to his archdeacon:

On Sunday afternoon I preached on the subject [of the Papal Aggression] giving such an explanation as I was able to. . . . I had a large Congregation, fully one third of my population, and a good muster of singers. The effect was like electricity. No sooner had I ended my sermon than the quire struck up with that beautiful hymn . . .

Soldiers of Christ arise
And put your armour on

now I think [that] shows us that even here our protestant people are alive to *Popish Insult.*

The public uproar began to abate after the middle of December . . . , and the dispute moved into the parliamentary arena. The Russell ministry introduced penal legislation in February 1851 that forbade the unauthorized use of any English or Scottish placename by any cleric and provided that any property transfer using illegal names would be void with the real estate concerned escheating to the Crown. For the next six months Parliament debated the Ecclesiastical Titles Bill in a spirit of political and religious acrimony. Russell lost control of the House, was forced out of office for a time, and ended the session with his majority in a shambles. . . .

. . . [B]road shifts in demography, politics, and religious life after the 1820s form the background to the Papal Aggression.

The English Roman Catholic community had experienced a twentyfold growth in numbers—from about 30,000 to about 750,000—between 1801 and 1851; much of the growth occurred within the thirty years after 1821. Because this rapid increase was largely the consequence of Irish immigration, English Roman Catholics appeared to pose both cultural and economic threats. Englishmen feared that alien Celts of an alien religion would swamp their traditional protestant culture and steal their jobs by working for lower pay. Thus traditional anti-catholicism was revived and merged with newer anti-Celtic racialist thought. And because early

Victorian economic thinking still viewed poverty as a moral category, the low income level of these new immigrants served to re-enforce the prejudices against them.

English political life after 1829, moreover, was marked by the renewal of disputes over religious issues in general and attacks on Roman Catholicism in particular. Debates over Irish and English church reform, parish rates, and education created animosity and suspicion on all sides. Roman Catholics participated as victims: Tories attacked Romanism as incompatible with English political institutions while liberals doubted that Romanism was compatible with the doctrine of progress. Thus religious tensions tended to increase during the period.

The English Roman Catholic Church simultaneously was revitalized and became militant in the late 1830s. It enjoyed the general revival of English religious life, the Irish immigrants put bodies in the pews, and the Oxford converts[12] brought intelligence, position, and enthusiasm into their new church. This militance alarmed protestants, for it took the forms of proclaiming the imminent conversion of England and importing the most extravagant examples of Italian rococo devotion. Sandalled Passionists[13] roamed Brompton and Oxford M.A.s prostrated themselves before the Benediction of the Blessed Sacrament; soon the big toe of St. Peter would be kissed in the Oratory. Against this apparently monolithic foe Englishmen contrasted a sadly fragmented protestantism. Anglicanism and Dissent[14] were divided; . . . on the left agnosticism, the earth sciences, and German higher criticism[15] threatened traditional beliefs and methodologies.

As far as the proximate causes for the Papal Aggression outcry are concerned, the consensus view maintains that 1850 was not an auspicious year in which to proclaim the new hierarchy. The hierarchy's creation had been preceded by five years of politico-religious problems at home and in Ireland, and the collapse of Anglo-French and Anglo-Italian relations. . . .

The accident of personality must also be taken into account. Lord John Russell's personality inclined him to anti-catholicism. A latitudinarian and memorialist in his euchrastic theology, he had a long history of battling against the high-church movement; by 1850 he sought to inflict crushing blows against both Puseyites[16] and ultramontanes.[17] Wiseman

---

[12]Those members of the Oxford Movement who converted to Roman Catholicism in the 1840s.

[13]One of several Roman Catholic religious orders that established missions in England during the 1840s and 1850s.

[14]Protestant nonconformity.

[15]Of the Bible.

[16]Tractarians.

[17]Supporters of the Papacy.

contributed the bombastic language of his pastoral, which provided the spark that set off the volatile mixture of English prejudices. A particularly adept practitioner of florid Victorian style, Wiseman outdid himself in pompous prose and failed totally to consider what the results of his missive might be. Newman's enthronement sermon also incited protestant hostility and demonstrated a lack of good judgment on the convert's part. Neither man's language reflected religious reality. While Wiseman's pastoral letter would have provoked a storm at any time, the convergence of these proximate elements resulted in a particularly nasty explosion. . . .

. . . There were two waves of protest. From October to December, 1850, England produced 2616 memorials to the Queen protesting the new hierarchy, bearing 887,525 signatures (roughly five percent of the English population). From March to July, 1851, England produced 1920 petitions to Parliament praying that the Ecclesiastical Titles Bill be made more stringent, bearing 348,590 signatures. The two must be treated separately, as we shall see. Thus I use "memorialists" to refer to the protesters of 1850, and "petitioners" to refer to the protesters of 1851. By looking at these sources we can draw up a geography of prejudice in Victorian England. . . .

The Victorian public meeting was a ceremony in which participants elected a chairman, moved and debated resolutions, and chose a committee to draft a petition. Almost any group could and did assemble in public meeting to express opinion on issues of the day—inhabitants of local areas, professional and trade societies, religious congregations and synods, voluntary organizations, chambers of commerce, *ad hoc* pressure groups, and Chartists.[18] Public meetings of towns and counties, meetings of the "people" (usually ratepayers or freeholders, but sometimes inhabitants) enjoyed a quasi-official status; custom obliged lords-lieutenant and mayors to summon meetings upon the application of freeholders or ratepayers. Most public meetings, of course, were carefully orchestrated events that had as much to do with the balance of local political power as with the purpose for which they were ostensibly called. . . . These meetings directed their addresses to the Queen or, more commonly, to the House of Commons. . . .

. . . [The] signatures [gathered at such meetings] are a broadly accurate measure—indeed the only countable measure—of public sentiment in 1850–1851. In order to speak accurately about public opinion one needs a good sample (which reflects precisely the social, political, sexual, religious, age, educational, etc., distribution of the population) and a measuring instrument that is reliable (one that produces the same response for the same subject each time that it is administered). Contemporary polling organizations can hardly meet these criteria; historians must

---

[18]Members of a political reform movement of workers.

make do with the evidence that has survived. But petitioning was a common way for the Victorians to express their opinion. . . . Thus the protest signatures are at least as good a measure of public opinion as are newspapers, which historians customarily use. . . .

. . . Wesleyan Methodists, quiet about protesting the hierarchy itself, contributed 73% of the petitions and 30% of the signatures in favor of making the Ecclesiastical Titles Bill more stringent. (Could it be that Wesleyans were likely to be more anti-catholic than pro-Anglican?) Anglicans, on the other hand, played a much more important role in 1850 than they did in 1851. In neither instance did non-Wesleyan Dissenters figure, except insofar as they may have participated in public meetings. Thus we must treat the two protest episodes separately and focus on Anglicans and Methodists in our analysis.

A map . . . showing how the memorialists were distributed by county suggests three, or possibly four, centers of memorializing. From Hampshire east along the south coast, we find the counties ranking second, third, sixth, thirteenth, and fourteenth in terms of signatures per thousand of population. From Northampton a second center of anti-catholicism extends northwest to include the first, seventh, ninth, tenth, fifteenth, seventeenth, and nineteenth ranking counties. Lancashire (ranking fourth) and Westmoreland (eighth) form a third locus; and from Devon east we see the counties ranking eleventh, twelfth, and sixteenth in memorialists. A map of petitioners . . . presents a different picture. Lancashire and Westmoreland retain their ranks of fourth and eighth; Gloucester moves from ninth to fifth; from Nottingham west we see three counties ranking first, second, and seventh. In the south, Surrey (third) and Kent (sixth) are the only major centers of petitioning. Those counties that did not participate significantly in the protests (note also Cornwall) form a band running southwest from East Anglia to Berkshire; and in the north is Northumberland and Durham. The Midlands and the agricultural west country appear to be the most inconsistent.

To what extent was opposition to Tractarianism a factor in the outcry against Papal Aggression? A minority did indicate its concern with Tractarianism; not quite a third . . . of the memorialists went beyond protest against the new hierarchy to deplore Romanizing tendencies within the Church of England. But over two-fifths . . . of the anti-Tractarians came from only three great towns; metropolitan London, Bristol, and Birmingham. These, with three more towns (the Plymouth area, Exeter, and Bolton) generated over half (51.37%) of the anti-Tractarian signatures. . . . Mass anti-Puseyite sentiment was a limited and localized phenomenon; we may conclude that Russell and *The Times* failed in their attempts to focus a great national outcry against Anglicanism's "unworthy sons."[19] The popular mind, after all, could

---

[19]Russell's term for Puseyites in his letter to the Bishop of Durham.

grasp papal pretensions more readily than Dr. Pusey's theology. Thus the Papal Aggression was a more purely anti-catholic phenomenon. . . .

. . . [If] the rapid increase in the number of Irish immigrants was a chief cause for the Papal Aggression outcry, [w]e would therefore expect that those counties with larger Irish-born populations would be more likely to memorialize than would those with smaller Irish populations. But such a relationship does not appear to exist. Only five of the twelve counties with the largest rate of Irish to total population were also among the twelve counties with the largest rates of memorialists and petitioners to total population. . . .

Religious practices in an age of faith must not be ignored, and it is therefore illuminating to compare protesting with these. . . .

. . . "[A]ttendance ratios"/ratios of church-attendance by sect over all attendances . . . guage . . . the relative strength of each sect vis-à-vis the rest. In an age of denominational militance, as the Victorian age was, sects will view the unchurched as a potentially fertile missionary field, but they will look upon each other as rivals and enemies. The attendance ratios allow us to examine this second view, for they exclude the unchurched from the ratios. (About half of the population, on the whole, was unchurched.) . . . With respect to memorialists, the interesting relations are with Anglicans, Wesleyans, and Roman Catholics. . . . Anglicans played an important role in memorializing, while Wesleyans and other Methodist sects were equally important in petitioning. The constant factor in both protests is the presence of Roman Catholics: the larger the proportion of Roman Catholic church-attendance to all church-attendance per county, the more likely the county was to memorialize or petition.

The important rivalries are not only between a specific sect and all sects, but also between two particular sects. That is, one might hypothesize that Wesleyans, for example, were more concerned with their numerical standing proportionate to Anglicans, Roman Catholics, or Methodist seceders than to other Dissenting sects. If so, then one would expect to find, for instance, that the greater the ratio was of Roman Catholic to Wesleyan church-attendances, the more likely the county was to memorialize. . . . [S]uch ratios . . . we may call "rivalry ratios," between Anglicans and Wesleyans, Roman Catholics and Wesleyans, Roman Catholics and Anglicans, and Wesleyans and other Methodists. There are weak positive relationships between memorialists and the ratios of Roman Catholics to Anglicans and Anglicans to Wesleyans, and a moderate relationship with the ratio of Roman Catholics to Wesleyans. The larger the ratio of Roman Catholic to Wesleyan church-attendance, the more likely the county was to memorialize. . . .

It seems clear that two factors—Roman Catholicness and Irishness— influenced memorializing and petitioning in different ways. The two are closely related. . . .

. . . [T]he larger the ratios of Roman Catholic and Anglican attendances to Wesleyan per county, the more likely the county was to memorialize. . . . Wesleyans tended to be influenced by both the presence of Irish and the presence of Roman Catholics . . . , whilst Anglicans were influenced by the presence of Irish alone in 1850. . . .

The quantitative evidence suggests that English reaction to the new Roman Catholic hierarchy was by no means monolithic. Anglicans participated in both cycles of protest, but Wesleyan Methodist exertions were more significant in 1851 than in 1850. The two cycles of protest show different geographical distributions: centers of memorializing in 1850 were more evenly distributed, while the Midlands were more important in 1851. (That suggests that the former may have been more spontaneous than the latter.) Anti-Tractarianism was not so important a factor in the protests as has been thought hitherto. Marked variations in local behavior appear when one breaks down the protests by county. Anglicans behaved differently than did Wesleyans, by and large, in reacting to the Papal Aggression. Most of the signatories probably were males. Although a few addresses are identified as from women's groups, one suspects that the vast majority of the meetings were all-male affairs.

. . . Englishmen, by and large, were optimistic at mid-century about the way their society had developed. . . . Britain appeared attractive indeed in comparison with the rest of the world. Continental Europe was too autocratic, too unstable, or too benighted; the only other independent English-speaking nation was too democratic. Thus, in the year of the Crystal Palace[20] middling and upper-class Englishmen saw themselves at the acme of political, cultural, and economic development, and believed that their institutions were patently superior to those of any other nation. But such optimism does not exhaust the sentiments of the Victorians at mid-century. . . . [A] deep vein of pessimism and uncertainty underlay that complacency. This was the tail end of a century or longer transition between the Old Society and our modern world, a century that saw social and economic dislocations, shifts in values, and the inevitable pain and human suffering. Excessive and oft-proclaimed optimism is a classic defense mechanism to protect against depression and despair. The Papal Aggression is a good example of how a people will react when it thinks that its deepest fears are real.

It was against this background that the grave post-1828 transformations worked themselves out. . . . The rapid growth in numbers of Irish immigrants, the revitalization of the English Roman Catholic Church, and the increase of denominationalism in domestic politics after Catholic Emancipation all tended to increase religious tensions in both private and public life. Those tensions, with respect to Roman Catholic Irish and "Romanizing" Puseyites, came to a head during the Russell ministry.

[20]Building in Hyde Park, London, and site of the Great Exhibition in 1851.

Simultaneously, foreign relations with both the Papacy and France, the Papacy's protector, had reached a new low. (These foreign issues did touch the consciousness of the middling classes through the support of liberalism in 1848 and through "Bonapartophobia.") Of course, personalities were important. Wiseman and Newman struck the worst possible tone, under the circumstances; Russell's pronouncements legitimized the popular uproar.

. . . Certainly traditional, latent anti-catholicism was the deep spring that fed Papal Aggression. The early Victorians knew their *Book of Martyrs*;[21] anti-catholicism was perhaps as deeply engrained in their national ideology as anti-communism is in the American. The series of grave crises that England faced from the excommunication of Queen Elizabeth to the Gunpowder Plot permanently tarred English recusants[22] with the brush of treason; the Glorious Revolution and eighteenth-century Jacobite[23] plots only confirmed that protestant vision. By the late eighteenth century English recusants could be granted toleration because they had become discreet in their religious practices and anglo-gallican in their politics. But the Gordon Riots[24] showed that anti-catholicism still persisted as a part of popular ideology. . . .

. . . Both Irishness and Roman Catholicism were [considered] symptoms of congenital inferiority. Irish were dirty, drunken, and lazy; Roman Catholics were ignorant, priestridden, credulous, and "feminine." But other sterotypes also combined to re-enforce each other. Italians—also Roman Catholics—were degenerate peasants, credulous, stealthy, untrustworthy; it was an Italian Pope and Curia who proclaimed the hierarchy. French—also Roman Catholics—were excitable, jacobinical, and expansionist; they were French troops that kept the Pope on his throne while he proclaimed the hierarchy. These attitudes are not modern scientific racism, for they refer to moral and cultural judgments, not biological or genetic ones. Nevertheless, Anglo-Saxon supremacists assumed that the Roman Catholic communion was the faith of the racially inferior because the racially inferior embraced it.

. . . [T]he growth of Irish immigration and the revitalization of the English Roman Catholic Church [are] important factors in anti-catholicism, but these elements influenced Englishmen in complicated ways. Different sects reacted to different threats and differently to the same threats. Wesleyan Methodists were unusually anti-catholic, but mainly for religious reasons. The score of years after the Great

[21]One of the most widely read books in the English language, published in 1563 by John Foxe (1516–1587).

[22]Roman Catholics who did not attend services of the Church of England.

[23]The Jacobites were supporters of the deposed English king, James II, and his descendants.

[24]Anti-Catholic riots in London in 1780.

Reform Act was a particularly trying time for that denomination. The maintenance of its self-defined role as daughter to the Establishment grew increasingly difficult in the face of the Church's own doctrinal evolution, and disputes over authority rent the denomination by mid-century. . . . Anti-catholicism, however, was a way of resolving the dilemma of a dissenting sect that would not dissent.

It is not surprising that Anglicans reacted differently than Wesleyans to the Papal Aggression, for the two differed in social composition, sacramental theology, and church order. Anglicans, the majority of church-goers, represented a cross-section of the population while Wesleyans tended to be middling and working-class. Anglicans emphasized baptism as the entry-rite into the Christian community while Wesleyans looked to the conversion experience. Anglicans accepted apostolic succession and priesthood while Wesleyans did not; and they were as ambiguous as Tractarians about civil establishment. Consequently, Anglicans reacted sharply in 1850 to the creation of the new Roman Catholic hierarchy, for it denied the validity of their orders, while Wesleyans, unaffected by Roman Catholic sacerdotal claims, petitioned Parliament to punish papists in 1851.

. . . Middling-class Dissenters, who associated Roman Catholic pretensions with aristocratic oligarchy and royal absolutism, were predisposed to be anti-catholic because of their struggle against the landed interest; and the landed interest, on the defensive against industrial "modernity," grew anti-catholic because militant Roman Catholicism was a symbol of modernity to the extent that it rejected the happy establishment in church and state.

. . . Anti-catholicism, as much as any other manifestation of public opinion, emerges from local contexts that must be understood in order to explain regional variations. The nature of local leadership, the history of local disputes, and the constellation of local outgroups probably determine whether and how the locality will react to a national event. . . .

Is God French?

EUGEN WEBER

Many European historians have turned from the study of theology and church politics to the sociology of religion. Examining parish registers, wills, sermons, visitation reports by clergy, diaries, letters, and tracts and pamphlets written for the populace, historians have attempted to describe both daily religious behavior and the thought of the masses. Eugen Weber here elucidates the meaning of religion to nineteenth-century French people.

France in the second half of the nineteenth century appeared to be a solidly Roman Catholic nation. In the census that Weber cites, over 98 percent of the French affirmed themselves Catholics, and there were certainly enough priests to minister to the spiritual needs of the populace. Yet today the major religion of the French is indifference. What developments (from the French Revolution on) does Weber discuss that reflect a decline of religiousness?

Did people reject supernatural religion altogether or did they just lose faith in the institutional Church? After all, it is not uncommon for sincerely religious people to stay away from churches. To what extent did Church attendance measure religious belief? What role did the Church play in the lives of people in nineteenth-century France? Weber describes a panoply of popular religious beliefs, including attitudes toward saints and miracles, for example. From the Middle Ages there has been perennial tension between the institutional view of religion and the popular attitude toward religious practice. How did the Church feel about the parishioners' veneration of saints and craving for the miraculous? What functions did miracles serve? The popularity of Lourdes is a marvelous example of the strength of popular devotion and the Church's desire to control its flock's religious expressions. On the other hand, how did the flock view the priest's functions? Could the priest be considered a magician? What Church rules and prohibitions did the French come to disregard?

Religion did not simply mean belief and practice; there was a commercial side to religion that Weber does not neglect. Thus the pilgrimage signified more than a possible cure for a crippling disease or improved chances for salvation. There was money to be made from pilgrims, and, for their part, the pilgrims could play tourist and enjoy their escape from a humdrum existence. Was the priest involved in the commercial aspects of religion?

Weber concludes this selection with a story that illustrates "the requiem of nineteenth-century religion." Perhaps Weber is a bit premature, for the 1890s unleashed a torrent of religious feeling in the virulent anti-Semitism that colored the notorious Dreyfus affair. But there is no doubt that the traditional faith of the peasantry had changed in dramatic ways and that the Church had lost its hold on the hearts and minds of many French people.

Eugen Weber, Peasants into Frenchmen. The Modernization of Rural France, 1870–1914 (Stanford: Stanford University Press, 1976), 339–356.

. . . In the mid-1870's 35,387,703 of the 36,000,000 people in France were listed in the official census as Catholics. The rest declared themselves Protestants (something under 600,000), Jews (50,000), or freethinkers (80,000). The secular clergy of the Catholic church alone included 55,369 priests, one for every 639 inhabitants. Roman Catholicism remained, as it had been in 1801, "the religion of the majority of Frenchmen."

Whatever else this meant, it meant that the Church was an integral part of life. It presided over all the major occasions in a person's life—birth, marriage, death—and over the welfare of the community and the conduct of its members. It helped the crops increase and the cattle prosper. It healed, taught, and preserved from harm. . . .

Religion provided spells and incantations, often written down and passed on preciously like amulets. These, like its ceremonies, were efficacious and protective. The peasant . . . was proud to recite his prayers. "He has prayers for thunder, for sickness, for going to bed at night. They are good, very good, these prayers, says he, though he doesn't understand them very well, since they are in French," or in Latin. The ritual lent solemnity to private and public occasions, as the term solemnization applied to ceremonies like marriage attests. This was particularly important in rites of passage. The first communion, the first time one received the Eucharist, was crucial—a "great matter for country children; many cannot find a job before they have done it." Marking admission into the world of workers and of earners—almost an adult world—the first communion and the preparation for it, the catechism, provided the basic initiation into the moral mysteries of life. "The children did not know how to read, so the priest was teaching them the catechism by heart [which was] full of extraordinary words and which they laughed at," recorded Charles Péguy.[1] They must have had a sense that obscure powers were properly invoked with obscure incantations. . . .

Was Christ's personal message communicated in many a village church? We cannot tell. Those sermons that one finds concern themselves with the proprieties and transgressions of everyday behavior. Policemen were less concerned with immanent justice than with infringements of petty human laws; and village priests seem to have taken a similar view. This was their civilizing function. Along with this, it was their duty to see that their flock observed all of the formal and routine religious rites. It is by the practice of such rites that adherence to religion is generally measured. When there is little participation, even on high holidays, or when it declines, religion is said to decay. Yet what did church attendance mean to churchgoers?

"Sunday, the peasants go to church . . . some moved by religious feeling, most by habit or by fear of what people say." One went to

---

[1]Essayist and poet, 1873–1914, from a working-class background.

church because it was the thing to do on Sunday, because it was one of the few social occasions of the week, because it was an opportunity for talking business or meeting friends, acquaintances, relatives. It was— especially for the women, once men had grasped at the opportunities that fairs held out—the sole occasion to escape the isolation in which many lived, the major recreation or diversion in a restricted life. Observance, business, and pleasure were combined. One went to mass wearing one's Sunday best. . . . Public announcements were made by the village crier as the congregation left the service, public sales were often timed to fall after it, one could slip off later to call on the notary or the doctor, or drop in to the tavern, circle, or café. Even if a majority did not attend the service but went about their work as on any other day, "a multitude of peasants gathered in front of the church, discussed politics, made deals, filled the taverns."

In a world where entertainment was scarce, church provided a certain festive diversion. Those attending might well "love the high mass, the rich ornaments, seeing a great many statues of saints in their churches." Writing about his grandmother, Charles Péguy presented church attendance as a treat for the lonely child raised in a woodcutter's hut in Bourbonnais in the early 1800's: "When she was good, she was allowed to go on Sunday to mass in the village—she wore her sabots[2] because one doesn't go to church barefoot, and she was happy because that's where everybody met, where they exchanged news, where one heard about deaths, marriages, births, where gossip flowed about what was going on, where servants were hired."

. . . But the belief and behavior of the peasants never ceased to oscillate between observance and transgression. Until the Revolution church attendance was compulsory, and religious sanctions that could cause serious social embarrassment menaced those who skipped their Easter duties. The elimination of constraints broke this decreed unanimity. Those who had been quietly uncommitted (as in Aunis-Saintonge, where the forced conversion of Protestants had made lukewarm Catholics) were free to fall away. Political divisions and internal schism during the 1790's confused many more, and deprived parishes of pastors or cut sections of a community off from the only priest. For a decade or more, at least until the Concordat of 1801,[3] a good number of young people grew up without catechism, whole communities did not attend church, and others ceased to celebrate traditional festivals. The Décadi[4] created the habit of working on Sunday. The absence of priests left marriages to civil authorities and

---

[2]Wooden clogs.

[3]Agreement between the pope and the French government re-establishing religious peace and recognizing Catholicism as the religion of the majority of the French.

[4]The ten-day week created during the French Revolution to replace the seven-day week.

led to prolonged delays before baptism, if the ceremony was performed at all.

Some communities came to rely on the services of laymen, who took over the functions of absent priests, performing baptisms, marriages, and burials. . . . Ad hoc arrangements of this sort could prove enduring. . . .

Canon Fernand Boulard doubts that the Revolution really affected rural religious practice very profoundly, or that much changed in this realm until the last decade or two of the nineteenth century. He may be right. But there were discordances where there had once been at least outward unity. Men who had acquired Church property and would not submit, men who had married in a civil marriage and would not seek absolution for their sin, became centers of local opposition. Not many cases of this kind of sturdy opposition developed in communities that remained cohesive, but it flourished in areas where, as in Burgundy, the memory of clerical harshness and exploitation survived, along with the fear of a reconstitution of their great domains. In Mâconnais . . . the devil appears as the hero in some local legends and triumphs over Christ, disgraced by the men who served him. The peasants had burned churches there in the Middle Ages and did so again in 1789, or stayed away thereafter. But even where the road had not been so prepared, hard times frayed clerical authority. Priests were forced to ask for help from their parishioners. Rival clergymen accused each other of the worst transgressions, diminishing still further the influence of the cloth. "People begin to separate religion from its ministers," asserted the *Statistique*[5] of Lot in 1831. But religion *was* its ministers, just as the state was bailiffs and gendarmes. And when, after 1830, liberal local mayors opposed the influence of priests loyal to the old order, they sought to sap their authority by encouraging the drift of men away from the sacraments.

We see that in the churches, as in the schools, non-attendance is a way of measuring ineffectiveness. The growing numbers of migrant workers going to the cities added to this trend. Urban workers worked Sundays and holidays, or did so very often. The more earnest the man, the more he worked. The less responsible were the more likely to get drunk during their free time. The Church did not see them either way. Like the Revolution, acquaintance with the city did not destroy religious sentiment. It simply made nonconformity possible or created another kind of conformity. Men who attended church at home because their peers did ceased to attend church where such attendance was exceptional. The city merely provided an opportunity for the collapse of practices "shallowly rooted in the personality." Returning migrants may well have lost whatever impulse to religious conformity they had left with. They did not necessarily bandy this about so long as the priest retained his influence in the community. But they were ready to welcome emancipation when it came.

[5]*Statistics*, a publication.

At any rate, all observers seem to have sensed the shallowness of faith behind the slackness of observance. In Beauce respectable farmers, "preoccupied by the care to augment their fortune, work to this end even on Sunday during the services, so that the churches are deserted." Not that they lacked respect for religion, "but they consider that the time they would spend in church would be lost for their work and their fortune." Not challenge, but indifference and hardheadedness. . . . "The absence of religious sentiment [in the countryside, especially] is such that there are communes where scarcely one marriage in six is blessed in church.". . .

Whether unconverted or disaffected, people lost their respect for Church rules and Church prohibitions. The proportion of civil marriages grew, the delays between birth and baptism became longer. Once set at 24 hours of birth, the outside limit for baptism was extended to three days in 1830, to eight days in 1887, to "the soonest possible time" in the twentieth century. In one Sologne parish the average delay between birth and baptism, which was 2.73 days in 1854, had stretched to 15.12 days by 1901; in 1950 it ran well over three months. Less fear for the newborn's life, fewer epidemics, greater closeness between husband and wife, who was increasingly expected to play a part in the ceremony, but also indifference to what the sacrament of baptism meant and to the authority of the priest. . . . One could do without the priest if one wanted to get married when he could not, or would not, perform the ceremony.

From the Church's point of view, every innovation only made things worse. The bicycle was blamed for enabling young people to avoid mass. Tourists, visitors, and returning emigrants felt increasingly free to speak of their indifference to religious practice or even their scorn of it. Military service side by side with "pagan" urban workers made some peasants ashamed of a show of piety as a mark of their bumpkin backwardness. Finally, with war in 1914 there came a culmination of the pressures toward detachment. . . .

Religion was an urban import, like education, and, just like education, it reflected the scholarship of the Counter-Reformation and the Enlightenment—the two at one, at least, in being alien to the countryside. Tridentine[6] and post-Tridentine missionaries, where they could, replaced familiar native rites and practices with new ones that were strange. These had no time to settle into tradition before the Revolution and the cascade of changes following it. Religious custom remained superficial, even though convention and the need for ritual kept it in being. In this respect, reputedly devout areas appear little better than incredulous ones. For the outwardly pious Solognot, religion was "an artificial system that he bore without understanding, lacking in efficacy and well above his preoccupations.". . .

---

[6]From the Council of Trent (1545–1563), which clarified doctrines and reformed the Roman Catholic Church.

Such comments may explain the frequent conjunction between indifference and some form of practice, as in Bourbonnais where peasants "have recourse to religion in all great circumstances, but following ancestral traditions rather than any real faith." Religion had didactic uses: "It fills the young with fear," and that was good and necessary, "but when we're dead we're dead," and that was common sense. Even those peasants who eschewed religious practice wanted a resident priest, for one thing, because he would teach the children to respect their parents and authority, but above all "for rites needed in social life and to ensure good crops, for festivals often connected with a healing saint." In short, the ritual and the ceremonies that were the very core of popular religion were fundamentally utilitarian. Accordingly, we might expect such pragmatic formalism to decline when its utility no longer seemed apparent, or when rival authorities and formalities beckoned.

This of course is advanced as merest supposition. I know no way of telling the spiritual hold that the Church had on people. At the visible level, however, its influence was based on practical services and subject to its ability to keep these up: consecration (in an officially acceptable sense), healing, protection, making wishes come true, and not least providing a center for traditional practices. In all these things, official religion drew generously on the popular cult of saints, of healing agencies and other useful "superstitions." Superstitions have sometimes been described as religions that did not succeed. Perhaps, in our case at least, it is they that should be called successful, since so much official religion depended on them and survived largely by indulging practices endorsed by popular belief. The people of Balesta in Comminges, noted the village teacher in 1886, "are the more religious, the more superstitious they are.". . .

We know about the widespread usage of the cross—about how the plowman signed himself before he drew the first furrow, and again before he sowed the first handful of grain; about how he would not cut a slice out of a loaf without first tracing a cross on it. But how far did this, or prayers, or kneeling in the fields when the Angelus[7] tolled, go beyond the propitiation of powers that were feared but little understood?. . .

Much that was expected of the priest indeed fell in the category of magic—white, of course, as when the priest said masses to cure animals that were under a spell, or when, during the traditional processions that wound their way through communal territory on Rogation Sunday,[8] he threw stones plastered with a small wax cross (priest's dung in Franche-Comté) into the fields to keep the storms and hail away. We have already seen the power over natural phenomena attributed to priests,

[7]A Roman Catholic prayer said three times daily upon the tolling of the Angelus bell.

[8]The Sunday before Ascension Day, which marked the supposed bodily ascent of Jesus to Heaven.

and the logical belief that some men of the cloth wielded more powers than others. . . . It seems quite natural that when, in the early 1890's, the bishop of Mende visited the village of Saint-Enimie (Lozère), his flock should find that his blessing of their valley made the almond harvest more abundant. . . . In Meuse several priests were held to sit on clouds, thus helping to disperse them; and the Abbé Chévin, of Bar-le-Duc, who died in 1900, was accused of having made a violent storm break over his own parish.

For those who connected Catholicism and sorcery, plainly, priests could be sinister figures, holding the powers of black magic as well. As a result of natural associations, the Limousins of the twentieth century still dreaded that "priests would usher death" into the homes they visited. The fear that stalked all the inhabitants of the countryside found in the church service not only appeasement but fuel. When sermons did not deal with public discipline, they frequently stoked the fires of brimstone and hell. That was the only way "to move such an almost savage populace," remarked a Breton. "A voice like thunder, dire threats, fists belaboring the pulpit, sweat running down his cheeks, the eloquent pastor fills his hearers with delicious terror."

Benoît Malon (another hostile witness) has denounced the obsessive effects this sort of thing could have on people, especially children, haunted throughout life by the dread of hell-fire, torments, retribution, and circumambient fiends. But priestly menaces were bound to be intimidating to the most sober when menace was the staff of everyday life. Living was marginal, disaster inexplicable and uncontrollable. . . . Where harm and ill-fortune were swiftly come by, nothing was easier than to claim that they were punishments of heaven. Long centuries of trying to mollify and coax the powerful conjured up a religion where fear almost excluded love, a faith bent to flatter and do honor to the heavenly lords in order to obtain their protection or avoid their ire. Power and irascibility were what impressed. The peasants would not work their cattle on the feasts of the nastiest saints, the ones most likely to resent and revenge any irreverence. . . .

God was far away. The saints were near. Both were anthropomorphic. Saints were intercessors. One did not address God directly, but prayed to saints to request his favors, rewarded them if the crop was good or the weather fair, even chastised them, as at Haudimont (Meuse), where Saint Urban, accused of permitting the vines to freeze on May 25, his own feastday, was dragged in effigy through the nettles around his church. The greatest saint of all, of course, was the Virgin, an unparalleled source of delivery from harm. The *gwerz* (ballad) made up when a new pilgrimage to her was launched in 1894 at Plounéour-Menez recited only recent and concrete miracles: saving men from falling, drowning, prison, and so on. These were the functions of a saint.

But the chief function of saints on earth was healing, and every malady was the province of a particular saint. The attribution could vary from region to region, with some local patron saint taking over duties another saint performed elsewhere; but it was a creation of popular design. The conjunction between saint and illness was determined by associations, some naively evident, others lost in the mists of time. Thus Saint Eutropius healed dropsy . . . ; Saint Cloud healed boils . . . ; Saint Diétrine dealt with herpes and scurf . . . ; Saint Aignan coped with ringworm and scurvy. . . . Berry had its own array of saints destined by alliteration or obscure fiat to heal. For the deaf there was Saint Ouen; for the gouty, Saint Genou; for crabbed and peevish women, Saint Acaire. . . . In Finistère Our Lady of Benodet healed aches, depressions, madness, or simplemindedness—disorders associated with the head. Benodet literally means head of Odet, that is, the mouth of the Odet river. . . .

Probably the most notorious saint born of popular whimsy and need was Saint Grelichon or Greluchon (from *grelicher*, which means to scratch or tickle). Saint Greluchon had started life as the funeral statue of a local lord of Bourbon-l'Archambault, Guillaume de Naillac, but we rediscover the figure in a recessed nook of that city's streets. Childless women came from afar to scratch a little dust from the statue's genital area and drink it in a glass of white wine. By 1880, when Sir Guillaume's lower parts had been scratched down to nullity, the dust was obtained from under the statue's chin. Finally, the statue—which had become a bust—was transferred to the museum for safekeeping.

. . . [M]iracle-working agents enlisted strong popular loyalties. So did the traditions that called for rites to be performed in scrupulous detail, or otherwise fail in their intent. At Maizey (Meuse) the relics of Saint Nicholas were carried in procession through the streets in May, and the following Sunday's services then had to be celebrated in a country chapel about a mile away. In 1889 the priest tried to avoid the chore and to say mass in his own church. This disturbed his flock, and most of the men in his congregation, dressed in their holiday clothes, marched to the designated chapel so that the rite would be carried out properly. On the other hand, it appears that the change of a patron saint was often treated with equanimity, as was a substitution of the supposedly sacred image itself. At Villeneuve-de-Berg (Ardèche) the blacksmiths had no statue of their patron, Saint Eloi, to parade on his feastday. They solved the problem routinely by borrowing Saint Vincent from the vintners' corporation, removing the statue's pruning knife, and replacing it with a little hammer. Similarly, in the Alps, at the feast of Saint Besse the saint's devotees brought medals "of him" bearing the legend "St.-Pancrace." When the discrepancy was pointed out to them, it bothered them not at all. The fact was, they said, the likeness was close, and the effects were the same. To the traditional mind the patron saint was secondary to the rite, and to the site as well.

We can see this in the cult of "good" [i.e. healing] fountains, a cult that was generally abetted by the clergy on the theory that the saints who protected the fountains would be given a share of the credit for their restorative powers. Yet popular customs connected with healing fountains were, as a student says, "often purely secular," and certain spas kept their appeal with or without the Church's blessing. . . . On Batz island, off the Breton coast, the old chapel dedicated to Saint Pol (de Léon) was shifted to the patronage of Saint Anne when, at the end of the nineteenth century, she was officially declared the patron saint of the peninsula. The pilgrimage continued as before. It was the place that mattered! . . .

Alphonse Dupront has written that all pilgrimages are made to a source of healing. But we should add that the pilgrims as often seek protection and favors, too. In Bresse one went to pray to Saint Anthony that one's pigs should "gain" during the year. In Bourbonnais shepherdesses attended the annual pilgrimage to Saint Agatha's shrine at Saint-Désiré "in the first place to divert themselves and to secure a blessed hazel switch" with which to control their herds and be free of the fear of wolves.

Conditions obviously varied depending on the stand of the local priest; but priestly decisions were interpreted without illusions. At Carnac (Morbihan) the pilgrimage to the shrine of Saint Cornelius (Cornély), patron of horned beasts, was very profitable. Oxen and calves were offered to him; they were made to kneel in adoration of his statue, which stood above the portal of the church, then blessed by the priest and auctioned off under the saint's banner. Then, in 1906, the priests refused to bless the gathered beasts. "They haven't been paid enough," explained a hawker selling his toys at the local fair. . . . [P]riests too galled or too rigorous to keep up traditional devotions were in minority. As a general rule, they accepted current beliefs in healing fountains, stones, and megaliths. For one thing, as all observers hastened to point out, the gifts offered to their patron saints contributed to clerical revenues. Saint Anthony was offered pigs' feet, Saint Eloi horses' tails, and Saint Herbot cows' tails. More important, many saints were offered the beasts themselves, calves, lambs, chicken, and other gifts in kind. These would be sold by the verger after the ceremony, and the revenue could rise to as much as 1,500 or 2,000 francs—riches for men whose yearly income was only half as much.

For some priests the launching of a new pilgrimage spot meant big business, like the shrine in Picardy, complete with publicity, signposts, hostels, and eateries, which had to be suppressed in 1882 by the bishop of Beauvais. Others were satisfied with a modest but regular income gained from the sale of some small item, like the *saint vinage*[9] at Miremont in Combrailles, a mixture of 10 liters of water and one liter of wine that was

---

[9]Reference to a process of making consecrated wine.

blessed by the priest and sold by the sexton at very moderate prices, and that was said to cure all cattle ills. . . .

That priests and their parishes profited from such religious undertakings does not make the undertakings any the less valid or the participants any the less sincere. Utility underlies most human enterprise, and in no way demeans it. The mother who trudged off carrying her child that it might be strengthened or healed was an admirable figure. The priest who sought funds to glorify the source from which such healing sprang—and perhaps its guardian as well—was human and perhaps even saintly.

But to return to pilgrimages: these were perhaps important above all as a form of access to the extraordinary. . . . The pilgrimage offered an excuse to leave the village, and with it, for a time at least, an inescapable fate. Pilgrimages were festive occasions involving food and drink, shopping and dancing. The most ancient pilgrimages coincided with great fairs; markets and sanctuaries went together. . . . Bakers and butchers, clothiers and peddlers, set up their stalls; people treated themselves to sweetmeats, wine, or lemonade, and purchased images, traditional cakes, and other ritual ex-votos to deposit in the sanctuary or tie to the branch of a nearby tree. The healing statue of Saint Stephen at Lussac-les-Eglises (Haute-Vienne) was invoked, like a good many others, by binding a ribbon on the statue's arm. The ribbons were bought from cloth merchants or from the stalls local women set up in the village streets. So were the wax limbs carried in the procession of Saint Amateur at Lamballe (Côtes-du-Nord); the "saffron-flavored cakes shaped like hens," sold to the devotees of Saint Symphorien at Vernègues (Bouches-du-Rhône); the yellow wax breasts offered by women to Saint Anthony's fountain near Brive (Corrèze); and the amulets or priapic figures, in cake or wax, sold from Normandy to Var at least since the seventeenth century. No wonder the peasants felt that priests were necessary because they made business go! And it is easy to dwell on the commercial aspects of religion. The point is that there was commerce because there were people, and people congregated because this was the only sort of festivity they knew.

"It's more a pleasure trip than a pious action," caviled an eastern teacher in 1888. What was wrong with its being both? At this unexalted level, the pilgrimage and traveling were one and the same thing. . . . Relations and friends met at pilgrimage places regularly every year, and such predictable gatherings were convenient in times when communications were rare and difficult. They also afforded welcome breaks, especially to women. The pilgrimage was chiefly a feminine activity—perhaps because it was the woman's only socially sanctioned means of escape from home and its daily routine. Men had opportunities to visit fairs or to travel to farther places. Their lives were far more varied than those of womenfolk. These found their opportunity in pilgrimages, which they often undertook alone over great distances. . . .

But let us hazard further. Even quite humble trips, for secular or devotional ends, took a person out of his element and opened up unfamiliar spheres. The extraordinary began much closer to home then than it would do today, and a trip of any kind was an understandable aspiration for those whose ordinary lives offered so little change.

What could be more extraordinary than the miraculous? Perhaps this was what humble people welcomed in the news of the great miracles of the time. Miracles promise deliverance from the routine unfolding of predictable destinies; and they create a sense of expectancy and excitement the more potent for being the more vague. Millenarianism, which embodies all this in its most extreme form, is commonly attributed to bafflement—a sense of privation and restraint with no conceivable relief in sight. The promise carried by evidence of supernatural forces heals bafflement and frustration, and reinforces hope. It also holds out an opportunity to escape from the commonplace into the realm of the prodigious, to wonder over marvels and possibilities beyond familiar ken. . . .

Whatever the explanation, the rural world was eager for miracles. . . . Most of the time rumors of local miracles did not go beyond a limited radius. In 1840 the Holy Virgin seems to have manifested herself in several places in Vendée. But this was treated as local superstition. In the early 1860's the Ursuline nuns of Charroux in Poitou discovered what they claimed to be the Sacred Prepuce, removed from the Infant Jesus at the circumcision and, in the words of Monsignor Pie, bishop of Poitiers, "the only part of Christ's body left behind when he ascended into heaven." The name Charroux was associated with *chair rouge* (the red meat of the cut-off prepuce!), and an elaborate festival in 1862 brought the fortunate convent into the public eye. . . .

At about the same time, in the fall of 1862, the sixteen-year-old daughter of a rural postman of Saint-Marcel-d'Ardèche began to preach, predict the future and promise miracles. The people came en masse from all surrounding communes until, in a few days, the furor died down.

In other cases the feverish excitement did not pass so quickly. When, in September 1846, two shepherd children guarding their herds on the deserted mountainside of La Salette saw an unnatural light and a tearful lady announcing the wrath of Christ in their own patois,[10] curious pilgrims hastened there at once. The veracity of the children was contested, especially by the Church authorities, but the enthusiasm was too great to stifle. The evidence makes clear that miracles were validated and imposed by popular opinion, which the authorities—civil and clerical—accepted only unwillingly and under pressure. In a notorious trial of 1857, concerned with the reality of the miracle of La Salette, the lawyers continually referred to the supernatural needs of the lower classes (explained presumably by their ignorance). It was wholly understandable,

---

[10]Local dialect.

they said, that the common people should believe in such things, but they expressed some surprise at finding members of the upper classes sharing these views.

This same division and the same pressure of popular need appear in the earliest stages of the first and perhaps the greatest modern pilgrimage site—Lourdes. In February 1858, eleven-year-old Bernadette Soubirous encountered a "Beautiful Lady" beside a stream. The local nuns, priests, and civil authorities, afraid of complications, refused to believe Bernadette's story. The local gendarme sought to tell "the people . . . that it is not in the nineteenth century that one lets oneself be carried away by such a belief." Yet belief was stronger than skepticism. It spread like wildfire. Within a few days large crowds, mostly women and children, began to gather at the grotto of Masabielle. By the beginning of March they numbered 20,000 (the population of Lourdes was less than a quarter of that). "Disorder caused in the name of God is none the less intolerable disorder," warned the gendarme. All his superiors clearly thought the same. The records are full of it: "disorder," "regrettable agitation," "preserve order," "undeceive the population," "regrettable facts." But the population did not want to be undeceived. For it, disorder was hope and holiday. "The population . . . wants to believe. When there are no miracles, it invents them; it insists on baring heads, kneeling, etc."

There were few priests, sometimes no priests, in the assembled crowds. The clergy, as the imperial prosecutor reported, "maintained an excessive reserve." But the ritual pilgrimages developed without their intervention and despite that of the civil authorities. It was several years before the bishop of Tarbes confirmed the miracles in 1862, proclaiming the authenticity of the Virgin's appearance and the healing virtues of the grotto's spring. But clearly the voice of the people preceded the voice of God. In 1867 a railway line became available. By 1871 the pilgrimage had become international, and in 1876 the great basilica was consecrated before 100,000 pilgrims—a new tide in the affairs of men, flowing in the wake of the railroads. . . .

What does all this tell us about religion? Conclusions do not come easily. That it was local and specific. That a peasant who did not believe in the Church, its foolishness or its saints, to quote a country priest, could share in local reverence and worship Saint Eutropius. That men who would not go to mass would undertake long pilgrimages to be healed or to have their beasts healed. And that, in one way or another, religious practices were interwoven with every part of life, but hardly in a manner that one would call specifically Christian. Leaving aside the entertainment that these practices offered, divinity was associated with vast unknown areas. God and saints—like fairies—possessed knowledge that was forbidden to men. They had to be propitiated and persuaded to perform tasks that men accomplish only imperfectly (like healing) or not at all (like controlling the weather). The more men came to master such tasks, plumb the unknown, shake the tree of knowledge, the less they needed intercessors.

The sales of the *saint vinage* at Miremont declined, to the despair of the sexton. In Sologne good Saint Viâtre, who had done so much to heal the local fevers (malaria), was badly hurt by the spreading use of quinine and by the drainage and sanitation projects beginning to show results in the 1880's. At Hévillers (Meuse) the priest read the Lord's Passion every day from May to September "to bring heaven's blessing on the goods of the earth"; then, before Christmas, the church treasurer went from door to door to collect grain in payment for this service. In the 1850's the treasurer got 800 lbs and more. By 1888 . . . he garnered only 330. Things were worse still in Périgord, where the popularity of Saint John the Baptist, whose accompanying lamb had made him the patron of the local sheepruns, declined with the century. . . .

. . . The observance of Rogation week declined—even in Brittany. The turn of the century saw fewer processions across the village fields with cross, banners, and bells to drive off evil spirits and to bless the crops. In the Limousin, where in 1876 many peasants still reckoned their age according to ostensions—great septennial processions with scores of villages in their entirety parading behind relics, drums, and banners— the emotional content gradually seeped away, and the penitents in their colorful costumes disappeared; and new religious groups that borrowed nothing from the old traditions meant little to the popular public. . . .

Local pilgrimages of the popular sort leveled off or declined. Some were domesticated into the Marian cult. Others were suppressed because they gave rise to scandalous practices, as when Morvan women seeking a cure for barrenness too often found it in adjacent woods; or because they always brought disorders, like the wrestlers' *pardon* of Saint Cadou at Gouesnac'h (Finistère) that never failed to end in fights and brawls. The mercantile activities that had grown around traditional devotions killed them, like trees stifled by ivy. Easter Sunday processions had to be given up in some places because the streets and squares were too crowded with stalls and carrousels. Tourists and sightseers helped to keep observances alive as pure pageantry, but finally, "when everyone wants to watch the procession, there is no one left to take part in it." Between the wars, automobiles denied the roads to those pilgrimages traditionally made on horseback, and the enclosure of fields discouraged them. In 1939 the *Courier du Finistère*[11] noted that the traditional procession stopped at the wires barring access to the ancient chapel of Saint-Roch at Landeleau. "What is the use in destroying the grass of a field to enter a building in ruins and without a roof?" No such reasoning could have been accepted half a century earlier.

Yet phosphates, chemical fertilizers, and schooling had spelled the

---

[11]A newspaper.

beginning of the end. In 1893, a drought year in Bourbonnais when many men were having masses said for their emaciated cattle (which died anyway), the priest reproached Henry Norre, a self-taught man who farmed not far from Cérilly, for not attending church. "I haven't got the time," he answered. "And really, I haven't got much confidence in your remedies for the beasts. My remedies are better; you can check." Daniel Halévy[12] quotes another story about Norre. This time the farmer returned from the railway station with a cartful of fertilizer and met the priest. "What are you carting there?" "Chemicals." "But that is very bad; they burn the soil!" "Monsieur le curé,"[13] said Norre, "I've tried everything. I've had masses said and got no profit from them. I've bought chemicals and they worked. I'll stick to the better merchandise." It was the requiem of nineteenth-century religion.

[12]French historian.
[13]Chief parish priest.

Men, Women, and Sex

EDWARD SHORTER

The nineteenth century was the last period in which traditional marriage could be found at all levels of Western society. As Edward Shorter describes it, traditional marriage entailed little affection between husband and wife. In Shorter's view, most husbands were uncaring or even quite brutal toward their wives, not loving. Why did men treat their women so severely? Why was wife beating commonplace? These were the "good old days," yearned for by nostalgic preachers and moralizers today. Yet in those days men were often more worried about the health of their animals than about their wives. It would have been an improvement had they treated their wives as they did their beasts.

For centuries theologians and other intellectuals taught that women were naturally inferior to men and that men were therefore to be dominant in marriage. Shorter cites many proverbs to show that the belief in male dominance was a part of peasant lore. How did the husband's supremacy manifest itself in practice? There was little battle between the sexes, for society dictated who the winner must be. The sad evidence of wifely submission was frequent and painful childbirth, hardly avoidable because of the lack of effective contraception and the wives' obligation to perform the conjugal duty. The husband had the legal right to sex on demand; the wife could not refuse him. Shorter believes that nineteenth-century wives did not enjoy intercourse. Where does Shorter get his evidence to support such a statement? Why did wives feel the way they did? Was their anti-eroticism a response to nineteenth-century conditions or part of an older female tradition? What does Shorter say about sexual practices?

Shorter's views have not gone unchallenged by other historians. Some feel that he does not substantiate his conclusions but generalizes wildly about different countries and times. Nevertheless, Shorter offers bold interpretations that have forced historians to re-examine the relations between the sexes.

. . . I shall describe the harm done to women by sexual activity over which they had no control. "No control?" wonders the twentieth-century reader. In our own time, a married woman who dislikes her husband's advances can leave the marriage, and an unmarried woman is usually able to avoid a man's embraces if she so wishes. But today we have the "modern"—even the "post-modern"—family, and things are very different from two hundred years ago, when the traditional husband's "conjugal rights" meant that the married woman could not in fact refuse intercourse.

Edward Shorter, *A History of Women's Bodies* (NY: Basic Books, 1982), 3–13, 15–16.

Put yourself in the shoes of the typical housewife who lived in a small town or village then. Neither she nor anyone else had any idea when the "safe" period for a woman was; and for her, any sexual act could mean pregnancy. She was obliged to sleep with her husband whenever *he* wanted. And in the luck of the draw, she would become pregnant seven or eight times, bearing an average of six live children. Most of these children were unwelcome to her, for if one single theme may be said to hold my story together, it is the danger to every aspect of her health that this ceaseless childbearing meant.

The first issue thus becomes men. What was going on in the minds of husbands to make them subject their wives to these endless births?

A male unconcern for the welfare of women lay in the nature of traditional marriage. Two decades of research in the history of the family has now clearly established that the assumptions of traditional marriage differed radically from those of modern marriage. Unlike the twentieth century, when the point of matrimony is generally thought to be the emotional gratifications of romance and companionship, people in earlier times married for reasons of "lineage": a man needed a wife to help him run the farm or to provide male children to whom he could pass along the patrimony. There was little emotional contact between man and wife; and in fact, men saw other men as their main "spiritual companions" and thus formed the basis of . . . "male bonding." Women, in their turn, did not even imagine that their husbands might somehow "understand" them, and saw as their main allies other women. This was the basis of "female bonding." Thus, with both men and women seeking their major sentimental allies outside the family, power relations inside were jarringly unequal. The woman had the status of "chief servant of her sons and of the farmhands," to quote one observer of Brittany. And the man was the "master of his little kingdom". . . .

I should like to make several points about family life then, and call the reader's attention to the anecdotal nature of the evidence that follows. Although one would like firm statistics on such things as wife beating, they are simply not to be had. I have worked for many years in the sources, and what follows is my general impression of relations between men and women—"anecdotal" to be sure, but I am convinced that it is nonetheless accurate.

The husband's overtowering supremacy appears in many rituals of daily life. At table, the closer one sat to the father's chair, the more status one had. In the farm kitchens of the Sauerland, the farmer would be at the head of the table, the other men sitting next to him on the bench against the wall, male children at the end. The women sat on stools across the table. A guest would usurp not the father's place at the head, but the mother's, and she and all the other females would bump down one place. An alternative arrangement would be for all the men to be seated at table, first the father, then the retired grandfather, then his unmarried brother, then the sons in order of their age, with the women all *standing*. Or, . . . the father might eat alone, served separately by his wife. "Nobody dares raise his voice in the father's presence."

So overawing was the authority of men that in Languedoc a wife would not open the door to searchers from the police when her husband was away, lest she dishonor his authority. His wife would call him "mister" . . . and fall silent in the presence of a guest. In the Limousin a wife would not accompany her husband to the market, would not "stand at his side during civil or religious ceremonies," and would address him with the polite *vous*.[1] The husband would not refer to her directly, would never say, "My wife did such-and-such," but, "The woman of this house did such-and-such." French peasant proverbs demonstrate that a man was boss by virtue of his gender:

- "A rooster no larger than your fist will get the best of a hen as large as a stove." (Lower Brittany)
- "A woman who doesn't fear her husband doesn't fear God." (Catalogne)
- "As a man you're strong as plaster if of your wife you aren't the master." (Languedoc)

A woman ethnographer who lived in a German village just before the First World War reported how intensely the "subordination of the woman" was drummed into a young bride's head right from the beginning of her marriage. She would find herself in a strange, already established household, where her mother-in-law and all the relatives were constantly inspecting her. Her new husband sharply criticizes her work, and she starts to get the impression that his good will depends not on her qualities as a woman but on her ability as a farm worker. . . . The custom is that a wife does not go out on her own, even if she pays for it out of her own money. It is like pulling teeth to persuade him to let her go on a small trip or a pilgrimage. He, for his part, goes out every Sunday afternoon with his neighbors to the tavern, and often spends the afternoon or evening there during the week. Actual authority in a particular marriage would depend more on the characters of the individual man and woman; but custom stipulated that affection and intimacy were unimportant in negotiating the pitfalls of married life. The man was master.

Moreover, the average husband in small towns and villages would beat his wife. Legally his right to do so was unclear, yet he certainly was responsible for his wife's actions—a responsibility in which was implicit the power to correct her physically. As a practical matter, wife beating was universal. Midwives saw a lot of domestic violence simply because they were so close to the family circle. Midwife Lisbeth Burger told of

[1] "You," as opposed to the more familiar *tu* (also meaning "you").

one husband who kept strongly urging his wife to get an abortion. She kept refusing.

> He: "Why don't you just go into town like everyone else and see the abortionist. Otherwise I'm leaving you."
>
> She: "No. If I'm really pregnant, then our child has a right to live and I won't touch it."
>
> He: "You dare to say that in my face! You dare disobey me! Who's the boss around here, you or me?"

Then "in a blind rage he grabbed her by the hair and started kicking her," saying, 'By God, I'll show you what's what around here'." Burger's account implies that this kind of marital scene occurred frequently in her practice.

The doctors, too, saw many beaten women. Eduard Dann in Danzig thought the reason that working-class wives did not drink brandy was that they suffered from the consequences of their husbands' drinking—"terrible beatings," among other things. The obstetrical literature often mentions in passing that a beating was the cause of a woman's miscarriage. . . .

Johann Storch of Gotha, investigating the cause of a maternal death in 1724, found that the mother had a broken rib, probably caused by a kick from the husband sometime during the pregnancy. . . .

These stories go on and on. The doctors were not particularly distressed by wife beating, but mentioned it casually along with other medical details.

The proverbs and jokes, which are a culture's very core, assumed that a husband would normally use force to correct his wife. In peasant France:

> • "Good or bad, the horse gets the spur. Good or bad, the wife gets the stick." (Provence)
>
> • "If your wife gets an attack of nerves, the best medicine is a good thrashing." (Provence)
>
> • Question: "What do mules and women have in common"? Answer: "A good beating makes them both better." (Catalogne)

Along with a husband's overt brutality to a wife went his apparent lack of concern over her illnesses, deliveries, and death. The point is important, for if men were uncaring at these crises, they would also be indifferent in general to a wife's physical welfare. . . .

If the cow kicks off, mighty cross.
If the wife kicks off, no big loss (Hesse)

. . . The underlying logic . . . is that farm animals were expensive, whereas a wife could easily be replaced with a new bride who would bring another dowry to the farm. Hence while the loss of a horse was a blow, the death of a wife definitely carried with it a silver lining.

Contemporary observers, moreover, confirm the cool emotional calculus that lay behind these proverbs. . . . A priest in the Marne region wrote in 1777, "The peasants of the parish worry more about their cows when they birth their calves than about their wives when they have babies." When Rudolf Dohrn was teaching obstetrics in Königsberg, he said, "A country doctor from Lithuania told me that the death of a wife in childbirth meant little to the peasant. When a cow dies, it is very painful to the peasant, but another wife he'll get easily.

The indifference of men to the physical welfare of women is most striking in regard to childbirth. . . . Midwife Burger was called urgently to the bedside of a mother in labor. "I knew there was no rush," she later wrote, "but I try to please when it's a young mother."

The peasant farmer awaited her. "It has to be a male child," he said, "an heir for the farm."

"And if it's a girl?" Burger asked.

"Then the devil take her," the farmer said.

. . . Thus the sex of the infant was crucially important for fathers, especially when it came to a boy who would carry on the family name. The rest was secondary.

We know that it was secondary because many traditional husbands showed themselves loath to pay the cost of a trained midwife or doctor. They felt the neighbor's help was good enough. . . . Wrote Dr. Flügel of the Frankenwald . . . , "There is very little attention paid to childbirth, in that not only many poor but also well-to-do dispense with a midwife in order to save money, letting their own wives give birth as best they can. Through such parsimony I have in the last few years been witness to several maternal deaths." . . .

Beneath this male torpor lay a massive indifference to the sufferings of wives which is the antithesis of "modern" family sentiment. . . . A middle-class London woman gave birth on 21 April 1770 and came down a few days later with a post-delivery infection, which had a nasty odor. This went on for several weeks. . . . [T]he husband refused to go into his wife's sickroom, leaving her with the other women, "upon account of the excessive heat and offensive smell which it afforded." So we may imagine the scene: the wife lying ill for weeks, the other women clustering about, the husband virtually refusing to see her because he didn't like the smell. The doctor did not comment on the husband's absence as unusual.

I am not trying to cast the husbands of traditional society as fiends but want merely to show what an unbridgeable sentimental distance separated them from their wives. Under these circumstances it is unrealistic to think that men would abstain from intercourse in order to save women from the physical consequences of repeated childbearing.

A modern hypothesis might be that the sex was so satisfying that women were willing to overlook its disadvantages. But no, intercourse in the traditional family was brief and brutal, and there is little evidence that women derived much pleasure from it.

The main characteristic of the sexuality of traditional men is its ruthless impetuosity. When a man desired his wife, he would take her—that was all there was to it. It fell, for example, always to the man to initiate intercourse. . . .

Impetuousness appears in men's refusal to abstain from intercourse during the mother's lying-in period. Stories abound of husbands mounting their wives just after they had delivered, heedless of the doctor's pleas. Sex too soon after delivery can give the mother an infection. Thus, we are not surprised to learn that, a couple of days after a smooth delivery, Frau Stengel had a slight fever and some bleeding. "Something is wrong here," thought midwife Burger.

"Did you get out of bed yesterday, Frau Stengel," she asked.

"Oh no, no that." The woman looked embarrassed. Burger kept pressing her until the truth came out.

"It's just that . . . my husband was . . . with me."

"That scoundrel, that wretch," cried Burger. And gave him an earful.

"What's a wife there for?" responded the husband.

This happened often among the common people, despite custom's prescribing much longer waits.

Nor is this impetuosity some particularly brutal "peasant" quality. The seventeenth-century Virginia gentleman William Byrd was given to taking his wife on the spur of the moment—for example, on the billiard table—and often referred in his diary to having "rogered" her or "given her a flourish." Perhaps Mrs. Byrd liked this. . . . It is more likely, however, that Byrd thought of sex as a regular body function, unconnected to romantic ardor. It "was marked by only the most perfunctory exhibitions of human connectedness or emotional intensity. Except on the rarest occasion, Byrd scarcely seemed to notice his wife's response to him.". . .

To the extent that couples departed at all from the "missionary position," they seem to have done so largely at the man's urging and for his benefit. Among the Latvian songs describing oral-genital sex—from both male and female viewpoints, the least common theme is a married woman expressing pleasure at her husband's performing cunnilingus upon her.

There are a number of references to the wives of peasants performing fellatio or masturbating them. A Finnish proverb suggests, for example, that after withdrawing his penis in *coitus interruptus*, a man should poke it into his wife's mouth. I found fewer references to men masturbating their wives. . . .

The best measure of men's impetuosity is the extent to which women had the right to say no. If a married woman could not refuse sex, she would be vulnerable indeed to her husband's desire. Does it sound as though Madame Dubost, at the age of forty-nine, had the right to refuse sex to Monsieur Dubost? She appeared at Lyon's Hôtel Dieu,[2] in July of 1812 with an extensive cervical cancer, bleeding and smelling awful. However her immediate problem was that she was pregnant, for despite her "advanced sarcoma," Monsieur Dubost had insisted upon intercourse. On 16 September she miscarried, and died shortly afterward. The wife of a wealthy burgher of Valognes suffered a continuous hemorrhage during pregnancy, and sent for Guillaume de la Motte, a man midwife. De la Motte examined her, then turned to the husband and made him promise to abstain from sex for the remainder of the pregnancy. "They were the prettiest promises in the world, but immediately for-gotten." Does it sound as though this woman had the right to avoid intercourse?

Few women did, not even when they had a grim pelvic condition . . . where the bones have grown too small for the infant's head to pass. Other women had hideous forceps deliveries, and were themselves mutilated and bedridden for months, only to become pregnant again! One hapless woman, who died in August 1797 while giving birth to her sixth child, had an unusually small pelvis. "Each delivery was very difficult. In the second she was delivered with forceps, in the fifth, when an arm was the presenting part, I delivered her with an arduous turning." The remarkable thing is that she kept getting pregnant. Because she felt the "joy of sex"? Or because her husband insisted on sleeping with her?

Thus we see the reality of "conjugal duties," a euphemism for the *task* of intercourse. The obligation existed on both sides. According to old German law, a husband who had refused his wife sex would lose the use of her dowry. She, however, in refusing *him* sex would find her dowry confiscated and herself totally penniless. We may ask how often husbands among the common folk refused to sleep with their wives. Probably not often. Moreover, in cohabiting with their wives they risked nothing. . . .

[The] question [of whether women enjoyed sex before 1900] can be approached from two radically opposed points of view—the man's and the woman's. As far as traditional men are concerned, women were raging volcanos of desire. The view that women need to have orgasm in order to conceive goes back to the second-century Greek physician Galen.

[2]Hospital.

After Saint Augustine,[3] in the fifth century, Christian doctrine was to glare suspiciously on the sensuality of both sexes. But after the late Middle Ages, the Catholic Church mistrusted the woman in particular, "the most dangerous of all the serpents." Classic medical views of the uterus reinforced this image of women's devouring sexuality. One writer said in 1597 that "the uterus has naturally an incredible desire to conceive and to procreate. Thus it is anxious to have virile semen, desirous of taking it, drawing it in, sucking it, and retaining it." As these views filtered down, the message was: women are furnaces of carnality, who time and again will lead men to perdition, if given a chance.

The point of much brutal male sexual behavior was to deny women this chance. Because the flame of female sexuality could snuff out a man's spirit, women had sexually to be broken and controlled. "Of women's unnatural, insatiable lust," said Robert Burton[4] in 1621, "what country, what village doth not complain." The French proverbs present women as "devourers of males.". . .

- "Satisfying a woman is like confessing to the devil." (Limousin)
- "You can't satisfy everyone and your wife too." (Picardy)

Thus the underlying male rationale for this ramrod impetuosity in sexual matters was to shatter a woman's natural sexual force before it could get the best of a man.

How about women? How did they feel about sex?

One preliminary point. Evidence on the subject of female sexuality, among middle-class and aristocratic women, starts to accumulate during the eighteenth and early nineteenth centuries, precisely at the time when modern attitudes toward family life, which value emotional expressiveness among women, begin to appear among these classes. So we must be on guard against taking these new sexual attitudes as in any way "traditional." At this time as well, a sort of premarital "sexual revolution" was accomplished among unmarried young women from the lower classes, in which sex before marriage began to be seen as an extension of personal happiness rather than as a way to "get a man" (or as a form of rape).

The people who interest us, however, are those vast numbers of married women from the popular classes who lived before the twentieth century. What was their "traditional" sexual response? Some bits of evidence . . . seem to go against my case. Yet I believe the overwhelming body of evidence suggests that, for married women in the past, sex was a burden to be dutifully, resentfully borne throughout life rather than a source of joy. . . .

---

[3]Bishop of Hippo in North Africa and Church theologian, 354–430.

[4]English clergyman and scholar, 1577–1646.

This theme of physical revulsion surfaces time and again in the world we have lost. In May 1693, de la Motte counseled two women who were unable to lubricate when their spouses wanted sex. His analysis was that "the sword was too big for the scabbard," but it is more likely that the women simply were not aroused. He advised them to lubricate their fingers with oil and manually to dilate their vaginas, which they did successfully. This male midwife made casual references to women who "vomit during coitus"—a symptom he ascribed to some anatomical relationship between the stomach and the uterus. As he treated none of these complaints as remarkable, they may well have been common.

When in the 1930s, Margaret Hagood interviewed women in the rural South of the United States, she got responses reminiscent of these seventeenth-century French peasants. One woman "has always hated" sex but "has never let her husband get the upper hand of her." Even when first married she would say, "Take your hands off me," if she thought sex too frequent. "Now since she has arthritis, which makes intercourse painful, he tries to be as considerate as possible and holds off as long as he can—usually two or three weeks." Another, older, woman said that "she supposes she is now like other women after the menopause—that is, she knows what is going on, but she feels nothing (a commonly held notion)." "I never enjoyed it one bit," said a third.

Salient in this revulsion against sex was fear of pregnancy. In 1925, Marie Stopes said of one of the women whom she interviewed in her birth control clinic in London, "She could hardly bear to hear an amiable note in her husband's voice for fear it should lead to sex indulgence, when she was at the mercy of his all too unreliable 'self control'." Emma Goldman, a noted radical intellectual, recalled the immigrant women she delivered in New York in the 1890s when she was a midwife, "During their labor pains some women would hurl anathema on God and man, especially their husbands. 'Take him away,' one of my patients cried, 'don't let the brute come near me—I'll kill him!' "

In fact, the predominant attitude toward sexuality among peasant and working-class women before the twentieth century—and afterward, in isolated communities—seems to have been quiet resignation. Lisbeth Burger's patients thought that "it was a sin to refuse him sex." And Marta Wohlgemuth, a young German doctoral student who lived in several Badenese villages just before the First World War, described the role of "Sunday afternoons" in the sexual subordination of the farm wife. The farmer is at the bar: "The farmer's wife remains at home. Tired from the week's work she sleeps a bit; then she does some knitting or reads in the Sunday religious magazines or in the Bible, and thus comes to the quiet submission which one sees so often on the faces of these women. . . . Revolt against the husband seldom occurs, and if so she regrets it, because for her it is a religious commandment that she practice obedience and self-effacement." It is for her similarly a religious commandment that "every year she bring a new child into the world."

Maria Bidlingmaier, who around the same time was observing life in other villages, confirmed the passive acceptance of sex which lay behind this docility. "The wife feels it as a burden to be married, although as a young woman she was robust and full of life. From this arises often a quiet bitterness toward her husband, who dominates her physically and exploits her powers. Already in the first year she is expecting. . . . Birth follows birth. . . .

"Under the pressure of her first years of marriage the wife drifts toward a quiet resignation to her fate. Some become unfeeling, hard, and inaccessible to all sentiment, interested only in gain. Others seek 'refuge and shelter' in the will of the Lord and His guidance."

Some of the working-class English women who responded, just before the First World War, to a Women's Co-operative Guild questionnaire, said they saw sex "only as a duty." "I submitted as a duty," wrote one woman in explaining why she had six children, "knowing there is much unfaithfulness on the part of the husband where families are limited." Another was explicitly anti-erotic: "I do wish there could be some limit to the time when a woman is expected to have a child. I often think women are really worse off than beasts. . . . If the woman does not feel well she must not say so, as a man has such a lot of ways of punishing a woman if she does not give in to him."

There is no shortage of quotes from around the turn of the century suggesting that married women dislike marital relations. The point I wish to make, however, is that this "Victorian" prudery and passivity are a continuation of negative female feelings about sex that reach far back into time, rather than being a creation of the nineteenth century.

. . . Traditional women were sexually cowed and emotionally brutalized by men. They found it impossible to escape intercourse, and sought solace for its unpleasant consequences only in the company of other women. Not until women solved the problems of abortion, contraception, and safe childbirth . . . would they be able to relax about marital sexuality.

Infanticide:
A Historical Survey

WILLIAM L. LANGER

It has been suggested that one cause of the population increase in the late nineteenth century was a decline in the practice of infanticide. By now infanticide is rare enough in Western civilization to merit newspaper coverage, and it is difficult to imagine how pervasive infanticide was until recently. William Langer briefly traces the history of the murder of children, looking at methods of killing as well as cultural assumptions that justified the disposal of unwanted infants.

In some societies infanticide was an acceptable practice. Other societies condemned infanticide, but saw large portions of the population disobeying the ban. What socioeconomic conditions induced parents to get rid of infants? What intellectual arguments defended the practice of infanticide? Why were cultures more likely to eliminate female rather than male infants? (Here infanticide becomes a part of the history of women.) Langer's account is depressing reading for those of us accustomed to revere infants, but there were some historical developments that made infanticide unacceptable. Which societies forbade the practice? When infanticide was illegal, it became a sex-linked crime—why did European courts punish mothers and not fathers?

The nineteenth century saw important changes in the history of infanticide. What role did the Industrial Revolution play in this story? Why did foundling hospitals, intended to alleviate the problem of unwanted children, not prove to be an effective reform? The situation in Victorian England became a public scandal, and English society moved to abolish infanticide. Who killed Victorian babies, and why? What ended the widespread practice?

Infanticide is linked to the history of the family, and other changes in the family are related to the successful but not total abolition of infanticide. People married more often for love than had been the custom; affection bound children to parents as well as husbands to wives. These have been gradual, long-term processes that are among the most significant changes in Western civilization.

Infanticide, that is, the willful destruction of newborn babes through exposure, starvation, strangulation, smothering, poisoning, or through the use of some lethal weapon, has been viewed with abhorrence by Christians almost from the beginning of their era. Although often held

William L. Langer, "Infanticide: A Historical Survey," *History of Childhood Quarterly,* I, No. 3 (Winter 1974): 353–362.

up to school-children as an abomination practiced by the Chinese or other Asians, its role in Western civilization, even in modern times, has rarely been suggested by historians, sociologists or even demographers.

Yet in these days of world population crisis there can hardly be a more important historical question than that of the chronically superfluous population growth and the methods by which humanity has dealt with it. Among non-Christian peoples (with the exception of the Jews) infanticide has from time immemorial been the accepted procedure for disposing not only of deformed or sickly infants, but of all such newborns as might strain the resources of the individual family or the larger community. At the present day it is still employed by so-called underdeveloped peoples in the effort to keep the population in reasonable adjustment to the available food supply. Among the Eskimos of Arctic Canada, for instance, many babies are set out on the ice to freeze if the father or elder of the tribe decides that they would be a continuing drain on the means of subsistence.

In ancient times, at least, infanticide was not a legal obligation. It was a practice freely discussed and generally condoned by those in authority and ordinarily left to the decision of the father as the responsible head of the family. Modern humanitarian sentiment makes it difficult to recapture the relatively detached attitude of the parents towards their offspring. Babies were looked upon as the unavoidable result of normal sex relations, often as an undesirable burden rather than as a blessing. More girls than boys were disposed of, presumably to keep down the number of potential mothers as well as in recognition of the fact that they would never contribute greatly to the family income. . . .

The attitude of the ancient Greeks in this matter is well reflected in the pronouncements of Plato and Aristotle. The former favored the careful regulation of all sex relations, so as to produce the most perfect type of human being, while Aristotle was more concerned with the problem of population pressure. With its limited resources, ancient Greece, according to a modern authority, "lived always under the shadow of the fear of too many mouths to feed." Neglect of this problem by many city-states was denounced by Aristotle as "a never-failing cause of poverty among the citizens, and poverty was the parent of revolution." He firmly contended that the size of the population should be limited by law and suggested that abortion might be preferable to exposure as a method of control.

In Hellenistic Greece, infanticide, chiefly in the form of exposure of female babies, was carried to such an extent that the average family was exceptionally small. Parents rarely reared more than one daughter, with the result that there was an altogether abnormal discrepancy in the numbers of the sexes.

The practice of the Hellenistic Greeks was continued under Roman rule and probably influenced Roman attitudes. After all, Rome itself was traditionally founded by the exposed youngsters, Romulus and Remus, who were saved from their certain fate by the nursing of a friendly wolf. Throughout the Republic and long after the authority of the father over his family had worn thin, unwanted children continued to be disposed of in the accepted way. It was thought altogether natural that proletarians, poverty-stricken and hopeless, should protect themselves from further responsibility. As among the Greeks, there was a marked disparity between the sexes, which suggests that many bastards and a substantial number of female infants were abandoned if not murdered by drowning. . . . Edward Gibbon, writing in the late eighteenth century on *The Decline and Fall of the Roman Empire*, denounced this exposure of children as "the prevailing and stubborn vice of antiquity," and charged the Roman Empire with being "stained with the blood of infants.". . .

A decisive change of attitude came with Christianity. The Church fathers were undoubtedly, in this respect as in others, influenced by Judaic Law which, while it did not mention infanticide specifically in the discussion of murder, was always interpreted by Rabbinical Law as an equivalent. . . . Increasingly, Christian leaders thundered against infanticide as a pagan practice and insisted that all human life be held inviolable. Yet it was only with the triumph of Christianity that the Emperor Constantine in 318 A.D. declared the slaying of a son or daughter by a father to be a crime, and only at the end of the fourth century that the Emperors Valentinian, Valens, and Gratian made infanticide a crime punishable by death.

While the contribution of Christian theologians to the adoption of a more humane attitude is obvious, it should be remembered that the later Roman Empire apparently suffered from progressive depopulation, due to devastating epidemics, recurrent famines and general disorder. Under the circumstances there was clearly no need to limit population growth. On the contrary, increased fertility was desired. Hence the repetition of the exhortation of the Bible: "Be fruitful and multiply." Until the late eighteenth century at least, when the great upswing of the European population set in, large families were the fashion, being regarded as the blessing of a benevolent deity.

Yet there can be little doubt that child murder continued to be practiced, even in the most advanced countries of western Europe. Lecky,[1] in his *History of European Morals* (1869), speaks of the popular distinction in the early Middle Ages between infanticide and exposure, the latter offense not being punishable by law: "It was practiced on a gigantic scale with absolute impunity, noticed by writers with most frigid indifference and, at least in the case of destitute parents, considered a very venial offence."

Until the sixteenth century, and in some places until much later,

[1]William E. H. Lecky, Irish historian and philosopher, 1838–1903.

the unenviable task of dealing with the problem was left to the Church authorities. In the hope of reducing the exposure and almost certain death of newborn children (especially girls), foundling hospitals were opened in the eighth century in Milan, Florence, Rome, and other cities. But these institutions proved to be ineffectual, since most of the children had to be sent to the country to be nursed, and the majority soon succumbed either through neglect or more positive action on the part of the wet-nurses.

Infanticide by out-and-out violence of various kinds was probably always exceptional. Throughout European history the authorities were baffled and frustrated primarily by the many cases of reputed suffocation, the "overlaying" or "overlying" of an infant in bed by its allegedly drunken parents. This could and surely did occur accidentally, but the suspicion, always present and usually warranted, was that of intentional riddance of an unwanted child. Since it was impossible to prove premeditated crime, the authorities contented themselves with the imposition of penance in the case of married women, who were condemned to live for at least a year on bread and water. The unwed mothers and the presumed witches, however, were to bear the brunt as examples and admonitions. A girl known to have committed infanticide in any form might be absolved by pleading insanity, but was otherwise condemned to suffer the death penalty, usually in the most diabolical imaginable manner. Medieval sources tell of women being tied in a sack, along with a dog, a cock, or some other uncongenial companion and thrown into the river for a supreme struggle for life. This method was probably never in general use, and in any case seems to have been abandoned by the end of the Middle Ages. A detailed analysis of the court and prison records of Nürnberg from 1513 to 1777 lists by name eighty-seven women executed for infanticide, all but four of them unmarried girls who had committed violent murder. Prior to 1500 the penalty in Nürnberg as in most of Germany was burial alive, often with gruesome refinements. During the sixteenth century the usual method was drowning, and after 1580 decapitation. Hangings were quite exceptional. It was hardly worse, however, than being buried alive, being drowned or decapitated, penalties which continued to be practiced, though less and less frequently, until the nineteenth century.

In any case, overlaying continued to be a vexing problem until modern times. In 1500, the Bishop of Fiesole set fines and penalties for parents who kept babies in bed with them. In the eighteenth century, a Florentine craftsman designed a basket frame . . . which would protect the child from smothering. An Austrian decree of 1784 forbade having children under the age of five in bed with parents, and Prussian legislation of 1794 reduced the age of the infants to two.

Government authorities were apparently no more successful than the clergy in checking the practice of overlaying, at least among married couples. One may safely assume that in the eighteenth and nineteenth centuries the poor, hardly able to support the family they already had, evaded responsibility by disposing of further additions. But by the eighteenth century another form of infanticide became so prevalent that governments were at their wits' end in their efforts to combat it. For reasons too complex and still too obscure, there was a marked increase in sexual immorality, in seduction, and in illegitimacy. The evidence suggests that in all European countries, from Britain to Russia, the upper classes felt perfectly free to exploit sexually girls who were at their mercy. As late as 1871, Mr. Cooper, the Secretary of the Society for the Rescue of Young Women and Children, testified before a Parliamentary Committee that at least nine out of ten of the girls in trouble were domestic servants: "in many instances the fathers of their children are their masters, or their masters' sons, or their masters' relatives, or their masters' visitors." To be sure, lords of the manor often recognized the offspring as their own and raised them as members of the family. But in the new factory towns foremen favored amenable girls for employment. Young aristocrats, too, were much to blame. When traveling they expected to find relaxation with the chamber maids of the inn. It seems to have been taken for granted that the upper classes were entitled to the favors of pretty girls of the lower classes and that fornication was looked upon as an inevitable aspect of lower class life.

Yet if a girl became pregnant, she was left to shift for herself. She at once became an object of obloquy and might well be whipped out of the village by the more fortunate members of her sex. Many sought anonymity and aid in the cities, where professional midwives would, for a pittance, not only perform an abortion or deliver the child, but would also undertake to nurse and care for it, it being fully understood that the mother would not need to worry further about it. Starvation or a dose of opiates would settle the child's fate in a matter of days.

Naturally all girls in trouble were not willing to resort to so drastic a solution. There was always the possibility, admittedly slim, that if the unwanted baby were left on the steps of a church or mansion, it might stir the sympathies of a stranger and be adopted by him, as was Tom Jones by Squire Allworthy.[2] Many young mothers therefore bundled up their offspring, and left them at churches or other public places. In the late seventeenth century, St. Vincent de Paul[3] was so appalled by the number of babies to be seen daily on the steps of Notre Dame that he appealed to ladies of the court to finance an asylum for foundlings. His efforts soon inspired others to similar action, and before long most large towns in Catholic Europe had established similar institutions. In England a retired sea captain, Thomas Coram, was so depressed by

[2]In *Tom Jones* (1749), a novel by Henry Fielding (1707–1754).
[3]French priest (1580–1660) famous for his charitable activity.

the daily sight of infant corpses thrown on the dust heaps of London that he devoted seventeen years in soliciting support for a foundling hospital. Eventually a group of his supporters petitioned the King to charter a Foundling Hospital so as "to prevent the frequent murders of poor, miserable infants at their birth," and "to suppress the inhuman custom of exposing new-born infants to perish in the streets."

The story of the foundling hospitals is too long and complicated to be more than sketched here. For a time they were the favorite charity of the wealthy and huge sums were expended in lavish construction and equipment. Although the London and Paris hospitals were the best known, the establishment at St. Petersburg, actively patronized by the imperial court, was undoubtedly the most amazing. . . . It was housed in the former palaces of Counts Razumovski and Bobrinski and occupied a huge tract in the very center of St. Petersburg. By the mid-1830s, it had 25,000 children on its rolls and was admitting 5000 newcomers annually. Since no questions were asked and the place was attractive, almost half of the newborn babies were deposited there by their parents. A dozen doctors and 600 wet-nurses were in attendance to care for the children during the first six weeks, after which they were sent to peasant nurses in the country. At the age of six (if they survived to that age) they were returned to St. Petersburg for systematic education. The program was excellent, but its aims were impossible to achieve. Despite all excellent management and professional efforts, thirty to forty percent of the children died during the first six weeks and hardly a third reached the age of six.

The chronicle of the hospitals everywhere was one of devoted effort but unrelieved tragedy. The assignment was simply impossible to carry out. Everywhere they were besieged by mostly unwed mothers eager to dispose of their babies without personally or directly committing infanticide. Even so, actual child murder appears to have continued to an alarming extent, due to the fear of many girls of being identified at the hospital. Napoleon therefore decreed (January 18, 1811) that there should be hospitals in every departement of France, and that each should be equipped with a turntable (*tour*), so that the mother or her agent could place the child on one side, ring a bell, and have a nurse take the child by turning the table, the mother remaining unseen and unquestioned.

Although it is agreed that Napoleon's provision of *tours* helped to diminish the number of outright child murders, it meant that the hospitals were swamped with babies. It was impossible to find enough wet-nurses for even a short period, and most of the infants had to be shipped off to the country at once. Relatively few survived the long journey over rough roads in crude carts, and those happy few generally succumbed before long due to the ignorant treatment or the intentional or unintentional neglect of their foster parents. Small wonder that Malthus[4] referred

[4.] Thomas Malthus (1766–1834), English economist.

to the asylums as "these horrible receptables," while others spoke freely of "legalized infanticide." In the years 1817–1820, the number of foundlings in charge of the Paris hospital, many of them brought in from the provinces, and, interestingly, about a third of them children of married couples, was about equal to a third of all babies born in Paris in that period. Of 4779 infants admitted in 1818, 2370 died in the first three months. It would be unjust, no doubt, to put the entire blame for this situation on the foundling hospitals. Many of the infants were diseased or half dead when they arrived, and we may well believe that prior to the nineteenth century many newborn babies would in any event have succumbed to the methods of clothing and feeding then still in vogue.

By 1830, the situation in France had become desperate. In 1833 the number of babies left with the foundling hospitals reached the fantastic figure of 164,319. Authorities were all but unanimous in the opinion that the introduction of the *tours* had been disastrous, that they had, in fact, put a premium on immorality. Thereupon the *tours* were gradually abolished until by 1862 only five were left. Instead, the government embarked upon a program of outside aid to unwed mothers. Presumably the growing practice of birth control and the advances made in pediatrics also contributed to the reduction in infant mortality.

The story of the foundlings in England was no less tragic than that of France. The London Foundling Hospital (opened in 1741) was intended for the reception of London children only, but the pressure for admissions soon became so great as to give rise "to the disgraceful scene of women scrambling and fighting to get to the door, that they might be of the fortunate few to reap the benefit of the Asylum." Under the circumstances Parliament in 1756 provided a modest grant on condition that the hospital be open to all comers, but that at the same time asylums for exposed or deserted young children be opened in all counties, ridings, and divisions of the kingdom. Parish officers promptly took advantage of the act to empty their workhouses of infant poor and dump them on the new hospices, while others had them shipped to London. By 1760, the London Hospital was deluged with 4229 newcomers, making a total of 14,934 admissions in the preceding four years. It was impossible to cope with the situation, and "instead of being a protection to the living, the institution became, as it were, a charnel-house for the dead." In 1760, Parliament reversed itself by putting an end to indiscriminate admissions and returned the care of the provincial foundlings to the parishes. The London Hospital soon became more of an orphanage than a foundling asylum. By 1850, it had only 460 children and admitted only 77 annually.

The parish officers were helpless in the face of the problem. A law of 1803 specified that charges of infanticide must be tried according to the same rules of evidence as applied to murder, while yet another law required that "it must be proved that the entire body of the child has actually been born into the world in a living state, and the fact of its having breathed is not conclusive proof thereof. There must be independent circulation in the child before it can be accounted alive." In other words, to kill a child by crushing its head with a hairbrush or hammer, or cutting its throat was technically not a crime, so long as its lower extremities were still in the body of the mother. Since the required evidence was all but impossible to obtain, infanticide could be committed almost with impunity. In any case, juries refused, even in the most flagrant cases, to convict the offender, holding that capital punishment was far too harsh a penalty to pay when the real culprit was usually the girl's seducer. So infanticide flourished in England. . . . Dr. Lankester, one of the coroners for Middlesex, charged that even the police seemed to think no more of finding a dead child than of finding a dead dog or cat. There were, he asserted, hundreds, nay thousands of women living in London who were guilty of having at one time or another destroyed their offspring, without having been discovered.

By the mid-century the matter had become one of public scandal. One doctor in 1846 commented on "the great indifference displayed by parents and others in the lower ranks of life with regard to infant life." Women employed in the factories and fields had no choice but to leave their babies in the care of professional nurses, sometimes called "killer nurses," who made short shrift of their charges by generous doses of opiates.

Worse yet was the revelation that some women enrolled their infants in Burial Clubs, paying a trifling premium until, after a decent interval, the child died of starvation, ill-usage, or poisoning. They then collected £ 3 to £ 5 by way of benefit. Cases were reported of women who had membership for their babies in ten or more clubs, reaping a rich return at the proper time.

The institution of "killer nurses" or "angel-makers" eventually became known as "baby-farming." By 1860, it had become the subject of lively agitation, both in lay and in professional circles. In 1856, Dr. William B. Ryan was awarded a gold medal by the London Medical Society for his essay on "Infanticide in its Medical-Legal Relations." He followed this two years later by an address on "Child Murder in its Sanitary and Social Bearings," delivered before the Liverpool Association for the Promotion of Social Science. . . .

A survey of the British press in the 1860s reveals the frequent findings of dead infants under bridges, in parks, in culverts and ditches, and even in cesspools. The *Standard* in 1862 denounced "this execrable system of wholesale murder," while the *Morning Star* in 1863 asserted that "this crime is positively becoming a national institution." In Parliament an outraged member declared that the country seemed to be reveling in "a carnival of infant slaughter, to hold every year a massacre of the Innocents."

In February, 1867, Dr. Curgeven, Dr. Ryan, and a formidable delegation of medical men from the elite Harveian Society called upon the Home Secretary with a lengthy list of specific recommendations for checking the increase in infanticide, with emphasis on the need for the registration of all child nurses and for annual reports on all "baby farms." The government acted with no more than its habitual alacrity, and it was only in 1870 that it was further pressed by the Infant Protection Society founded by Dr. Curgeven and when the country was shocked by the news that in Brixton and Peckham two women were discovered to have left no fewer than sixteen infant corpses in various fairly obvious places. The women were tried for murder and one of them was convicted and executed. Parliament at long last set up a committee to study the best means "of preventing the destruction of the lives of infants put out to nurse for hire by their parents." It can hardly have come as a surprise to the members that babies commonly died through being given improper or insufficient food, opiates, drugs, etc. In many baby-farms they were in crowded rooms, with bad air, and suffered from want of cleanliness and willful neglect, resulting in diarrhea, convulsions, and wasting away. The evidence was more than enough to induce Parliament to pass in 1872 the first Infant Life Protection Act providing for compulsory registration of all houses in which more than one child under the age of one were in charge for more than twenty-four hours. Each such house was required to have a license issued by a justice of the peace, and all deaths, including still-births, which had not previously been recorded, were to be reported at once. The penalty for violation of the law was to be a fine of £ 5 or imprisonment for six months.

Less was heard or written about infanticide in the last quarter of the nineteenth and in the twentieth century. This was certainly a reflection of the beneficial results of the abolition of the *tours* in France, Belgium, and other countries, and of the increasingly stringent regulations in Britain. But credit must also be given to the growing public interest in maternity and child care, and to the progress in pediatrics which contributed to the reduction of the high infant mortality rate. Finally, consideration must also be given to the adoption and spread of contraceptive practices, even among the lower classes. Nonetheless, infanticide continued and still persists, albeit on a much lower scale. The ignorance and recklessness of many young people, and initially the expense and inconvenience of contraceptive devices made the unwed mother and the illegitimate child a continuing social problem. Only since the Second World War has the contraceptive pill, the intrauterine devices, and the legalization of abortion removed all valid excuses for unwanted pregnancy or infanticide. To the extent that these problems still exist, at least in western society, they are due primarily to carelessness, ignorance, or indifference.

A Woman's World:
Department Stores and
the Evolution of
Women's Employment,
1870–1920

THERESA M. McBRIDE

So much a fixture of Western society today, the department store is actually a quite recent innovation. It first appeared in mid-nineteenth-century Paris, revolutionizing the retail trade. How did department stores differ from traditional retail businesses? What new merchandising principles did the new stores espouse? What did the French novelist Émile Zola mean in claiming that the department store helped bring about a "new religion"? How did department stores change attitudes to and patterns of consumption?

Theresa M. McBride depicts the department store as the "world of women," of female customers and employees. The work and lives of the female clerks especially interest McBride. Who were the female clerks? Why did they choose to find employment in department stores, where the hours were long, the pace often frantic, the rules stifling, fines and dismissal constant threats, and the supervision intense? What could they hope for in their careers? It would be difficult to imagine female employees now tolerating being locked up in dining halls, forced to live in company apartments, and having their sexual lives the subject of department store concern. But the department store owners mixed capitalism with old-fashioned paternalism, combining the pursuit of profit with the enforcement of morality. The owners believed it a necessity to concern themselves with the behavior of female clerks after work.

What were the lifestyles of the female clerks? How did they spend their lives in the evenings and on Sundays? Did other women of the same social background envy their jobs and status? How did the clerks form part of the new urban leisure culture? What major changes occurred by World War I that affected women's employment in department stores?

Theresa M. McBride, "A Woman's World: Department Stores and the Evolution of Women's Employment, 1870–1920, *French Historical Studies* X (Fall 1978): 664–683.

In the 1840s Aristide Boucicaut[1] took over a small retail shop for dry goods and clothing in Paris. This shop became the "Bon Marché," the world's first department store, and soon the idea was emulated by other commercial entrepreneurs throughout the world. The department store helped to create a "new religion," as Emile Zola[2] described the passion for consumption nurtured by the department stores' retailing revolution. As churches were being deserted, Zola argued, the stores were filling with crowds of women seeking to fill their empty hours and to find meaning for empty lives. The cult of the soul was replaced by a cult of the body— of beauty, of fashion. The department store was preeminently the "world of women," where women were encouraged to find their life's meaning in conspicuous consumption and where they increasingly found a role in selling. Thus, the department store played a highly significant role in the evolution both of contemporary society and of woman's place in that society.

The department stores came to dominate retail trade by introducing novel merchandising principles. Most obviously, they were much larger than traditional retail establishments and united a wide variety of goods under one roof; specialization was retained only in the *rayons* or departments into which the stores were divided. Department store entrepreneurs throughout the world evolved the techniques of retailing between the 1840s and 1860s, which included the important innovation of fixed pricing, and eliminated bargaining from a sale. Fixed pricing was a revolutionary concept because it altered the customary buyer-seller relationship, reducing the buyer to the role of passive consumer, whose only choice was to accept or reject the goods as offered at the set price. Even the buyer's desire for certain items was created through the tactics of large-scale retailing: publicity, display of goods, and low prices of items. The salesperson became a simple cog in the giant commercial mechanism; instead of representing the owner, the salesclerk became a facilitator, helping to create an atmosphere of attention and service while the merchandise "sold itself."

The low mark-up of the large stores allowed lower prices (hence the name—Bon Marché)[3] and helped to attract crowds of customers from throughout the city. The department stores could not simply depend upon the traditional bourgeois clientele of smaller shops (the upper classes ordered goods from their own suppliers) and had to attract customers from among the petite bourgeoisie. By catering to the budgets and the "passion for spending" of the petite bourgeoisie, the department

[1]Merchant and philanthropist, 1810–1877.

[2]Novelist, 1840–1902.

[3]Cheap.

stores brought increasing numbers of people into contact with modern consumer society.

A significant part of the department stores' merchandising revolution was the presentation. Exhibits in the spacious galleries of the stores, large display windows, publicity through catalogs and newspaper advertising shaped illusions and stimulated the public's desires for the items offered. The salesperson was herself part of that presentation, helping to create an atmosphere of service and contributing to the seductiveness of the merchandise.

In order to attract customers and facilitate a heavy volume of sales, the department stores needed a new kind of staff. Whereas the shop-keeper could rely upon family members and a loyal assistant or two, the department store became an employer on the scale of modern industrial enterprises. In the 1880s the Bon Marché employed twenty-five hundred clerks; the Grands Magasins du Louvre . . . by 1900 had a staff of thirty-five hundred to four thousand, depending on the season. Smaller provincial stores typically employed several hundred people. The Nouvelles Galeries in Bordeaux, for example, had 554 employees in 1912, divided into sales (283), office staff (60), and stock control (211). In 1906, by comparison, more than half of all commercial enterprises in France employed no more than five people (54 per cent), and two-thirds had ten or fewer employees. The average number of employees was 2.8. With such a large number of clerks, the entrepreneur could not expect to treat them like family members nor to encourage their . . . hope that they might some day take over control of the store.

Beyond simple size, the department stores were innovators in the ways in which they recruited, trained, and treated their employees. The fixed price system and the practice of allowing customers to browse freely meant that a large percentage of the work force were simply unskilled assistants, who brought the items to the customers and took their payments to the cashiers. Costs were minimized by paying very low base salaries. But loyalty and diligence were assured by a highly graduated hierarchy in which the top ranks were achieved only through intense competition. Entrepreneurs like Boucicaut realized that in order to create the proper atmosphere in their stores they would have to reward top salespeople by the payment of commissions on sales and by allowing them to enjoy a high level of status and responsibility. The department stores formalized the system of recruitment, promotion, and rewards to create a group of employees who would espouse the interests of the firm as their own or be quickly weeded out.

Women were a crucial element in this system. In fact, although women did not form the majority of the stores' work force until after 1914, women dominated certain departments and came to symbolize the "world of women," as the department store was described. Women were both the clerks and the customers in this market place, for the mainstays of the new stores were fashions and dry goods. Women were scarcely new to commerce, but their role was expanding and changing in the late nineteenth century. A parliamentary investigation into the Parisian food and clothing industries found women clerks throughout those industries, and the report's conclusions insisted upon the importance of the unsalaried work of women who were *patronnes*[4] or who shared that responsibility with their husbands. Typically, several members of the family worked in family-run businesses, so that daughters also received some early work experience. Most shops could not have survived without the contributions of female family members. For the women themselves, this kind of work was both an extension of their domestic role and an important experience in the world of business. While the department stores involved women in commercial activity in a very different way, traditional commercial roles continued to be exercised by the wives and daughters of shopkeepers well into the twentieth century.

One of the best descriptions of the new store clerks emerges from the investigations of Emile Zola for his novel, *Au bonheur des dames*,[5] in which the young heroine secures employment with a large department store closely modelled after the Bon Marché and the Grands Magasins du Louvre. Zola's heroine Denise is the carefully sketched model of the female clerk: young, single, and an immigrant to Paris from a provincial store.

Denise was hired at the store after the management assured itself of her experience and her attractiveness. In the first few days, she learned to adjust to the pace of work, the supervision of older saleswomen, and to the competitiveness of the older clerks who tried to monopolize the sales. Most beginners like Denise spent much of their time arranging displays of merchandise and delivering items to customers. During peak seasons, many clerks started as temporary help "with the hope that they would eventually be permanently hired," but only a small proportion of them survived this period of "training." During the first year, beginners received little more than room and board. But if the debutante could withstand the low salaries, long hours, and often heavy-handed surveillance of other salesclerks, she had a chance to enter the ranks of the relatively well-paid saleswomen.

At the highest level of the sales hierarchy were the department heads, *chefs de rayons*, and their assistants, whose responsibilities included not only sales but also the ordering of merchandise for their own divisions and the hiring and supervision of salespersonnel. Salespeople

[4]Employers.
[5]*The Paradise of Women.*

provided information about merchandise, and once items were sold, took them to be wrapped, and delivered the payment to the cashier. Saleswomen and men were generally divided into different departments: men sold male clothing, household furnishings, and even women's gloves and stockings, while women handled baby clothing and women's dresses, reflecting the pattern in the industry as a whole. Significantly, men made up the majority of department heads and assistants, though a few women managed to win out against the intense competition to head departments.

Department stores employed many women who were not sales clerks. There were office staffs of women who carried on the ordering, advertising, and the mail-order business. In addition, the largest stores employed hundreds of seamstresses, who were clearly distinguished from the sales force by the designation *ouvrière*[6] (rather than "employee"). The seamstresses received none of the benefits of the employees, such as free lodging or medical care, and the market provided by the department stores for the handwork of the domestic garment-making workers kept the institution of "sweated" labor alive well into the twentieth century.

The proportion of women employed in the department stores steadily increased after a large strike by clerks in 1869. In part, employers recruited women because they represented a tractable labor force. Department stores gradually replaced some male clerks with female clerks who were more "docile" and "lacking in tradition" and who, consequently, would be less eager to strike. But there were other reasons for recruiting women clerks. Women were cheaper to hire than men and readily available because of the narrowing of other employment options for women. The spread of public education for women provided a pool of workers who were reluctant to work as seamstresses or domestics. And women workers impressed employers with their personal qualities of "politeness," "sobriety," and even a "talent for calculation."

Considering both the obvious advantages of a female work force and the important traditional role of women in commerce, it seems inevitable that women should have been hired as clerks in the new department stores. But women salesclerks were recruited from different sources than other female workers and remained a distinctive group through the period of the First World War. Why women clerks replaced men when the occupational opportunities expanded in commerce is, then, not so simple a question.

Department store clerks were very different from the largest group of women workers in the late nineteenth century—domestic servants. The young women who came to work in the Parisian *grands magasins*[7] were recruited from the cities and towns of France, while the domestic servants

[6]Worker.
[7]Department stores.

came from the countryside. Over half (53 per cent) of the female clerks who lived in the Parisian suburbs in 1911 and worked in Parisian stores had been born in Paris. Zola noted that one-third of the Bon Marché's saleswomen were native Parisians and that this was a larger percentage than among the male clerks. Salesmen were undoubtedly more mobile both geographically and socially. Both male and female employees who were not native Parisians had generally moved there from some provincial city where they had completed the essential apprenticeship in another store.

Department store clerks, like other commercial employees, often came from the ranks of urban shopkeepers and artisans. Children of shopkeepers frequently worked for a time in the large stores to learn commercial skills before returning to work in the family business. Over half of the shopgirls living with parents were from employee or shopkeeping families. . . . The occupational backgrounds of French clerks were primarily the urban, skilled occupations. A few even came from possible middle-class backgrounds, having parents who were teachers or *commerçants,*[8] but these were rare. In general, a clerk was not a working-class girl working her way out of poverty but more typically a lower-middle-class girl whose father was himself commercially employed, if not a shopkeeper.

Department store clerks were young. But unlike other women workers, who might begin their working lives at eleven or twelve, store clerks were rarely under seventeen years old. The Parisian *grands magasins* selected women only after a period of training, and thus the majority of the work force were in their early twenties. . . . Domestic servants and seamstresses included a wider range of ages because women could be employed at much younger ages in those occupations and could go back to work in small shops or as charwomen or seamstresses after their families were grown.

The career of the sales clerk, however, could be very short. Apart from the attrition due to marriage, the occupation simply wore some women out. Stores rarely hired anyone over 30, and the unlucky woman who lost her job after that age might be permanently retired. Younger women were more attractive, stronger, and cheaper to employ than older, more experienced women.

The life of the department store clerk was monopolized by the store. About half of the unmarried women were housed by the stores. The Bon Marché had small rooms under the roof of the store, while the Louvre housed its employees in buildings nearby. The rooms provided by the Bon Marché for their female employees were small with low ceilings; each contained a simple bed, table, and chair. But though these rooms were unadorned and sometimes overcrowded, they were often

[8]Tradespeople.

better than the rented room a young clerk could expect to find on her own. The lodgings at the Bon Marché included social rooms, where the management provided pianos for the women and billiard tables for the men. Visitors of the opposite sex were not allowed there, not even other employees. A concièrge kept track of the employees, and her permission had to be requested in order to go out at night. Such permission was nearly always granted as long as the eleven o'clock curfew was respected. Although department store entrepreneurs were innovators in retailing practices, their attitudes toward employees retained the strong flavor of paternalism that was typical of small-scale retailing. In small shops, the woman employee was almost a domestic, living in and working with other members of the family in the shop. Store managers of the department stores acted "in loco parentis"[9] at times, too, by exercising strong control over the lives of their saleswomen to preserve respectable behavior and to protect the public image of their firms.

The practice of housing female employees on the premises illustrates a variety of capitalistic and paternalistic motivations. There was considerable advantage to having salesclerks housed nearby, given the long hours they were expected to work. Employers also expressed . . . concern about the kind of . . . behavior, such as drinking, which could result from a lack of supervision. Women and young male clerks were both the victims and the beneficiaries of this system; adult men were allowed much greater freedom. The offer of housing and other benefits was combined with the opportunity to more closely control the lives of salespeople. Because of the economic advantages of insuring a well-disciplined work force, department store owners prolonged the paternalism of shopkeepers long after the size of the new enterprises had destroyed most aspects of the traditional relationship.

Department store clerks were surrounded by their work. Not only housed in or near the store but also fed their meals there, the women were never allowed out of the store until after closing. The large dining halls where employees took their midday meal were an important features of the first department stores, and one contemporary described them as follows: "At each end of the immense dining halls were the department heads and inspectors; the simple male employees were seated in the center at long tables. Only the opening out of newspapers and the low hum of voices broke the silence, and everyone was completely absorbed in eating, for all were required to finish [in an hour]. . . . " Female clerks ate in a different room, separately from the men. There were three sittings to accommodate the large number of employees, the first one beginning at 9:30 A.M. The break was closely supervised, and each employee had less than an hour, calculated from the time she left her post until she returned there. Although employees

[9]In the place of the parents.

only rarely complained about the food they were served, much criticism was levelled at the conditions under which employees were forced to eat. Despite protests, women employees were never allowed to leave the store nor to return to their rooms during their breaks. At the Galeries Lafayette, they were locked into their dining hall during the meal. This kind of control indicates more strongly the "severity" than the "paternal indulgence" which managerial policy espoused.

Work rules throughout the store were very strict. Employees were dressed distinctively as a way of identifying them and making them conscious of their relationship to the store. Until after 1900, male employees were required to arrive at work wearing a derby or "melon," and the women were uniformly dressed in black silk. Surveillance by inspectors and supervisors assured that employee behavior was as uniform as their dress. Employees were expected to begin work at 8 A.M., and penalties were imposed on the tardy. At the Magasins Dufayel, a clerk was fined 25 centimes for being five minutes late; if she were two hours late, she could lose an entire day's wage. The average workday lasted twelve to thirteen hours, for the department stores did not close until 8 P.M. in the winter and 9 P.M. in the summer. During special sales or while preparing displays for the new season, clerks frequently had to work overtime without any special compensation. Although clerks in small shops often worked even longer hours, work in the department stores was judged more tiring by two parliamentary investigators in 1900, who argued that the large crowds attracted to the new stores quickened the pace of work.

By 1900 the workday for most female clerks had been reduced in accordance with an 1892 law setting a ten-hour maximum for women. The length of the clerk's workday had aroused much concern about the women's health, but their situation was still . . . better than that of the thousands of seamstresses who worked in sweatshop conditions in Parisian attics for little pay. Even before the reform, the workday of the salesgirl had been the envy of domestic servants, whose freedom was much more limited and whose employers did not allow the few hours of leisure which shopgirls enjoyed.

Characteristic of the way in which reforms were effected was the campaign for Sunday closing. In the 1890s . . . the large department stores began to adopt the practice of remaining closed on Sundays, giving most of their work force a day off. Although some employees were still needed to mount special expositions, prepare for sales, or unload deliveries, Sunday closing assured virtually all the women clerks a day off per week. The campaign for Sunday closing . . . inspired the most significant level of employee organization seen in this period. Concerted pressure was exerted by the predominantly male unions who occasionally solicited the support of women clerks and at times took up issues which were specifically female ones, such as the practice of locking up the women in their dining hall. As with other reforms, the chief opponents of reform were those who were concerned about the autonomy and survival of small shops that remained open longest in order to compete with the department stores. Overall, the challenge to the department store owners' authority was slight.

The authority of the employer, evident in the rigid work rules . . . was . . . obvious in the firing policies. The threat of termination was an excellent tool for shaping docile, hard-working employees, and employers did not use it sparingly. At the Bon Marché, the new recruits were quickly sized up in terms of their suitability as Bon Marché employees; among the four hundred new employees who were hired in 1873, 37 per cent were fired in the first five years. Most firings came without warning or compensation. Commonly, employers were not required to provide their employees with advance notice of termination, and employees lived with the sense of insecurity.

In the "severe yet beneficent" approach, however, there were also sweeter inducements to employee loyalty. Entrepreneurs like Boucicaut of the Bon Marché or Cognacq[10] of the Samaritaine knew that the success of their ventures depended in large part upon the formation of loyal employees. The department stores offered numerous incentives of various kinds. Compensation was high compared to other female salaries. Though young clerks received little more than their room and board, the average salary of a top saleswoman was three hundred to four hundred francs per month around 1900. Even a single woman could live very comfortably in Paris on a salary of that level. By contrast, the average wage of a woman employed in industry in 1902 was two francs per day, and the best industrial salaries scarcely exceeded three francs. Thus, a working woman rarely achieved an income of 75 francs per month, compared to the average saleswoman's income of 75 francs per week.

Clearly the averages conceal an enormous range of salaries, since the greater part of the total was earned in commissions. All of the stores gave 1 or 2 per cent commissions on sales, . . . and, in addition, employees received discounts on merchandise purchased at the store. These incentives inspired many employees to associate their own interests with those of the firm but also to go into debt over their purchases of clothing and household items.

Long-term employees received the greatest advantages, such as the benefits from the provident fund begun by the Boucicaut family. After five years' service the store invested an annual sum on behalf of each employee. After 1886 a woman with 15 years of service could begin to draw benefits after the age of forty-five. The benefits averaged six hundred to fifteen hundred francs per year, depending on the individual's salary and length of service. . . . The fund paid death benefits to employ-

[10]T.E. Cognacq, 1839–1928.

ees' families, and women clerks could draw a small sum from it when leaving the store to be married. At the Grands Magasins du Louvre, the store contributed two hundred francs per year to a similar fund. The Louvre also sponsored employee savings plans and invested in vacation homes for employees. In addition, Cognacq of the Samaritaine subsidized the building of inexpensive apartments on the outskirts of Paris, and the Boucicaut family built a hospital.

As a result, . . . department store owners earned a . . . reputation for philanthropy. . . . A parliamentary committee in 1914 reluctantly concluded that the department stores treated their employees better than family-run shops, even though the report . . . was generally hostile to large-scale retailing.

Critics of the department stores emphasized the destruction of the familial relationship between employer and employee in large-scale commerce, but store owners were scarcely indifferent to the quality of employees' family lives. Women employees received paid maternity leaves (up to six weeks at the Louvre)—an important innovation. Employers also promoted larger families by awarding gifts of two hundred francs for the birth of each child. The Samaritaine . . . ran a day nursery for the children of employees in 1890s.

Employers took an interest in the employee's welfare to prevent harm to the public image of the firm. Disreputable or disruptive behavior by employees was punished by disciplinary action, including firing. Informal liaisons among employees were strongly discouraged, and upon discovery employees were forced to "regularize" their relationship or face immediate dismissal. Relationships among employees of the same store were not encouraged for fear that they would disrupt the work atmosphere. . . . In spite of such disapproval, marriages among employees were probably common. Once formalized, the relationship between two employees received the blessings of the management in the form of a monetary gift (generally one hundred francs). Whether employers induced women to retire after marriage is impossible to determine, but the percentage of married women in their work force was low.

Employer investment in employee productivity produced plans for paid sick leave, health care, and annual vacations. Most stores assured their employees of several sick days per year, and the Bon Marché employees could be admitted to the Boucicaut hospital for long-term illnesses. The Louvre sent several employees each year to a store-owned estate in the countryside for a "cure." Commercial employees were also among the first workers to receive annual paid vacations, although at first many of these so-called vacations were actually unpaid leaves during the dead seasons of January–February and August–September. . . . [P]aid holidays of several days to two weeks became common for department store employees in the early 1900s.

The combination of paternalistic motivations and publicity seeking also inspired the organized choral groups supported by the Bon Marché. The employee groups "le Choral" and "l'Harmonie" presented regular public concerts for employees, customers, and invited guests in the great galleries of the store. A winter concert could draw an audience of several thousand. Employees were also encouraged to participate in other uplifting types of leisure activities, such as the free language lessons offered in the evening hours.

In spite of these programs, employee life was scarcely ideal. What seemed like a life of ease and relative glamour often more closely resembled the hardships of other working-class women in the nineteenth century. Like domestic servants, shopgirls worked long hours and were heavily supervised. The lodgings in the "sixième étage"[11] of the department stores were . . . little better than that of the "chambres de bonnes."[12]

Commercial employees, like other Parisian working women, had levels of mortality which were strikingly high. Employees often suffered from tuberculosis and other respiratory diseases. The high level of mortality was not easy to explain, but no one disputed the fast pace of work and long hours, which could produce fatigue and reduce the employee's immunity to certain diseases. Thus, the first protective legislation dealt directly with the problem of fatigue, requiring that a seat be provided for every female employee in the store. The legislation could not assure, however, that the clerks would actually be allowed to rest during the day. Noted an investigator in 1910:

> Among other examples, last October I saw a new salesgirl who remained standing from 8 A.M. to 7 P.M. near a sales table full of school supplies in the midst of an indescribable jostling, in a stuffy atmosphere, without stopping, often serving several customers simultaneously, accompanying them to the cashier and hurrying to return to her station; she was constantly under the threat of a reprimand from her department head, and with all of that, she had to be always smiling, amiable, even when the excessive pace of work rendered that especially difficult.

Street sales represented the worst abuse of employees, since they required a similar regimen but completely out-of-doors, even in the winter. These sales . . . were an important part of retailing, but the consequences for employees could be tragic. Several saleswomen wrote to *La Fronde*[13] in 1898: "One of our fellow workers died last winter from an illness contracted when she was required, as we ourselves are, to work outside exposed to all kinds of weather." Even once Sunday closing was secured, the long, unrelieved days of work contributed to tuberculosis, anemia, and a variety of nervous disorders. The pace of work and

---

[11]The sixth floor (the seventh floor, counting the ground floor).

[12]The maids' rooms.

[13]The first newspaper run entirely by women.

the crush of customers induced a level of stress which combined with the inadequate diet of most shopgirls gave rise to a variety of gastrointestinal problems. The medical reports stress the obvious dangers in shop work of tuberculosis and other long-term disabilities, but they also asserted a connection between the physical environment and the morally degrading aspects of work for women.

Social observers in the nineteenth century often felt that female employment offered . . . too many opportunities for the sexual abuse of women. . . . The low salaries of most women made it impossible for them to support themselves without male companionship, which a girl acquired "at the price of her honor and her dignity." Some salesgirls could be seduced by wealthy customers or lecherous supervisors. . . . [T]he shopgirl was the victim of the role she had to play—an attractive amiable "doll," who was forced "to maintain an eternal smile." Whether or not she was sexually promiscuous, the salesgirl's role inspired moralists to imagine her debauchery.

A typical salesclerk was probably planning to marry a young employee or shopkeeper, and thus the suggestion of a sexual relationship might simply be a prelude to marriage. Salesgirls often came to the department stores with the hope of finding better suitors there. The inescapable fact that most salesclerks were young and single meant that their culture was that of young, urban, single people, whose attitudes and behavior were different from their middle-class employers.

The single state was almost a condition of employment, as it was with domestic service. Employees complained that the practice of providing housing inhibited their freedom to marry. About two-thirds of the female employees of the Louvre in 1895 were unmarried. In 1911, in the suburbs of Paris, only 14 per cent of the saleswomen were married. But the clerks hoped that work "was only a temporary occupation for them" and that they would ultimately retire from the occupation upon marriage. . . .

The young single employee . . . helped to create a new urban leisure culture in the years before the First World War. This culture included the attendance at concerts and sporting events. Employees took up bicycling, which itself allowed for freer sociability and a new style of courting. Employees also frequented cafés and certain restaurants. Musical groups and organized activities at the department stores were clearly intended to lure employees away from such public entertainments, but they did not succeed. Employees continued to use more of their leisure time in their own ways.

Women employees could expect to have the use of their Sundays and a few evening hours . . . between closing and curfew time. Department store clerks generally purchased their own evening meal at a restaurant, and thus they developed the habit of public dining. Whole chains of inexpensive restaurants . . . were established to supply inexpensive meals to a new class of consumers—clerks and office employees. Cheap but respectable, such establishments catered to the limited budgets of employees and office clerks and were located near the banks and stores. Shop girls could also dine inexpensively in the Latin Quarter, where, "needless to say, a woman alone is the commonest of sights and you will not hesitate to enter any of these establishments," according to the author of *A Woman's Guide to Paris*. Unlike the working classes, who frequented cafés mainly at mid-day, employees, especially the male clerks, were highly visible in the evenings in the cafés and restaurants of central Paris.

Leisure for the female clerk also included Sunday strolls in the parks, mixing with young soldiers, servant girls, and bourgeois families. Shopgirls were said to "shine" in their leather boots and stylish hats, which set them apart from the other working girls. The salesgirl's dress expressed the ambiguity of her position. On the street, employees' appearances showed a preoccupation with their public image; most of the women tried to dress attractively in spite of the cost. "The employees seem the queens of the urban proletariat. When one encounters them in the street, it is difficult to distinguish them from ambitious petit bourgeois: they wear hats, gloves, and fine boots. This is a necessity, it seems, in their occupation, but it costs them dearly." The stylish clothes of the shopgirl suggest two things about the experience of store clerks before 1914. The salesclerk herself was affected by the retailing revolution of the department stores and seduced by the attractiveness of current fashions. But the salesclerk's behavior was also the result of her ambiguous social position, a status which was complicated by the enormous range of salaries and benefits within the sales hierarchy. Zola suggested that the department store clerk was "neither a worker nor a lady. . . [but] a woman outside." Monsieur Honoré of the Louvre suggested that young clerks were recruited from the working classes because they were attracted by the idea of escaping a life of manual labor. But the reality is more complex than the desire of a working-class girl to become a bourgeoise. The department stores did offer their employees an important chance for mobility—the owners of the four major department stores had started their careers as simple employees. But for most clerks, and especially for a woman, the possibility of becoming a shop owner was distant. Instead, one could hope to be promoted in the store's hierarchy, although even this kind of promotion was more difficult for women to achieve than for men.

The reality of mobility is impossible to assess precisely, but one can gain an impression of what a female salesclerk may have achieved by her experience in a department store. Most salesclerks came from the petite bourgeoisie and in particular from employee families. Moreover, the young women who found suitors most often married other employees. During the 1880s, when the city of Paris gathered data on marriages, the percentage of female clerks who married male employees was between 45 and 50 per cent. The intermarriage of clerks was the result of their associations at work and also of their desire for a respectable life. Rather than raising them into the middle class, their endogamy helped to form an independent lower middle class culture. Through marriage, employees tied their lives and their fortunes together, forming a group whose experiences and aspirations were significantly different from those above and below them.

The transition from shopkeeping to modern merchandising did not represent an easy process for employees. It was the male department store clerks who organized the first union and mounted the largest and earliest strikes of employees. Again in 1919 and 1936, department store clerks, by this time predominantly female, contributed heavily to the labor struggles of those crisis years. Employer paternalism, which had characterized the first generation of department stores, earned the employers a reputation for philanthropy, but it . . . enclosed the salesclerk in an interlocking structure of life and work that was difficult to escape.

Inevitably, fashions in clothing and in retailing changed, and the First World War accelerated the pace of those changes. The era of live-in clerks ended. Women came to predominate in the ranks of department store employees. Declining salaries and benefits during the war years were only partially restored by the wave of strikes in 1919. Female clerks gained a forty-eight hour week in 1917 but never recovered their élite status among working women.

As department store work evolved, so did the work experience of most women. By 1920 clerical work in offices as well as shops was much more common for women. Whereas in 1906 only one woman in ten worked as an employee, by 1936 one in every three was employed as a clerk. From the feminization of clerical work resulted the "deprofessionalization" of the clerk: lower salaries, the influx of unskilled labor, and declining benefits. The evolution of department store work since the 1840s has thus been an example of broader social changes. This "paradise of women," as Zola described the department store in the 1880s, became truly feminized only after the First World War, but the experience of female salesclerks in the first generation of department stores suggests much about the changing character of work and the place of women in that transformation.

CONTEMPORARY EUROPE (WORLD WAR I–PRESENT)

One might argue that the twentieth century has been the worst of centuries in the history of Western civilization. Mass murder and widespread torture, easier owing to new technologies, have made prior epochs seem remarkably humane. Totalitarianism and genocide are two of this century's contributions to humankind, while nuclear catastrophe, now apparently a permanent specter looming ominously offstage, may be the third. Few are the regions of Europe that have not experienced the sequence of recent horrors that include World War I, fascist and Communist brutalities, World War II and the Holocaust, and the terrorism that currently punctuates the rhythm of modern life.

These developments have markedly influenced the social history of contemporary Europe, for the lives of millions have been altered dramatically in short periods of time. (The significance of the long duration becomes less noticeable in the contemporary era.) Warfare in the twentieth century has become total, involving entire populations, soldiers and civilians alike. Because Europe in the twentieth century has become more closely knit through economic ties, travel, and communications systems, occurrences in one country create ripples throughout the continent. Localism and agricultural self-sufficiency are things of the past, changes in the economy very quickly affect everyone, and consumers share a common culture. One of the ideals of modern citizenship is keeping abreast of the news, made readily available by the mass media, because we have come to realize that individuals and societies can no longer go their own way with impunity; we are all, in every aspect of our lives, at the mercy of changes that take place far from us. The peasant in an isolated village, eking out an existence in total ignorance of the outside world, is fast becoming extinct.

III

CONTEMPORARY EUROPE (WORLD WAR I—PRESENT)

'Play Up! Play Up! and Win the War!' Football, the Nation and the First World War, 1914–15

COLIN VEITCH

*The English, like all the other combatants, entered World War I with great
expectations. Unable to predict either of the devastating effects of machine guns and
poison gas or the horrors of life in the trenches, they believed that the war would be
glamorous, the victory quick and easy. The war, in short, was in the minds of many
analogous to a football (soccer) match, played with good sportsmanship, according to
the rules, and may the better side win! As Colin Veitch shows, this romantic view
of warfare and of sports was well-evidenced in Captain Nevill's kick of a football
at the beginning of the Battle of the Somme, a battle that in its first day produced
nearly 60,000 British casualties and served, in its carnage, to kill both Nevill and
the idea that war could be sport. What was the "athleticism" in English society that
led Nevill to offer his grand gesture?*

*Veitch emphasizes that sports in late nineteenth- and early twentieth-century
England had a class character. In what different ways did the ruling class and the
working class look at sports, especially football matches? How do you explain the
differences in their attitudes and their play? What issues were debated when the
Football Association determined at the beginning of the war to continue scheduling
games? Why did the games cease in 1915?*

*The English were united by patriotism but divided by class. Football, "only"
a game, was the occasion for class conflict and, according to some, a model for the
conduct of war. Sport in England thus had a dual nature: it could maintain class
consciousness and class divisions and it could stir up fervor for the war effort. Sport
in this essay becomes a means to understand differing patterns of thought in English
society as well as the optimism that so characterized life in the years prior to the
Great War.*

7:30 a.m., 1 July 1916. Along an eighteen mile front in Picardy the first
attack line of the British Fourth Army, more than 500,000 men all-told,
crouched in their trenches. Laden with equipment, they awaited the sig-

Colin Veitch, "'Play Up! Play Up! and Win the War!' Football, the Nation and the
First World War 1914–15," *Journal of Contemporary History* 20 (July 1985): . . . . 363–376.

nal to clambor out over the parapet and begin their advance across no man's land to occupy the shattered German lines. A seven-day bombardment had pounded the Germans with more than 1,500,000 shells; nine high explosive mines, tunnelled deep beneath their positions, had exploded between 7:20 and 7:28 a.m., hurling enormous clouds of earth and smoke 4000 feet into the air. Little opposition was anticipated. As the officers' whistles shrilled, a soldier in the Montauban sector noted:

> As the gun-fire died away I saw an infantry man climb onto the parapet into no man's land, beckoning others to follow. As he did so he kicked off a football; a good kick, the ball rose and travelled well towards the German line. That seemed to be the signal to advance.

Thus began the blackest day in the entire history of the British army. By nightfall, 57,470 casualties had been sustained; 19,240 officers and men were dead.

The gallant and defiant actions of the infantryman in question, Captain Nevill of the East Surrey Regiment, have not gone unnoticed by social, military and sports historians alike. The incident has become legendary, as research has revealed that Nevill bought four footballs on his last leave in London, and offered a prize to the first of his platoons to dribble a ball into the German positions which they were to attack. The winning platoon, however, were not able to claim their prize. Captain Nevill was killed during the assault along with many of his men. As an appropriate epitaph to him, two of the footballs were recovered, and are now enshrined in British military museums. To complete the legend, an anonymous elegy was composed to commemorate the incident:

> *On through the heat of slaughter*
> *Where gallant comrades fall*
> *Where blood is poured like water*
> *They drive the trickling ball*
> *The fear of death before them*
> *Is but an empty name*
> *True to the land that bore them*
> *The SURREYS play the game.*

The incident can be variously represented as illustrative of the indomitable British spirit, a celebration of defiant English pluck, the ultimate proof that the British believed war to be just another game, or simply that football was the common thread that bound together a group of men facing the most severe challenge of their lives. There are some elements of truth in all of these explanations, but none of them do justice to the complexity of the interrelationship between team games and trench warfare in the Great War of 1914–18. The Nevill incident is but one popularized example of sport and battle from the war. . . . [I]t symbolizes the intensity of the relationship whilst masking the clarity. It has passed into British folklore as illustrative of the national sporting character; an act of bravado that was shared by a group of men united in their devotion to sport. . . . [I]ncidents such as this have been used to gloss over some very real and pertinent British disunities concerning sport and the war. . . .

To understand the place of team games in wartime British society it is necessary to review briefly some crucial developments in sport and education that took place during the nineteenth century. At this time, the private educational establishments known as the 'public schools', which catered almost exclusively to the fee-paying sons of the country's titled and wealthy, began to encourage the introduction of games into the curriculum for distinct moral and educational purposes. Games as recreational pastimes, it must be said, were by no means new to the schools. What was unique was the didactical purpose behind their introduction. Eminent educationalists began to realize that through the employment of team games they could foster discipline and self-control in their often unruly charges, whilst simultaneously contributing to the character development of the young boy, who was being groomed by the schools to take his privileged position in the ever-expanding British Empire. The belief in the simple linear equation 'games build character' blossomed. In the following years, it became self-supporting and self-generating as the influential products of the public school system left their 'alma maters', taking with them their enthusiasm for games, and the resolute conviction that participation in football, cricket and other manly sports inculcated valuable character traits. Team sports, they believed, taught loyalty, consideration and selflessness, whilst simultaneously generating courage, strength and pluck. Organization of the games by the boys themselves encouraged responsibility and fostered their abilities both to lead by example and to obey with gentlemanly deference. Regulation of the sports brought with it an appreciation for order, good form and fair play. Above all, the game was to be played to the utmost of one's abilities—victory was to be accepted with humility, and defeat with unembittered integrity. Significantly, these characteristics were held to mould the boy for later life, fostering patriotism and preparing him for the moral and military battles he might have to face in the wider world. Together, these beliefs will be taken to comprise an educational ideology called 'athleticism', which had an enormous influence on British thought and practice in the Victorian and Edwardian eras that researchers are only recently beginning to appreciate.

Football, in a variety of forms and guises, was the major winter game of the public schools, and was therefore accorded the ability to develop those admirable characteristics previously highlighted. Hard knocks and good lessons were amongst the benefits that were held to accrue from a wholesome and manly game of football; both would stand the young boy in good stead once he embarked on his chosen career. For many young public schoolboys, the chosen path was entry into the officer corps of the British army. As this institution, too, was dominated by members of the country's social élite, it is hardly surprising that the qualities valued most highly for a potential officer were those which were being honed on the cricket field or football pitch. In 1857, for instance, Sir John Burgoyne wrote:

> At a public school will be found one set of boys, who apply to their studies, and make the greater progress in them, another set take to cricket, boating, fives, swimming etc. Now, of the two, I should decidedly prefer the latter, as much more likely to make good officers.

Another officer stated that, although knowledge of the principles of gunnery was desirable, 'activity of body, proficiency in field sports and qualification for commanding men' were all of 'almost equal importance to the artilleryman in the field'. As British military influence spread into remote quarters of Africa, the Far East, and the Indian sub-continent, so there developed a familiar stereotype of the schoolboy-sportsman-soldier, patriotically doing his duty throughout the Empire. As Head-master Haslam of Ripon School made clear in his address on Speech Day in 1884, it was participation in games which was to a great degree responsible for this admirable and plucky product:

> Wellington said that the playfields of Eton won the battle of Waterloo, and there was no doubt that the training of the English boys in the cricket and football field enabled them to go to India, and find their way from island to island in the Pacific, or to undergo fatiguing marches in Egypt. Their football and cricket experiences taught them how to stand up and work, and how to take and give a blow.

These sentiments were reiterated in Henry Newbolt's *Vitai Lampada*. Written on the eve of the Boer war in 1898, it can be seen as the ultimate poetic expression of the ideological transfer held to take place between public school playing-field and the battlefield:

> *There's a breathless hush in the Close tonight*
> *Ten to make and the match to win —*
> *A bumping pitch and a blinding light,*
> *An hour to play and the last man in.*
> *And it's not for the sake of a ribboned coat,*
> *Or the selfish hope of a season's fame*
> *But his Captain's hand on his shoulder smote —*
> *Play up! Play up! And play the game!*
>
> *The sand of the desert is sodden and red —*
> *Red with the wreck of the square that broke —*

The Gatling's jammed and the Colonel dead,
And the regiment blind with dust and smoke.
The river of death has brimmed his banks
And England's far and Honour a name,
But the voice of a schoolboy rallies the ranks;
Play up! Play up! And play the game!

. . . As late as 1911, the *Standard* was reminding its readers that 'in some lonely sentry box on the Empire's frontier, up there on the Khaiber or the Bolan, there a clean-cheeked, smooth-haired boy will handle his half-hundred wind-baked ruffians as if they were the Second Eleven, and he their Captain'.

It was, then, understandable that *The Times* should publish the following poem[1] two weeks after war had been declared in 1914:

Lad, with the merry smile and the eyes
Quick as hawk's and clear as the day,
You, who have counted the game the prize,
Here is the game of games to play.
Never a goal—the captains say—
Matches the one that's needed now:
Put the old blazer and cap away—
England's colours await your brow .

The historical evidence, then, would appear if not to sanction and justify the bravado of Captain Nevill on the Somme, certainly to allow an explanation of the action to be advanced. Indeed, several researchers have cited the incident as an eccentric act, stemming from an ideological immersion in athleticism. Nevertheless, no one has yet shown that Nevill had actually been educated at a public school, nor have they attempted to account for the actions of his men, who were most unlikely to have been reared in their youth by an educational force intent on moulding their characters through games. The reiteration of the Nevill incident then, has contributed to the propagation of a misleading myth regarding contemporary British attitudes towards sport and war in the years of the Great War. . . . [F]ootball did indeed play a vital part in the early stages of the war in shaping British responses to the conflict, but for several months its contribution was neither jingoistic nor laudatory. Instead, football proved to be the medium through which vocal elements of the middle and upper classes launched an embittered literary attack upon the working-class reaction to the national crisis. The game itself became the weapon in a war of words that was the crystallization of strong feelings over the social changes which had occurred in football in the previous thirty years.

[1]By R.E. Vernede.

The public schools had nurtured the game of football behind their venerable walls during the nineteenth century, and it had been on the impulse of a group of ex-public schoolboys that the fledgling Football Associations had been formed in 1863. Teams of old boys had dominated the first ten years of national competition in the FA Cup from its inception in 1871, but that had been their zenith. From that point on, although the gentlemen and amateurs educated at the public schools continued to retain their administrative power, they were never again to dominate the game on the field as before. Football, or 'soccer' as it had become known, had been rapturously embraced by the working classes, and the teams emerging from the industrial heartlands of England — particularly Manchester, Birmingham, Wolverhampton and Blackburn — began to gain ascendancy. This social diffusion of football brought with it ethical and ideological turmoil for those who had been reared on the game in the closeted environments of the public schools. They had been taught to value, in Vernede's words, 'the game the prize', rather than the result. Football, like other team games, was to be played in a spirit of sportsmanlike good conduct, where rivalry was good-natured and the quality of the game surpassed the result in importance. The vast intrusion of the lower classes into the game, bringing with them the ultimate bane of the amateur gentleman ethos — the *professional* footballer — was held to be totally detrimental to the progress and practice of football.

... [T]he bitter and often bigoted viewpoints that are recorded in this debate are invariably those of a section of the population who felt themselves and their beliefs and values to be threatened by the challenge from the new working men's teams. Nevertheless, this literary onslaught was to set the tone for football's role in the opening months of the war. The *Badminton Magazine* clearly illustrated the root of the discord in 1896:

> ... the artisan differs from the public-school man in two important points: he plays to win at all costs and, from the nature of his associations, he steps onto the football field in better training ... his strong desire to win leads him to play up to the rules (and) to indulge in dodges and tricks which the public school man is apt to consider dishonourable, while it is difficult for him to realise that you can be defeated with honour.

In 1911, another gentlemanly viewpoint was recorded, this time in response to the referee's power to award a penalty kick for a foul close to the goal. As this ruling had been incorporated into the game in 1891, the twenty years intervening perhaps make this comment all the more significant; 'It is a standing insult to sportsmen to have to play under a rule which assumes that players intend to trip, hack, and push their opponents and behave like cads of the most unscrupulous kidney.' Alongside professionalism, and a lack of sportsmanship, the act of spectating was the third element of soccer's unholy trinity identified by the defenders of the old school game. Conveniently forgetting the large crowds of boys that used to crowd the sidelines during their own school and house matches, the most vocal of the adherents to the amateur, upper-class game took exception to the huge crowds which were attending the Saturday matches. Football, they felt, was a game to be played, not watched. Benefits were derived from participation, not observation; large-scale mass support, particularly when the home crowds were so partisan, was simply another travesty of the game that was to be endured by the purists. On the eve of war, then, all was far from well in the arena of British football. Class divisions were prominent, and were the root of several internal divisions within the Association. The three main areas of contention identified here were to achieve an embarrassing notoriety following the outbreak of the war.

Vernede's poem appeared in *The Times* on 19 August 1914. Its sentiments and its language both place it firmly in the mould of athleticism, for despite its adoption of football as the metaphor for warfare, the game chosen by the poet was distinctly upper-class and amateur. The references to blazers, caps and colours, together with the allusion to the game itself being the prize, all mark the poem as being undeniably aimed at the products of the public schools, who had been reared on these particular trappings and ethics of game-playing. Though the response was obviously not directly related to the poet's appeal, the public school and university men responded to the nation's plight with alacrity. *The Times* appealed to its own readership: 'All Varsity men, Old Public School Boys—men who are hardened to the soldiers' life by strenuous pursuit of sport should enlist at once'. *TP's Weekly* was one of several magazines which carried advertisements from the War Office for these young men to enlist as junior officers for the duration of the war, and some 37,000 of these were swiftly commissioned. More than 20,500 of these men had previous Officer Training Corps experience, and were characterized by one of their commanding officers thus:

> They are the figures of the British youth with the principles of honour, manhood, justice and courage instilled into them, and with a very real idea of what sacrifices of ease and luxury and possibly of life are demanded today.

The formation of these essential characteristics was naturally attributed, in part, to the football field: '. . . even today there are amongst us those who really imagine that Wellington trained his officers between the goal-posts'.

Advocates of athleticism, then, saw football as a cardinal virtue which had helped shape the manly English characters of those young men now being called upon to defend their country. Their praise, however, extended once again only to the amateur game. The professional game administered by the Football Association received short shrift from an often hostile press, contributors to which were incensed by the decision to continue to play the scheduled league games despite the crisis of war. In a column headed 'Duty Before Sport', the *Evening News* published the following announcement:

> This is no time for football. This nation, this Empire has got to occupy itself with more serious business. The young men who play football and the young men who look on have better work to do. The trumpet calls them, their country calls them, the heroes in the trenches call them. They are summoned to leave their sport, and to take part in the great game. That game is war, for life or death.

The renunciation of football and enlistment to 'play the greater game' for King and country shot to disproportionate prominence in the early months of the war. Recruitment for Kitchener's 'New Armies'[2] was based exclusively on a voluntary basis. Consequently, a vocal minority saw it as expedient to the national effort that the Football Association should be forced to abandon its programme of games, and encourage players and spectators alike to sign up. Such responses from the amateur clubs and associations only served to embitter the 'unpatriotic' stance of the professional footballers. On 2 September, Mr. Philip Collins, Vice-President of the Hockey Association and Chairman of the England Selection Committee, had suggested that all coming matches for the season be abandoned, as this would release some 40,000 able-bodied men for army service. Two days later, all rugby clubs in Kent were asked by the association to scratch their fixtures and encourage enlistment. The following day, the Rugby Football Union announced its intention of forming a corps of rugby players, and in a column headed 'Patriotism Before Sport', invited volunteers to send applications to Twickenham, the traditional home of English international rugby. Perhaps the most notable contribution on this topic appeared one week later, penned by none other than the redoubtable cricketer Dr W.G. Grace:

> The fighting on the Continent is very severe and will probably be prolonged. I think the time has arrived when the county cricket season should be closed, for it is not fitting at a time like the present that able-bodied men should play day after day, and pleasure-seekers look on.

Conscious of its somewhat delicate position in the limelight of the nation's press, the Football Association put its complete administrative structure at the disposal of the War Office, and offered the use of all league club grounds for recruitment and training. It was announced that Glasgow would form a battalion of football players and followers, and

---

[2]The raising of 2½ million men by voluntary recruitment during the period September 1914 to March 1915 to supplement the professional army.

that recruiting rallies would be held at soccer grounds during the half-time interval on match days. One poster displayed at a London ground encouraged fans with the words:

> Do you want to be a
> Chelsea Die-Hard?
> If so
> Join the 17th Battalion
> Middlesex Regiment
> 'The Old Die-Hards'
> And follow the lead given
> by your favourite Football Players

These acts, however, were insufficient to quell the protests, which reached a sensational peak on 8 September when one F. N. Charrington, an East End Temperance worker, sent a telegram to the King, asking for the playing of football to be banned during the war. Earlier that year, George V had been the first reigning monarch to attend a Cup Final, and had also become the honorary patron of the Football Association. In a diplomatically-worded reply, the King's Personal Secretary told Charrington '. . . the doings of the Association will be carefully followed having regard to the King's position as its patron'. This incident appears to have toughened the resolve of the Management Committee of the league, who stated: 'The committee are even more decidedly of the opinion that in the interests of the people of this country, football ought to be continued'.

The defiant stance of the FA was a source of considerable disappointment to the army's recruiting officers:

> It has a moral effect . . . These professional footballers of England are the pick of the country for fitness. Nobody has a right to say that any body of men are not doing their duty, and there may be excellent domestic reasons why every one of these thousands of players does not enlist. But when the young men week after week see the finest physical manhood of the country expending its efforts kicking a ball about, they can't possibly realise there is a call for every fit man at the front.

The controversy was fuelled by the publication in the same issue of the following poem, 'The Game' by A. Lochhead. A close reading of the first stanza in particular reveals the poet's bias:

> Come, leave the lure of the football field
> With its fame so lightly won,
> And take your place in a greater game
> Where worthier deeds are done.
> No game is this where thousands watch

The play of a chosen few;
But rally all! if you're men at all,
There's room in the team for you.

. . . .

Then leave for a while the football field
And the lure of the flying ball
Lest it dull your ear to the voice you hear
When your King and country call.
Come join the ranks of our hero sons
In the wider field of fame,
Where the God of Right will watch the fight
And referee the game.

... *The Times* reported in a bitter tone that recruitment drives at football league matches were having dismal results, despite large crowds. On Saturday, 21 November, only six volunteers came forward from the crowd at the game between Cardiff and Bristol Rovers, while at the Arsenal ground in London, a call for recruits yielded only one man. It was noted that there was a 'growing feeling that professional and spectacular football is incompatible with successful recruiting'. These observations ignored the fact that the month of November had been a highly successful one for the nation in recruiting terms. More than 160,000 men had come forward, a substantial increase over the months of September and October.

The controversy over the depicted unpatriotic response of the professional footballers and their spectators was no doubt fanned, albeit unconsciously, by the actions and press coverage of their amateur and educated counterparts, the public school sportsmen. The call for the formation of a public school battalion met with an overwhelming reaction in September 1914, and within days 1,950 ex-public school and university men had enlisted to serve alongside their peers. A reporter pointed out, 'They are all of the well-to-do class, and are paying their own expenses', and noted that most wore their old school caps or colours as they paraded from Hyde Park to Victoria Station, en route to Epsom Downs for training. Their dutiful and enthusiastic patriotism was celebrated in 'The Recruits', by I. Gregory Smith:

O! Hearts ever youthful, like schoolboys at play,
So be it with you in the thick of the fray;
In the crash and the smoke and the roar of the fight
Be it yours, if it need be, to die for the Right!

Even in death, sporting imagery followed these young men. The obituary for Mr. Julian Martin Smith, who achieved posthumous fame for being the first volunteer to fall in action, noted that at Eton 'his athletic record was remarkable'. . . . For the benefit of its readers, *The Times Educational Supplement* actually constructed a 'league table' of the public schools' contribution to the war effort.

Whilst this thinly veiled struggle between the values and expectations of two polarized social classes was continuing to gain attention, there were more conciliatory attempts being made to persuade the youth of the nation that their footballing skills were an advantageous preparation for war. Sir Robert Baden-Powell in his enormously influential unofficial training manual for the war, wrote that new recruits must be taught:

> . . . from the first that they are like . . . players in a football team: each has to be perfect and efficient, each has to adhere patiently to the rules and to play in his place and play the game—not for his own advancement or glorification, but simply and solely that at all costs his side may win.

Admiral Lord Charles Beresford, too, chose to remain aloof from what had become a dispute of distinctly acidic rhetoric, and in his appeal adopted reason in preference to rancour:

> I cast no stones. The men who play football, cricket and other games are our finest specimens of British manhood. I put it to them to consider—they are fit, strong, healthy and as sportsmen they are cheery; health makes vigour, cheeriness makes pluck—I put it to them that we must now all be prepared to stand by our country and to suffer for our country.

Professional football finally fell into line on 24 April 1915. The 'Khaki Cup Final' was played at the Old Trafford ground in Manchester between Chelsea and Sheffield United, the latter club winning by the only goal of the game. As he presented the cup and medals to the teams, Lord Derby effectively closed the debate on wartime professional soccer with the words, 'You have played with one another and against one another for the Cup; play with one another for England now'. Thus ended eight months consternation for the patriotic British reading public. . . . [L]ater that year . . . the men of the First Battalion of the 18th London Regiment had gone into action at Loos, led by men kicking a football. At last Britain's national game could claim total concord with the war effort, without the skeleton of active professional soccer at home in the cupboard. This was a far more desirable image—the British sportsman-soldier leading the fight against the Hun—and it undoubtedly quietened the former critics. It also set the tone for future British war-reporting, which embraced the national sporting stereotype with renewed vigour. Nevertheless, the furore over the continuation of the game during the early months of the war had highlighted the Victorian legacy of intense social differentiation within the nation, particularly in regard to attitudes towards and valuation of team games and their contribution to the formation of national character. In particular, it reveals the extent to which the most vocal of the critics—especially those who raised their objections within the columns of *The Times*—distorted the situation to give credence to their assault on what was essentially an attack on their comprehension of the working-class ethos of sport. Their tirades ignored the fact that the vast majority of working-class soccer was amateur, and that many of the more than 300,000 players registered with amateur teams had already enlisted in the forces. They paid scant attention to claims by the Football Association that they were employing only 5,000 professionals, of whom 2,000 were already with the forces, and only a further 600 were unmarried, and therefore being encouraged to enlist. Although the Football Association's claim that their organization had recruited 500,000 men by the end of 1914 remains unsubstantiated, there is little doubt that their administrative machinery was of invaluable assistance to the War Office in the early months of the war. Once again, this received little acknowledgement from the patriotic protesters who saw the continuation of the game as the ultimate national evil. In these regards, there would appear to be some justification in the equally antagonistic claims of the *Athletic News*, which spoke out strongly in support of the professionals:

> The whole agitation is nothing less than an attempt by the classes to stop the recreation on one day in the week of the masses . . . What do they care for the poor man's sport? The poor are giving their lives for this country in thousands. In many cases they have nothing else . . . there are those who could bear arms, but who have to stay at home and work for the Army's requirements, and the country's needs. These should, according to a small clique of virulent snobs, be deprived of the one distraction that they have had for over thirty years.

By mid-1915, the battle of words was all but over, but the real war was far from won. Sport was to maintain its ascendancy in the forefront of British thought and expression throughout the remaining years of the conflict, and continued to be used to typify the genetic strength of British manhood. This paper has attempted to search beneath that glossy veneer presented by the contemporary literature, and show that the undercurrents which brought sport into the forefront of the nation at war were powerful, deeply-rooted and not nearly as neatly delineated as some authors, poets, journalists, and even historians would have us believe. The role of sport within the confines of British society in the first world war and, in particular, the gallant actions of young men such as the courageous Captain Nevill are far too important to an understanding of British social history to be left unchallenged and misunderstood.

The Price of Glory: Verdun 1916

ALISTAIR HORNE

If war is Hell, then the Battle of Verdun, from February to December, 1916, was the deepest circle. The French and Germans sustained approximately one million casualties. The horrors of the battle can scarcely be imagined, but Alistair Horne does manage to immerse us in the sights, smells, and feelings that this, the most destructive battle in history, evoked. Historians of warfare have begun to move from descriptions of military maneuvers and biographies of generals and heroes to reconstructions of war from the perspective of the ordinary soldier. This is what Horne does in this powerful, moving essay.

How did the battlefield appear? What was the approach march like? Horne frequently refers to colors, something that historians of warfare tend to ignore, save when discussing uniforms or flags. The odors of Verdun were overwhelming; the living mixed promiscuously with the dead. Indeed, Verdun was an open cemetery, with ghastly and mutilated corpses of both men and animals prominent everywhere. Filth and disease contributed to the enormous suffering. Above all this was the nearly constant artillery bombardment raining death on those who could do little to protect themselves from indiscriminate shells. What does Horne mean by the statement that "Verdun was the epitome of a 'soldier's battle' "? What was the fate of the wounded? Did the French support services do a commendable job in treating the wounded or in feeding and aiding the soldiers in the front lines?

Why does Horne consider the runners, ration parties, and stretcher-bearers to have been the greatest heroes of Verdun? How did the high probability of death or mutilation and the constant, seemingly unendurable suffering affect the soldiers physically and mentally? Did the saying that "there are no athiests in a foxhole" ring true at Verdun? Do you think, after reading this selection, that the suffering and deaths of the soldiers were meaningless, mere sacrifices on the altar of nationalism?

. . . Although from March to the end of May the main German effort took place on the Left Bank of the Meuse, this did not mean that the Right Bank had become a 'quiet sector'. Far from it! Frequent vicious little attacks undertaken by both sides to make a minor tactical gain here and there regularly supplemented the long casualty lists caused by the relentless pounding of the rival artilleries. Within the first month

Alistair Horne, *The Price of Glory: Verdun 1916*, (New York: Penguin Books, 1964), 185–201.

of the battle the effect of this non-stop bombardment, by so mighty an assemblage of cannon, their fire concentrated within an area little larger than Richmond Park,[1] had already established an environment common to both sides of the Meuse that characterized the whole battle of Verdun. The horrors of trench warfare and of the slaughter without limits of the First War are by now so familiar to the modern reader that further recounting merely benumbs the mind. The Battle of Verdun, however, through its very intensity—and, later, its length—added a new dimension of horror. Even this would not in itself warrant lengthy description were it not for the fact that Verdun's peculiarly sinister environment came to leave an imprint on men's memories that stood apart from other battles of the First War; and predominantly so in France where the nightmares it inspired lingered perniciously long years after the Armistice.[2]

To a French aviator, flying sublimely over it all, the Verdun front after a rainfall resembled disgustingly the 'humid skin of a monstrous toad'. Another flyer, James McConnell, (an American . . .) noted after passing over 'red-roofed Verdun'—which had 'spots in it where no red shows and you know what has happened there'—that abruptly

> there is only that sinister brown belt, a strip of murdered nature. It seems to belong to another world. Every sign of humanity has been swept away. The woods and roads have vanished like chalk wiped from a blackboard; of the villages nothing remains but grey smears. . . . During heavy bombardments and attacks I have seen shells falling like rain. Countless towers of smoke remind one of Gustave Doré's[3] picture of the fiery tombs of the arch-heretics in Dante's 'Hell'. . . . Now and then monster projectiles hurtling through the air close by leave one's plane rocking violently in their wake. Aeroplanes have been cut in two by them.

. . . The first sounds heard by ground troops approaching Verdun reminded them of 'a gigantic forge that ceased neither day nor night'. At once they noted, and were acutely depressed by, the sombre monotones of the battle area. To some it was 'yellow and flayed, without a patch of green'; to others a compound of brown, grey, and black, where the only forms were shell holes. On the few stumps that remained of Verdun's noble forests on the Right Bank, the bark either hung down in strips, or else had long since been consumed by half-starved pack-horses. As spring came, with the supreme optimism of Nature, the shattered trees pushed out a new leaf here and there, but soon these too dropped sick and wilting in the poisonous atmosphere. At night, the Verdun sky resembled a 'stupendous *Aurora Borealis*', but by day the only splashes of colour that one French soldier-artist could find were the rose tints

---

[1] In London.

[2] Of 11 November 1918, ending hostilities on the Western Front.

[3] French illustrator and painter (1832–1883), famous for his illustrations of books, including Dante's *Divine Comedy*.

displayed by the frightful wounds of the horses lying scattered about the approach routes, lips pulled back over jaws in the hideousness of death. Heightening this achromatic gloom was the pall of smoke over Verdun most of the time, which turned the light filtering through it to an ashy grey. A French general, several times in the line at Verdun, recalled to the author that while marching through the devastated zone his soldiers never sang; 'and you know French soldiers sing a lot'. When they came out of it they often grew crazily rapturous simply at returning to 'a world of colour, meadows and flowers and woods . . . where rain on the roofs sounds like a harmonic music'.

A mile or two from the front line, troops entered the first communication trenches; though to call them this was generally both an exaggeration and an anachronism. Parapets gradually grew lower and lower until the trench became little deeper than a roadside ditch. Shells now began to fall with increasing regularity among closely packed men. In the darkness (for obvious reasons, approach marches were usually made at night) the columns trampled over the howling wounded that lay underfoot. Suddenly the trench became 'nothing more than a track hardly traced out amid the shell holes'. In the mud, which the shelling had now turned to a consistency of sticky butter, troops stumbled and fell repeatedly; cursing in low undertones, as if fearful of being overheard by the enemy who relentlessly pursued them with his shells at every step. Sometimes there were duckboards around the lips of the huge shell craters. But more often there were not, and heavily laden men falling into the water-filled holes remained there until they drowned, unable to crawl up the greasy sides. If a comrade paused to lend a hand, it often meant that two would drown instead of one. In the chaos of the battlefield, where all reference points had long since been obliterated, relieving detachments often got lost and wandered hopelessly all night; only to be massacred by an enemy machine-gunner as dawn betrayed them. It was not unusual for reliefs to reach the front with only half the numbers that set out, nor for this nightmare approach march to last ten hours or longer.

One of the first things that struck troops fresh to the Verdun battlefield was the fearful stench of putrefaction; 'so disgusting that it almost gives a certain charm to the odour of gas shells.' The British never thought their Allies were as tidy about burying their dead as they might be, but under the non-stop shelling at Verdun an attempt at burial not infrequently resulted in two more corpses to dispose of. It was safer to wrap the dead up in a canvas and simply roll them over the parapet into the largest shell-hole in the vicinity. There were few of these in which did not float some ghastly, stinking fragment of humanity. On the Right Bank several gullies were dubbed, with good cause, '*La Ravine de la Mort*'[4] by the French. Such a one, though most of it in French hands,

---

[4]"The Ravine of Death."

was enfiladed by a German machine gun at each end, which exacted a steady toll. Day after day the German heavies pounded the corpses in this gully, until they were quartered, and re-quartered; to one eye-witness it seemed as if it were filled with dismembered limbs that no one could or would bury. Even when buried,

> shells disinter the bodies, then reinter them, chop them to pieces, play with them as a cat plays with a mouse.

As the weather grew warmer and the numbers of dead multiplied, the horror reached new peaks. The compressed area of the battlefield became an open cemetery in which every square foot contained some decomposed piece of flesh:

> You found the dead embedded in the walls of the trenches, heads, legs, and half-bodies, just as they had been shovelled out of the way by the picks and shovels of the working party.

Once up in the front line, troops found that life had been reduced, in the words of a Beaux Arts[5] professor serving with the Territorials,[6] 'to a struggle between the artillerymen and the navvy, between the cannon and the mound of earth.' All day long the enemy guns worked at levelling the holes laboriously scraped out the previous night. At night, no question of sleep for the men worn out by the day's shelling (it was not unknown for men in the line to go without sleep for eleven days). As soon as darkness fell, an officer would lay out a white tape over the shell ground, and the 'navvies' began to dig; feverishly, exposed, hoping not to be picked up by enemy flares and machine guns. By dawn the trench would probably be little more than eighteen inches deep, but it had to be occupied all day, while the enemy gunners resumed their work of levelling. No question of latrines under these conditions; men relieved themselves where they lay, as best they could. Dysentery became regarded as a norm of life at Verdun. Lice, made much of by combatants on other fronts, receive little mention. With luck, by the second morning the trench might have reached a depth of barely three feet.

Over and again eye-witnesses at Verdun testify to the curious sensation of having been in the line twice, three times, without ever having seen an enemy infantryman. On going into the line for the first time, one second-lieutenant who was later killed at Verdun, twenty-six-year-old Raymond Jubert, recalled his Colonel giving the regiment instructions that must have been repeated a thousand time at Verdun:

---

[5] From the École Nationale Supérieur des Beaux-Arts in Paris.

[6] The French Territorial Army was composed of veterans and older citizens. They usually took secondary jobs, thus freeing front-line troops for combat.

You have a mission of sacrifice; here is a post of honour where they want to attack. Every day you will have casualties, because they will disturb your work. On the day they want to, they will massacre you to the last man, and it is your duty to fall.

Battalion after battalion decimated solely by the bombardment would be replaced in the line by others, until these too had all effectiveness as a fighting unit crushed out of them by the murderous shelling.[7] After nights of being drenched by icy rain in a shell-hole under non-stop shelling, a twenty-year-old French corporal wrote:

> Oh, the people who were sleeping in a bed and who tomorrow, reading their newspaper, would say joyously—'they are still holding!' Could they imagine what that simple word 'hold' meant?

The sensation provoked by being under prolonged bombardment by heavy guns is something essentially personal and subjective; first-hand accounts cover a wide range of experience. To Paul Dubrulle, a thirty-four-year-old French Jesuit serving as an infantry sergeant at Verdun, whose journals are outstanding for their un-embellished realism, it seemed as follows:

> When one heard the whistle in the distance, one's whole body contracted to resist the too excessively potent vibrations of the explosion, and at each repetition it was a new attack, a new fatigue, a new suffering. Under this régime, the most solid nerves cannot resist for long; the moment arrives where the blood mounts to the head; where fever burns the body and where the nerves, exhausted, become incapable of reacting. Perhaps the best comparison is that of seasickness . . . finally one abandons one's self to it, one has no longer even the strength to cover oneself with one's pack as protection against splinters, and one scarcely still has left the strength to pray to God. . . . To die from a bullet seems to be nothing; parts of our being remain intact; but to be dismembered, torn to pieces, reduced to pulp, this is a fear that flesh cannot support and which is fundamentally the great suffering of the bombardment. . . .

. . . More than anything else, it was the apparently infinite duration of the Verdun bombardments that reduced even the strongest nerves. Sergeant-Major César Méléra, a tough adventurer, who had sailed around the world in peacetime and who appeared little affected by the horrors of war, describes his experience of Verdun shell-fire initially with an unemotional economy of words: 'Filthy night, shells.' Three

---

[7]To us this kind of futile sacrifice symbolizes the First War mentality. Yet one must always remember the dilemma facing the French at Verdun. . . . By 1916 both sides had already experimented successfully with 'thinning out' the forward areas to reduce shell-fire casualties. But in the cramped space at Verdun where the loss of a hundred yards might lead to the loss of the city the risk of any such thinning out could not be taken by the French. Similarly the Germans, always attacking, could not avoid a permanent concentration of men in the forward lines. (Author's note.)

days later he was confiding to his diary that the night bombardment made him 'think of that nightmare room of Edgar Allan Poe, in which the walls closed in one after the other.' The following day: 'Oh how I envy those who can charge with a bayonet instead of waiting to be buried by a shell,' and, finally, the admission:

> Verdun is terrible . . . because man is fighting against material, with the sensation of striking out at empty air. . . .

. . . With the steadily increasing power of the French artillery, experiences of the infantryman on both sides became more and more similar. In June a soldier of the German 50th Division before Fort Vaux declared that 'the torture of having to lie powerless and defenceless in the middle of an artillery battle' was 'something for which there is nothing comparable on earth. ' Through this common denominator of suffering, a curious mutual compassion began to develop between the opposing infantries, with hatred reserved for the artillery in general. To Captain Cochin on the Mort Homme,[8] it seemed as if the two artilleries were playing some idiotic game with each other, to see which could cause the most damage to the two unhappy lines of infantrymen.

What the P.B.I. felt about their own gunners may be gauged from a French estimate that out of ten shells falling on a Verdun trench, 'on an average two were provided by the friendly artillery'. Sergeant Élie Tardivel tells how in June seven men from a neighbouring platoon had just been killed by a single French 155 shell:

> I met the company commander; I told him I had brought up some grenades and barbed-wire; I asked where I was to put them. He replied: 'Wherever you wish. For two hours our own guns have been bombarding us, and if it goes on I shall take my company and bombard the gunner with these grenades!'

Emotions between the infantry and gunners resembled those sometimes held towards the heavy-bomber crews of World War II, whom the ground troops viewed as sumptuously quartered well away from the enemy, making brief sorties to spray their bombs indiscriminately over both lines. A French company commander, Charles Delvert, describes passing two naval batteries en route for Verdun:

> Not a single man on foot. Everybody in motors. The officers had a comfortable little car to themselves. . . . I looked at my poor troopers. They straggled lamentably along the road, bent in two by the weight of their packs, streaming with water, and all this to go and become mashed to pulp in muddy trenches.

---

[8]The "Dead Man," a hill between the town of Verdun and the front line that was the scene of ferocious combat.

Other infantrymen were irked by the impersonal casualness with which the heavy gunners crews emerged from their comfortable shelters to fire at targets they could not see, 'appearing to be much less concerned than about the soup or the bucket of wine which had just been brought.'

This picture is to some extent endorsed by the artillery themselves. Staff-Sergeant Fonsagrive, serving with a 105 mm. battery wrote in his journal during the peak of the March battle on the Right Bank; 'the fine weather continues, the days lengthen; it is a pleasure to get up in the morning. . . . ' Watching the planes dog-fighting overhead, there was plenty of leisure time for day-dreaming about wives and families. Later, Fonsagrive notes with some vexation:

> One day when, quietly sitting underneath an apple tree, I was writing a letter, a 130 mm. shell landed forty metres behind me, causing me a disagreeable surprise.

. . . Not all French gunners, however, were as fortunate as Sergeant Fonsagrive. When death came from the long-range German counter-battery guns, it came with frightening suddenness. A gunner sipping his soup astraddle his cannon, a group of N.C.O.s playing cards would be expunged by an unheralded salvo. In action, the field artillery particularly had even less cover than the infantry; often reduced still further by officers of the old school of that notably proud French arm, *'La Reine des Batailles'*,[9] who believed (and there were still many like them) that to take cover under fire was almost cowardice. Casualties among some batteries were in fact often at least as high as among the infantry. Captain Humbert, a St Cyrien[10] of the 97th Infantry Regiment, testifies to the effect of the German artillery's systematic sweeping of the back areas, knowing that the French field batteries must all be there:

> Nobody escapes; if the guns were spared today, they will catch it tomorrow. . . . Whole batteries lie here demolished. . . .

Lieutenant Gaston Pastre, though also a heavy gunner, provides a very different picture to Fonsagrive. Arriving at Verdun in May, he found the unit he was relieving had lost forty per cent of its effectives; 'If you stay here a month, which is normal,' they warned him, 'you will lose half of yours too.' The reverse slopes up to Fort St Michel on the Right Bank, where Pastre's battery was sited, were crammed with every calibre of gun; it was 'nothing more than one immense battery, there are perhaps 500 pieces there. ' A wonderful target for German saturation fire—anything that falls between Fort Michel and the road is good.' There

---

[9]"The Queen of Battles."
[10]St. Cyr was the principal French Military academy.

were generally only two periods of calm in the day; between 4 and 6 a.m. and between 4 and 7 p.m. when, like subhuman troglodytes, the French gunners emerged from the ground to repair the damage. For the rest of the time, to move from one shelter to another—a distance of about twenty yards—required considerable courage. By night the solitary road from Verdun came under constant fire from the German gunners, certain that French munition columns must be coming up it nose to tail. It presented 'a spectacle worthy of Hell', in which men not killed outright were often hurled off their gun carriages by shell blast, to be run over and crushed by their own caissons in the dark.

Next to the incessant bombardment, the stink of putrefaction, and the utter desolation of the battlefield, Verdun combatants testify again and again to the terrifying isolation, seldom experienced to the same degree in other sectors. Verdun was the epitome of a 'soldier's battle'. Within an hour or less of the launching of each organized attack or counter-attack, leadership over the lower echelons ceased to play any significant role. Company commanders would lose all but the most spasmodic and tenuous contact with their platoons, often for days at a time. The situation where one French machine-gun section found itself holding a hole in the front two hundred yards wide with its two machine guns for several days in complete detachment from the rest of the army, was by no means unique. To add to this demoralizing sense of isolation, the tenacious curtain of smoke from the bombardment meant that the front line frequently could not see the supporting troops behind; nor, worse still, could their rockets of supplication asking for the artillery to bring down a barrage, or cease shelling their own positions, be seen at the rear. Countless were the true heroes of Verdun, fighting small Thermopylaes[11] in the shellholes, who remained unsung and undecorated because no one witnessed their deeds.

> After twenty months of fighting, where twenty times I should have died [Raymond Jubert admitted] I have not yet seen war as I imagined it. No; none of those grand tragic tableaux, with sweeping strokes and vivid colours, where death would be a stroke, but these small painful scenes, in obscure corners, of small compass where one cannot possibly distinguish if the mud were flesh or the flesh were mud.

Of all the participants qualifying for the title of hero at Verdun, probably none deserved it more than three of the most humble categories: the runners, the ration parties, and the stretcher-bearers. As a regular lieutenant in charge of the divisional runners at Souville stated, simply: 'The bravery of the man isolated in the midst of danger is the true form

---

[11]Thermopylae was a small mountain pass in Greece where the Persians in 480 B.C. annihilated a Spartan army to the last man.

of courage.' With telephone lines no sooner laid than torn up by shell-fire, and the runner become the sole means of communication at Verdun, the most frequently heard order at any H.Q. was 'send two runners'. From the relative protection of their holes, the infantry watched in silent admiration at the blue caps of the runners bobbing and dodging among the plumes of exploding T.N.T. It was an almost suicidal occupation. Few paths were not sign-posted by their crumpled remains, and on the Mort Homme one regiment lost twenty-one runners in three hours.

Perhaps demanding even more courage, though, was the role of the *cuistot*,[12] *ravitailleur*,[13] or *homme-soupe*,[14] as the ration parties were variously called, in that it was played out in the solitariness of night.

> Under danger, in the dark, one feels a kind of particular horror at finding oneself alone. Courage requires to be seen [noted Jubert]. To be alone, to have nothing to think about except oneself . . . to have nothing more to do than to die without a supreme approbation! The soul abdicates quickly and the flesh abandons itself to shudders.

On account of the shelling, motor transport could approach no closer than a cross-roads nicknamed 'Le Tourniquet'[15] at the end of the *Voie Sacrée*.[16] The massacre of the horses, unable to take cover upon the warning whistle of a shell, had become prohibitive. Thus all rations for the men at the front had to come up on the backs of other men. The *cuistots*, three or four to a company, were generally selected from among the elderly, the poor shots, and the poor soldiers. One of the most moving pictures printed in *L 'Illustration*[17] during the war was of one of these unhappy *cuistots* crawling on his stomach to the front at Verdun, with flasks of wine lashed to his belt. Each carried a dozen of the heavy flasks, and a score of loaves of bread strung together by string, worn like a bandolier. They often made a round trip of twelve miles every night; even though, bent under their loads, at times they could barely crawl, let alone walk, in the glutinous mud. The arrived, collapsing from fatigue, only to be cursed by comrades, desperate from hunger and thirst, on finding that the flasks of precious *pinard*[18] had been punctured by shell fragments, the bread caked with filth. Frequently they never arrived. Fixed enemy guns fired a shell every two or three minutes on each of the few well-known routes with the accuracy of long practice. . . .

[12]Cook.
[13]Carrier of supplies.
[14]Soup man.
[15]The turnstile.
[16]The "Sacred Way," the road that took the French soldiers to Verdun.
[17]A French newspaper.
[18]Wine.

For all the gallantry and self-sacrifice of the *cuistots*, hunger and thirst became regular features at Verdun, adding to the sum of misery to be endured there. Twenty-two-year-old Second-Lieutenant Campana notes how he dispatched a ration party of eight men one night in March. The following morning five came back—without rations. That night another eight set out. None returned. The next night some hundred men from all companies set forth, but were literally massacred by violent gunfire. After three days without food, Campana's men were reduced to scavenging any remnants they could find upon the bodies lying near their position. Many had been decomposing for several weeks. The experience was more the rule than the exception; so too, as winter sufferings gave way to a torrid summer, was this spectacle:

> I saw a man drinking avidly from a green scum-covered marsh, where lay, his black face downward in the water, a dead man lying on his stomach and swollen as if he had not stopped filling himself with water for days. . .

Worst of all was the lot of the stretcher-bearers, which usually fell—until the supply was used up—to the regimental musicians. The two-wheeled carts that comprised the principal means of transporting the wounded on other French sectors proved quite useless over the pock-ridden terrain at Verdun; the dogs used to sniff out the wounded went rabid under the shelling. Unlike the runners or the *cuistots*, when carrying a wounded man the unhappy *musiciens-brancardiers* [19] could not fling themselves to the ground each time a shell screamed overhead. Often the demands simply exceeded what human flesh could obey. Response to pleas for volunteers to carry the wounded was usually poor, and the troops at Verdun came to recognize that their chances of being picked up, let alone brought to medical succour, were extremely slim.

During the Second World War, there were cases when the morale of even veteran British Guardsmen suffered if, in the course of an action, they were aware that surgical attention might not be forthcoming for at least five hours. On most Western battlefields, it was normally a matter of an hour or two. Surgical teams and nursing sisters, copiously provided with blood plasma, sulfa-drugs, and penicillin, worked well forward in the battle area, so that a badly wounded man could be given emergency treatment without having to be removed along a bumpy road to hospital. For the more serious cases, there was air transport direct to base hospital, possibly hundreds of miles to the rear. In contrast, at Verdun a casualty—even once picked up—could reckon himself highly fortunate if he received any treatment within twenty-four hours. During the desperate days of July, the wounded lingered in the foul, dark, excrement-ridden vaults of Fort Souville for over six days before they could be evacuated.

---

[19]Musician–stretcher-bearers.

Poorly organized as were the French medical services, demand far outstripped supply almost throughout the war, but several times at Verdun the system threatened to break down altogether. There were never enough surgeons, never enough ambulances, of course no 'wonder drugs', and often no chloroform with which to perform the endless amputations of smashed limbs. If a casualty reached the clearing station, his ordeals were by no means over. Georges Duhamel, a doctor at Verdun . . . , vividly describes the chaos in one of these primitive charnel houses in 'La Vie des Martyrs'.[20] Arriving during the early stages of the battle, he noted in despair, 'there is work here for a month.' The station was overflowing with badly wounded who had already been waiting for treatment for several days. In tears they beseeched to be evacuated; their one terror to be labelled 'untransportable'. These, not merely the hopelessly wounded, but those whose wounds were just too complicated for the frantic surgeons to waste time probing, or who looked as if they would be little use to the army again, were laid outside in the bitter cold. It was not long before German shells landed among this helpless pile, but at least this reduced the doctors' work. Inside, the surgeons, surrounded by dustbins filled with lopped-off limbs, did the best they could to patch up the ghastly wounds caused by the huge shell splinters.

Later Duhamel and his team were visited by an immaculate Inspector-General who told them they really ought to plant a few flowers around the gloomy station. As he left, Duhamel noticed that someone had traced 'Vache'[21] in the dust on the brass-hat's car.

At the clearing stations the backlog of even the partially repaired mounted alarmingly as, with the constant demand of the *Voie Sacrée* supply route, all too few vehicles could be spared for use as ambulances. British Red Cross sections appeared on the front . . . and later American volunteers. Though the crews drove twenty-four hours at a stretch, unable to wear gasmasks because they fogged up, still there seemed to be more wounded than the ambulances could hold. Meanwhile in the overcrowded, squalid base hospitals, those who had survived so far were dying like flies, their beds immediately refilled. Clyde Balsley, an American very badly wounded with the 'Lafayette Squadron', noted in contrast that

> the miracles of science after the forced butchery at Verdun . . . made a whole year and a half at the American Hospital pass more quickly than six weeks in the [French] hospital at Verdun.

The wounded in these hospitals lived in terror of the periodical decoration parades; because it had become a recognized custom to reward a man about to die with the *Croix de Guerre*.[22] Of slight compensation were

[20]*The Life of the Martyrs.*
[21]Swine.
[22]Military Cross.

the visits of the 'professional' visitors, such as the patriotic, exquisite, 'Lady in Green', described by Duhamel, who spoke inspiredly to the *grands mutilés*[23] of

> the enthusiastic ardour of combat! The superb anguish of bounding ahead, bayonet glittering in the sun. . . .

Equipment in these hospitals was hopelessly inadequate, but at Verdun the situation was exacerbated still further by the poisonous environment, virulently contaminated by the thousands of putrefying corpses. Even the medically more advanced Germans noted the frequency of quite minor wounds becoming fatal. Gas gangrene, for which an effective cure was not discovered till a few weeks before the Armistice, claimed an ever-increasing toll; during the April fighting on the Right Bank, one French regiment had thirty-two officers wounded of whom no fewer than nineteen died subsequently, mostly from gas gangrene. In an attempt to reduce infection of head wounds, Joffre[24] issued an order banning beards; the *poilus*[25] complained bitterly, and still the wounded died. After the war, it was estimated that, between 21 February and the end of June, 23,000 French alone had died in hospitals as a result of wounds received at Verdun. How many more died before ever reaching hospital can only be conjectured.

So much for the physical; and what of the spiritual effects of this piling of horror upon horror at Verdun? Many were affected like the young German student, highly religious and torn with doubts about the morality of war, who wrote home shortly before being killed at Verdun on 1 June:

> Here we have war, war in its most appalling form, and in our distress we realize the nearness of God.

As in every war men confronted with death who had forgotten, or never knew how, began to pray fervidly. Sergeant Dubrulle, the Jesuit priest, was revolted above all by the hideous indignities he had seen T.N.T. perpetrate upon the bodies God had created. After one terrible shelling early in the battle when human entrails were to be seen dangling in the branches of a tree and a 'torso, without head, without arms, without legs, stuck to the trunk of a tree, flattened and opened', Dubrulle recalls 'how I implored God to put an end to these indignities. Never have I prayed with so much heart.' But, as day after day, month after month, such entreaties remained unanswered, a growing agnosticism

---

[23]Badly disabled.

[24]Joseph Joffre (1852–1931), French commander in chief, 1911–1916.

[25]French soldiers.

appears in the letters from the men at Verdun. Later, on the Somme, even Dubrulle is found expressing singularly non-Catholic sentiments:

> Having despaired of living amid such horror, we begged God not to have us killed—the transition is too atrocious—but just to let us be dead. We had but one desire; the end!

At least this part of Dubrulle's prayer was answered the following year.

For every soldier whose mind dwelt on exalted thoughts, possibly three agreed with Sergeant Marc Boasson, a Jewish convert to Catholicism, killed in 1918, who noted that at Verdun 'the atrocious environment corrupts the spirits, obsesses it, dissolves it'.

Corruption revealed itself in the guise of brutalization. . . .

It was indeed not very exalting to watch wounded comrades-in-arms die where they lay because they could not be removed. One Divisional Chaplain, Abbé Thellier de Poncheville, recalls the spectacle of a horse, still harnessed to its wagon, struggling in the mud of a huge crater. 'He had been there for two nights, sinking deeper and deeper', but the troops, obsessed by their own suffering, passed by without so much as casting a glance at the wretched beast. The fact was that the daily inoculation of horror had begun to make men immune to sensation. Duhamel explains:

> A short time ago death was the cruel stranger, the visitor with the flannel footsteps . . . today, it is the mad dog in the house. . . . One eats, one drinks beside the dead, one sleeps in the midst of the dying, one laughs and one sings in the company of corpses. . . . The frequentation of death which makes life so precious also finishes, sometimes, by giving one a distaste for it, and more often, lassitude.

A period of conditioning on the Verdun battlefield manufactured a callousness towards one's own wounded, and an apathetic, morbid acceptance of mutilation that seem to us—in our comfy isolation—almost bestial. Captain Delvert, one of the more honest and unpretentious of the French war-writers, describes his shock on approaching the Verdun front for the first time, when his company filed past a man lying with his leg shattered by a shell:

> Nobody came to his assistance. One felt that men had become brutalized by the preoccupation of not leaving their company and also not delaying in a place where death was raining down.

In sharp contrast to the revolted and tortured Dubrulle, young Second-Lieutenant Campana recounts how, at the end of his third spell in the line at Verdun, he cold-bloodedly photographed the body of one of his men killed by a shell that hit his own dugout, laid open from the shoulders to the haunches like a quartered carcass of meat in a butcher's window.

He sent a copy of the photograph to a friend as a token of what a lucky escape he had had.

Returning from the Mort Homme, Raymond Jubert introspectively posed himself three questions:

> What sublime emotion inspires you at the moment of assault?
> I thought of nothing other than dragging my feet out of the mud encasing them.
> What did you feel after surviving the attack?
> I grumbled because I would have to remain several days more without *Pinard*.
> Is not one's first act to kneel down and thank God?
> No. One relieves oneself.

This kind of moral torpor was perhaps the commonest effect of a spell at Verdun, with even the more sensitive—like Jubert—who resisted the brutalizing tendency admitting to a congelation of all normal reactions. Jubert also recalls the man in his regiment who, returning from the front, was overjoyed to find his house on the outskirts of Verdun still intact; but, on discovering that all its contents had been methodically plundered, he simply burst into laughter.

To troops who had not yet been through the mill at Verdun, passing men whom they were about to relieve was an unnerving experience; they seemed like beings from another world. Lieutenant Georges Gaudy described watching his own regiment return from the May fighting near Douaumont:

> First came the skeletons of companies occasionally led by a wounded officer, leaning on a stick. All marched, or rather advanced in small steps, zigzagging as if intoxicated. . . . It was hard to tell the colour of their faces from that of their tunics. Mud had covered everything, dried off, and then another layer had been re-applied. . . . They said nothing. They had even lost the strength to complain. . . . It seemed as if these mute faces were crying something terrible, the unbelievable horror of their martyrdom. Some Territorials who were standing near me became pensive. They had that air of sadness that comes over one when a funeral passes by, and I overheard one say: 'It's no longer an army! These are corpses!' Two of the Territorials wept in silence, like women.

Most of the above accounts come from the French sources. For, compressed in their hemmed-in salient and hammered by an artillery that was always superior, maintained and succoured by organization that was always inferior, things were almost invariably just that much worse for the French. But, as time went on, the gap between the suffering of the opposing armies became narrower and narrower, until it was barely perceptible. By mid April German soldiers were complaining in letters home of the high casualties suffered by their ration parties; 'many would rather endure hunger than make these dangerous expeditions for food'. General von Zwehl, whose corps was to stay at Verdun, without relief, during the whole ten months the battle lasted, speaks of a special 'kind of psychosis' that infected his men there. Lastly, even the blustering von Brandis, the acclaimed conqueror of Douaumont[26] for whom war previously seems to have held nothing but raptures, is to be found eventually expressing a note of horror; nowhere, he declares, not even on the Somme, was there anything to be found worse than the 'death ravines of Verdun'.

[26]The major fortress at Verdun.

Inflation in Weimar Germany

ALEX DE JONGE

The most celebrated instance of prices spiraling out of control is the hyperinflation in Weimar Germany in 1923. At the outbreak of World War I, the dollar was worth four marks; by November 1923, a person would need four trillion marks to purchase one dollar. To put this unprecedented devaluation of Germany's currency into perspective, consider the Price Revolution of the sixteenth century. This great period of inflation began in Spain and prices rose highest there, approximately 400 percent over the course of the century. Contemporaries had difficulty understanding the causes, not to mention the effects of that increase—significant to be sure, but small compared to the hyperinflation of 1923.

The German inflation was much more rapid and, obviously, intense. What were the reasons behind the hyperinflation? The Nazis found it easy and comfortable to blame the allied powers of the First World War and the Treaty of Versailles. Why? Many Germans came to believe the Nazi interpretation. Why would they not? After all, a man who should have known better, the director of the Reichsbank, implemented a solution for inflation that would have been laughable had it not been ridiculous: the use of printing presses to churn out more and more currency.

Hyperinflation had profound effects upon the German social fabric. How did the hyperinflation cause social chaos? What were its effects on morality, on the Germans' sexual behavior? Was it a coincidence that virulent anti-Semitism appeared at this time? Alex de Jonge offers dramatic and often pitiable stories of the wreckage of lives that resulted from the economic disequilibrium. Yet some benefited from hyperinflation. Which groups suffered and which prospered? What ended the period of hyperinflation?

The year 1923 has a special and dreadful connotation in German history, for it was the year of the great inflation. If defeat, abdication and revolution had begun to undermine the traditional values of German culture, then the inflation finished the process so completely that in the end there were no such values left. By November 1918 there were 184.8 marks to the pound. By late November 1923 there were 18,000,000,000,000. Although the mark was eventually "restored," and the period of inflation succeeded by a time of relative prosperity for many people, life for anyone who had lived through the lunatic year of 1923 could never be the same again.

Alex de Jonge, *The Weimar Chronicle. Prelude to Hitler* (NY: New American Library, 1978), 93–105.

Such a cataclysmic loss of a currency's value can never be ascribed to a single cause. Once confidence goes, the process of decline is a self-feeding one. By late 1923 no one would hold German money one moment longer than it was really necessary. It was essential to convert it into something, some object, within minutes of receiving it, if one were not to see it lose all value in a world in which prices were being marked up by 20 percent every day.

If we go back beyond the immediate cause of hyperinflation—beyond a total lack of confidence in a currency that would consequently never "find its floor," however undervalued it might appear—we find that passive resistance in the Ruhr[1] was a major factor. Effective loss of the entire Ruhr output weakened the mark disastrously, encouraging dealers to speculate against it, since the balance of payments was bound to show a vast deficit. Confidence in the currency could only begin to be restored when resistance ended late in 1923.

It has been the "patriotic" view that reparations were also a significant factor. Certainly they constituted a steady drain upon the nation's resources, a drain for which it got no return. But reparations alone would not have brought about hyperinflation. There were still other causes. Sefton Delmer[2] believes that the true explanation lay in Germany's financing of the war. She had done so very largely on credit, and was thereafter obliged to run a gigantic deficit. There were other more immediate causes, such as a total incomprehension of the situation on the part of Havenstein, director of the Reichsbank. Failing to understand why the currency was falling, he was content to blame it upon forces beyond his control—reparations—and attempted to deal with the situation by stepping up the money supply! . . .

By October 1923 it cost more to print a note than the note was worth. Nevertheless Havenstein mobilized all the printing resources that he could. Some of the presses of the Ullstein newspaper and publishing group were even commandeered by the mint and turned to the printing of money. Havenstein made regular announcements to the Reichstag to the effect that all was well since print capacity was increasing. By August 1923 he was able to print in a day a sum equivalent to two-thirds of the money in circulation. Needless to say, as an anti-inflationary policy, his measures failed.

. . . Certainly [inflation] had its beneficiaries as well as its victims. Anyone living on a pension or on fixed-interest investments—the small and cautious investor—was wiped out. Savings disappeared overnight.

---

[1]Belgian and French troops occupied the Ruhr Valley early in 1923 because the Germans had not delivered coal as the reparations agreement stipulated.

[2]A German newspaper reporter.

Pensions, annuities, government stocks, debentures, the usual invest-ments of a careful middle class, lost all value. In the meantime big business, and export business in particular, prospered. It was so easy to get a bank loan, use it to acquire assets, and repay the loan a few months later for a tiny proportion of the original. Factory owners and agriculturalists who had issued loan stock or raised gold mortgages on their properties saw themselves released from those obligations in the same way, paying them off with worthless currency on the principle that "mark equals mark." It would be rash to suggest . . . that the occupation of the Ruhr was planned by industrialists to create an inflation which could only be to their benefit. Yet we should remember that Stinnes,[3] the multi-millionaire, had both predicted that occupation and ended up the owner of more than 1,500 enterprises. It should also be remembered that some businessmen had a distinctly strange view of the shareholder. He was regarded by many as a burdensome nuisance, a drag upon their enterprise. He was the enemy and they were quite happy to see him wiped out to their benefit. Inflation was their chance to smash him. Witness the behavior of a banker at a shareholders' meeting at which it was suggested he should make a greater distribution of profit: "Why should I throw away my good money for the benefit of people whom I do not know?"

The ingenious businessman had many ways of turning inflation to good account. Thus employees had to pay income tax weekly. Employers paid their tax yearly upon profits which were almost impossible to assess. They would exploit the situation of a smaller businessman, obliged to offer six to eight weeks of credit to keep his customers, by insisting on payment in cash. The delay between paying for the goods and reselling them eroded any profit the small man might make, while the big supplier prospered.

Whether or not the industrialists actually caused inflation, their visi-ble prosperity made them detested by an otherwise impoverished nation. Hugo Stinnes became an almost legendary embodiment of speculation and evil. Alec Swan[4] remebers how hungry Germans would stare at prosperous fellow countrymen in fur coats, sullenly muttering *"Fabrikbe-sitzer"* (factory owner) at them. The term had become an insult and an expression of envy at one and the same time.

Hyperinflation created social chaos on an extraordinary scale. As soon as one was paid, one rushed off to the shops and bought absolutely anything in exchange for paper about to become worthless. If a woman had the misfortune to have a husband working away from home and sending money through the post, the money was virtually without value

[3]Hugo Stinnes, speculator.

[4]An Englishman who lived in Germany during the 1920s.

by the time it arrived. Workers were paid once, then twice, then five times a week with an ever-depreciating currency. By November 1923 real wages were down 25 percent compared with 1913, and envelopes were not big enough to accommodate all the stamps needed to mail them; the excess stamps were stuck to separate sheets affixed to the letter. Normal commercial transactions became virtually impossible. One luckless author received a sizable advance on a work only to find that within a week it was just enough to pay the postage on the manuscript. By late 1923 it was not unusual to find 100,000 mark notes in the gutter, tossed there by contemptuous beggars at a time when $50 could buy a row of houses in Berlin's smartest street.

> A Berlin couple who were about to celebrate their golden wedding received an official letter advising them that the mayor, in accordance with Prussian custom, would call and present them with a donation of money.
>
> Next morning the mayor, accompanied by several aldermen in pic-turesque robes, arrived at the aged couple's house, and solemnly handed over in the name of the Prussian State 1,000,000,000,000 marks or one half-penny.

The banks were flourishing, however. They found it necessary to build annexes and would regularly advertise for more staff, especially bookkeepers "good with zeros." Alec Swan knew a girl who worked in a bank in Bonn. She told him that it eventually became impossible to count out the enormous numbers of notes required for a "modest" withdrawal, and the banks had to reconcile themselves to issuing banknotes by their weight.

By the autumn of 1923 the currency had virtually broken down. Cities and even individual businesses would print their own notes, secured by food stocks, or even the objects the money was printed on. Notes were issued on leather, porcelain, even lace, with the idea that the object itself was guarantee of the value of the "coin." It was a view of the relationship between monetary and real value that took one back five hundred years. Germany had become a barter society; the Middle Ages had returned. Shoe factories would pay their workers in bonds for shoes, which were negotiable. Theaters carried signs advertising the cheapest seats for two eggs, the most expensive for a few ounces of butter which was the most negotiable of all commodities. It was so precious that the very rich, such as Stinnes, used to take a traveling butter dish with them when they put up at Berlin's smartest hotel. A pound of butter attained "fantastic value." It could purchase a pair of boots, trousers made to measure, a portrait, a semester's schooling, or even love. A young girl stayed out late one night while her parents waited up anxiously. When she came in at four in the morning, her mother prevented her father from taking a strap to her by showing him the pound of butter that she had "earned." Boots were also highly negotiable: "The immense paper value of a pair of boots renders it hazardous for the traveler to leave them outside the door of his bedroom at his hotel."

Thieves grew more enterprising still in their search for a hedge against inflation.

> Even the mailboxes are plundered for the sake of the stamps attached to the letters. Door handles and metal facings are torn from doors; telephone and telegraph wires are stolen wholesale and the lead removed from roofs.

In Berlin all metal statues were removed from public places because they constituted too great a temptation to an ever-increasing number of thieves. One of the consequences of the soaring crime rate was a shortage of prison accommodation. Criminals given short sentences were released and told to reapply for admission in due course.

It was always possible that one might discover an unexpected source of wealth. A Munich newspaperman was going through his attic when he came upon a set of partly gold dentures, once the property of his grandmother, long since dead. He was able to live royally upon the proceeds of the sale for several weeks.

The period threw up other anomalies. Rents on old houses were fixed by law, while those on new ones were exorbitantly high. As a result in many parts of Germany housing was literally rationed. If one were fortunate enough to live in old rented property, one lived virtually free. The landlord, however, suffered dreadfully: to repair a window might cost him the equivalent of a whole month's rent. Thus yet another of the traditional modes of safe investment, renting property, proved a disaster. Hitherto well-to-do middle-class families found it necessary to take in lodgers to make ends meet. The practice was so widespread that not to do so attracted unfavorable attention suggesting that one was a profiteer. . . . Real property lost its value like everything else. . . . More telling is a famous song of inflation:

> *We are drinking away our grandma's*
> *Little capital*
> *And her first and second mortgage too.*

As noted in the famous and highly intelligent paper the *Weltbühne*,[5] the song picked out the difference between the "old" generation of grandparents who had scraped and saved carefully in order to acquire the security of a house, and the "new generation" for whom there could be no security any more, who "raided capital" or what was left of it, and

---

[5]The *World Arena,* a left-wing journal.

were prepared to go to any lengths to enjoy themselves. Where their parent's lives had been structured with certainties, the only certainty that they possessed was that saving was a form of madness.

Not all Germans suffered, of course. Late in 1923 Hugo Stinnes did what he could to alleviate the misery of his fellow countrymen by the magnanimous decision to double his tipping rate in view of the inflation. Along with rents, rail fares were also fixed and did not go up in proportion to inflation. Consequently, travel appeared absurdly cheap. Alec Swan recalls crossing Germany in the greatest style for a handful of copper coins. Yet even this was beyond the means of most Germans. A German train in 1923 would consist of several first-class carriages occupied entirely by comfortable foreigners, and a series of run-down third-class carriages crammed to bursting with impoverished and wretched Germans.

Although the shops were full of food, no one could afford it except foreigners. Germans often had to be content with food not normally thought of as fit for human consumption. In Hamburg there were riots when it was discovered that the local canning factory was using cats and rats for its preserved meats. Sausage factories also made much use of cat and horse meat. Moreover, . . . some of the most famous mass murderers of the age used to preserve and sell the meat of their victims in a combination of savagery and an almost sexual obsession with food that mythologizes much of the darkness and the violence that were latent in the mood of Weimar.

If 1923 was a bad year for the Germans it was an *annus mirabilis*[6] for foreigners. Inflation restored the sinking morale of the army of occupation; small wonder when every private found himself a rich man overnight. In Cologne an English girl took lessons from the *prima donna* of the opera for sixpence a lesson. When she insisted that in future she pay a shilling, the *prima donna* wept with delight. Shopping became a way of life: "All through that autumn and winter whenever we felt hipped we went out and bought something. It was a relaxation limited at home, unlimited in the Rhineland."

Germany was suddenly infested with foreigners. It has been suggested that the English actually sent their unemployed out and put them up in hotels because it was cheaper than paying out the dole. Alec Swan stayed with his family in a pension in Bonn. They had moved to Germany because life was so much cheaper there. . . .

To find oneself suddenly wealthy in the midst of tremendous hardship proved rather unsettling. Inflation corrupted foreigners almost as much as the Germans. The English in Cologne could think of nothing else.

[6]Extraordinary year.

They talked with sparkling eyes and a heightened color, in the banks, the streets, the shops, the restaurants, any public place, with Germans standing around gazing at them.

Scruples were on the whole overwhelmed by the sudden onslaught of wealth and purchasing power beyond one's dreams.

As Alec Swan put it:

You felt yourself superior to the others, and at the same time you realized that it was not quite justified. When we went to Bellingshausen, which was a sort of wine place near Königswinter, we would start drinking in the afternoon. I would always order champagne and my Dutch friend would shake his head in disapproval. We'd have two ice buckets: he with some Rhine wine and me with German champagne. It was really rather ridiculous for a chap of my age to drink champagne on his own.

Being as wealthy as that was an extraordinary feeling, although there were many things you couldn't get in Germany. It was impossible to buy a decent hat, for instance. But you could have any food you wanted if you could pay for it. I haven't eaten anything like as well as that in my life. I used to go to the Königshalle (that was the big café in Bonn) at eleven o'clock in the morning for a *Frühschoppen*[7] and a *Bergmann's Stückchen*, a large piece of toast with fresh shrimps and mayonnaise. For a German that would have been quite impossible.

I paid two million marks for a glass of beer. You changed as little money as you could every day. No, one did not feel guilty, one felt it was perfectly normal, a gift from the gods. Of course there was hatred in the air, and I dare say a lot of resentment against foreigners, but we never noticed it. They were still beaten, you see, a bit under and occupied.

My mother did buy meat for three or four German families. I remember I bought an air gun, and, when I grew tired of it, I gave it to my German teacher's son, with some pellets. Some time later the woman came to me in tears saying the boy had run out of pellets, and they could not afford to buy any more.

On another occasion Swan, all of twenty-two at the time, took the head of the Leipzig book fair out for a meal and looked on incredulously as the elderly and eminent bookseller cast dignity to the winds and started to eat as if he had not had a meal in months.

Stories of money changing and currency speculation are legion. *Bureaux de change*[8] were to be found in every shop, apartment block, hairdresser's, tobacconist's. An Englishman named Sandford Griffith remembers having to visit a number of cities in the Ruhr which had local currencies. He stopped at a dealer's to change some money, but when

---

[7]Lunchtime drinking.

[8]Foreign exchange offices.

he produced a pound note the dealer was so overcome by such wealth that he simply waved a hand at his stock of currency and invited the astonished Englishman to help himself. Foreigners acquired antiques and *objets de valeur*[9] at rock-bottom prices. A favorite trick was to buy in the morning with a down payment, saying that one would fetch the rest of the money from the bank. By waiting until the new exchange rate had come out at noon before changing one's money into marks, an extra profit could be made on the amount that the mark had fallen since the day before.

The population responded to the foreign onslaught with a double pricing system. Shops would mark their prices up for foreigners. It would cost a tourist 200 marks to visit Potsdam, when it cost a German 25. Some shops simply declined to sell to foreigners at all. In Berlin a . . . tax on gluttony was appended to all meals taken in luxury restaurants.

Foreign embassies were also major beneficiaries of inflation, giving lavish banquets for virtually nothing. Indeed the *Weltbühne* noted with great resentment the presence of foreign legations of nations so insignificant that they would never hitherto have dreamed of being represented in Germany. The spectacle of foreigners of all nations, living grotesquely well and eating beyond their fill in the middle of an impoverished and starving Germany did not encourage the Germans to rally to the causes of pacificism and internationalism. The apparent reason for their inflation was there for all to see, occupying the Ruhr.

The surface manifestations of inflation were unnerving enough, but its effect upon behavior, values and morals were to reach very deep indeed, persisting for years after the stabilization of the mark, right up to the moment when Hitler came to power. The middle class—civil servants, professional men, academics—which had stood for stability, social respectability, cultural continuity, and constituted a conservative and restraining influence was wiped out. A French author met a threadbare and dignified old couple in spotless but well-worn prewar clothes in a café. They ordered two clear soups and one beer, eating as if they were famished. He struck up a conversation with the man, who spoke excellent French and had known Paris before the war. "Monsieur," the man replied, when asked his profession, "I used to be a retired professor, but we are beggars now."

There was a general feeling that an old and decent society was being destroyed. If the year 1918 had removed that society's political traditions and its national pride, 1923 was disposing of its financial substructure. In response, people grew either listless or hysterical. A German woman

[9]Valuables.

told Pearl Buck[10] that a whole generation simply lost its taste for life—a taste that would only be restored to them by the Nazis. Family bonds melted away. A friend of Swan, a most respectable German whose father was a civil servant on the railways, simply left home and roamed the country with a band. It was a typical 1923 case history. Young men born between 1900 and 1905 who had grown up expecting to inherit a place in the sun from their well-to-do parents suddenly found they had nothing. From imperial officer to bank clerk became a "normal" progression. Such disinherited young men naturally gravitated toward the illegal right-wing organizations and other extremist groups. Inflation had destroyed savings, self-assurance, a belief in the value of hard work, morality and sheer human decency. Young people felt that they had no prospects and no hope. All around them they could see nothing but worried faces. "When they are crying even a gay laughter seems impossible . . . and all around it was the same . . . quite different from the days of revolution when we had hoped things would be better."

Traditional middle-class morality disappeared overnight. People of good family co-habited and had illegitimate children. The impossibility of making a marriage economically secure apparently led to a disappearance of marriage itself. Germany in 1923 was a hundred years away from those stable middle-class values that Thomas Mann[11] depicted in *The Magic Mountain*, set in a period scarcely ten years before. Pearl Buck wrote that "Love was old-fashioned, sex was modern. It was the Nazis who restored the 'right to love' in their propaganda."

Paradoxically, the inflation that destroyed traditional German values was also largely responsible for the creation of that new, decadent and dissolute generation that put Berlin on the cosmopolitan pleasure seeker's map, and has kept it or its image there ever since. It was no coincidence that 1923 was the year that the Hotel Adlon first hired gigolos, professional male dancers, to entertain lady clients at so much per dance. It was also a period when prostitution boomed. A Frenchman accustomed enough to the spectacle of Montmartre[12] was unable to believe his eyes when he beheld the open corruption of Berlin's Friedrichstrasse. Klaus Mann[13] remembers:

> Some of them looked like fierce Amazons strutting in high boots made of green glossy leather. One of them brandished a supple cane and leered at me as I passed by. "Good evening, madame" I said. She whispered in my ear: "Want to be my slave? Costs only six billion and a cigarette. A bargain. Come along, honey."

[10]An American writer, 1892–1973.

[11]German author (1875–1955) and winner of the Nobel Prize in literature in 1929.

[12]District in Paris.

[13]German writer, 1906–1949.

. . . Some of those who looked most handsome and elegant were actually boys in disguise. It seemed incredible considering the sovereign grace with which they displayed their saucy coats and hats. I wondered if they might be wearing little silks under their exquisite gowns; must look funny I thought . . . a boy's body with pink lace-trimmed skirt.

Commercial sex in Berlin was not well organized and was considered by connoisseurs to be inferior to that of Budapest, which had the best red-light district in Europe. But in Berlin there was no longer any clear-cut distinction between the red-light district and the rest of town, between professional and amateur. The booted Amazons were streetwalkers who jostled for business in competition with school children. . . .

Along the entire Kurfürstendamm powdered and rouged young men sauntered, and they were not all professionals; every schoolboy wanted to earn some money, and in the dimly lit bars one might see government officials and men of the world of finance tenderly courting drunken sailors without shame. . . .

At the pervert balls of Berlin, hundreds of men dressed as women, and hundreds of women as men danced under the benevolent eyes of the police. . . . Young girls bragged proudly of their perversion. To be sixteen and still under suspicion of virginity would have been considered a disgrace in any school in Berlin at the time.

Another visitor was struck by what he referred to as Berlin's "pathological" mood:

Nowhere in Europe was the disease of sex so violent as in Germany. A sense of decency and hypocrisy made the rest of Europe suppress or hide its more uncommon manifestations. But the Germans, with their vitality and their lack of a sense of form, let their emotions run riot. Sex was one of the few pleasures left to them. . . .

In the East End of Berlin there was a large *Diele* (dancing café) in which from 9 P.M. to 1 A.M. you could watch shopkeepers, clerks and policemen of mature age dance together. They treated one another with an affectionate mateyness; the evening brought them their only recreation among congenial people. Politically most of them were conservative; with the exception of sex they subscribed to all the conventions of their caste. In fact, they almost represented the normal element of German sex life.

. . . There was a well-known *Diele* frequented almost entirely by foreigners of both sexes. The entertainment was provided by native boys between 14 and 18. Often a boy would depart with one of the guests and return alone a couple of hours later. Most of the boys looked undernourished. . . . Many of them had to spend the rest of the night in a railway station, a public park, or under the arch of a bridge.

Inflation made Germany break with her past by wiping out the local equivalent of the Forsytes.[14] It also reinforced the postwar generation's appetite for invention, innovation and compulsive pleasure seeking, while making them bitterly aware of their own rootlessness. It is not surprising that cocaine was very much in vogue in those years. The drug was peddled openly in restaurants by the hat-check girls, and formed an integral part of the social life of Berlin.

Inflation was also taken as evidence that the old order was morally and practically bankrupt. Capitalism had failed to guarantee the security of its citizens. It had benefited speculators, hustlers, con men and factory owners. It had spawned Hugo Stinnes, but had done nothing for the common good. The need for an alternative system appeared universally self-evident, and until one came along the thing to do was to enjoy oneself, drink away grandma's capital, or exchange one's clothes for cocaine: a dinner jacket got you four grams, a morning coat eight.

Inflation and the despair that it created also acted as the catalyst of aggression. It was at this time that anti-Semitism began to appear in Berlin. An attractive German lady remembers walking through a prosperous suburb with a Jewish friend when someone called to her in the street, "Why do you go around with a Jew? Get yourself a good German man." In one sense she found it understandable. The ordinary German was very slow to adjust to the special situation of inflation, and in 1923 anyone who was not very quick on their feet soon went under. Jews were better at economic survival in such situations than were other Germans— so much so, she says, that by the end of inflation they had become terribly conspicuous. All the expensive restaurants, all the best theater seats, appeared to be filled by Jews who had survived or even improved their position.

One can imagine that Germans who had lost their own status might have resented the spectacle. One old conservative I spoke to added a second reason for the rise of anti-Semitism in a Prussian society which had traditionally been quite free of it. The arguments advanced are his own, and tell us something of his prejudices. He believes that the Weimar Republic was too liberal with regard to immigration from the East, admitting thousands of Jews from Galicia and the old Pale of settlement,[15] persons who, in his words, were "Asiatics, not Jews." They found themselves in a strange anonymous town, free of all the ethical restraints imposed by life in a small community where their families had lived for several generations. They tended therefore to abandon all morality as they stepped out of their own homes, morality being strictly a family affair. They would sail as close to the wind as the law would allow, for they had no good will, no neighborly esteem to lose. The gentleman in question is convinced that their mode of doing business during the

[14]A prosperous bourgeois family in novels by John Galsworthy (1867–1933).
[15]The Pale was an area where Jews were permitted to live in Russia.

inflation did a great deal to create or aggravate more generalized anti-Semitic feelings.

Yet precisely these immigrants were to prove a mainstay of the republic. An old Berlin Jew who had spent some time in prewar Auschwitz told me that it was just these Eastern Jews who offered the most active and effective resistance to National Socialism. They were activists where native Berliners, Jew and Gentile alike, were more inclined to remain on the sidelines.

Certainly the period saw a rise in pro-National Socialist feelings. The first Nazi that Professor Reiff[16] knew personally was a schoolboy in his last year. The young man's father, a small civil servant, had just lost everything through inflation, and as a result his son joined the party. Pearl Buck records the views of an antimonarchical businessman worried by inflation, who said of the Nazis: "They are still young men and act foolishly, but they will grow up. If they will only drop Ludendorff and his kind, maybe someday I'll give them a chance."

For many people, who felt that they had lost all zest for a life rendered colorless by war and poverty, who could see that they lived in a world in which *Schieber*[17] won and decent folk lost, a new ideology combining patriotism and socialist anticapitalism seemed to be the only viable alternative to a totally unacceptable state of financial chaos and capitalist *laissez-faire*. The shock of inflation had made people mistrustful of the past, immensely suspicious of the present, and pathetically ready to have hopes for the future. It was perfectly clear to them that new solutions were needed, equally clear that until such solutions should appear they could put their trust in nothing except the validity of their own sensations.

The mood of the inflationary period . . . endured well beyond inflation itself to become the mood of the Weimar age, a blend of pleasure seeking, sexual and political extremism, and a yearning for strange gods.

> It was an epoch of high ecstasy and ugly scheming, a singular mixture of unrest and fanaticism. Every extravagant idea that was not subject to regulation reaped a golden harvest: theosophy, occultism, yogism and Paracelcism.[18] Anything that gave hope of newer and greater thrills, anything in the way of narcotics, morphine, cocaine, heroin found a tremendous market; on the stage incest and parricide, in politics communism and fascism constituted the most favored themes.

It was indeed a time for the revaluation of all (devalued) values.

The mood of 1923 persisted long after inflation ended, which is why

---

[16]Professor of Economics who lived in Berlin during the Weimar period.

[17]Profiteers.

[18]Doctrines associated with the Swiss physician and alchemist, Paracelsus (1493–1541).

the manner of its ending is offered here as a postscript, for nothing was restored but the currency.

Restoration of confidence was only possible when passive resistance in the Ruhr ended in the autumn of 1923. At the same time, the Reichsbank appointed Hjalmar Schacht to deal with inflation. He was an extremely able man with a clear grasp of essentials. He realized that his main problem was to restore confidence both within and without Germany, and to try to prevent people from spending money as soon as it came into their hands. He established a new currency, based on the notional sum total of Germany's agricultural wealth, the *Roggen-Mark* (rye mark). This had the effect of restoring psychological confidence in the currency. He combined the move with a gigantic bear trap laid by the Reichsbank to catch the speculators who would regularly build up huge short positions in marks, in the almost certain expectation that the mark would continue to fall against the dollar: i.e., they sold marks they hadn't got, knowing that they could buy them for a fraction of their present value when the time came to meet the demand. When the mark stopped falling, thanks to the Reichsbank's engineering, they had to rush to close their positions, and were forced to buy marks which had actually begun to go up. Many speculators lost the entire fortunes which they had built up over the year.

Schacht's measures sufficed to stop the rot, but in the period between the ordnance declaring the new currency and the appearance of the first notes, there was an interim of pure chaos in which, as Lord d'Abernon noted, "four kinds of paper money and five kinds of stable value currency were in use. On November 20, 1923, 1 dollar = 4.2 gold marks = 4.2 trillion paper marks. But by December the currency was stable." The last November issue of the weekly *Berliner Illustrirter Zeitung*[19] cost a billion marks, the first December issue 20 pfennigs. Confidence seemed to have been restored overnight. Germany could breathe again. . . .

---

[19]The *Berlin Illustrated Newspaper.*

Violence and Terror in Twentieth-Century Ireland: IRB and IRA

MICHAEL LAFFAN

During the Middle Ages, many social and political groups had recourse to violence to attain their aims; the right to use force was not restricted to one particular group or institution. Beginning in early modern Europe, the emerging nation states gradually achieved recognition as the sole and legitimate source of violence. National systems of justice and taxation diminished the strength of local loyalties and curbed the power of the nobility, thereby instilling a national consciousness that in the nineteenth century became full-blown patriotism. Central governments relied on armies and police to enforce their legitimacy. No longer could any nobleman or town claim the right to raise troops.

Despite the acceptance of the state's legal monopoly of force, the twentieth century has seen various social and political organizations resort to violence and terror to promote their goals. The paramilitary freicorps in Germany after World War I, the Ku Klux Klan in the United States, and the Palestine Liberation Organization are examples. Indeed, extra-legal terrorism has become part of daily existence in the modern world. Ireland, having the longest continuous history of terrorism in this century, is a case in point. In this essay, Michael Laffan traces the history of the Irish Republican Brotherhood and the Irish Republican Army, as well as their current successor, the Provisional Irish Republican Army. What have been the goals of these groups? Why have they felt it necessary to use violence? How did they select their targets? Why did they sometimes resort to indiscriminate violence? What is distinctive about the use of violence and terror by these small groups in Ireland? The IRB and IRA often lacked public backing for both their goals and methods, yet they claimed to speak for the Irish population. What arguments did they offer to defend their use of terror on behalf of a public that disagreed with them? How did they manage at times to secure popular acquiesence, if not wholehearted support? What myth served to legitimize and glorify the IRA?

The legal government, Great Britain, first fought the IRA in Ireland and today combats the Provisional IRA in Northern Ireland. What mistakes has the British government made? What strategies of the IRB and IRA met with success? Did these groups have a program for social reform, or were they only concerned with politics?

Laffan adroitly details the shifts in the fortunes of these Irish extra-legal

Michael Laffan, "Violence and Terror in Twentieth-Century Ireland: IRB and IRA," in *Social Protest, Violence, and Terror in Nineteenth- and Twentieth-Century Europe*, ed. Wolfgang J. Mommsen and Gerhard Hirschfeld (New York: St. Martin's Press, 1982), 155–173.

groupings. How did major events, such as World War I, the creation of the Irish free state, and World War II, affect the fate and politics of the IRA? Where do Laffan's sympathies lie? How, for example, does he feel about the Provinsional IRA? Does terrorism work?

Twentieth-century Ireland has had a long history of small groups using force to undermine the established order and overthrow the power of the state. Its experience has been unusual on two counts. With rare exceptions the aim of such groups has been purely nationalist and political, they have had little interest in ideological, social or economic questions; and, again with rare exceptions, they have belonged to what was effectively one organisation, the *Irish Republican Brotherhood* (IRB) and the *Irish Republican Army* (IRA). These bodies have successively (the IRB until 1916, the IRA since 1919) exercised a near monopoly of the use of violence on any large scale or with any consistency.

Other groups, such as the two *Ulster Volunteer Forces* (one between 1912 and 1914, the other since 1966) or the *Blueshirts* in the 1930s, have used force or the threat of force to further their objectives, and in the case of both the UVFs have achieved important results, but they have never seriously challenged the central role of the IRB/IRA. Agrarian unrest, often leading to violence and intimidation, was endemic until the 1930s but it was on a small scale compared with the land wars of the nineteenth century. Left-wing groups prepared to use force have appeared from time to time but, most notably in 1916 and the early 1930s, were subsumed into the nationalist movement, while with the exception of the great Dublin lock-out of 1913/14 industrial unrest has tended to be non-violent. In contrast, ever since its formation in 1858 the *Irish Republican Brotherhood* has planned or waged war on the British presence in Ireland.

This consistency of aim has been matched by flexibility of means. The forms which IRB/IRA violence have taken in this century have varied from a set piece rebellion in 1916, through widespread guerrilla warfare in 1920/21, civil war in 1922/23, a bombing campaign in England in 1939/40, attacks on British forces in Ulster in the 1950s and a terror campaign in the 1970s, to isolated outbursts of intimidation and assassination. Despite its 120-year-old suspicion of politics and politicians the IRB/IRA has occasionally co-operated uneasily with constitutional movements, though it has only been happy when playing a dominant role.

Since the 1790s when French revolutionary ideas inspired Irish radicals, Irish rebel and terrorist movements have been concerned almost single-mindedly with ending British rule in Ireland. From then until the withdrawal of British forces from most of the island in 1922 their objective was a simple one, however frequently other issues such as the struggle for the land might become enmeshed in the national, political question, sometimes sharpening and strengthening it, sometimes blunting and deflecting it. As will be argued below, with the establishment of the Irish Free State in 1922 and the relegation of those nationalists still living under British rule to the role of a beleaguered minority, the IRA's targets became more diffused.

Wolfe Tone, the father of Irish nationalism in the 1790s, denounced the connection with England as 'the never-ending source of all our political evils', and over a hundred years later one of his disciples declared that 'it is not bad government that ails Ireland, it is foreign government, and till foreign government is ended Ireland cannot prosper'. In the intervening century most Irishmen showed a remarkable consistency in their distaste for the British connection and the *Act of Union* of 1800,[1] associating them, sometimes fairly, with British exploitation and duplicity. In the course of the nineteenth century the removal of other grievances, economic, social and religious, merely focussed attention on the fact that most Irishmen felt different from Englishmen and wanted to have a much louder voice in running their own affairs. Ireland developed a tradition of discontent, although as far as the great majority was concerned this was far from being a tradition of insurrection.

The proclamation of the Irish Republic in Easter Week 1916 referred to the Irish people having risen 'six times during the past three hundred years'. The first two such risings, in 1641 and 1690, could be fitted into such a pattern only with considerable difficulty, the third, in 1798, was a major catastrophe in which as many as 30,000 may have perished, while the remaining three, in 1803, 1848 and 1867 were botched, pathetic farces.

In the long run, for those who demanded Ireland's separation from Britain, this record of failure was unimportant. What mattered to them was that subjection to British rule was not accepted passively, that there was a tradition of resistance, and that they themselves should carry on the tradition. The dead hand of the past pointed out to the living what their task must be. In the peroration of the most famous of his speeches Pearse,[2] twentieth-century Ireland's leading exponent of the nationalist tradition, proclaimed that 'life springs from death; and from the graves of patriot men and women spring living nations. . . . they have left us our Fenian[3] dead, and while Ireland holds these graves Ireland unfree shall never be at peace'. Soon afterwards he was to argue 'that the national demand of Ireland is fixed and determined; that that demand has been made by every generation; that we of this generation receive it as a trust

---

[1]Merger of the kingdoms of Great Britain and Ireland into the United Kingdom.

[2]Padraig Pearse (1879–1916) was a leader of the 1916 Easter Rebellion, after which the British executed him.

[3]Referring to the IRB.

from our fathers; that we are bound by it; that we have not the right to alter it or to abate it by one jot or tittle'. Two years later de Valera[4] told his followers 'Sinn Fein[5] wished to keep the people true to the ideals sanctified by the blood of twenty-five generations—ideals which the mass of the Irish people at no time really compromised'.

Historically this was utter rubbish, politically it was a powerful myth which legitimised and ennobled the activities of the IRA and its political counterpart, *Sinn Fein*. Most of the country was prepared to follow the moderate *Irish Parliamentary Party* and seek its limited goals, and until after 1916 views such as those expounded by Pearse and de Valera were held only by a small minority—but they were held passionately and fiercely. To this minority compromise was anathema, politics and Irish politicians were suspect, and they believed firmly that the British government, always treacherous in its dealings with Ireland, would yield only to force. These men plotted, talked or dynamited, or else waited for the time when they or their successors in the next generation could strike again. From 1858 onwards most of them were members of the secret *Irish Republican Brotherhood* which sought a fully independent Irish republic and regarded force as the only means of bringing this about.

By the early years of this century the IRB had fallen on hard times. The most recent rebellion receded further into the past, the organisation was infiltrated by government spies, numbers and morale were falling, and the Land Acts[6] were bringing about a social revolution in Ireland while the political revolution remained as far away as ever; in fact the removal of so many material grievances—the policy of 'killing Home Rule[7] with kindness'—seemed likely to blunt the demand for separation and independence. There was no sign that the Irish people were prepared to follow radical leaders using radical means. The situation worsened after 1910 when the Liberal government, dependent on Irish votes in the House of Commons, committed itself to the prompt introduction of *Home Rule*. For many IRB men this lack of widespread support, this clear absence of a pre-revolutionary situation, were reasons enough for postponing indefinitely any new rising; all the more when one clause of the 1873 IRB constitution declared that the organisation should 'await the decision of the Irish Nation, as expressed by a majority of the Irish people, as to the fit hour of inaugurating war against England'. This was an extraordinary self-denying ordinance for a revolutionary body, and it reflected awareness that lack of public support had helped doom earlier insurrections. . . .

[4]Eamon de Valera (1882–1975), later Prime Minister of Ireland.

[5]"Ourselves Alone," Irish nationalist party, founded in 1905.

[6]Series of acts that reformed the system of land tenure and ultimately allowed many peasants to gain ownership of land.

[7]Limited independence for Ireland.

About this time,[8] however, the IRB's fortunes began to revive. The key figures in this development were Tom Clarke, a middle-aged veteran of the dynamite campaign of the 1880s and of a subsequent 15-year penal sentence, and two young Ulstermen, Bulmer Hobson and Denis McCullough. They began purging the hive of drones, and the story has it that McCullough even forced out his own father. Soon the IRB was better placed to avail of improving circumstances, and by 1912 its numbers had increased to over 1500.

The opportunity for action came from an unlikely source. The Ulster unionists, who dreaded the prospect of subjection to a Catholic-dominated *Home Rule* parliament in Dublin and were unreconciled by the limited powers such a parliament would enjoy, formed their own private army, the *Ulster Volunteers*, and threatened to rebel against the Crown so that they might remain the Crown's most loyal subjects. Their leader Sir Edward Carson declared 'we will shortly challenge the Government to interfere with us if they dare, and we will with equanimity await the result . . . They may tell us if they like that that is treason. It is not for men who have such stakes as we have to trouble about the cost.' His claim that the government would not dare to interfere with what was illegal was vindicated; it temporised and compromised.

This action by their deadly enemies appealed to the imagination of many Irish nationalists both inside and outside the ranks of the IRB, it made physical force once more respectable, made it seem daring, heroic and successful. Carson brought guns back into Irish life, and the IRB was determined that some of the guns should be in its hands. At the IRB's instigation a rival *Irish National Volunteer* force was formed in November 1913. . . . Within a short time the Irish Volunteers' numbers had risen to about 180,000, and small quantities of arms were provided for them.

The formation of a private army under IRB influence was followed closely by the outbreak of war in Europe, and this provided a further incentive to action. A key group within the IRB . . . decided that as in the past 'England's difficulty was Ireland's opportunity' and that a rebellion must be staged while Britain was distracted by war with Germany. . . . The awkward facts that in economic terms Ireland did well out of the war, and that spreading disillusionment with the Irish Parliamentary Party was not transformed into support for a rising, did nothing to deter men like Pearse and Clarke who felt that they, rather than the majority of the population, recognised and represented the national will.

Although they prepared the rising carefully and secretly and were naturally anxious to maximise its chances of success, the rebels did not regard success as essential. When at a late stage their plans miscarried, an arms shipment from Germany was intercepted, Volunteer leaders outside

[8]1908.

the plot learned of it and tried to stop the insurrection, and it became clear that the British authorities were on their guard, they went ahead even though they knew that . . . 'we are going out to be slaughtered'. For most of them their determination that a rebellion should take place, that their generation should not betray the tradition of the 'protest in arms', was the most important consideration. Pearse, the rebel commander-in-chief, courted martyrdom.

Only about 1,500 Irish Volunteers fought for the newly-proclaimed Irish Republic, and apart from a few incidents in the countryside the rising was confined to Dublin. 450 people were killed and 2,500 wounded. Initially it was rejected with horror by the great mass of the Irish population, a common reaction being 'the British will never grant Home Rule now!' When the rebels surrendered and were marched off under arrest Dublin housewives rushed into the streets with food and drink, not for the prisoners, but for their guards. Gradually opinion changed. Realisation that the rebels had fought bravely and honourably and that the rising had not been an ignominious fiasco like its predecessors inspired pride as well as condemnation. . . . As the leaders of the rising had intended, the Irish people were jolted out of their complacency and were forced to re-examine tactics—violence and rebellion—which they had come to associate with unhappy phases of the past.

Even more than the fighting itself, the government's response swung public opinion behind the rebels and helped redeem the tarnished image of violence. Over three thousand people were arrested, many of them having little or no sympathy with the insurrection. Sixteen men were executed, a few at a time, over a period of ten days. The result was instant canonisation. . . .

The Easter rising was itself partly the result of a myth, of a distorted image of Ireland forever renewing the struggle against British oppression. Its leaders soon became mythological figures themselves, their images sacrosanct and inviolable. Their cult still thrives. Within a short time not only the young but also the staid and the cautious began to gloss over their initial opposition to the rising and to give it their retrospective support, even veneration.

This development is one of the most important in modern Irish history. A small group of men, deciding that they represented the national interest and the national will, struck against the system supported, or at least accepted, by the overwhelming majority of the people. After their deaths their aims and methods won widespread approval. This posthumous success inspired others to emulate their achievement, and it has been the model for all subsequent Irishmen committed to the use of violence. Today the *Provisional IRA* likes to see itself as following the example given by Clarke and Pearse, confident that public opinion will support it eventually, however belatedly. Another objective of later rebels and terrorists, also modelled on the pattern of 1916 and also successful at times, was to force the government of the day into such repressive measures that the repression would seem, and would be, an even greater evil than the initial provocation; the public's resentment would shift from the IRA to the government. Their traditional dislike of alien rule had led the Irish people to sympathise with those who defied authority and the IRA could benefit from the national tendency to be 'agin' the government'.

However successful the rising had been in transforming Irish opinion, in military terms it was a failure and for the rest of the Great War it was clear that another rebellion was impossible. It was also unnecessary. From a military standpoint the best way to pursue the struggle begun in 1916 would be to consolidate and build on the newly won public sympathy so that when the time came for the next round Ireland would experience a genuine national uprising. One immediate problem was that the obvious means for doing this were repugnant to many of the rebels. When *Sinn Feiners* in Ireland decided to contest by-elections as a way of building up an organisation and arousing support and enthusiasm, the surviving imprisoned Volunteer leaders were hostile. They had long regarded politics as a demeaning activity and, accustomed to disparaging their own generation, they were not prepared to put their trust in the electorate's change of heart. De Valera complained that 'we are not willing that what has been purchased with our comrades' blood should be lost on a toss throw with dice loaded against us', and when one of the prisoners was run—successfully—against the Irish Party candidate, he and virtually all his colleagues raised strong objections. Their supporters back home were not deterred, and they won a series of spectacular election victories. Their success disarmed the purists, even though many continued to regard politics with suspicion and to feel it was no more than a tactical expedient, a second-best to fighting. Nonetheless the Volunteers proved remarkably successful politicians, a mass *Sinn Fein* party was built up in 1917, and in the 1918 general election it eliminated the Irish Party. . . .

De Valera and other Volunteers were elected to the highest posts in the party, and de Valera soon showed himself temperamentally more of a politician than a soldier. The effective takeover of the political leadership by the fighting men was a return to an old Irish pattern in which violence and political activity often interacted on each other. On the whole the political and the military wings of the movement co-operated harmoniously, although the soldiers' contempt for mere politicians was matched by some *Sinn Feiners'* alarm at the Volunteers' bellicosity. . . .

The political phase which lasted throughout 1917 and 1918 overlapped with a steady revival of the Irish Volunteers (soon more widely known as the Irish Republican Army, or the IRA) and also, though on a small scale, of the IRB. In the eyes of most of the Volunteers the establishment of a large-scale force committed to rebellion made a secret society like the IRB redundant, and many were influenced by the Catholic Church's hostility towards secret societies. Nonetheless the IRB survived, its head still nominally president of the Irish Republic (a title later to be enjoyed by de Valera after his election as president of the Dáil, the Irish parliament established by Sinn Fein MPs in January 1919). After the Easter rising the IRB played a relatively minor role and was significant mainly because Michael Collins, its guiding force, controlled so much else as well. From 1919 onwards the active units of the IRA, a small minority of the total, occupied a position comparable to that held for so long by the IRB and shared many of its claims and attitudes.

The Anglo-Irish war of 1919–21 was basically a guerrilla campaign in which the use of terror played an important part in removing dangerous enemies, weakening British morale and deterring civilians from helping the government forces. Unlike the Easter rising it was a modern war, dirty and ungentlemanly. Policemen were shot in Dublin streets and in country lanes. Most of the IRA's victims were, like their killers, Irish Catholics (the police suffered far more heavily than the army; in the two and a half years of fighting the losses were respectively 405 and 150). Many were well-known and popular in their neighbourhoods, and initially the normal response to what were seen as brutal and cowardly murders was revulsion and condemnation. *Sinn Feiners* felt that a few gunmen in Dublin and Tipperary were blackening the movement's good name. . . .

The war began on a small scale and escalated slowly; in the first eighteen months, from January 1919 to June 1920, only sixty members of the crown forces were killed. Gradually the IRA's scale of activities was extended. In November 1920 Collins's 'squad' killed twelve officers in Dublin, most of them engaged in intelligence work, while sixteen policemen were killed in a battle in Co. Cork. Over a hundred IRA men were captured after the destruction of the Dublin *Custom House*, the centre of local government, in May 1921. Isolated killings continued, sometimes representing the settling of private grievances rather than attacks on 'enemies of the Republic'. Assassination was not a policy characteristic of the IRA, although there were exceptions. . . .

The IRA was delighted by the government's response to its attacks, a response criticised by *The Times* as 'collective punishment'. When policemen and soldiers were ambushed the whole neighbourhood was often proclaimed a military district, fairs and markets were banned, curfews imposed, and the innocent were punished with the guilty. In retaliation for the killing of a policeman Limerick was subjected to military rule and to the imposition of permits needed for entering and leaving the city. The failure of a general strike in protest against these measures in no way diminished local resentment. There was little to choose between the terror imposed by the IRA and that imposed by the crown forces (the latter often in the form of 'official reprisals'), but the IRA had the double advantage of being the under-dogs and of being 'our lads'. Among many Irishmen, though certainly not all, the IRA acquired a romantic image which was enhanced by the panache and courage often shown in incidents such as prison escapes and arms raids. In late 1919 the police inspector general lamented that 'the general public is apparently prepared to suffer rather than condemn the criminal acts of the rebel fanatics'.

Long before the end of the war Irish public opinion had been radicalized yet again. After 1916 the government's clumsy response to the rising encouraged widespread support for the rebels' aims and a sympathy with the idea or the memory of violence. The reality of violence, when it returned in less romantic circumstances in 1919, shocked people initially, but once again the authorities' blind and indiscriminate reaction . . . closed the nationalist ranks behind the IRA. By and large people supported the IRA, or at least did not support the government, and fallen volunteers such as Kevin Barry were promptly incorporated into the republican mythology and became the heroes of ballads. . . . Between them, the IRA and the British government succeeded in identifying the IRA with nationalism and patriotism.

The authorities went to extreme lengths in polarising Irish opinion between the British army and the IRA. Late in 1919 the *Dáil*, the *Sinn Fein* party and other political bodies were banned. They continued to function underground, and particularly in 1920 succeeded in playing a significant political and administrative role in the conflict, but unable to act with their earlier effectiveness they could not rival the power and appeal of the IRA. . . .

Despite the important role played by the Sinn Fein politicians and administrators, ultimately it was the IRA, the flying columns in the South and Collins's squad in Dublin, which undermined British determination and drove Lloyd George's[9] government to the truce of July 1921 and the lengthy negotiations which followed.

The signing of a compromise treaty in December 1921 created new problems for the IRA. Until then its task had been uncomplicated—the achievement of an independent republican Ireland—and the means were the defeat of the British government and its agents. Even though the treaty conceded merely a Free State with a governor general representing the crown instead of an Irish Republic, and even though it left the island partitioned, it was good enough for the great majority of Irishmen who wanted nothing more than peace. The Church, the middle classes and the press were solidly in its favour. However most of the active units of the IRA were opposed to the treaty, as was a large minority of the political leadership (three out of seven members of the *Dáil* cabinet, including de Valera, and 57 out of 121 in the *Dáil*). The IRB command, probably through Collins's influence, threw its weight behind the settlement, although most of the rank and file were opposed to it.

Those who had been reared in the Fenian tradition, who had been 'out' in 1916 or else wished they had been, who had seen the change

[9]David Lloyd George (1863–1945), British Prime Minister, 1916–1922.

in public opinion after the rising, who had seen the people rally around those 'gunmen' who had been denounced at the beginning of the Anglo-Irish war, who had seen these gunmen extract concessions from the British which mere politicians could never have won, and who were yet dissatisfied with these concessions, could not be expected to accept a cabinet majority of one in favour of the treaty or a *Dáil* majority of seven. Later, in June 1922, popular endorsement in a general election also left them unmoved. Rejecting compromise they continued to demand a republic free of any formal connection with Britain. . . .

The section of the IRA which rejected the treaty now reverted to its normal role, that of a minority prepared to resort to arms to impose its vision of Ireland on the short-sighted majority. . . .

Collins, the most dangerous of all the 'gunmen', emerged as the chairman of the provisional government which began taking over power from the British in January 1922. Despite all his attempts to control the country it gradually slid towards anarchy, with rival groups of soldiers seizing barracks, munitions and strategic points. . . .

Full-scale fighting broke out in June, and with 1916 still in mind the anti-treaty rebels holed themselves up in buildings in Dublin and waited until they were blasted out. But this time, although a considerable minority of Irishmen opposed the treaty with passion there was no swing of public opinion in their favour. Soon the anti-treaty IRA was forced to retreat to the hills where it waged a guerrilla war. In the course of the fighting Collins was killed in an ambush.

The republicans refused to acknowledge the legitimacy of the *Free State*, and saw the members of the government as traitors and British agents; in return, they were viewed as anarchists, utterly negative and destructive. As the killing and devastation dragged on, both sides' ferocity increased, surpassing that of the recent fight against the British. The IRA launched an assassination campaign against members of the *Dáil* and in response the government began executing its prisoners. In all 77 were shot, three times the number executed during the Anglo-Irish war. Naturally this ruthlessness intensified existing opposition to the government and the treaty, but surprisingly it did not make such opposition more widespread; in general public opinion was prepared to acquiesce in executions and atrocities by an Irish administration which it would never have accepted from the British. For the third time in seven years the IRA had succeeded in provoking the government into repressive measures, but this time the tactic failed to mobilise support for the rebels. . . .

By early 1923 the IRA rebels were defeated but instead of surrendering they buried their weapons and waited for a suitable time to resume the struggle. This did not come about until 1939, the campaign was then abandoned within a year and the IRA had to wait until 1956 for the third round. This in turn petered out after five years, and not until the 1970s did the IRA again become a significant force. The heroic decade between the formation of the *Irish Volunteers* in 1913 and the end of the civil war in 1923 was followed by a return to the traditional policy of waiting patiently for better days.

The IRA regarded itself, with much justification, as heir to the IRB tradition. It was significant that it had retained its title, just as the republicans' political wing retained the name *Sinn Fein*, both of which had been abandoned by the majority who accepted the treaty. Their task was now much harder than it had been. The British had left most of Ireland, and in the six counties remaining under their rule nationalists of all kinds were outnumbered two to one by unionists. The citizens of the *Free State* seemed content with a government which did not share the IRA's zeal for a united Irish republic, and in the 1923 elections *Sinn Fein* won only 44 of the 153 *Dáil* seats. . . .

In the early 1920s the IRA was not a secret army, rather an open army defeated in the field whose members were known to the victorious government. It engaged in sporadic acts of violence . . . but these reflected frustration in the aftermath of defeat, not the beginning of a new campaign.

Relations between the IRA and the republican 'government' headed by de Valera worsened gradually. The anti-treaty politicians wanted power, but their policy of abstention from the *Dáil* doomed them to impotence. The IRA purists became suspicious that the *Sinn Feiners* might compromise their principles; in 1925 an army convention accused the republican government of developing into a mere political party and it set up an independent executive which was 'given the power to declare war'. . . .

In the course of the next two years de Valera and his more pragmatic colleagues left *Sinn Fein*, formed their own *Fianna Fail* party, entered the *Dáil* and became the official opposition, while the rump *Sinn Fein* went into a prompt decline and became no more than an adjunct of the IRA. De Valera and his followers were denounced as compromisers and traitors who had succumbed to the fatal lure of politics.

The 1920s witnessed a small but steady series of violent incidents. The IRA carried out arms raids, attacked and sometimes killed policemen who investigated them too closely, and later began intimidating prison warders, court witnesses and jurors. To a large extent these were spontaneous and uncoordinated measures and were often defensive in intent, designed to prevent the movement being destroyed by the *Free State* authorities. The IRA was not waging a campaign to bring down the *Cumann na nGaedheal*[10] government or the political system, much though it hated both. . . .

In the early 1930s the tempo of IRA attacks increased dramatically, illegal drillings, arms raids and assaults (several fatal) on the police became more common. The government was forced to adopt harsh

[10]Gaelic Party.

measures; the IRA and many allied organisations were banned, their members were rounded up in larger numbers and special military tribunals were established to try cases of politically motivated violence. This response to increased IRA provocation made the government look awkward and ridiculous as well as repressive and probably contributed to its defeat by *Fianna Fail* in the 1932 elections. In a way this could be seen as another success for the policy of goading the authorities into unpopular, self-destructive actions, but there were many other causes of their defeat. The impact of the Depression, *Cumann na nGaedheal's* bungled and negative campaign, *Fianna Fail's* superior organisation and the simple desire for a change all played a part.

The 1932 elections and the peaceful transfer of power to those who had been defeated in the civil war less than ten years earlier were decisive events in the consolidation of Irish democracy. They were also significant in the history of the IRA.

Most IRA men regarded de Valera as a renegade, but at least he had recently been a fellow-rebel against the treatyite government and he still shared their rhetoric and many of their views. . . . The ban on the IRA was lifted, the military tribunals were suspended and police surveillance was eased. De Valera intensified the previous government's policy of whittling away at the restrictions imposed on Irish sovereignty by the treaty, and one by one he removed its more obnoxious clauses. But he made it clear that he was going to move cautiously and peacefully, and he no longer talked about 'the Republic' which remained, along with reunification, the IRA's main objective.

IRA members were in a dilemma. De Valera was achieving many of their aims by peaceful means, and while they could and did reject his argument that with *Fianna Fail* in power they were no longer necessary, they realised there was no point in fighting another round against so sympathetic a government. Under the circumstances it is not surprising that the IRA was tempted to settle old scores, and applying the principle of 'no free speech for traitors' some of its members turned on the now powerless *Cumann na nGaedheal* party, attacking its leaders and disrupting its meetings. . . .

By 1933 de Valera, the poacher turned gamekeeper, was securely in power. In his new position he resented his former colleagues' lawlessness but he found it difficult to turn on them; after all, he had deserted them, not they him, and they still held many objectives in common. In its rejection of majority rule and democratic procedure the IRA was firmly in the 1916–19 tradition, and de Valera's support of the anti-treaty forces in 1922 showed that he shared the IRA's view that violence was justifiable against an Irish as well as against a British administration. . . . The IRA may have been a small minority but it was the direct successor of that other small minority whose resort to violence had established the state. Democratic politicians democratically elected occupied their positions because in 1921 the British had yielded to force when earlier they would not yield to reason. . . .

. . . Gradually the basic incompatibility between de Valera's methods and those of the IRA became clearer, especially when some IRA elements began flirting with socially radical ideas, involving themselves in land disputes and in attempts to stop government strike-breaking. Once again policemen who harried the IRA were killed, and the crisis came when the IRA alienated itself decisively from public opinion by acts of stupid brutality. In March 1936 in County Cork the retired Admiral Somerville, who had acted as referee for local men wanting to join the Royal Navy, was shot dead on his own doorstep by an IRA group which had taken literally authorisation by the local command to 'get him'. Not long afterwards a 'traitor' was killed. The government's much-criticised indulgence of the IRA came to an end, and within a short time it was banned and its leaders arrested. Police pressure increased as its sympathisers in the cabinet lost their patience, and by the end of the decade the IRA's situation was no better than it had been under the *Cumann na nGaedheal* government before 1932. De Valera was now seen as another British collaborator, even more dangerous than his predecessors in office.

Some IRA men felt that as long as the Republic or a United Ireland remained distant goals the organisation should concern itself with economic and social problems and that only in this way could they acquire a mass following. (A mass following, of course, was viewed by the leadership with grave suspicion; in that direction lay the danger of becoming yet another political party.) Throughout the 1920s and 1930s the more radical members of the IRA, in particular Peadar O'Donnell, tried to move the organisation to the left. . . . In 1934 the IRA radicals made another attempt to form a left-wing political party, the *Republican Congress*, but the army council opposed the move bitterly and warned that 'this Party will, in course of time, contest elections and enter the Free State Parliament'. . . . As had been the case with the mass *Sinn Fein* party in 1917, and even with the *Irish Parliamentary Party* before it, divisive issues which would distract from a single-minded concentration on nationalist objectives were suspected and condemned. First and foremost the IRA remained an organisation dedicated to resuming, some day, the struggle with Britain.

By 1937 the Irish political system had been consolidated and opponents as well as supporters of the treaty were quite content to work within the framework established in 1922. The *Free State* had been officially ended and the treaty had been so dismantled that only the formal acknowledgement of the 'republic' was missing; this step (delayed until 1949) lost much of its importance once the crown had been removed from the constitution. Attacking the Southern state no longer seemed worthwhile and from the late 1930s onwards the IRA began to concentrate on the continuing British presence in Northern Ireland.

All Irish nationalists, North and South, regarded partition as the latest example of British cunning, and the border itself as a blatant gerrymander. Few Irishmen could understand why Britain was so appalled by the prospect of a united Ireland containing a Protestant minority of 26 per cent and so satisfied with an artificial Northern Ireland containing a Catholic minority of 33.5 per cent. A justifiable sense of grievance at how Ireland had been partitioned between 1920 and 1925 helped lure many young men into the IRA's ranks, but for many years its attention was centred on the easier target in the South rather than on the North.

This relative neglect of the North is one of the main ironies of Irish history during the inter-war years; after all, as the imperfections of the *Free State's* position were gradually removed, one might have expected a concentration of energies in an effort to drive out the 'British occupying forces' from Ulster. But *Sinn Fein* and the IRA had always been weak in the North. . . . [F]or most of the 1920s and 1930s the Northern units of the IRA saw their role as a defensive one, protecting the Catholic minority against the Protestant majority. The violent riots of 1935 showed the necessity of such protection.

North or South of the border, no-one could deny that the IRA's record since 1922 had been pitiful. It had survived and preserved its much-valued continuity, and if circumstances should improve there were men prepared to utilise them. The more active spirits felt that this was quite insufficient, and that more drastic steps were called for. In the late 1930s these men won the day and, led by Sean Russell, took over the leadership of the organisation.

For years Russell had demanded an attack on Britain, arguing that this would both intimidate the British public into abandoning Northern Ireland and unite Irishmen behind the IRA. . . . Many of Russell's colleagues argued that Northern Ireland was a more natural as well as an easier target—after all, the IRA's grievance was the presence of British troops in Ulster, not in England. He paid no attention, purged his opponents, and went ahead with his plans. Apart from the Anglo-Irish war, Russell's bombing campaign in 1939–40 was to be the IRA's only sustained exercise in terror until the 1970s. It was an utter failure. The preparations, training and finance were all inadequate, little respect was paid to the master plan, and local IRA units in Britain decided on the targets. From January 1939 onwards bombs went off at electrical lines, power stations, left luggage offices, the London underground, banks, cinemas and other public places. . . . Care was taken not to attack individuals, and in the first seven months of the year, in the course of 127 attacks, only one person was killed and 55 injured. But in Coventry in August a bomb went off in the wrong place killing five people and injuring sixty. The British government introduced emergency legislation, Irishmen were deported and checks made on travellers between Britain and Ireland. The bombers were steadily rounded up (in separate raids the arrests included the 16 year-old Brendan Behan and his 77 year-old grandmother) and the campaign faded out in early 1940.

The outbreak of the Second World War created new difficulties for the IRA. De Valera was anxious above all to preserve Irish neutrality and he regarded the bombing campaign in England and the IRA's links with Germany as a grave embarrassment. This was compounded by a flamboyant, melodramatic coup in December 1939 when the magazine fort in the Phoenix Park in Dublin was raided and a million rounds of ammunition were seized. The government and the Irish army were mortified, but so were the local IRA commanders who could not cope with such an unexpected windfall. The government's response was immediate and effective—so much so that it is said more weapons and ammunition were recovered from raids on IRA arms stores all over the country than had been taken from the magazine. From then on the army and police were relentless in their attacks on the IRA. Its leaders were on the run until they were rounded up and imprisoned or interned; during the war over five hundred were interned and six hundred convicted under the *Offences against the State Act*, six IRA men were executed and three died as a result of hunger strikes. IRA action dwindled away.

The *coup de grace* came with the Stephen Hayes affair. Hayes succeeded Russell as chief of staff, but under the special wartime circumstances proved spectacularly ineffective—to such an extent that some of his more impatient and aggressive colleagues in the North decided that he was a British agent deliberately destroying the organisation. In June 1941 they kidnapped him, held him prisoner for ten weeks, tortured him, tried him and sentenced him to death, but allowed him to write out a lengthy confession, in the style of the Stalinist purges, before his execution. Hayes lingered over the extravagant details of this confession. Eventually he managed to escape and fled, his legs still chained together, to the sanctuary of a Dublin police station. He was safe from his former captors, but spent the rest of the war in prison. Once the full, farcical details were made public it was hard for people to view the IRA seriously any longer. The arrests continued and by the end of the war, for the first time, continuity in the IRA's leadership had been broken. De Valera, the rebel of the civil war, had done what the British and the *Cumann na nGaedheal* governments had been unable to do.

The postwar history of the IRA, which will be treated briefly, almost as a postcript, was one of mixed fortunes in which the problems and opportunities encountered in the 1920s and 1930s repeated themselves. The main change, mentioned above, was a new concentration on Northern Ireland. The lure of politics continued. In 1946 Sean MacBride, one of the most prominent IRA leaders of the inter-war years, formed a new party, and two years later joined in coalition with the survivors and successors of the 1920s treatyite government. As in 1932 there were short-term gains for the extremists when one of their former colleagues came to power, and the remaining IRA prisoners were released, but the fact remained that once again a republican had 'sold out', had recognised the status quo and its institutions.

Between 1956 and 1962 a new attack was launched against British forces in Ulster. By this time the benefits of the welfare state and the lessening of sectarian tensions had weakened Northern Catholics' faith both in a united Ireland and in the IRA as their protector, and significantly the driving force for the new campaign came from South of the border. Once again it proved a miserable failure. In the five years it lasted 18 people were killed (in gruesome contrast the total during the 1970s would be over a hundred times as great) and the IRA statement calling off the campaign admitted that 'foremost among the factors motivating this course of action has been the attitude of the general public whose minds have deliberately been distracted from the supreme issue facing the Irish people—the unity and freedom of Ireland'.

There followed, in the 1960s, a return to the minority position of the 1920s and 1930s, a flirtation with left-wing ideas. Attention turned to questions such as housing and trade union organisation, and the IRA gave its support to the civil-rights movement, but this attitude was dropped promptly when national and sectarian problems re-emerged at the end of the 1960s. In August 1969 the Catholics' old fears were revived as Protestant mobs attacked their ghettoes and rendered 3,000 of them homeless. The *Provisional IRA* was formed a few months later when the traditionalist rank and file, disenchanted with the way in which their leaders' pacifism and social conscience had led to the Catholic areas being undefended (and the embarrassing slogan IRA = I Ran Away) decided to revert to the time-honoured aim of driving the British out and reunifying the island. All questions of social reform would be left aside until those first objectives had been achieved. As ever, the fact that the revived IRA was soon rejected by most Irish nationalists, on both sides of the border, carried no weight; what was new in the 1970s was the IRA's inability to win any parliamentary seat in any election, North or South.

The *Provisional IRA* has shown a new ruthlessness which had been lacking in the half-hearted campaign of 1956–62, or in Russell's bombing attacks in 1939/40; lacking often in the Anglo-Irish war of 1919–21. No matter how much the IRA might be sustained by its long tradition its tactics have naturally more in common with those of modern terrorist groups such as Irgun,[11] EOKA,[12] the FLN[13] or the PLO[14] than with those

[11]National Military Organization, a Jewish movement organized in 1931 to create a Jewish state in what was then Palestine.

[12]National Organization of Cypriot Struggle, Greek Cypriot organization that intended to unite Cyprus with Greece.

[13]National Liberation Front, formed in 1954 to win Algeria's independence from France.

[14]Palestine Liberation Organization, conglomeration of Palestinian groups that aim to destroy Israel.

of its Irish predecessors. One former member describes the *Provisionals'* attitude most revealingly:

> The Army Council's first target was to kill thirty-six British soldiers—the same number who died in Aden.[15] The target was reached in early November 1971. But this, the Army Council felt was not enough: I remember Dave [O'Connell], amongst others, saying: 'We've got to get eighty'. Once eighty had been killed, Dave felt, the pressure on the British to withdraw would be immense. I remember the feeling of satisfaction we had at hearing another one had died.

However brutal and politically blind the *Provisional IRA* might be, however far removed its members are from the self-sacrifice of Pearse or the pragmatism of Collins, they remain unworthy heirs to an unbroken tradition going back to the mid-nineteenth century. Even their political obtuseness is a result of their divorce between Ireland and Irishmen, of their contempt for majority opinion and in particular for those who pander to majority opinion, politicians; and such attitudes have a long history in the IRB/IRA. However much ordinary Irishmen might disapprove of their actions, the mere fact that the *Provisionals* represent, however misguidedly, the present generation in the age-old fight against the British enemy has won them a certain sympathy; they are regarded as stupid and cruel, but their hearts are felt to be in the right place. . . .

Irish attitudes are ambivalent. The same person will deplore the *Provisionals* when they plant bombs in restaurants or kill children in crossfire, but applaud them when they escape from jail. Almost all non-unionist Irishmen regard British policy towards Ireland, at any period, with a well-merited distrust, and any movement which can identify itself with the long tradition of active opposition to the British presence in Ireland can draw on latent support.

As an Irish political scientist has argued,

> it seems reasonable to admit the claim of the Provisional IRA . . . as the true descendant of the unreconstructed Irish republican tradition of the mid-nineteenth century . . . they have a legitimacy of sorts . . . in politics you do not have to be illegitimate to be a bastard.

[15]Now South Yemen, independent of Great Britain since 1967.

The Nazi Camps

HENRY FRIEDLANDER

The Nazi death camps by themselves are sufficient to differentiate the twentieth century from all that had come before. The Germans murdered, with a callous equanimity that makes one shudder, approximately eleven million people. This figure does not include those killed in warfare, even the masses of civilians fallen victim to indiscriminate terrorist airplane bombardments or those civilians killed because of resistance to the Nazis. Historians use the term "Holocaust" to refer to the systematic extermination of the Jews, the primary target of Nazi barbarity. Of the eleven million killed in the German effort to "purify" Western civilization, six million were Jews and one million of those were children. What groups, besides the Jews, went to the Nazi camps? What was the difference between concentration camps and extermination camps?

Henry Friedlander explains that the camps before 1939, heinous though they were, did not match in numbers or brutality those after 1939, and especially those functioning after 1942. How exactly did World War II affect the development of the Nazi camps? Who ran the camps? How were they organized? What was life like at the camps for the prisoners who arrived there? What was the relationship between the camps and German industries? How did camps in Western Europe differ from those in Eastern Europe?

Why did the Nazis, after experimenting with various methods of exterminating masses of people, reach the conclusion that the killing centers provided the most effective means of attaining "the final solution"? What methods of murder did the Germans prefer at the death camps? How did Auschwitz, the best known of the camps, earn its infamous reputation?

The Nazis established camps for their political and ideological opponents as soon as they seized power in 1933, and they retained them as an integral part of the Third Reich until their defeat in 1945. During the 1930s, these concentration camps were at first intended for political enemies, but later also included professional criminals, social misfits, other undesirables, and Jews.

During World War II, the number of camps expanded greatly and the number of prisoners increased enormously. Opponents from all occupied

Henry Friedlander, "The Nazi Camps," in *Genocide: Critical Issues of the Holocaust*, ed. Alex Grobman and David Landes (Los Angeles: The Simon Wiesenthal Center, 1983), 222–231.

countries entered the camps, and the camps were transformed into an empire for the exploitation of slave labor. Late in 1941 and early in 1942, the Nazis established extermination camps to kill the Jews, and also Russian POWs and Gypsies. These camps had only one function: the extermination of large numbers of human beings in specially designed gas chambers. The largest Nazi camp, Auschwitz-Birkenau, combined the functions of extermination and concentration camp; there, healthy Jews were selected for labor and, thus, temporarily saved from the gas chambers. In this way, small numbers of Jews survived in Auschwitz and other Eastern camps. In 1944–1945, as the need for labor increased, surviving Jews were introduced into all camps, including those located in Germany proper.

In the United States, the term "death camp" has frequently been used to describe both concentration and extermination camps. It has been applied to camps like Auschwitz and Treblinka—killing centers where human beings were exterminated on the assembly line. But it has also been applied without distinction to camps like Dachau and Belsen—concentration camps without gas chambers, where the prisoners were killed by abuse, starvation, and disease.

Six Nazi concentration camps existed on German soil before World War II: Dachau, near Munich; Sachsenhausen, in Oranienburg near Berlin; Buchenwald, on the Ettersberg overlooking Weimar; Flossenbürg, in northern Bavaria; Mauthausen, near Linz in Austria; and the women's camp Ravensbrück, north of Berlin. Other camps like Esterwegen, Oranienburg, or Columbia Haus had existed for a few years, but only the permanent six had survived; they had replaced all other camps. Dachau opened in 1933, Sachsenhausen in 1936, Buchenwald in 1937, Flossenbürg and Mauthausen in 1938, and Ravensbrück in 1939.

These camps, officially designated *Konzentrationslager* or KL, and popularly known as Kazet or KZ, were originally designed to hold actual or potential political opponents of the regime. A special decree had removed the constitutional prohibition against arbitrary arrest and detention, permitting the political police—the Gestapo—to impose "protective custody" *(Schutzhaft)* without trial or appeal. The protective custody prisoners—mostly Communists and Socialists, but sometimes also liberals and conservatives—were committed to the camps for an indefinite period. The camps, removed from the control of the regular prison authorities, were not run by the Gestapo; instead, they were administered and guarded by the Death Head Units of the black-shirted SS *(Schutzstaffel)*,[1] a private Nazi party army fulfilling an official state function.

[1]Élite guard.

Reich Leader of the SS Heinrich Himmler appointed Theodor Eicke as Inspector of the Concentration Camps and Commander of the Death Head Units. Eicke had been Commandant of Dachau; he had built it into the "model camp." Eliminating unauthorized private murders and brutalities, he had systematized terror and inhumanity, training his SS staff and guards to be disciplined and without compassion. From the prisoners, Eicke demanded discipline, obedience, hard labor, and "manliness"; conversion to Nazi ideology was neither expected nor desired. Eicke issued rules that regulated every area of camp life and that imposed severe punishments for the least infraction. His petty rules were a perversion of the draconic training system of the Prussian army. This system accounted for the endless roll calls (the *Appell*), the introduction of corporeal punishment (the *Pruegelstrafe*), and the long hours of enforced calisthenics. The SS added special refinements to this torture: suspending prisoners from trees, starving them in the camp prison (the *Bunker*), and shooting them while "trying to escape." In this system, labor was only another form of torture.

When Eicke became Inspector, he imposed the Dachau system on all concentration camps. Every camp had the same structure; every camp was divided into the following six departments:

1. The *Kommandantur*. This was the office of the commandant, a senior SS officer (usually a colonel or lieutenant-colonel and sometimes even a brigadier general) assisted by the office of the adjutant. He commanded the entire camp, including all staff, guards, and inmates.

2. The Administration. The administrative offices were charged with overseeing the camp's economic and bureaucratic affairs. Junior SS officers directed various subdepartments, such as those for supply, construction, or inmate properties.

3. The Camp Physician. This office was headed by the garrison physician and included SS medical officers and SS medical orderlies. The camp physician served the medical needs of the SS staff and guards; he also supervised medical treatment and sanitary conditions for the inmates.

4. The Political Department. This office was staffed by SS police officers (not members of the Death Head Units), who were assigned to the camps to compile the dossiers of the prisoners and to investigate escapes and conspiracies. They took their orders from both the commandant and the Gestapo.

5. The Guard Troops. These were the military units assigned to guard the camp. Quartered in barracks and trained for combat, they served under their own SS officers. They manned the watch towers and the outer camp perimeter. Officially, they had contact with the prisoners only when they accompanied labor brigades as guards.

6. The *Schutzhaftlager*. The protective custody camp was the actual camp for the prisoners; surrounded by electrified barbed wire, it occupied only a small fraction of the entire camp territory. It was headed by a junior SS officer (captain

or major) as protective custody camp leader. He was assisted by the senior SS noncommissioned officer; this roll call leader *(Rapportführer)* supervised the day-by-day running of the camp. Under him, various SS men served as block leaders in charge of individual prisoner barracks and as commando leaders in charge of individual labor brigades.

The SS hierarchy of the protective custody camp was duplicated by appointed inmate functionaries. But while the SS were always called "leader" *(Führer)*, the inmate functionaries were called "elders" *(Aeltester)*. The chief inmate functionary, for example, was the camp elder, corresponding to the SS role call leader. The functionary corresponding to the block leader was the block elder, who was in charge of a single barrack. He was assisted by room orderlies, the so-called *Stubendienst*. The functionary corresponding to the commando leader was the *kapo* in charge of a single labor brigade. He was assisted by prisoner foremen, the *Vorarbeiter.* In large labor brigades with several *kapos*, the SS also appointed a supervising *kapo (Oberkapo)*. (The unusual title *kapo*, or *capo*, meaning head, was probably introduced into Dachau by Italian workers employed in Bavaria for road construction during the 1930s. During World War II popular camp language, especially as spoken by non-German inmates, transformed *kapo* into a generic term for all inmate functionaries.) In addition, inmate clerks, known as *Schreiber,* performed a crucial task. The camp clerk assisted the roll call leader and supervised the preparation of all reports and orders. Clerks also served in labor brigades, the inmate infirmary, and various SS offices.

Until 1936–1937, the prisoners in the concentration camps were mostly political "protective custody prisoners" committed to the camps by the Gestapo. At that time, the category of "preventive arrest" . . . was added to that of "protective custody." The Criminal Police, the Kripo, and not the Gestapo, thereafter sent large numbers of "preventive arrest prisoners" to the camps. These included the so-called professional criminals. . . . They were rounded up on the basis of lists previously prepared; later, the police simply transferred persons who had been convicted of serious crimes to the camps after they had served their regular prison terms. The Gestapo and Kripo also used preventive and protective arrest to incarcerate the so-called asocials, a group that included Gypsies, vagabonds, shirkers, prostitutes, and any person the police thought unfit for civilian society. Finally, the Gestapo sent to the camps those whose failure to conform posed a possible threat to national unity; this included homosexuals as well as Jehovah's Witnesses.

In the concentration camps, the inmates lost all individuality and were known only by their number. Shorn of their hair and dressed in prison stripes, they wore their number stitched to their outer garment (during the war in Auschwitz non-German prisoners usually had this number tattooed on their forearm). In addition, the arrest category of each prisoner was represented under his number by a color-coded triangle. The most common were: red for political prisoners, green for professional criminals, black for asocials, pink for homosexuals, and purple for Jehovah's Witnesses. Inmate functionaries wore armbands designating their office. The SS used mostly "greens" for the important offices, but during the war the "reds" often replaced them and in some camps even non-German inmates were appointed *kapos* and block elders.

Before 1938, Jews usually entered the camps only if they also belonged to one of the affected categories. In the aftermath of the *Kristallnacht*[2] in November, 1938, the police rounded up the first large wave of Jewish men. Approximately 35,000 Jews thus entered the camp system, but most were released when their families were able to produce valid immigration papers for them.

In 1938, after the roundups of criminals, asocials, Jews, and Jehovah's Witnesses, and after the waves of arrests in Austria and the Sudetenland, the camp population reached its highest point for the prewar years. But after the release of large numbers, it sank again to approximately 25,000 by the summer of 1939.

World War II brought substantial changes to the Nazi concentration camp system. Large numbers of prisoners flooded the camps from all occupied countries of Europe. Often entire groups were committed to the camps; for example, members of the Polish professional classes were rounded up as part of the "General Pacification Operation" and members of the resistance were rounded up throughout western Europe under the "Night and Fog Decree."[3] To accommodate these prisoners, new camps were established: in 1940, Auschwitz in Upper Silesia and Neuengamme in Hamburg; in 1941, Natzweiler in Alsace and Gross-Rosen in Lower Silesia; in 1942, Stutthof near Danzig; in 1943, Lublin-Maidanek in eastern Poland and Vught in Holland; in 1944, Dora-Mittelbau in Saxony and Bergen-Belsen near Hanover.

By 1942, the concentration camp system had begun to develop into a massive slave labor empire. Already in 1939, the SS had established its own industries in the concentration camps. These included the quarries at Mauthausen, the Gustloff armament works at Buchenwald, and a textile factory at Ravensbrück. During the war this trend continued; every camp had SS enterprises attached to it: forging money and testing shoes at Sachsenhausen, growing plants and breeding fish at Auschwitz, and producing fur coats at Maidanek. In addition, the SS rented out prisoners for use as slave labor by German industries. The prisoners were worked to death on meagre rations while the SS pocketed their

[2]"Night of the Broken Glass," Nazi anti-Jewish riots, 10 November 1938.
[3]Order issued 7 December 1941 to seize "persons endangering German security."

wages: Both SS and industry profited. I. G. Farben established factories in Auschwitz for the production of synthetic oil and rubber; Dora-Mittelbau was established to serve the subterranean factories of central Germany. However, the largest expansion came with the creation of numerous subsidiary camps, the *Aussenkommandos*. For example, Dachau eventually had 168 and Buchenwald 133 subsidiary camps. Some of these—like Mauthausen's Gusen—became as infamous as their mother camp. The growing economic importance of the camps forced a reorganization. Early in 1942, the Inspectorate of the Concentration Camps, previously an independent SS agency, was absorbed by the agency directing the SS economic empire. It became Department D of the SS Central Office for Economy and Administration (*SS Wirtschafts-Verwaltungshauptamt,* or WVHA); chief of WVHA Oswald Pohl became the actual master of the camps.

After 1939, the concentration camps were no longer the only camps for the administrative incarceration of the enemies of the regime. They lost their exclusivity to a variety of new institutions: ghettos, transit camps, and different types of labor camps. In eastern Europe, the German administration resurrected the medieval ghetto, forcing the Jews to live and work behind barbed wire in specially designated city districts. These ghettos served as temporary reservations for the exploitation of Jewish labor; eventually everyone was deported and most were immediately killed.

The Germans did not establish ghettos in central or western Europe, but a variety of camps existed in most occupied countries of the West. In France, camps appeared even before the German conquest. There the French government incarcerated Spanish Republican refugees and members of the International Brigade.[4] After the declaration of war, these camps received large numbers of other aliens: Jewish and non-Jewish anti-Nazi German and Austrian refugees; Polish and Russian Jews; Gypsies and "vagabonds." The largest of these camps was Gurs, in the foothills of the Pyrenees; others included Compiègne, Les Milles, Le Vernet, Pithiviers, Rivesaltes, and St. Cyprien. After the German conquest, these camps were maintained by the French and the inmates were eventually deported to Germany or Poland.

Most Jews from western Europe went through transit camps that served as staging areas for the deportations to the East: Drancy in France, Malines (Mechelen) in Belgium, and Westerbork in Holland. Theresienstadt, established in the Protectorate of Bohemia and Moravia, served the dual function of transit camp and "model" ghetto.

Captured Allied soldiers found their way into POW camps: the Oflags for officers and the Stalags for the ranks. Their treatment

---

[4]Foreigners who fought under the auspices of the Soviet Union for the Republicans during the Spanish Civil War.

depended in part on the status of their nation in the Nazi racial scheme. Allied soldiers captured in the West, even Jews, were treated more or less as provided by the Geneva Convention. Allied soldiers captured in the East, however, did not receive any protection from international agreements. Camps for Red Army POWs were simply cages where millions died of malnutrition and exposure. Prisoners identified as supporters of the Soviet system—commissars, party members, intellectuals, and all Jews—were turned over by the *Wehrmacht*[5] to the SS Security Police, who either shot them or sent them to concentration camps.

Labor camps had appeared immediately after the start of the war. Hinzert in the Rhineland was opened for German workers and was later transformed into a Buchenwald subsidiary for former German members of the French Foreign Legion. Similar camps appeared in Germany for workers imported from the East *(Ostarbeiter)* and in most European countries for a variety of indentured workers, such as those for Jews in Hungary.

Most important were the Forced Labor Camps for Jews in the East. Hundreds of these camps, ranging from the very small to the very large, were established in Poland, the Baltic states, and the occupied territories of the Soviet Union. These forced labor camps were not part of the concentration camp system, and they were not supervised by WVHA. Instead, they were operated by the local SS and Police Leaders, Himmler's representatives in the occupied territories. While executive authority rested with the SS Security Police, the camps could be run by any German national: police officers, military officers, or civilian foremen. Although the supervisors were always German, the guards were usually non-German troops. Some of these were racial Germans *(Volksdeutsche)*, but most were Ukrainians, Latvians, and other eastern European nationals recruited as SS auxiliaries.

Conditions varied from labor camp to labor camp. Some were tolerable and others resembled the worst concentration camps. Like the Jews in the ghettos, those in the labor camps were eventually deported and killed; some labor camps, like Janowska in Lemberg, also served as places for mass executions. Only a few camps, economically valuable for the SS, remained in operation. In late 1943, WVHA seized them from the SS and Police Leaders and turned them into regular concentration camps: Plaszow near Cracow in Poland, Kovno in Lithuania, Riga-Kaiserwald in Latvia, Klooga and Vaivara in Estonia; other camps, like Radom, became subsidiaries of these or older concentration camps.

World War II also changed the function of the concentration camp system. On the one hand, it became a large empire of slave labor, but on the other, it became the arena for mass murder. During the war, persons sentenced to death without the benefit of judicial proceedings

---

[5]The German military.

were taken to the nearest concentration camp and shot. Large numbers of inmates no longer able to work were killed through gas or lethal injections. Thousands of Russian POWs were killed in the concentration camps, while millions of Jews were systematically gassed in Auschwitz and Maidanek.

In 1943 and 1944, large numbers of Jews entered the concentration camp system. Many had been selected for labor upon arrival at Auschwitz; others had been prisoners in labor camps and ghettos that were transformed into concentration camps. These Jewish prisoners were retained only in the East. Germany itself was to remain free of Jews, and this included the camps located on German soil. But as the front lines advanced upon the Reich and the need for labor increased, Jewish prisoners were introduced into all camps, including those located in Germany proper. Eventually, Jews made up a large proportion of inmates in all concentration camps.

The end of the war brought the collapse of the concentration camp system. The approach of the Allied armies during the winter of 1944–1945 forced the evacuation of exposed camps. The SS transported all prisoners into the interior of the Reich, creating vast overcrowding. On January 15, 1945, the camp population exceeded 700,000. Unable to kill all the inmates, the SS evacuated them almost in sight of the advancing Allies. Inmates suffered and died during the long journeys in overcrowded cattle cars; without provisions and exposed to the cold, many arrived at their destination without the strength necessary to survive. Others were marched through the snow; those who collapsed were shot and left on the side of the road.

As the Russians approached from the East and the Anglo-Americans from the West, cattle cars and marching columns crisscrossed the shrinking territory of the Third Reich. The forced evacuations often became death marches; they took a terrible toll in human lives, killing perhaps one-third of all inmates before the end. Even camps like Bergen-Belsen, not intended for extermination, became a death trap for thousands of inmates. Thus, the Allies found mountains of corpses when they liberated the surviving inmates in April and May, 1945.

In 1941, Hitler decided to kill the European Jews and ordered the SS to implement this decision. After the invasion of Russia, special SS operational units, the *Einsatzgruppen,* killed Communist functionaries, Gypsies, and all Jews. These mobile killing units roamed through the countryside in the occupied territories of the Soviet Union, rounding up their victims, executing them, and burying them in mass graves. The units consisted of members of the Security Police and of the SS Security Service, recruited for this purpose by Reinhard Heydrich and his Central Office for Reich Security (*Reichsicherheitshauptamt,* or RSHA). They were supported by units of the German uniformed police and they used native troops whenever possible; local Lithuanian, Latvian, Estonian, and Ukrainian units participated in these massacres whenever possible. To increase efficiency, the Technical Department of RSHA developed a mobile gas van, which was used to kill Jewish women and children in Russia and Serbia. But the troops did not like these vans; they often broke down on muddy roads.

The *Einsatzgruppen* killings were too public. Soldiers and civilians watched the executions, took photographs, and often turned these massacres into public spectacles. The killings also demanded too much from the SS troops. They found the job of shooting thousands of men, women, and children too bloody. Some were brutalized; some had nervous breakdowns. To maintain secrecy and discipline, the SS leaders searched for a better way. They found the perfect solution in the extermination camps, where gas chambers were used to kill the victims. These killing centers were installations established for the sole purpose of mass murder; they were factories for the killing of human beings.

Murder by gas chamber was first introduced in the so-called Euthanasia program. Late in 1939, Hitler ordered the killing of the supposedly incurably ill. The program was administered by the Führer Chancellery, which established for this purpose the Utilitarian Foundation for Institutional Care, whose headquarters was located in Berlin at Tiergartenstrasse 4 and was known as T4. The victims (the mentally ill, the retarded, the deformed, the senile, and at times also those with diseases then considered incurable), chosen by boards of psychiatrists on the basis of questionnaires, were transferred to six institutions—Bernburg, Brandenburg, Grafeneck, Hadamar, Hartheim, and Sonnenstein—where specially constructed gas chambers were used to kill the patients. This radical ideological experiment in murder involved German nationals, and public protests forced the Nazi leadership to abort it in 1941. However, the program continued for adults and particularly for children on a smaller scale throughout the war, especially for the murder of ill concentration camp prisoners under the code designation 14f13.

Killing centers using gas chambers appeared late in 1941. In western Poland, the governor of the annexed area known as the Wartheland established a small but highly efficient killing center at Kulmhof (Chelmno) for the extermination of the Lodz Jews. A special SS commando, formerly occupied with killing mental patients in East Prussia, operated the installation. Using gas vans and burning the bodies, the commando killed at least 150,000 persons. In eastern Poland, the Lublin SS and Police Leader Odilo Globocnik headed the enterprise known as Operation Reinhard. Its object was to concentrate, pillage, deport, and kill the Jews of occupied Poland. He established three extermination camps: Belzec, Sobibor, and Treblinka. To operate these killing centers, he requested the services of the T4 operatives. A number of these, including the Kripo officer Christian Wirth, traveled to Lublin to apply their know-how to the murder of the Jews. Augmented by SS and police recruits with backgrounds similar to those of the T4 personnel, and aided by Ukrainian auxiliaries serving as guards, they staffed the extermination camps and, under the overall direction of Wirth, ran them with unbelievable efficiency.

Belzec opened in March, 1942, and closed in January, 1943. More than 600,000 persons were killed there. Sobibor opened in May, 1942, and closed one day after the rebellion of the inmates on October 14, 1943. At least 250,000 persons were killed there. Treblinka, the largest of the three killing centers, opened in July, 1942. A revolt of the inmates on August 2, 1943, destroyed most of the camp, and it finally closed in November, 1943. Between 700,000 and 900,000 persons were killed there. These three camps of Operation Reinhard served only the purpose of mass murder. Every man, woman, and child arriving there was killed. Most were Jews, but a few were Gypsies. A few young men and women were not immediately killed. Used to service the camp, they sorted the belongings of those murdered and burned the bodies in open air pits. Eventually they, too, were killed. Very few survived. Kulmhof and Belzec had only a handful of survivors. Sobibor and Treblinka, where the above-mentioned revolts permitted some to escape, had about thirty to forty survivors.

The method of murder was the same in all three camps (and similar in Kulmhof). The victims arrived in cattle wagons and the men were separated from the women and children. Forced to undress, they had to hand over all their valuables. Naked, they were driven towards the gas chambers, which were disguised as shower rooms and used carbon monoxide from a motor to kill the victims. The bodies were burned after their gold teeth had been extracted. The massive work of mass murder was accomplished by unusually small staffs. Figures differ (approximately 100 Germans and 500 Ukrainians in the three camps of Operation Reinhard), but all agreed that very few killed multitudes.

Thus, mass murder was first instituted in camps operated outside the concentration camp system by local SS leaders. But the concentration camps soon entered the field of mass murder, eventually surpassing all others in speed and size. The largest killing operation took place in Auschwitz, a regular concentration camp administered by WVHA. There Auschwitz Commandant Rudolf Hoess improved the method used by Christian Wirth,[6] substituting crystalized prussic acid—known by the trade name Zyklon B—for carbon monoxide. In September, 1941, an experimental gassing, killing about 250 ill prisoners and about 600 Russian POWs, proved the value of Zyklon B. In January, 1942, systematic killing operations, using Zyklon B, commenced with the arrival of Jewish transports from Upper Silesia. These were soon followed without interruption by transports of Jews from all occupied countries of Europe.

The Auschwitz killing center was the most modern of its kind. The

---

[6]SS Major (1885–1944) who carried out gassings on incurably insane Germans in 1939.

SS built the camp at Birkenau, also known as Auschwitz II. There, they murdered their victims in newly constructed gas chambers, and burned their bodies in crematoria constructed for this purpose. A postwar court described the killing process:

> Prussic acid fumes developed as soon as Zyklon B pellets seeped through the opening into the gas chamber and came into contact with the air. Within a few minutes, these fumes agonizingly asphyxiated the human beings in the gas chamber. During these minutes horrible scenes took place. The people who now realized that they were to die an agonizing death screamed and raged and beat their fists against the locked doors and against the walls. Since the gas spread from the floor of the gas chamber upward, small and weakly people were the first to die. The others, in their death agony, climbed on top of the dead bodies on the floor, in order to get a little more air before they too painfully choked to death.

More than two million victims were killed in this fashion in Auschwitz-Birkenau. Most of them were Jews, but others also died in its gas chambers: Gypsies, Russian POWs, and ill prisoners of all nationalities.

Unlike the killing centers operated by Globocnik and Wirth, Auschwitz combined murder and slave labor. RSHA ran the deportations and ordered the killings; WVHA ran the killing installations and chose the workers. From the transports of arriving Jews, SS physicians "selected" those young and strong enough to be used for forced labor. They were temporarily saved.

Those chosen for forced labor were first quarantined in Birkenau and then sent to the I. G. Farben[7] complex Buna-Monowitz, also known as Auschwitz III, or to one of its many subsidiary camps. Periodically, those too weak to work were sent to Birkenau for gassing from every camp in the Auschwitz complex; they were simply replaced by new and stronger prisoners.

A similar system was applied in Lublin-Maidanek, another WVHA concentration camp with a killing operation. But it closed much earlier than Auschwitz; it was liberated by the Red Army in the summer of 1944. Auschwitz continued to operate even after all other extermination camps had ceased to function. But when the war appeared lost, Himmler ordered the gassings stopped in November, 1944. Only a few hundred thousand Jews survived as slave laborers in Auschwitz and other concentration camps. Those who survived the evacuation marches of early 1945 were liberated by the Allied armies.

---

[7]The huge German chemical and dye trust.

The Soviet Family
in Post-Stalin Perspective

PETER H. JUVILER

Major developments have taken place in the Soviet family since the dictator, Joseph Stalin, died in 1953. Peter H. Juviler discusses four major areas of change: (1) parental choice in determining the number of children; (2) marital choice in deciding to remain unmarried and to divorce; (3) women's liberation in questioning sex roles; and (4) familial authority in defining the relationship between husband and wife.

Families in the Soviet Union have become smaller. Why? What are the implications for society of families with fewer children? How did World War II affect the family? Another current trend is a higher divorce rate. Why are more couples divorcing than ever before? Are there pronounced differences between rural and urban families with respect to the number of children and the frequency of divorce?

Citizens in Western Europe and the United States might consider the women's liberation movement in the Soviet Union to be rather paradoxical because of the comparative lack of political and personal freedom for both Soviet men and women, but Juviler believes that women have acquired more freedom in recent years—from their husbands if not from the state. Why does Juviler say that the term women's emancipation may be a more appropriate description than women's liberation for the changes taking place? How has work affected women's family lives? What complications in family life have been brought about by increased emancipation?

What has impeded the achievement of equality between wife and husband? What determines who wields the most authority in the home? How has Soviet law treated the relationship between husband and wife?

Omnipresent in the background lurks the Soviet state. What policies toward the family did Stalin's government pursue? To what extent has the state in more recent times changed its attitudes toward family life? Exactly what type of family would the government deem to be ideal?

How do you think the developments that Juviler describes in the Soviet family compare to recent trends and changes in Western societies, including the United States?

A leading Soviet women's advocate recently quoted to her readers a letter from the spouse of a field geologist. The geologist was away on

Peter H. Juviler, "The Soviet Family in Post-Stalin Perspective," in *The Soviet Union Since Stalin*, ed. Stephen F. Cohen, Alexander Rabinowitch, and Robert Sharlat (Bloomington: Indiana University Press, 1980), 227–33, 235–44.

expeditions much of the time, leaving her husband at home to raise their eight-year-old son. The couple became estranged and subsequently divorced. The situation just described is symptomatic of some current trends in Soviet family life. The family is small, with only one child. The marriage has ended in divorce. The divorce came about because of tensions created by the wife's independence and by conflicts of roles and of authority between the spouses.

Low birth rates, high divorce rates, and parental neglect of children caused the Soviet regime concern as early as the 1930s. These concerns remain today. But since Stalin, new conflicts have come to the fore in family life, brought on by massive social changes. The regime has been seeking new ways of responding to family needs and shortcomings. Some of the social and policy changes affecting Soviet families (outside of the most traditionalist areas of the country) are the subject of this chapter.

Parental choice about how many children to raise continues to affect the demography and the labor-force availability in the USSR. The birth rate, in turn, is closely connected with other crucial aspects of change: a growing legal freedom and personal assertion of *marital choice*—especially choices to stay single and to divorce; the drawn-out growing pains of *women's liberation* in the face of persistent women's inequality in the home; and the slow drift of *authority in the family* from patriarchal to more democratic patterns.

This account touches on rural as well as urban, non-Russian as well as Russian, families. Generalizations about trends in freedom of choice since Stalin refer both to regime policy and to the actual behavior of family members, for families typical of the great mass of outwardly conforming Soviet citizenry. . . .

Had the original Marxist and Bolshevik expectations for the family and its "withering away" been realized, there would be no such issues of family life and policy. After the Stalinists restored the family to honor, the watchword became not the eventual "withering away" of the family but its "strengthening." Now, roughly 94 percent of Soviet people live with some form of residential or budgetary tie to the 60 million families they form. Nuclearization of these families into units of no more than two generations was on the rise in tsarist cities. Increasing urbanization since then has multiplied the number of nuclear families. City families today average only 3.5 persons. Not only nuclearization but falling birth rates account for their small size, as well as for the small size of rural families, which now average 4.0 persons for the USSR. Indeed, live birth rates have been steadily dropping during this century: 45.5 (per thousand population) in 1913; 31.2 in 1940; 24.9 in 1960; and only 18.1 in 1977.

If this trend keeps up, families will not even be reproducing themselves in the fairly near future. The population will then level off and decline, and the shortage of labor power will become ever more serious, according to many Soviet demographers. Basic to this present trend is the drastically declining fertility of women—not their capacity to have children but their desires, their choices as to how many children to raise. Some changes associated with this diminishing fertility have not yet run their course by any means.

First, the fertility of rural women is dropping toward that of city women in many parts of the USSR. Second, urbanization has long been associated with smaller families; the USSR, today 62 percent urban, will be 75–80 percent urban by the year 2000. . . .

Soviet women must have two or three children each in order to guarantee an adequate labor force, according to the prevailing opinion of demographers. But women stubbornly choose to have only one or two, on the average, for the whole of the USSR. Their exercise of parental choice confronts the demographers and the Communist Party, all the way up to the general secretary, who expressed strong concern, with the prospect of an aging population and a labor shortage.

Yet unlike Stalin, the present regime has turned aside suggestions that it return to the compulsive legislation of parental and marital choice in order to increase birth rates and preserve the family. Under Stalin, nontherapeutic abortions were banned in 1936 and divorce fees were raised. Wartime losses in people and births prompted new laws to protect the family as a childbearing unit and to raise the disastrously low wartime birth rate. The decree of July 8, 1944, barred paternity suits and forbade the recognition of a nonhusband's paternity, even when he voluntarily acknowledged it. The decree was meant, on the other hand, to encourage unmarried women to have children, in a situation where there were only two men for every three women of childbearing age, owing to the loss of 20 million men in the war. Thus, though only registered marriage gave rise to paternal rights and obligations under the 1944 decree, the state undertook to give unmarried mothers a grant for every child born to them out of wedlock and to care for such children in state homes. Family allowances for all mothers went up, and more nurseries and kindergartens were ordered. But sharp cuts in allowances in 1947 took the noncompulsive heart out of the severe new family law. The 1944 decree included other intended protection for the family based on registered marriage: a new, complicated, and expensive divorce procedure in two courts.

Buttressed by such a restrictive law, the Soviet family came to be seen by the ideologues as an essential replenisher of labor power and a psychological bulwark of Stalin's authoritarian system, a "microcosm of the new socialist order," alongside the redisciplined school and the mass youth organizations.

More and more women reacted inarticulately to Stalin's compulsion by having illegal abortions. Couples circumvented the divorce barriers through de facto divorces and marriages unprotected by law. As for advocates of women's rights and interests, their voices had long been stilled by the abolition of the Zhenotdel, the Women's Department of the Central Committee, in 1930, and then, by the climate of conformity and terror under Stalin.

By 1954, less than a year after Stalin's death, an articulate movement began pressing for family law reform, especially for equality of extramarital children, easier divorce, and an easing of women's conditions of life. The revival of research and a limited leeway for the discussion of sensitive social issues opened up channels of public debate on matters of family life (excepting the political ones such as freedom of religious upbringing). Out of the debates and party decisions have come measures reducing the compulsion on parents to have more children, while continuing to try to hold parents responsible for the proper upbringing of their children. The party leadership considers "an effective population policy" to be a matter of some urgency. Lawyers and demographers have considered the possibility of compulsive "demographic legislation," such as a new abortion ban, to reverse the lifting of the old abortion ban in 1955, but the party, apparently, has sided with the majority view that a new set of compulsive laws would not serve the party purposes.

The family law reform of 1968 permitted the voluntary acknowledgment of extramarital paternity. It opened up a narrow field for paternity suits in some cases of noncasual liaisons, removed the documentary stigma of illegitimacy by no longer crossing out the father's name in the old birth certificate and permitting the mother to enter a patronymic and her own last name as the father's, for a child born out of wedlock. The partial restoration of women's rights and equality was furthered by prohibiting husbands from divorcing wives during pregnancy or less than a year after childbirth, and by more extensive spouse support and property division clauses.

Instead of compelling parental choice, the regime is trying to raise the incentive to have more children by easing the financial and childcare burdens of parenthood. . . .

When it comes to parental choice as to how to raise children, the state has become, if anything, less permissive since Stalin. Part of the regime's concern is with the role of faulty upbringing in aggravating the persistent problems of juvenile delinquency and crime. . . .

Criminologists cite failures of the family as educator as "a leading cause" of juvenile lawbreaking. Hence, while the post-Stalin regimes have liberalized juvenile punishment in courts and labor colonies, they have also increased the range and severity of the criminal and administrative responsibility of parents who neglect, abuse, or contribute to lawbreaking by their children.

New since Stalin, also, is the effort to mobilize a whole network of nonjudicial social agencies such as the commissions on juvenile affairs, comrades' courts, social counselors, and committees in work places to help the family and the school. The intervention of these amateur agencies is uneven in reach, effectiveness, and sensitivity to the needs of individual juveniles and their families. But whatever the impact, work places are involved in influencing wayward parents more than they are in most other countries.

In short, the authority of the state over the family has not faded since Stalin. Rather, it has assumed new forms—in some ways more compulsive than they had been, in some ways less so. The attempt to compel fertility has been abandoned, at least for now. The complex social changes helping to lower birth rates touch many sides of family life, from marriage and divorce to women's liberation and equality.

Marriage formalities in the USSR made the institution of marriage seem a casual affair indeed until recently. After years of experimentation with "wedding palaces" and new ceremonials even in humbler surroundings, secular ceremonials, complete with bridal gowns and wedding parties, are again becoming popular in Soviet cities. . . .

Yet the tide of legal divorces flows unabated. . . . A simplified divorce procedure, involving only one court, went into effect January 1, 1966. The 1968 reform added a provision for the simple registration of divorce without court trial on the condition of payment of a fifty-ruble fee and a three-month waiting period, when there is mutual consent and when there are no minor children of the marriage.

By 1977, 902,000 families were dissolving by divorce annually. . . . [T]his is one divorce for every three marriages on the average for the USSR. . . .

Divorces directly reduce fertility, since couples avoid having children when they feel divorce coming on. They may remain unmarried for years after divorce. Less than half of divorced women remarry, and a half-million children of broken marriages remain fatherless.

Unmarried Soviet men and women, both divorced and single, form a huge untapped "reserve" of increased fertility. One in five men over twenty are unmarried as are nearly two in five women (38 percent). . . .

A large jump in divorce rates . . . occurred after the liberalization of divorce procedures in 1965, effective January 1, 1966. . . . There is little doubt that recent rises are related to urbanization and to social and economic change in the USSR.

Chances are that a divorce will be initiated by the wife rather than by the husband. The husband's alcoholism, and the drunken bedlam and violence to wife and children accompanying his drinking, is the most frequent cause given by wives to the court to explain the breakup of the marriage. It is the top reason in nearly half the cases. Incompatibility, a rubric including all kinds of problems from sex to fights over housework, is the second reason. Infidelity is the third most frequent reason given for petitioning for divorce.

Experts tend to dismiss these reasons as clues to what really accounts for the rush to divorce these days. Drunkenness is hardly new in Russia. Neither are the side effects of urbanization. Family ties have been loosening, rather, because the family is losing functions that kept it together. . . . Upbringing is transferred increasingly to other agencies: schools, youth organizations, and informal peer groups. The family has also been losing its functions of economic production. The restraints of religion, extended family influences, community mores, and the former victorianism of the Stalinist regime, whereby divorce was a blot on the career of a party member, have all eroded.

The marriage union has become more fragile, more dependent on mutual accommodation, respect, attraction of the spouses, an arrangement more of pleasure and less of necessity. Ironically, this approach toward the socialist ideal of "finally cleansing family relations from material calculation," though not fully achieved, has already helped destabilize the family, increase divorces, and lower the birth rate. . . .

. . . [R]ising divorce rates in the USSR reflect a "desire for more choice in every area of life." . . . The era of strong official disapproval of divorce has ended. Alternative housing is increasingly available for divorcés. People are becoming more self-centered, more absorbed by hope and striving for a happier and more comfortable personal life. They defer less than their grandparents did to the authority of church, state, morality, or tradition in their choices of when to marry and divorce. They act in ways familiar to urban families in other industrialized countries—at least, their expectations run in roughly the same direction, though less trammeled by tradition. Without trying rashly to attribute a specific share of cause to the women's liberation movement, one must add that in its Soviet form, too, it has probably contributed to divorce rates, and it has certainly led to falling birthrates.

The term "women's liberation" . . . indicate[s] that in the Soviet Union, as well as in the West, the question of changing sex roles, of greater female equality, has been a burning issue, both before the late thirties and after Stalin.

Women's emancipation may be a better term to use for this development, in the sense that it was initiated from above, not from below. Barely in power, the Bolsheviks hastened to legislate women's full equality of family, economic, and civil status, *in the law* . Bolshevik leaders saw this as a blow to the old authoritarian social order and a way to right a historic wrong to women. "Liberation" implies a feminist movement. Feminism had always been a minor aspect of the Russian revolutionary movement and its Marxist segment. . . .

. . . The family existed in Soviet family law and policy as a relic to be used for child rearing and mutual support of its members until the society at large could find resources with which to take over the motherly, housewifely, and welfare functions of the family. The family code of 1926 actually increased the economic claims of family members on each other, in the face of the growing unemployment of women. The proletarian-toned first five-year plan of 1928–32, with its collectivization of peasant households and attacks on parental authority, probably undermined family stability more than did any conscious family policies of the Bolsheviks.

Constituting nearly half the industrial labor force by World War II, women took much of the home-front effort on their shoulders. . . . Today 51.5 percent of workers and employees are women. . . .

Some women work because they have to in order to supplement the family income. Others work because they want to. The more skilled the worker category and the more creative the work they do, the more likely women are to rank work satisfaction first, satisfaction of being with other workers (a typical office worker's reason) second, and material considerations last.

Work fulfills an original Bolshevik aim: it makes women more independent. . . .

The rub is that the Bolsheviks envisaged a woman fully independent of the family, emancipated "from kitchen and frying pan." Instead, women still work a "double shift" and encounter many other costs in their division of roles, work, and authority with men. As a Soviet expert has pointed out, "Women's emancipation is a great achievement of our epoch. But a price must be paid for that great achievement. The price includes complications of relations between the sexes." These complications often involve conflicts over the nature of femininity, over the division of labor in the family, and over authority in the family. One of the reasons there are so many Soviet expert sources to quote on this problem, aside from the greater post-Stalin possibilities of discussing social problems openly, is that the regime has been virtually forced to give attention to women's role-conflict because of its toll in divorce, reduced fertility, and neglected children.

The wider question of feminism and femininity in the USSR falls beyond the range of this inquiry into the status of the Soviet family. Suffice it to say that many men, and some women too, lament the alleged passing of the tender, modest, motherly "keeper of the hearth" and resent the "masculinity" of the younger generation of hard-swearing, smoking, drinking, promiscuous women, whose strong aggressiveness is concealed by the svelte new superficial image beaming attractively out of the TV set, movie screen, and magazine cover. The crisis of sexual identity is exacerbated by the fact that a man's mentors are mainly his mother and female teachers. It reaches into families to cause divorce.

Larisa Kuznetsova, a leading publicist and women's advocate, cautions women not to be ashamed of the new strength they have gained as a natural adaptation of their old femininity to changed social circumstances. However, she also sees the danger of a woman's losing all of the feminine difference so important to men. . . .

Femininity but with shared authority—that is the demand of the new

Soviet woman whom Kuznetsova represents. Can one imagine such an outlook under Stalin?. . . .

Division of labor in the family was not a simple question even then. It has now become the central family issue. The "double shift chronically overburdens women, making them nervous and destroying their femininity, youthfulness and beauty." But today Soviet women are farther than ever from the illiterate, dependent drudges of old. Working women are as educated as their male coworkers, whose further on-the-job training and greater advancement they subsidize with the liberation of their husbands from most housework. Again and again, surveys by Soviet researchers record women's expectations from marriage: love, respect, trust, common interests, companionship, consideration, sexual fulfillment, and help with the housework. Yet women end up doing two to three times as much housework as men. . . .

When, in an experiment, mothers working in an Odessa construction organization received a daily hour off, they spent it on more housework. Husbands of these women shared housework evenly in only 8.6 percent of the families and helped to raise the children in 28.4 percent. . . .

A recent survey of 4,000 working youths and married couples with and without children in Taganrog shows what happens to women's free time after marriage and motherhood. The appearance of children spells the end of free time for the wife. For example, on "cultural" activities at home unmarried men spend 9.0 hours a week and women, 9.4 hours. Married men spend 11.15 hours and married women, 13.5. But after children appear, married men spend 15.4 hours at "cultural" pastimes in the home, while married women spend only 5.3. The mother reads on the average 1.65 hours; the father, 5.6 hours. Mother watches TV 3.15 hours a week; father, 9.25 hours. While the wife is cleaning, washing clothes, cooking, and changing diapers, the husband is either out somewhere or, if at home, comfortably lying on the couch, reading or watching television.

As in this country, there are many women who put family and home ahead of work. They do not resent being one of the many women holding disproportionately low-paid or low-ranked posts within their trades and professions. Nor do they mind that their children's gradeschool readers brim with sex-role stereotyping of women and little girls, and that the females do the housework in the stories. It is probably a matter of indifference to these nonliberated women that many of the proposed solutions for their double burden promise simply to reduce it, or to remove them from production and pay them to tend their babies, rather than shift some of that burden to their husbands.

But for the well-educated working woman, the "second shift" grows intolerable. She will *not* assume the duties of a servant, as she is expected to do, while her husband turns to drink or outside social life and self-improvement. "The husband and wife often determine domestic duties virtually in open combat, the wife taking the offensive and the husband defending himself—supported by the traditions that say housework degrades a man." Until this conflict is resolved, the number of divorces will not drop, nor will the depression of birth rates.

As many Soviet sociologists see it, the basic demographic problem is created not by divorces, but by the unwillingness of most women to pay the "price" of large or even medium-sized families. Women are "in rebellion." New interests crowd out home, children, and family. Women feel, increasingly, the need for "self-expression, personal improvement, equality with other people in all spheres of life, for respect for their person, for freedom of behavior and choice." There are not enough grandmothers and child-care facilities, despite the enormous expansion of nurseries and kindergartens. Besides, parents are unprepared to cope with family difficulties and to raise children. Divorces are producing millions of single-parent families along with additions to the 20 million bachelors and unmarried women twenty to forty years old. Annually, 700–800,000 children appear to be raised only by their mothers, owing to illegitimate births, divorces, and husbands' deaths. Husbands' indifference also raises the "price" of a second and third child. The response of women is simply to stage a slowdown in childbearing.

Together, divorces and drops in birth rate help bring women's "second shift" to the level of a major national issue for the government, the major issue in family policy. . . .

It is hard to imagine a Stalinist regime allowing its experts to write about "women in rebellion" and demanding equality. No less hard to imagine under Stalin would have been serious inquiry into the final determinant of choice among family members: the division of authority in the family. . . .

Under the 1977 Soviet constitution, the division of authority within the family is equal, as it has been since 1917 but with a very important difference. Family law proclaims the equality of men and women in family relations. The constitution speaks of the full equality of "spouses" in family relations. Women tend to be less than equal in nonregistered conjugal relationships because of limitations on claiming the paternal support of the father of a child when the father does not voluntarily acknowledge his paternity. In sum, spouses may claim legal protection of equality in family relations only where the law says such relations exist. The law enforces woman's freedom of choice to give her body to her husband or to withhold. A husband who forces his attentions on an unwilling wife is liable to prosecution for rape—if she brings charges. The law does recognize one element of inequality in the family: the position of head of the collective-farm household, who is responsible for the fulfillment of tax and certain other household obligations to the state. Otherwise, the government has ignored suggestions that it recognize a head of every family.

The census takers, on the other hand, insist on naming a head of every household: the one whom family members name as head, whether or not the family actually has an active single holder of more authority than others. Only 28.5 percent of all families in 1970 listed women as heads. Moreover many such women heads are widows or unmarried mothers. . . .

The conflicts over doing housework involve not simply a particular division of labor but also perceptions of authority in the family. Husbands and wives often give different answers on questionnaires asking them who is the head of the family. . . .

Family heads in the sociological sense have the right of giving orders and making decisions. Other family members have the obligation to carry out the head's decisions and to minister to family needs. Soviet researchers see the family in transition from the autocratic type, with one head of household, to the biarchic type (spouses share authority), or the democratic type (either spouses share all authority or they decide together with the children). The proportion of autocratic families diminishes and the proportion of democratic families increases, as the survey moves from a small town to a medium city and to a metropolis like Moscow.

Some headships are purely formal. They are recognized and the head is listened to, but nobody carries out his orders and the wife is actually in control. In any event, the younger and better educated the family, the less likely it is to have a head. When a head is recognized, men are accorded the authority of head because they are "breadwinners," while the most frequent reason for according headship to a woman is that she cares for the family (the last consideration in recognizing a man's headship). To earn her authority, the woman must work in the family; to earn his, the man must be the main earner, in many cases.

Regardless of headship, the wife will generally play a larger role than the husband in spending money, even large sums of money, for the family, and in the upbringing of children. Many parents have little time for children. And a recent survey prompted the conclusion that parents pay "insufficient attention to the upbringing of children in a majority of cases, especially the father." Just as the post-Stalin Soviet state has not solved the problem of division of labor, so it has not been able to prevail on or encourage the majority of parents to exercise effective authority over their children.

. . . The present division of authority in the Soviet family, to the extent that one can generalize about it, supports the appraisal that women's freedom of choice has increased faster in education and employment since Stalin than it has in areas less susceptible to state control such as decision making and authority within the family.

The nature of the state's interaction with the family has changed considerably since Stalin. State involvement with the family continues to be intense. But the compulsion has shifted from women to men, as freedom, or relative freedom, of parental and marital choice has been restored in post-Stalin reforms of abortion rules, laws on marriage and divorce, paternity, and birth registration.

Watching the present trend toward zero population growth and ever smaller families, the Soviet regime has decided, for now at least, to avoid renewing compulsive efforts at birth stimulation and to increase parental incentives to choose to have a second or third child.

There are virtually no signs yet of legal or educational support for the idea that men should take on at least a share of domestic chores, if not an equal one. The trend in Soviet state policy has been to try to lighten women's double burden of outside and domestic work without shifting some of the burden on to men's shoulders, the latter a step many deem essential to the final liberation of women.

Women are seeking and exercising greater social freedom; they evince a "desire for more choice in every area of life." That choice must be exercised at the expense of the past authority of the state and of their spouses. Women's changing view of the meaning of femininity, where it crops up, tends to exacerbate family conflicts. These conflicts often begin not in unequal burdens alone, but in women's new resistance to the double burdens. The conflicts originated in the very growth of equality and independence envisaged by Bolshevik (and other Russian) revolutionaries.

Divorce is one way for women to assert their freedom. Divorce is not mainly a man's game any more. Registered divorces have risen to new heights of one for every three marriages in the USSR, two for every three marriages in the big cities. Soviet sociologists may no longer cite low Soviet divorce rates, as they once did, to show the superiority of the socialist over the bourgeois way of life.

Another act of choice and independence by women has been to desist from having more than one or two children. This "rebellion" by women in the family is what has created the government's sense of crisis and has drawn its attention to women's double burden and the need to lighten it. The fall in birth rate, the smaller family size, and increased freedom of choice have had an ambivalent impact. Soviet believers in large families lament that this assertion of choice produces families too small for proper upbringing and too many self-centered only children. The chauvinists among Soviet men find the new claims of women to be an unsettling nuisance, if not a serious threat to their sense of their own identity and sex roles. Other people, especially females, have welcomed the new family trends as signs of transition to an era in which women will take their lives and choices into their own hands, approach full equality, decide family size along with their husbands on the basis of a couple's wishes, and not because of spontaneous nature or reasons of state. That women are in rebellion is all to the good for these observers, both male and female.

Division of authority in the family is hard to define and measure.

From the little information available, it seems that Soviet families are in transition from (1) the traditional authoritarian structure of a single male head (or female when the male is missing), to (2) personal authority based on contributions and individual qualities or merely formal male authority and much participation, to (3) a democratic structure of decision making and work sharing. To complicate the picture, women hold considerable power, even under male headships, by spending the family money. A family may make decisions democratically but will still leave much of the housework to the wife.

In all three regards—equality, choice, and authority—the post-Stalin course of Soviet families and their interaction with the state authority over them, as well as the position of women in the families, seem to indicate that Soviet society is slowly becoming less repressive and relationships more equalitarian.

Forbidden Death

PHILIPPE ARIÈS

During the Romantic era of the late eighteenth and nineteenth centuries, death rep-
resented a sudden rupture between the dying person and the immediate family. The
same development of sentiment and affection that saw people marrying for love and
parents adoring their children had a similarly profound effect on society's attitude
toward death. Family members seemed more anxious about the final departure
of spouses and offspring than about their own deaths; overburdened with grief,
they have left us evidence of their intense bereavement in literature, diaries, and
lachrymose funerary monuments.

Ariès argues that this Romantic view gave way in the twentieth century to a
death revolution, in which death became something shameful and forbidden. What
exactly does he mean? How has society interdicted death? What role has the hospital
played in the death revolution? What does Ariès say constitutes an acceptable death?
Customs have changed as well as attitudes. What innovations have appeared in
funeral rites and ceremonies?

What does it mean to say that death has replaced sex as a taboo and has become
the new pornography? What are the implications of this development? Is this
taboo more prevalent in the United States than in other Western countries? Ariès
does offer specific comments about American attitudes toward death. How does the
American way of death differ from the European?

With his books, Western Attitudes toward Death: From the Middle Ages
to the Present *and* The Hour of Our Death, *Ariès opened up a new subject*
for study, the history of attitudes toward death. Now, no one would deny the
importance of a society's collective feelings toward this event in life shared by all
people. Why do you suppose historians virtually ignored the history of death for
so long? How do Ariès's remarks about death help us understand the twentieth-
century world and the process of social change?

During the long period . . . from the Early Middle Ages until the mid-
nineteenth century, the attitude toward death changed, but so slowly
that contemporaries did not even notice. In our day, in approximately
a third of a century, we have witnessed a brutal revolution in traditional ideas and feelings, a revolution so brutal that social observers
have not failed to be struck by it. It is really an absolutely unheard-of
phenomenon. Death, so omnipresent in the past that it was familiar,

Philippe Ariès, *Western Attitudes toward Death: From the Middle Ages to the Present*
(Baltimore: The Johns Hopkins University Press, 1974), 85–103.

would be effaced, would disappear. It would become shameful and forbidden.

. . . It . . . seems that this revolution began in the United States and
spread to England, to the Netherlands, to industrialized Europe; and we
can see it today, before our very eyes, reaching France and leaving oil
smudges wherever the wave passes.

At its beginning doubtlessly lies a sentiment already expressed during the second half of the nineteenth century: those surrounding the
dying person had a tendency to spare him and to hide from him the
gravity of his condition. Yet they admitted that this dissimulation could
not last too long, except in such extraordinary cases as those described
by Mark Twain in 1902 in "Was it Heaven or Hell?" The dying person
must one day know, but the relatives no longer had the cruel courage to
tell the truth themselves.

In short, at this point the truth was beginning to be challenged.

The first motivation for the lie was the desire to spare the sick person,
to assume the burden of his ordeal. But this sentiment, whose origin we
know (the intolerance of another's death and the confidence shown by
the dying person in those about him) very rapidly was covered over by
a different sentiment, a new sentiment characteristic of modernity: one
must avoid—no longer for the sake of the dying person, but for society's
sake, for the sake of those close to the dying person—the disturbance
and the overly strong and unbearable emotion caused by the ugliness of
dying and by the very presence of death in the midst of a happy life, for
it is henceforth given that life is always happy or should always seem
to be so. Nothing had yet changed in the rituals of death, which were
preserved at least in appearance, and no one had yet had the idea of
changing them. But people had already begun to empty them of their
dramatic impact; the procedure of hushing-up had begun. . . .

Between 1930 and 1950 the evolution accelerated markedly. This was
due to an important physical phenomenon: the displacement of the site
of death. One no longer died at home in the bosom of one's family, but
in the hospital, alone.

One dies in the hospital because the hospital has become the place
to receive care which can no longer be given at home. Previously the
hospital had been a shelter for the poor, for pilgrims; then it became a
medical center where people were healed, where one struggled against
death. It still has that curative function, but people are also beginning to
consider a certain type of hospital as the designated spot for dying. One
dies in the hospital because the doctor did not succeed in healing. One no
longer goes to or will go to the hospital to be healed, but for the specific
purpose of dying. American sociologists have observed that there are
today two types of seriously ill persons to be found in hospitals. The most
archaic are recent immigrants who are still attached to the traditions of
death, who try to snatch the dying person from the hospital so he can die

at home, *more majorum;*[1] the others are those more involved in modernity who come to die in the hospital because it has become inconvenient to die at home.

Death in the hospital is no longer the occasion of a ritual ceremony, over which the dying person presides amidst his assembled relatives and friends. Death is a technical phenomenon obtained by a cessation of care, a cessation determined in a more or less avowed way by a decision of the doctor and the hospital team. Indeed, in the majority of cases the dying person has already lost consciousness. Death has been dissected, cut to bits by a series of little steps, which finally makes it impossible to know which step was the real death, the one in which consciousness was lost, or the one in which breathing stopped. All these little silent deaths have replaced and erased the great dramatic act of death, and no one any longer has the strength or patience to wait over a period of weeks for a moment which has lost a part of its meaning.

From the end of the eighteenth century we had been impressed by a sentimental landslide which was causing the initiative to pass from the dying man himself to his family—a family in which henceforth he would have complete confidence. Today the initiative has passed from the family, as much an outsider as the dying person, to the doctor and the hospital team. They are the masters of death—of the moment as well as of the circumstances of death—and it has been observed that they try to obtain from their patient "an acceptable style of living while dying." The accent has been placed on "acceptable." An acceptable death is a death which can be accepted or tolerated by the survivors. It has its antithesis: "the embarrassingly graceless dying," which embarrasses the survivors because it causes too strong an emotion to burst forth; and emotions must be avoided both in the hospital and everywhere in society. One does not have the right to become emotional other than in private, that is to say, secretly. Here, then, is what has happened to the great death scene, which had changed so little over the centuries, if not the millennia.

The funeral rites have also been modified. Let us put aside for a moment the American case. In England and northwestern Europe, they are trying to reduce to a decent minimum the inevitable operations nec- essary to dispose of the body. It is above all essential that society—the neighbors, friends, colleagues, and children—notice to the least possible degree that death has occurred. If a few formalities are maintained, and if a ceremony still marks the departure, it must remain discreet and must avoid emotion. Thus the family reception line for receiving condolences at the end of the funeral service has now been suppressed. The outward manifestations of mourning are repugned and are disappearing. Dark clothes are no longer worn; one no longer dresses differently than on any other day.

[1]According to the custom of the great ("social betters").

Too evident sorrow does not inspire pity but repugnance, it is the sign of mental instability or of bad manners: it is *morbid*. Within the family circle one also hesitates to let himself go for fear of upsetting the children. One only has the right to cry if no one else can see or hear. Solitary and shameful mourning is the only recourse, like a sort of masturbation. . . .

In countries in which the death revolution has been radical, once the dead person has been evacuated, his tomb is no longer visited. In England for example, cremation has become the dominant manner of burial. When cremation occurs, sometimes with dispersal of the ashes, the cause is more than a desire to break with Christian tradition; it is a manifestation of enlightenment, of modernity. The deep motivation is that cremation is the most radical means of getting rid of the body and of forgetting it, of nullifying it, of being "too final." Despite the efforts of cemetery offices, people rarely visit the urns today, though they may still visit gravesides. Cremation excludes a pilgrimage.

We would be committing an error if we entirely attributed this flight from death to an indifference toward the dead person. In reality the contrary is true. In the old society, the panoply of mourning scarcely concealed a rapid resignation. How many widowers remarried a few short months after the death of their wives! On the contrary, today, where mourning is forbidden, it has been noted that the mortality rate of widows or widowers during the year following the spouse's death is much higher than that of the control group of the same age.

The point has even been reached at which . . . the choking back of sorrow, the forbidding of its public manifestation, the obligation to suffer alone and secretly, has aggravated the trauma stemming from the loss of a dear one. In a family in which sentiment is given an important place and in which premature death is becoming increasingly rare (save in the event of an automobile accident), the death of a near relative is always deeply felt, as it was in the Romantic era.[2]

A single person is missing for you, and the whole world is empty. But one no longer has the right to say so aloud.

The combination of phenomena which we have just analyzed is nothing other than the imposition of an interdict. What was once required is henceforth forbidden.

The merit of having been the first to define this unwritten law of our civilization goes to the English sociologist, Geoffrey Gorer. He has shown clearly how death has become a taboo and how in the twentieth century it has replaced sex as the principal forbidden subject. Formerly children were told that they were brought by the stork, but they were admitted to the great farewell scene about the bed of the dying person. Today

[2]The late eighteenth and nineteenth centuries.

they are initiated in their early years to the physiology of love; but when they no longer see their grandfather and express astonishment, they are told that he is resting in a beautiful garden among the flowers. Such is "The Pornography of Death"—the title of a pioneering article by Gorer, published in 1955—and the more society was liberated from the Victorian constraints concerning sex, the more it rejected things having to do with death. Along with the interdict appears the transgression: the mixture of eroticism and death so sought after from the sixteenth to the eighteenth century reappears in our sadistic literature and in violent death in our daily life.

This establishment of an interdict has profound meaning. It is already difficult to isolate the meaning of the interdict on sex which was precipitated by the Christian confusion between sin and sexuality (though, as in the nineteenth century, this interdict was never imposed). But the interdict on death suddenly follows upon the heels of a very long period—several centuries—in which death was a public spectacle from which no one would have thought of hiding and which was even sought after at times.

The cause of the interdict is at once apparent: the need for happiness—the moral duty and the social obligation to contribute to the collective happiness by avoiding any cause for sadness or boredom, by appearing to be always happy, even if in the depths of despair. By showing the least sign of sadness, one sins against happiness, threatens it, and society then risks losing its *raison d'être*. . . .

The idea of happiness brings us back to the United States, and it is now appropriate to attempt to understand the relationships between American civilization and the modern attitude toward death.

It seems that the modern attitude toward death, that is to say the interdiction of death in order to preserve happiness, was born in the United States around the beginning of the twentieth century. However, on its native soil the interdict was not carried to its ultimate extremes. In American society it encountered a braking influence which it did not encounter in Europe. Thus the American attitude toward death today appears as a strange compromise between trends which are pulling it in two nearly opposite directions. . . .

. . . In America, during the eighteenth and the first half of the nineteenth centuries, and even later, burials conformed to tradition, especially in the countryside: the carpenter made the coffin (the coffin, not yet the "casket"); the family and friends saw to its transport and to the procession itself; and the pastor and gravedigger carried out the service. In the early nineteenth century the grave was still sometimes dug on the family property—which is a modern act, copied from the Ancients, and which was unknown in Europe before the mid-eighteenth century and with few exceptions was rapidly abandoned. In villages and small towns the cemetery most frequently lay adjacent to the church. In the cities, once again paralleling Europe, the cemetery had in about 1830 been situated outside the city but was encompassed by urban growth and abandoned toward 1870 for a new site. It soon fell into ruin. . . .

The old cemeteries were church property, as they had been in Europe and still are in England. The new cemeteries belonged to private associations. . . . In Europe cemeteries became municipal, that is to say public, property and were never left to private initiative.

In the growing cities of the nineteenth century, old carpenters or gravediggers, or owners of carts and horses, became "undertakers," and the manipulation of the dead became a profession. Here history is still completely comparable to that in Europe, at least in that part of Europe which remained faithful to the eighteenth-century canons of simplicity and which remained outside the pale of Romantic bombast.

Things seem to have changed during the period of the Civil War. Today's "morticians," whose letters-patent go back to that period, give as their ancestor a quack doctor expelled from the school of medicine, Dr. Holmes, who had a passion for dissection and cadavers. He would offer his services to the victim's family and embalmed, it is said, 4,000 cadavers unaided in four years. . . . Why such recourse to embalming? Had it been practiced previously? Is there an American tradition going back to the eighteenth century, a period in which throughout Europe there was a craze for embalming? Yet this technique was abandoned in nineteenth-century Europe, and the wars did not resurrect it. It is noteworthy that embalming became a career in the United States before the end of the century, even if it was not yet very widespread. . . . We know that it has today become a very widespread method of preparing the dead, a practice almost unknown in Europe and characteristic of the American way of death.

One cannot help thinking that this long-accepted and avowed preference for embalming has a meaning, even if it is difficult to interpret.

This meaning could indeed be that of a certain refusal to accept death, either as a familiar end to which one is resigned, or as a dramatic sign in the Romantic manner. And this meaning became even more obvious when death became an object of commerce and of profit. It is not easy to sell something which has no value because it is too familiar and common, or something which is frightening, horrible, or painful. In order to sell death, it had to be made friendly. But we may assume that "funeral directors"—since 1885 a new name for undertakers—would not have met with success if public opinion had not cooperated. They presented themselves not as simple sellers of services, but as "doctors of grief" who have a mission, as do doctors and priests; and this mission, from the beginning of this century, consists in aiding the mourning survivors to return to normalcy. The new funeral director ("new" because he has replaced the simple undertaker) is a "doctor of grief," an "expert at returning abnormal minds to normal in the shortest possible time." They are "members of an exalted, almost sacred calling."

Thus mourning is no longer a necessary period imposed by society; it has become a *morbid state* which must be treated, shortened, erased by the "doctor of grief."

Through a series of little steps we can see the birth and development of the ideas which would end in the present-day interdict, built upon the ruins of Puritanism, in an urbanized culture which is dominated by rapid economic growth and by the search for happiness linked to the search for profit.

This process should normally result in the situation of England today . . . : the almost total suppression of everything reminding us of death.

But, and this is what is unique about the American attitude, American mores have not gone to such an extreme; they stopped along the way. Americans are very willing to transform death, to put make-up on it, to sublimate it, but they do not want to make it disappear. Obviously, this would also mark the end of profit, but the money earned by funeral merchants would not be tolerated if they did not meet a profound need. The wake, increasingly avoided in industrial Europe, persists in the United States: it exists as "viewing the remains," the "visitation." "They don't *view* bodies in England."

The visit to the cemetery and a certain veneration in regard to the tomb also persist. That is why public opinion—and funeral directors—finds cremation distasteful, for it gets rid of the remains too quickly and too radically.

Burials are not shameful and they are not hidden. With that very characteristic mixture of commerce and idealism, they are the object of showy publicity, like any other consumer's item, be it soap or religion. Seen for example in the buses of New York City in 1965 was the following ad, purchased by one of the city's leading morticians: "The dignity and integrity of a Gawler. Funeral costs no more. . . . Easy access, private parking for over 100 cars." Such publicity would be unthinkable in Europe, first of all because it would repel the customer rather than attract him.

Thus we must admit that a traditional resistance has kept alive certain rituals of death which had been abandoned or are being abandoned in industrialized Europe, especially among the middle classes.

Nevertheless, though these rituals have been continued, they have also been transformed. The American way of death is the synthesis of two tendencies: one traditional, the other euphoric.

Thus during the wakes or farewell "visitations" which have been preserved, the visitors come without shame or repugnance. This is because in reality they are not visiting a dead person, as they traditionally have, but an almost-living one who, thanks to embalming, is still present, as if he were awaiting you to greet you or to take you off on a walk. The definitive nature of the rupture has been blurred. Sadness and mourning have been banished from this calming reunion.

Perhaps because American society has not totally accepted the interdict, it can more easily challenge it; but this interdict is spreading in the Old World, where the cult of the dead would seem more deeply rooted.

During the last ten years in American publications an increasing number of sociologists and psychologists have been studying the conditions of death in contemporary society and especially in hospitals. . . . [T]he authors have been struck by the manner of dying, by the inhumanity, the cruelty of solitary death in hospitals and in a society where death has lost the prominent place which custom had granted it over the millennia, a society where the interdiction of death paralyzes and inhibits the reactions of the medical staff and family involved. These publications are also preoccupied with the fact that death has become the object of a voluntary decision by the doctors and the family, a decision which today is made shamefacedly, clandestinely. And this paramedical literature, for which, as far as I know, there is no equivalent in Europe, is bringing death back into the dialogue from which it had been excluded. Death is once again becoming something one can talk about. Thus the interdict is threatened, but only in the place where it was born and where it encountered limitations. Elsewhere, in the other industrialized societies, it is maintaining or extending its empire. . . .

Leisure and Technological Civilization

GEORGES FRIEDMANN

Twentieth-century civilization, unlike that of previous eras, is essentially technological. In this essay, Georges Friedmann examines the role of leisure, which he says has given new attractions and possibilities to our modern technological society. What specific cultural traits define a technological civilization? The notion of time is crucial to an understanding of leisure. How did "floating" or "dormant" time mark pre-machine societies? What is the difference between spare time and working time? Between spare time and free time?

Friedmann believes that the goal of modern life is happiness but that societies have been unable to bring it about. The result has been disequilibrium, seen most ominously in drug abuse. Why has modern civilization not been successful in converting spare time into happiness? What are the threats to leisure? What is the campaign to humanize leisure?

Naively, intellectuals believed that a short work week would allow workers time to appreciate high culture—art, painting, literature—but to their chagrin they have seen workers use their leisure time to engage in more work. So the acquisition of spare time has not created leisure. Why? What characterizes the life of the "after-work man"? What have been the effects, both positive and negative, of the mass media in determining how people spend their spare time?

The new environment of man in industrialized societies is characterized by an increasingly extensive and tightly woven web of techniques, of which industrial mechanization—the whole complex of production machinery and equipment contained in the workshops and offices of industrial enterprises—is but a part. Considered as a whole, this environment, composed of all the technical factors (production, transport, communications, relations, entertainments) which have transformed and are still transforming man's way of existence at every moment, continually invading new sectors (work, home, consumption, leisure, etc.), subjects the individual to the pressure of a multitude of stimuli, possibilities and attractions hitherto non-existent, which take root in modern society, proliferate, and build up what we know as a technical environment.

Georges Friedmann,"Leisure and Technological Civilization," *International Social Science Journal* 12 (1960): 509–520.

Technical environments in differently organized societies possess, despite disparities, certain analogous features, both in the functioning of their institutions and in individual behaviour patterns. It is from the sum total of 'cultural traits' . . . that a civilization is built up. In the present-day world it is the combination of culture traits (such as the scientific organization of labour, mass production, mass media, publicity, consumer attitudes, mass tourism, leisure occupations, etc.) common to different industrialized societies that constitutes what we call a *technological civilization*. There have . . . been civilizations which have lived and died untouched by the technical discoveries made by other human groups; but this kind of isolation is likely to become increasingly rare in any part of the world. Technological civilization, with its stupendous machinery for mass communication, is by nature universal.

Besides providing increasing quantities of more and more highly perfected productive machinery and consumer goods, a technological civilization also gives rise to what we may call spare time, i.e. time that is 'spared' and, at least on the face of it, clearly differentiated from working time. This is made possible by the organization and discipline of work, the division of labour, the structure of industrial enterprises, and the cohesion of the armies of industrial workers. The fact that the mass invasion of factories and offices is regulated by a rigid time-table means that tens, or hundreds of millions of people have at their disposal a certain amount of time which, to the outside observer, appears to be available, unoccupied.

This sharp division of time is not natural to the human species. It is a new phenomenon, which has emerged with increasing clarity during the past fifty years in the economic and technical context of the current phase of the industrial revolution, characterized by mass production and the 'scientific organization' of labour. In pre-machine societies, . . . the most varied aspects of everyday life were pervaded by . . . 'floating' or 'dormant' time; the notion of duration was entirely different from that of the inhabitants of the world of jet planes, television and automation. There was no sharp dividing line between the interminable working hours and those not devoted to work. In the absence of any definite criterion, the length of the working day was not fixed in advance. In essentially peasant societies, which pay no attention to time-by-the-clock, spare time is dependent upon the slow cycles of cultural, seasonal and social rhythms that have been established gradually over many years.

Industrial revolutions have introduced abruptly, in the space of less than a century, a virtual dichotomy between working time and spare time; but they did not, concomitantly or necessarily, produce spare time. During the first industrial revolution, the main emphasis was laid, as Marx pointed out, on the fact that the length of the working day was indeterminate. English and French 'machine-facturers', at the beginning of the nineteenth century, seem to have worked on the principle of reducing spare time to the absolute minimum. Working hours in industry—as described by factory inspectors at the time—were, as we all know, inhuman. Fifteen or sixteen hours' work a day, in insanitary buildings, do not even allow the time needed for physiological recuperation, let alone leisure. The 60-hour week became general in the United States of America from 1860 onwards; in European industries, not until 1900. Shortly afterwards, a series of factors—the most important of which were the rationalization of production introduced in the United States from 1880 onwards, the adoption . . . of methods of scientific management, the pressure exercised by labour parties and trade unions, and finally, social legislation—led to the measuring of the working day in terms of *output* rather than *hours* worked. The introduction of the 8-hour day, after 1919, coupled with the gradual reduction of the working week to five and a half or even five days, particularly in the Anglo-Saxon countries, set the seal on the acquisition of the right to spare time and led to the emergence, in the technological civilization, of a newcomer—*the after-work man*.

Since the thirties, holidays with pay have become a reality for the workers of industrially advanced countries; and the introduction of weekly and yearly periods of time off or 'vacations' is undoubtedly one of the basic features of the technological civilization. It implies potentially . . . the acquisition of leisure by the lower-income classes of our societies. The radical, age-old antithesis between those who do nothing but work and those who simply 'do nothing' is now being obscured by the emergence of all kinds of in-between situations. The alternating rhythm of work and non-work in industry, offices, shops, workyards, services, etc., tends to affect all the members of modern industrialized societies; only among rural communities do we still find large islands of resistance, but even these are being gradually undermined by the spread of industrialization into the country districts. It is true that in places where small-holdings predominate, the pattern and rhythm of life are still dictated by the natural environment: peasant families cannot easily leave their farms for a whole day, even on Sundays, and in any case, they would be loath to do so. Nevertheless, there is no escaping the fact that the destruction of the traditional rural environment and what has been called the 'de-countrifying' of the countryside constitute the only means whereby country people can gain access to spare time.

Industrial revolutions tend to unify the world, and we repeat that technological civilization is by nature universal. Labour legislation aims at the same things in all countries, economically advanced and underdeveloped alike. There are, however, important differences between the two groups of countries: for the one, leisure occupations are an important part of social life; whereas for the other—in the *bidonvilles* and *gour-bivilles* of North Africa, the *faveles* of Brazil, the shanty towns of North America and the *bustees* of India[1]—mass media assail, as it were, populations that have been uprooted from their traditional environments and have not yet been integrated into the new environment of modern societies, and these people are often profoundly influenced by the most blatant 'patterns' of the mass media even before they enjoy the rudiments of material well-being (houses, food, clothing) and fundamental education.

We are living in an age of transition. Technical change brings in its wake, everywhere, spare time, all the possibilities of leisure and the pursuit of happiness, of the 'good life' as expressed in terms of the material and moral conditions of the new environment. At the end of the eighteenth century, happiness . . . was 'a new idea' in Europe; whereas in our day the constant, universal search for happiness is one of the most significant features of technological civilization. Despite all differences of country, socio-cultural patterns and historical inheritance, despite the different ways of life and traditions, despite the diversity of social origins, systems of training, professions and income, hundreds of millions of our contemporaries are drawn alike to the facilities, the comforts, the objectives and the forms of escape offered by technological civilization. A kind of hedonism, the principal patterns of which are diffused all over the globe, pervades societies with widely differing traditions and structures: mass exoduses by car, travel, basking in the sun at the seaside or among the mountain snows, 'functional' homes, clothes, comforts, etc. . . . [I]t is already apparent that the increasingly urgent and feverish pursuit of happiness by the twentieth-century masses is one of the major sociological facts of our epoch.

This quest is by no means always crowned by discovery, achievement and satisfaction. For another significant feature of technological civilization is that, though it holds the key to happiness, though happiness is theoretically possible, neither societies nor individuals are equipped to make it a reality. Modern societies do not possess enough institutions conducive to the realization of happiness, while individuals cannot transform their free time into genuine leisure unless they are able to dominate, master and convert to their own ends (instead of being enslaved by them) all the countless instruments, machines and gadgets of technological civilization. To avoid becoming the slaves of modern techniques and gadgets and to use them, to however small an extent, as a means to developing their personality, improving their physical and moral well-being and exploiting their potentialities to the full is no easy matter for the vast majority of people in the practical circumstances of their everyday life. This failure to master modern techniques doubtless explains (at least

[1] Slums.

to some extent) why there is not more positive evidence of happiness in the United States of America and Europe, even among the classes with a high or medium standard of living; and why, on the contrary, those very classes show so many obvious symptoms of disequilibrium, minor and major neurosis, discontent and constant craving for drugs of all kinds.

There are numerous other handicaps which prevent a technological civilization from converting spare time into happiness. To begin with, it is unprepared for the advent of leisure man. In pre-machine civilizations— which we must, of course, be careful not to idealize—feast days, when all members of the group assemble, are compounded of religious rites rich in emotional substance, and accompanied by the relaxation of social taboos, and genuine manifestations of folk art. Thus feast days have a deep inner significance, and work, too, is permeated with ceremonial of which it constitutes in fact an integral part. On the other hand, societies born of industrial revolutions have no leisure institutions of their own. . . . [T]he values of mass leisure are not yet capable of filling the void created by the introduction of the 40-hour week. Is it perhaps due to these defects in the organization of leisure that the conquest of spare time seems so precariously founded and is so often challenged? Or should we not mention in this connexion the existence of other handicaps but for which it would be impossible to explain why leisure, so recent a by-product of industralization, is already threatened on all sides with reduction and decay?

To begin with, owing to the ever-growing size of urban and suburban areas in all industrial societies, a certain proportion of spare time and energy goes in travelling. This is a problem to which sociologists, demographers, psychiatrists, and economists, to say nothing of town planners and administrators, are devoting increasing attention. Whatever their type of occupation, workers from suburbs (and where, nowadays, do the suburbs end?), scores of millions of them all over the world, have no time, after spending hours travelling to and from their work, to engage in many kinds of recreation, let alone develop their personalities. Many of them, according to numerous surveys made, scarcely even have time to relax. This is the common fate of the vast armies of commuters all over the world, from Chicago to Sao Paulo, from Paris to Moscow.

Then again, certain types of work may poison the potential benefits of free time in advance by their effect on the personality. . . . A study of the leisure occupations of employees at the Postal Cheque Centre in Paris whose jobs are completely routine (a counterpart of the repetitive piecemeal tasks perfomed by specialized workers in industry) shows that on leaving the office, these clerks are either much more active or, on the contrary, withdraw into themselves, in a sort of apathy. These conclusions are interesting but not surprising. Depending on temperament, family environment, cultural level, and how much energy they have left after work and the travelling it involves, some try to find compensation, whilst others take refuge in abstention, indifference or despondency. . . . Many workers and employees doing routine high speed jobs not involving any responsibility find that their free time is ruined by fatigue, more mental than physical, so intense as to make them totally unable to enjoy themselves, or even to recuperate their strength. Other reports, on the contrary, speak of the pursuit of extreme forms of compensation for the disintegrating effects of piecemeal factory jobs on the personality. Both types of reaction tend to prevent workers from using their leisure for enriching their personality and improving their cultural standards.

Thus, the first battlefield, so to speak, in the campaign to humanize leisure in an industrial civilization is that of the time actually spent at work; the second, that of the time spent away from work, threatened from within by all kinds of factors that encroach on it, eat it away and poison it.

It should be noted in passing that for many people technological civilization brings with it not only more opportunities (as a result of improved transport facilities) for contacts, recreation, spectatorship and participation, and all the stimuli of publicity and environmental pressures, but also new obligations and new dangers of dispersion of energy. Think, for instance, of all the administrative intricacies of bureaucracy (those involved in France, for example, in membership of the social security system or in merely obtaining an identity card); or again, of the obligations and duties relating to family and domestic matters or, in certain countries, to social, political and para-cultural activities. While industrialization in our societies tends, by cutting down working hours, to increase the amount of free time it is also apt to restrict it in a variety of ways. In order to avoid a dangerous confusion of terms, we therefore think it necessary to make a careful distinction here between spare time and 'free time', and to use the latter exclusively to denote the time—unperturbed by all the obligations and duties mentioned above—during which people are free to express and, if they have the capacity and the means to do so, to develop their personality.

Here, in connexion with these obligations and duties, something should be said about all the different kinds of work people do in their homes, from the *bricolage*[2] of the French to the 'do-it-yourself' activities of the Americans. For some workers and employees, activities such as these play a *compensatory* role, and help to repair the psychological damage done by repetitive, piecemeal jobs. These types of work have certain indisputable advantages, namely that they involve manual skill and the handling of tools and materials, they are undertaken voluntarily, and they are subject to no time limit. But they have their limitations as well, for money considerations enter into them to the extent that though such

[2]Tinkering, puttering about.

work is unpaid, it is frequently undertaken as a means of saving money so that more can be spent on consumer goods; and it tends to cut people off from social intercourse, and prevent them from taking advantage of the cultural facilities provided by the community. Even gardening really comes into the odd-job category. It has advantages which we would not dream of belittling—it is far healthier, for instance, to put up pea-sticks than to go pub-crawling—but all the same small gardens, in industrial or mining towns often result in (or even aim at) keeping workers tied to their environment by constituting yet another domestic obligation. Can gardening really be said to make a positive contribution either to culture or to freedom?

Let us pause to consider the intermediate zone of activities which, though they do not actually come into the category of work, encroach on people's spare time. They represent a curious assortment, all of them involving some degree of constraint, and include all the odd-jobs done for money, or for neighbours, blackleg work, and second (or even third) jobs.

The philosophers, theoreticians and moralists of our industrial societies, rejoicing at the shortening of the working week, hoped and even asserted that the workers, in their two or three days off a week, or even during their evenings, would devote most of their time to the joys of genuine culture, music, painting, reading good books, going on pilgrimage to the shrines of art. But observation shows that, both in prosperous societies like the United States, France and Great Britain, and in poor countries like Poland and Yugoslavia and under-developed regions of Argentina and Brazil, for a variety of reasons many workers, employees and minor officials in fact spend their extra leisure on working, trading and speculating! We are faced with what might be described as the infiltration of work into out-of-work hours.

The extreme forms of this 'decay' of spare time include all kinds of blackleg work, from odd-jobs for others, petty domestic and money-making jobs to recognized or admitted second jobs, taking up every moment of spare time. In advanced industrialized societies (the only ones with which we are concerned here), workers in all sectors are liable— under the presure of various social 'ideals', out of a desire to 'keep up with the Joneses' or as a result of constant incitement to new (or greater) needs—to seek to earn more money in order to buy more comforts, more domestic appliances, larger homes, etc. . . .

This, then, is another aspect of the battle for free time. Taking place in the heart of an industrial society, it is indissolubly bound up both with the economic structure and behaviour patterns of that type of society; and with the production-consumption cycle which Henry Ford, in 1920, rightly described as the basis of American prosperity—though he failed to perceive how precarious it was, or the dangers inherent in it. Be that as it may, the average citizen of modern society—the common man— imprisoned in this rigid cycle is in danger, even with automation to help him both in his work and outside it, of becoming another Sisyphus[3] condemned for ever to bear a crushing burden which kills his aspirations to culture and philosophy and delivers him up, in his time off . . . to the disruptive effects of mass media gone mad.

In a world where the Big Two[4] build up their systems in an effort to produce more and more through the application of technical progress and to win the race for supremacy in *per capita* consumption, it is not surprising that leisure-time man, still not very sure of himself, should yield to the victorious assault of consumer-man, ever responsive to the suggestion of new 'needs'. . . . [A]mong the working classes, the lure of consumer goods is stronger, in many individuals and families (and pressure in this connexion is exercised mainly through the family group) than their aversion to the fatigue and regimentation of work. Only social groups imbued with a strong hedonist spirit, backed by a lively tradition of games and 'festivals' could put up an effective barrier to the process of the decay of leisure; and it is doubtful whether any such groups exist, or can exist within a technological civilization in Europe or the United States. It is only in the societies of Africa, Asia and Oceania, governed by customs and traditions, where work is closely bound up with ceremony, magic and ritual (and even there, of course, only until the material and moral effects of industrialization begin to be felt) that the producer-consumer mentality fails to overcome an attitude of congenital indifference.

It is therefore not surprising, in the last analysis, that in advanced industrial societies, the potential acquisition of spare time should not suffice to create leisure. In order to make leisure a living reality, to transform it, in fact, into really free time, certain institutions must be established, and certain values introduced. This being so, we may well ask whether the prospects of leisure in a technological civilization are not fated to recede for ever in a vicious circle. . . .

Mass production is one of the main 'ingredients' of a technological civilization. Since the beginning of the century, both the flood of objects produced and the behaviour of the consumers for whom these objects cater have been in a state of constant evolution which in turn, owing to the laws of the market and the pressure of advertising, leads to perpetual shifting and re-adaptation on both sides. As the Americans say, 'the customer is always right', but at the same time industry, including the cultural commodities industry, exerts a strong and many-sided influence on the consumer; so that technological civilization, in all the advanced countries of the world, tends to create an environment characterized, in varying degrees, by the same basic features. We find producer-consumer man surrounded by the same system of industrial techniques, the same

---

[3]In Greek mythology, the god Zeus condemned Sisyphus to push up a hill a gigantic stone that would always roll down again.

[4]The United States and the Soviet Union.

transport, communications and leisure institutions not only from Massachusetts to California, but also from Stockholm to Milan. Traditional forms of recreation, ancient festivals and folk arts, undermined by the unending succession of innovations, are disintegrating and disappearing. And, under the pressure of omnipresent publicity, standardized information services, the compulsive attraction of new kinds of comfort and travel and the feverish pursuit of new forms of escape, real or imaginary, whole societies are being drawn towards identical leisure occupations.

In this break-up of the traditional environment, mass media play an essential but at the same time an ambivalent part. On the one hand, they can be used for disseminating information, arousing curiosity and fostering new interests, improving education, widening people's horizons, and making them conscious of their links with their region, their country and their planet, developing their taste and their intellectual and artistic interests (for example, their taste for music), bringing them, in short, in a hundred different ways, into *closer touch* with the world around them, with art and thought. Surveys made in the French countryside report cases of small landowners and agricultural labourers, some of whom have never been outside their own villages, being passionately interested in, genuinely inspired by, a film about exploration along the Upper Niger, or a broadcast about some hitherto completely unknown sport, such as fencing or horse-racing. On the other hand, these same media are capable of distorting, vulgarizing and misrepresenting facts in very way.

Let us look for a moment sympathetically, and without condescension . . . at the cultural 'consumer goods' disseminated by the mass media in industrialized societies. Let us observe the ways in which very large numbers of men and women in fact spend their spare time— on films, television programmes, broadcast variety shows, and popular magazines which are (their producers say) 'adapted' to the taste of the masses and which, in turn, 'appeal' to them. It must be admitted that anarchy is one of the great dangers in the commercial production of cultural commodities. . . . Another obvious danger, judging from the experience of the dictatorships (Third Reich, Fascist Italy), or single-party regimes with an official ideology (USSR, People's Republic of China) is that the State can monopolize the production of mass media and abuse them to put across doctrines, beliefs, information and ideologies, thus 'mass manufacturing' people's minds, to meet the needs of the moment.

In this connexion . . . a word should be said about the terrifying power wielded by mass media in modern societies as an instrument of propaganda. Individuals can be psychologically (emotionally and intellectually) conditioned to accept a war or support a dictatorship, or to buy a new product or experience a new need. In other words, mass media can be used, with calculated effect, to accelerate the maturing of new demands. . . .

Another aspect of cultural consumption which deserves mention here is that young workers, coming out of their factories at Paris, Frankfurt or Milan are likely to see the same cinema and television programmes, hear on the radio the same variety shows, songs and jazz records, and look at the same magazines as the son (or daughter) of their foreman, engineer, overseer and middle-class adolescents in general. Workers are to be found more and more often, during their holidays with pay, frequenting the same organized holiday clubs, sunbathing on the same beaches as the middle classes. It is true of course that, in office and factory, the social relations and even the tensions and conflicts created by their job-status still persist; but outside the place of work, mass media tend to dispel 'proletarian culture' and 'class consciousness' (to speak in Marxist terms). The worker, once outside the factory gates, becomes a consumer, like millions of other members of industrialized society. This is a fact which is emerging more and more clearly, and which may well have immense repercussions on the future of our societies. During several recent trips to Yugoslavia, the USSR and Poland, I was struck by the extent to which young people were influenced and sometimes even naïvely fascinated by these mass media products from the West—a universal feature of technological civilization everywhere, irrespective of differences of economic structure.

The character of leisure, in a technological civilization, is necessarily determined by the impact of mass media on the 'after-work man'. What is this 'after-work man' like? And in what physical and psychological state does he approach his leisure? . . .

It is true that . . . the problem of leisure is not linked with work alone. Leisure is bound up with society as a whole, its demographic and professional structure, its historical and cultural context. . . .

In this general introduction we must confine ourselves to defining the place played by leisure in a technological civilization, and indicating the main influence to which it is subject. In this connexion, there is no denying that large numbers of men and women working in industry, commerce, agriculture, offices and even in the tertiary services are reduced, by the time they finish work, to a psycho-physiological condition in which they both need compensation in leisure and find it difficult to obtain. . . .

Nevertheless, it would be unrealistic to ignore the far-reaching developments now taking place, despite all the hostile influences enumerated above, in the active use of leisure. This includes all the wide variety of ways whereby individuals, after finishing work, seek to satisfy their need for participation and creation, with results ranging from complete failure to full self-expression. They take the form of odd-jobs and craft work at home; widespread 'amateur' artistic activities, encouraged by the mass media; competitions of all kinds, whether or not organized for publicity purposes; successful recreational clubs; mass exoduses at week-ends and holidays; the multiplication of leisure clubs—all these speak the same language. Only peevish moralists or intellectuals clinging to the splendours of the past . . . and out of touch with the times can assert that the average modern man is doomed, after finishing work, to apathy and debasement. On the contrary, experience shows, despite all the obstacles enumerated, his capacity for resistance and, above all, the opportunities to which he has access.

The crux of the problem of compensation and non-participation lies in the isolation of modern man in the large urban agglomerations characteristic of industrial civilization. Returning to his family after work, to his villa or flat in the suburbs, he stays at home because he is tired, or because the recreational clubs he could join, and the social, political, trade union or cultural activities he could take part in are too far away. So he decides to 'abstain'. But, just as he is about to shut himself up in his home, to yield to the bane of solitude, he is exposed, through the newspapers and magazines lying on his table, through his radio or television set, to the clamour of mass media—an intermingling of stimuli of all kinds, a boundless universe of diverse possibilities. . . .

. . . The impact of television varies according to the educational level—primary, secondary, or university; those in the last category long proved more reluctant to invest in a set. . . .

. . . One of the most important aspects, as regards its influence on the use of leisure and its potential cultural effects is, I think, the capacity of mass media to stimulate viewers (or listeners) to undertake new activities. Information previously beyond people's reach for geographical, economic or social reasons—such as concerts, lectures, travel broadcasts, programmes dealing with well-known art centres, etc.—may, when of a sufficiently high standard, though perhaps not immediately, arouse curiosity and stimulate activity in otherwise unknown fields. New centres of interest are obviously fostered by the presence of the whole family together in the home and by the discussions which may thus take place on such subjects (with the emphasis varying according to socio-professional status) as domestic and international politics, sport, education, the theatre, opera and documentary programmes. Naturally, this survey of stimuli, and of the conditions in which they operate, must also include the repercussions of television on reading habits among groups of different cultural levels, and for different categories of reading (books, newspapers, magazines). In this respect, the influence of mass media does not appear on the whole to be favourable. . . .

Past and Present in a Greek Mountain Village

JULIET DU BOULAY

The village of Ambéli, in Euboa in east-central Greece, could in the 1960s boast only 144 people and 35 houses. The village was poor and, because there was no effective transportation system, lacked any regular communication with the outside world. Yet this traditional village has experienced great social change since the 1940s.

More significant for Ambéli than the initial Nazi occupation of Greece were the two civil wars, from 1943 to 1945 (between resistance groups and the Nazis and among the partisan groups as well) and from 1947 to 1949 (between Communist guerillas and the royal government). These were dangerous and bitter times for the villagers. To what extent were they involved in the civil wars? One important consequence was the evacuation of the villagers to Katerini in 1949. How did the evacuation affect them? What had been the basic features of traditional village life? Was the village modernized? That is, did there appear new economic and social patterns that we associate with modernity? Did the inhabitants of Ambéli consider the new developments—in social relations and in values, for example—to have been important?

Juliet du Boulay points out that there have been successive waves of emigration from the village in the twentieth century but that the most recent emigration is of a different type. What has been the effect of this emigration, both on the emigrants and on the Greeks remaining in Ambéli? What future awaits the villagers?

. . . [T]he entry in the present century of the Greek nation into the world of industry and commerce, and its gradual transformation from a subsistence to a consumer society, have had repercussions which have penetrated into the remotest corner of Greek rural life, and which have affected very deeply this traditional world view. The effect of this movement has been to change not so much the central elements of the value system as the ways in which they are interpreted; but this does not mean that this change is superficial, for it amounts in many respects to the setting up of new values which are often, although they are not always recognized to be so, antithetical to the old.

Communications with the outside world, and contact with its values,

Juliet du Boulay, *Portrait of a Greek Mountain Village* (Oxford University Press, 1974), 233–252.

have been achieved in two main ways—war and emigration. The participation of villagers in the Balkan Wars from 1912 to 1914, in the campaign in Asia Minor from 1920 to 1922,[1] in the Albanian campaign against the Italians in 1940, and later against the Germans in 1940–1, all tended to enlarge their horizons beyond that of traditional village culture. But it is emigration which has effected the deeper alteration to village thinking and incalculably changed the villagers' way of life.

The first significant instance of emigration was that to America at the beginning of this century. Many of the villagers of Ambéli were heavily in debt, others wanted to buy land, others to seek their fortunes permanently elsewhere—and several men left the village from 1905 to 1908, although most returned in 1912 at the outbreak of the Balkan Wars. Emigration also took place in the 1930s to America, but ended with the entry of Greece into World War II, and after that there was no further emigration from Ambéli until 1960 when there began the great exodus of young men to Canada, Germany, the United States, Australia, and Belgium, as well as recruitment of men for the Merchant Navy.

There was a great difference, however, between the earlier types of emigration and the later, for whereas in the former cases the migration ideally involved return, in the latter it was, and was intended to be, permanent. In earlier years the *émigré*[2] went abroad in order to send money home to his wife and children, to buy land, possibly a house, or houses, returning eventually himself to take up his old way of life on a stronger financial basis; and while some did leave the village for good, these were only people who could not be supported on the land and resources available. Anyone, therefore, who was already established in the village, went abroad to secure rather than to abandon his inheritance. In the post-1960 emigrations, however, the focus has been the reverse, and not one of these *émigrés* had—or has—any intention of ever returning to live in the village. They come back periodically, to see their parents and to have a holiday, but they have no thought at all of taking up permanent residence in the village; and those who are forced, as some are, to return and stay for some months because of difficulties with their visas or work permits, are discontented and oppressed by what they see as the narrowness and lack of culture (. . . meaning in this context the frequenting of cinemas, nightclubs, dance halls and restaurants), and resolute in their determination to get away for ever.

The men who emigrate as bachelors usually marry Greek girls whom they meet either abroad or on a trip back to their village, and many of these couples then settle permanently in their new country, and one by

[1]Against the Turks.
[2]Emigrant.

one organize the emigration also of their brothers, sisters, and cousins. Of those who emigrated after they had married and settled in Ambéli, some have managed to leave their children with relatives and take their wives with them to work, and all intend, on returning to Greece, to abandon the village and buy a building plot near some relatively urbanized centre in the plains. While these people are abroad they send money to their parents and thus in a sense support the village, but this money is not enough to provide for a real continuance of the traditional culture; nor is it enough to establish a house: it is to keep two unambitious and undemanding old people from destitution until they finally leave the village and go to live with a married son or daughter elsewhere. And although some men, though not all, send home money to help with their sisters' dowries, these dowries in fact also work against the continued existence of the village, for they enable the girls to marry 'well', into a different and, to however small an extent, more polished community. Thus while the tendency of the earlier types of emigration was in the long run to strengthen the village, the later type is destroying it.

. . . [W]hile the earlier emigrations, taking place from a firm basis in village culture and a belief in its value, were a confirmation of that culture, rather than a challenge to it, the post-1960 emigrations took place from a village that was already losing confidence in its own inherited way of life—that had looked beyond the confines of its own culture and found what it saw attractive. The situation therefore arose in which the village the *émigré* left behind him perpetuated, because of its remoteness and isolation, a vital life in its traditional patterns; yet nevertheless at the same time it held the seeds of a totally foreign growth which was to flower, in the *émigré*, into a total disillusion with his rural origin. And while this disillusion did not compromise the commitment of those who were kept in the village by lack of opportunity to leave, it was an image of the failure of these patterns in the most crucial sense to offer fulfillment to an entirely new generation. Thus it seems that at some time around 1950 there occurred the beginnings of a deeply hidden but very central collapse of village confidence—a collapse which even by 1966 had not affected the villagers' sense of the intrinsic validity of their inherited way of life, but which cast doubt on the viability of that way of life in terms of the future, and in terms, therefore, of that most important aspect of Greek life, the children.

As time goes on this particular balance is likely to change more and more. The *émigré* of 1960 was impelled by hope of better things outside, rather than by disillusion from within. The *émigré* of 1970 goes because, 'This isn't a life'. . . . And yet this paradox, whereby the village survives in its own village-centered terms even while it fails completely in terms of the outside world, is never likely to be finally resolved, for the degree of emigration has by now taken the situation too far. In many of the larger or less remote towns and villages of Greece, the recent pattern has been one of increasing modernization whereby the world moves in before the inhabitants move out. This has not proved possible in Ambéli, and it is not going to be the infiltration of the modern middle-class ethos which will eradicate the traditional patterns still remaining to it, but final depopulation.

Of the earlier emigrations and the contact of village men with war and invasion, two general effects on village life may be isolated. One has been to highlight in many ways the traditional polarity of male and female roles, among the older married couples, by deepening the discrepancy between the experience of the men and that of their wives. The other has been to provide a basis for the older generations from which they can understand and sympathize with the younger ones who want to leave the village and make a new life for themselves elsewhere. Experimentalism and ambition, in terms of the ability to adventure into completely new worlds, are characteristics not foreign to the people of Ambéli. The result of this is that the village as a whole helps its sons to emigrate, its daughters to marry out, and in the most practical terms understands, while it laments, the permanent departure of its children from the family hearth.

Apart from the emigration discussed above, the political events which had the greatest impact in recent times were the two outbreaks of civil war in 1944 and 1947, with the consequent evacuation of the whole village to Kateríni for one year, from November 1949 to November 1950.

The two great periods of civil war, when fighting was generalized throughout all Greece and extended even into the towns, were in 1943 until February 1945, and in 1947 to 1949. However, during the whole period from 1942 to 1950 there was a state of disturbance in various parts of Greece with guerrilla bands operating in the mountains. During the first period the fighting was relatively localized between rival Resistance bands all over the country, interspersed with actual Resistance activity. During the second period, however, the Communist guerrillas involved the villagers by both persuasion and terrorism and, especially after the American involvement in Greece in 1947, were themselves hunted by the National Army in the mountains.

The villagers' involvement in the civil war was, primarily, caused by the position of their village in the wooded mountains which were to become ideal refuges for the Communist guerrilla fighters or *andártes* . . . as they came to be called. . . . With the development of the guerrilla movement . . . the village split naturally into Left and Right, with those of the Left helping the Communists out of sympathy, those of the Right out of fear—neither however, at any rate in the beginning, aware of the real political movements in which they were so disastrously taking part. The villagers were, as always, the victims of the struggles of others rather than the active element of the struggle itself.

It was not surprising that the villagers were at first in ignorance of the real issues of the conflict, for this ignorance was a state shared initially also by the Greek Government in exile, and by the Allies. EAM/ELAS[3] was initially the Resistance group which provided most of the effective partisan opposition to the Germans, and as such was given aid by the Allies—money and arms. It came quite rapidly, however, under the control of the Greek Communist Party (KKE) and thus became involved in a struggle with EDES, a Resistance organization operating mainly in northwestern Greece, which, orginally Republican, became increasingly Rightist under the control of General Napoleon Zervas. Straightforward opposition to the invaders was thus confused with the struggle for power between these two rival groups, and the villages all over Greece were involved in this confusion.

There is no doubt that when Resistance groups all over the country were formed at the beginning of the occupation, they were formed in answer to an intense popular resolution to evict the Germans. However, from the way in which the villagers now remember those days, it seems that later events overwhelmed this initial fervour, and that EAM/ELAS came eventually to exercise a hold over village imaginations in the opportunity it offered for adventure and excitement, and as a catalyst for the villagers' own private passions or generalized political leanings, rather than as a revolutionary cause to which they were dedicated. During the civil war which followed the evacuation of Greece by the Germans, several of the villagers actively enlisted with the *andártes*, some because they were forced to, others as a means of implementing private grudges, others as a result of an ill-timed spirit of heroism or a general sympathy with the Left. It is said that one man joined the Communists with the express intention of killing a rival inheritor of his father's; there was a young boy who involved himself with the first outbreak of civil war and then found himself too deeply involved to draw back. There was a boy of thirteen who was taken from his home at night by the *andártes* and retrieved only at the last moment by his mother who pleaded with the leader that her son was too young to be of any use to them. . . .

The nature of the movement first began to reveal itself in Ambéli when speakers for the Communist Party had come round the villages exhorting disbelief in the Church and proclaiming the joys of communal living. A fat woman speaker, who scratched her behind as she was talking, made a particular impression on the villagers, ever, as is their

[3]EAM, the National Liberation Front, was the name of the political Resistance coalition which was set up at the beginning of the occupation, and is usually referred to in conjunction with ELAS . . . , the National Popular Liberation Army which refers to the guerrilla bands which first began operations in the mountains in the summer of 1942. (Author's note.)

nature, ready for a joke; and there was a man who appalled them by cutting tobacco on an icon in demonstration of the hallowness of faith. Still clearer to them were the political implications of the open fighting which broke out in the streets of Athens between ELAS and the liberating British troops in December 1944; but by that time those who had involved themselves with the *andártes* found it too late to withdraw.

The *andártes* only stationed themselves permanently in the village after it was evacuated in 1949, but before that they made periodic swoops for food, for conscription, or for revenge. It was a time of terror for all, both Left and Right, for betrayal was rife, and death was threatened from the *andártes* for opposition or refusal to help, while severe beatings were courted by villagers who came under suspicion of the Government troops. The slower-minded villager ran the risk of being beaten up by both parties for not being quick enough to evade accusation; the cunning one had a soft answer ready at all times. One old man told me how he used to watch his sheep on the mountain sides, and from time to time unidentifiable groups of men would approach him and ask roughly, 'What are you?' 'I'm a shepherd,' he would insist, feigning ignorance of the real implications of the question, 'I'm a shepherd'; while to me he said, 'How did I know what to say? You couldn't tell who they were, and if you said the wrong thing you might have got killed. That was how I escaped.' In the village at night the same thing would happen. A family sitting at its evening meal would be terrified by a thunderous knocking at the door. Trembling, the head of the house would open it, 'Welcome!' he would say. To me he explained, 'To the *andártes*, "You're welcome!" To the Government troops, "You're welcome!" What could we do? We wanted to live.'. . .

In Ambéli there were six deaths during that time. Four of these were young men who had joined the *andártes* and were shot by the army at varying times; the other two were inhabitants of the village, Royalists, who were killed by the Communists. The first was, it is said, popular with nobody, for he was a bully and also—a thing insupportable in such a period and never at any time considered admirable—a betrayer of people in the village to those outside. The *andártes* came for him one night early in the civil war, bound his hands, took him, chalk-white and trembling, from the village, and later killed him on the mountain slopes. They took his wife a few nights later, but released her when, as they say, the entire village rushed after them begging for her life and for those of her four children whom they were thus making destitute. The second of these men, however, was universally popular, and nobody could believe that the man with whom they had laughed a moment before, as he made jokes with them outside the church, had been taken and shot where he stood. At the same time as this was happening, other *andártes* were at work setting fire to his widow's house and burning in it everything she possessed. People still remember how the oxen bellowed from within the conflagration, and how the widow and her five children, all under the age of eight, left the next day for Kateríni with nothing but the clothes they wore. It was in the autumn of 1949 that this occurred, and the barbarity of this act is explained by the villagers as being the result of the long years of fighting and suffering, the increase of passion, and the deepening of bitterness.

Immediately following this event, the order went out that the entire village should be evacuated, and within a week this was done, carried out by the army with mules and men temporarily conscripted from the surrounding villages, and the villagers lodged in Kateríni in rooms commandeered from local families. It was a hard time, for although they had brought with them enough wheat to give them bread for that year and into the subsequent year to last them until the harvest, they were not able to bring down the straw which was then vital to the animals, and many of the villagers returned to Ambéli in November of 1950 with their flocks depleted by half. However, this year was noticeable in a positive sense for one thing, in that it 'woke up'—to use their own terminology— the villagers to an awareness of a standard of living and a range of ambitions of which they had until then been hardly aware. This new awareness coincided, after the return to the village, with a period of national economic expansion, and from that date is observable a noticeable degree of social change. In response to any question referring to the beginnings of new ways of thought and new customs in the village, the answer is almost invariably—'After we returned from Kateríni'.

In the old days, the people of Ambéli had been primarily shepherds, and 2,000 to 2,500 head of sheep and goats are reported to have grazed on their mountains before 1955. . . . Agriculture was practised intensively, with up to twelve or thirteen acres of wheat being sown per family . . . and owing to the number of grazing animals and the fact that almost all the villagers owned at least a few animals and some as many as 200, the sowing had to be organized on a community basis in special areas set aside for certain crops. . . .

The normal houses included, in the days before 1940, the joint family, which would split up either on the death of the father, or on the development of quarrels or the birth of more children than the house could adequately contain. A common size for such families is said to have been eight. Therefore to the high degree of integration created by the communal co-operation over the land was added the more particularized focus of smaller groups, integrated through kinship and common interest, and related outwards to the community by their various affinal links.

These large families provided the manpower to make complete exploitation of the properties possible, and consequently the land had a value immediately realizable in economic terms. Small children would herd the goats and sheep and watch the cows, one or two men would go to the forest, the remaining members of the family would go to the fields or do any other necessary tasks. There was therefore great competition over land, considerable variation of wealth within the village, and a hierarchy of prestige according to the pre-eminence of a few families. . . .

The standard of living is said to have been the same for both rich and poor. All families would work equally hard, wear the same sort of clothes, eat the same sort of food. But the rich families had more prestige, more gold coins tucked away in their wooden chests, could afford to give their daughters good dowries, to pay workmen, have more animals, and perhaps more yards of material in the sleeves and skirts of the men's dress, and finer trimmings on the women's best clothes. . . . All the villagers slept in the same way, rolled up in rugs in rows upon the floor, and each family ate in the same way from one big dish set on a rug in front of the hearth, while the pig had to be driven away again and again, and the cocks crowed from the beams above. . . .

The German conquest of mainland Greece in April 1941, the stoppage of imported wheat, and the appropriation of the existing stocks by the invaders, had by the winter time brought famine to much of Greece. In Athens there was a period when hundreds of people a day died of starvation, the bodies being collected by carts which went round scouring the streets, and all over the land the townspeople flocked to the country offering jewellery, clothes, anything they had, for bread. The people of Ambéli, though better off than those of other villages owning less land, found their bare subsistence livelihood threatened, and from February until the harvest in June 1942 they eked out their meagre stocks of wheat and maize with roasted roots, and ate wild greens till their stomachs revolted at them. . . .

The ten years from 1940 to 1950 marked a serious run-down of social and economic activity. Marriages were reduced to a minimum and the resin trade stopped totally until 1945, although the people of the villages were able after 1943 slowly to begin saving a little money here and there by trading locally and by intensive cultivation of their land. Otherwise their lives were concerned chiefly with the perils and tensions of the Italian and later the German occupying troops, and the *andártes*. These empty years formed a break between the old world and the new, and this period can be seen now as the turning-point from which the Greek community as a whole departed from a way of life which accorded coherently with itself and with the system of values it embodied and by which it was organized, to one which, in adjusting to new economic and social conditions, was forced into tension and paradox and the abdication from the totality of many of the former beliefs.

After 1950 everything was to change. The previous living standards had not been due to lack of money only, but also to lack of knowledge, and after personal experience in Kateríni of living in separate rooms, of sleeping in beds, of wearing shoes and socks regularly to work, the villagers decided that they would continue in this way. They began to partition their houses to keep the animals in one half and themselves in the other; to buy clothes and household implements that they had previously done without; they began to use paraffin lamps instead of oil wicks, and to have coffee, sugar, and tinned milk as everyday necessities instead of rare luxuries. At the same time as these household improvements were going on, farming methods were also changing. Tin cups for collecting the resin became more popular, and replaced the wasteful scrapes in the ground at the foot of the trees. Instead of the wooden ploughs tipped with iron, which frequently broke, iron ploughs began to be used, and instead of oxen, horses and mules began to be bought. . . . The advent of fertilizer revolutionized the wheat farming and by 1956 all the villagers were using fertilizer in both the autumn and the spring and had quadrupled their crop.

After 1950 the claims of the school for the attendance of the children became more stringent, and families found that they increasingly lost their children as goat-, sheep-, and cow-herds to the demands of education. There had, since the school was started at the turn of the century, been a law that all boys should attend, and in 1916 school was made compulsory for girls as well. But parents needed the children to guard the herds, the children did not enjoy school anyway, the community was poor, and the teachers sympathetic. During the troubled times from 1940 to 1950 the school functioned only sporadically. . . . But after 1950 the rule governing school attendance became more strict, and this was later matched by the parents' own wish that their children should, unlike so many of themselves, be literate.

The loss of the children to the school, of the growing daughters to the marriages which blossomed in the years of release after 1950, and after 1960, of the men to the ships and countries abroad, coincided with the easier farming conditions as a result of fertilizer and resulted in the gradual selling, chiefly from 1958 until 1963, of the flocks of sheep and goats, until only two flocks were left. Resin gathering, however, still continued, and in 1965 the stabilizing of the resin prices at 4 drs. a kilo by government subsidy ensured a regular cash income for all those who owned forests and were able, or willing, to work them.

As a consequence of all this, the standard of living within the village and expectations from the outside world began to change, and instead of extreme physical hardship and a high degree of self-sufficiency, people began to reduce their hours of toil in the fields, to live more comfortably in their homes, and to develop a way of life involving increasing dependence on more modernized communities and a gradual acquaintance with urban ways of life.

One of the most significant features to arise from this change was an altered form of self-interest, and a very radical shift in the balance of forces which kept the community together. Ironically, with the entry into village life of material improvements and wider ambitions, the whole structure of the community life began to disintegrate, and inroads began to be made into the traditional pattern which were to result eventually in emigration and depopulation.

Before the war the necessity for reciprocity over the fields and animals, and for a high degree of interdependence in the internal affairs of the village because of the lack of amenities, meant that the interests of the village as a whole forced upon its inhabitants a certain degree of mutual co-operation. Self-interest in a narrow sense had to give way to the good of the community, and within the joint family individualism had to be strictly suppressed for the group as a whole to be able to function. . . .

Before 1950, joint families and a system of patronage linked the family groups to the outside community by relationships of marriage and obligation; the pre-eminence of the kindred, marriage into a hierarchy of prestige and wealth associated with possession of the land, the unquestioning acceptance of the agricultural and pastoral life and of the related values of independence and honour, were all values which kept the community solidly rooted in itself and in its environment; and these factors resulted in a total system in which the interests of the various families and those of the community coincided to a very great degree. Today the reverse applies, and the increasing reliance on the outside world, the diversification of ambitions, the decreasing value of the land and the increasing dependence on cash, the fragmentation of the family group, the dispersal of the flocks and the incomplete exploitation of the farms, the rise of individualism and the weakening of traditional ties between the family, its kin, and its land, all involve the different families of the community in interests which basically diverge from those of their neighbours. The same force, that of self-interest in terms of the survival of the family, still persists; but the changed economic and social scene now provides an environment in which the impulses of generation and survival no longer act towards the exclusiveness and solidarity of the community, but flow outwards to cause village society to identify itself more and more with the nearby towns. Thus, along with a higher standard of living, a divergence of aims and a latitude for the individual are being brought into village life that act against a united social organization, and towards the breakdown of many of the traditional curbs on hostility and quarreling.

The villagers' unanimous verdict on the worsening of social relations in recent years has been referred to earlier, and expressed in the phrase, 'The community has fallen into a state of hatred'. . . . Two other phrases express the same idea. In the older days, the villagers say, 'People were on good terms with one another' . . . , whereas now, 'Hatred exists'. . . .

One cause for this change from, as the villagers put it, love to hatred, or, as it may otherwise be put, from social solidarity to fragmentation, lies in the altered form of self-interest already discussed. Another lies in the altered value now given to the concept of 'advancement' or 'progress', for because of the increasing attraction of the way of life presented by the outside world, the terms in which progress is defined now relate exclusively to that outside world. While in the old days progress could be realized within the terms of village life, it can now be realized only by leaving that life for good. Thus the only really prestigious individual is one who has left the village. . . .

. . . Now that the whole traditional way of life has been devalued, envy continues to work and competition is as fierce as ever, but failing any outlet in a struggle for the effective attainment and retention of wealth and prestige, it is forced to express itself increasingly in words and actions which result in gossip and quarrels. At the same time there exists to a much lesser extent the traditional bar to unlimited quarreling which was in earlier times provided by the villagers' need of one another. It is partly as a result of this that the word used to describe relationships within the village in the present day is not 'love' but 'hatred'. . . .

A further effect of the focusing of ambitions in terms realizable outside the village rather than within it, coupled with the inability of the villagers to exploit their properties fully and the levelling out of financial inequality in the crisis of 1940, is a radical change in the values attributed to the land. Land, it is frequently said, is immortal—it cannot die, it is always a secure investment; the man of property will live in the knowledge of the acres he has behind him, with their potential productivity and their possible monetary value should the wheel of fortune turn and Ambéli become accessible to timber merchants or building prospectors. Yet as he finds himself in the reality of the present economic moment the villager realizes that he is in possession of a commodity which he is not able to sell or fully to exploit, and which has no value as a dowry for his daughters or a legacy for his sons. Thus although people are still thought of as rich or poor in accordance with the property they own, this is an assessment guaged in unreal terms according to past standards of prestige which are not applicable to the present day. . . .

The alteration in the value placed on land is not the only factor which has affected this change in prestige values, although it is an important one. The break-up of the family through emigration and marriage out of the village has resulted in prestige being centred not in the good name of the house but in individual achievement, while the low esteem in which the village is held means that prestige through the marriage alliance is no longer achieved through the linking of the honour and wealth of two families, but by casting off for ever the bonds of village life. In this situation the part played by cash becomes increasingly important, for land can no longer be given in dowries. . . . At the same time, the cost of food, clothes, schoolbooks, and the extra expenses involved in higher education (which is becoming a necessity for girls as well as for boys and is another way in which the traditional dowry is being replaced) takes up a very large proportion of family incomes. Thus although the economic situation in Greece began to improve dramatically in the mid-1950s and has retained the same momentum until the present day, the expectations of the villagers are, as time passes, overreaching more and more their actual financial capabilities. In comparison with the past they are, materially speaking, infinitely better off. In comparison with the modern competitive world they are barely holding their own, and their self-respect suffers accordingly. If poverty may be judged by the discrepancy between what people have and what they want, the villagers of Ambéli today are probably poorer than they have ever been. . . .

"Urban Man." Hugh Thomas, *A History of the World*. Reprinted with the permission of Hamish Hamilton, Ltd., London.

"Popular Anti-Catholicism in England, 1850–1851." D.G. Paz, "Popular Anti-Catholicism in England, 1850–1851," *Albion* 11, 4 (Winter, 1979): 331–359. Reprinted with permission.

"Is God French?" Reprinted from *Peasants into Frenchmen: The Modernization of Rural France, 1870–1914*, by Eugen Weber, with the permission of the publishers, Stanford University Press. ©1976 by the Board of Trustees of the Leland Stanford Junior University.

"Men, Women, and Sex." From *A History of Women's Bodies* by Edward Shorter. Copyright ©1982 by Basic Books, Inc., Publishers. Reprinted by permission of the publisher.

"Infanticide: A Historical Survey." William L. Langer, "Infanticide: A Historical Survey," *History of Childhood Quarterly*, I, no. 3, (Winter, 1974), pp. 353–362. Reprinted with permission.

"A Woman's World: Department Stores and the Evolution of Women's Employment, 1870–1920." Theresa M. McBride, "A Woman's World: Department Stores and the Evolution of Women's Employment, 1870–1920," *French Historical Studies*, X (Fall 1978), 664–683, as revised by Richard M. Golden and by Theresa M. McBride. Reprinted by permission of the author and the editors of *French Historical Studies*.

"'Play Up! Play Up! and Win the War!' Football, the Nation and the First World War, 1914–15." Colin Veitch, "'Play up! Play up! and Win the War!' Football, the Nation and the First World War, 1914–15," *Journal of Contemporary History*, vol. XX, no. 3 (July 1985). Reprinted with permission.

"The Price of Glory: Verdun 1916." Alistair Horne, *The Price of Glory: Verdun 1916*, 1962, Macmillan Publishers, Ltd., pp. 185–210. Copyright ©Alistair Horne. Reprinted with the permission of the author.

"Inflation in Weimar Germany." Alex de Jonge, *The Weimar Chronicale. Prelude to Hitler*, 1978, New American Library, pp. 93–105. Copyright ©Alex de Jonge. Reprinted with permission of the author.

"Violence and Terror in Twentieth-Century Ireland: IRB and IRA," by Michael Laffan. From *Social Protest, Violence and Terror in Nineteenth- and Twentieth-Century Europe*, edited by Wolfgang J. Mommsen and Gerhard Hirschfeld, pp. 155–173. ©Wolfgang J. Mommsen and Gerhard Hirschfeld 1982 and reprinted by permission of St. Martin's Press, Inc.

"Violence and Terror in Twentieth-Century Ireland: IRB and IRA," by Michael Laffan. From pp. 155–73 *Social Protest, Violence and Terror in Nineteenth- and Twentieth-Century Europe* by Wolfgang J. Mommsen and Gerhard Hirschfeld. Reprinted by permission of Macmillan, London and Basingstoke.

"The Nazi Camps," Henry Friedlander. Reprinted from *Genocide: Critical Issues of the Holocaust*. Ed. Alex Grobman and Daniel Landes. Los Angeles, Ca., and Chappaqua, N.Y., 1983. By permission of the Simon Wiesenthal Center and Rossel Books.

"The Soviet Family in Post-Stalin Perspective," by Peter H. Juviler. Stephen F. Cohen, Alexander Rabinowitch, and Robert Sharlet, eds., *The Soviet Union Since Stalin*, 1980, Indiana University Press, pp. 227–233, 235–244. Reprinted with permission.

"Forbidden Death." From Philippe Ariès, *Western Attitudes Toward Death: From the Middle Ages to the Present*, 1974, The Johns Hopkins University Press, pp. 85–103. Reprinted with permission.

"Leisure and Technological Civilization." Georges Friedmann, "Leisure and Technological Civilization," *International Social Science Journal*, no. 12, 1960, (pp 509–520). ©Unesco 1960. Reproduced by permission of Unesco.

"Past and Present in a Greek Mountain Village." Juliet du Boulay, *Portrait of a Greek Mountain Village*, 1974, pp. 233–252. Edited selection reprinted by permission of Oxford University Press.